THE TRANSATLANTIC PERSUASION

THE
TRANSATLANTIC
PERSUASION

THE LIBERAL-DEMOCRATIC MIND
IN THE AGE OF GLADSTONE

ROBERT KELLEY

ALFRED · A · KNOPF   NEW YORK
1969

JN
216
K4.7

THIS IS A BORZOI BOOK
PUBLISHED BY ALFRED A. KNOPF, INC.

First Edition

To my wife
ROSALIE
and to our children
SANDRA, BRIAN, ALISON, *and* DORCAS

PREFACE

A number of debts, intellectual and personal, have been contracted since I began working on this book some ten years ago. Most signally, there has been the example of the works of Richard Hofstadter. He has taught me through his writings —as he has so many of us—to be alive to many considerations in history that, taken together, have given us a new way of looking at American politics and culture. I am sure the influence of his approaches to history will be evident in the pages that follow. I am grateful, too, for his encouragement of this project early and late, and for the painstaking care he gave to reading and commenting upon some key sections of the work.

Books of this sort, which seek both to describe and to interpret a wide range of historical experience, are heavily dependent on the works of other scholars. My debt to a great many fellow historians—such names as John Vincent and Donald Southgate in British history, Marvin Meyers and Lee Benson in United States history, and J. M. S. Careless in Canadian history only begin the list—will be obvious in the text. In seeking for explanations of matters that run somewhat beyond the usual beat for historians, I have often found penetrating instruction in the works of men in other disciplines. Of these, perhaps my largest obligation is to Gordon Allport and his discussion of the nature of prejudice.

Many friends and colleagues have provided invaluable assistance as this work has proceeded. My colleague John New read the entire manuscript and gave me valuable advice; Frank Thistlethwaite, Vice-Chancellor of East Anglia University, Norwich; Kenneth McNaught and Richard Helmstadter of Toronto University; and Otis L. Graham, Jr., of the University of California, Santa Barbara, have read various sections of it and discussed its findings with me. Then there are those who have provided encouragement and the benefit of their views at various stages along the road, sometimes in connection with the articles that from time to time have appeared on some of the key figures in the book: Merle Curti, University of Wisconsin; R. B. McCallum, Master, Pembroke College, Oxford; J. G. Kellas, Glasgow University; Donald Meyer, Connecticut Wesleyan; Joseph Stonehouse, Labour Party Agent in York, England; Maurice Smith, Whitehall, London; Richard Rapson, University of Hawaii; Frances Herrick, Mills College; Joseph G. Rayback, former editor of *The Historian;* Roderick Nash, Felice A. Bonadio, Leonard Marsak, C. Warren Hollister, Otey Scruggs, Alexander DeConde, Morton Borden, Stephen N. Hay, Larry L. Adams, A. Russell Buchanan, Alexander Callow, Alfred Gollin, Charles B. Spaulding, and Walter Mead of the University of California, Santa Barbara; and my graduate and undergraduate students through the years. Of these, I am especially indebted to Steven L. Allaback of the University of Connecticut; Mrs. Sigrid Jan Morris, now of the Peace Corps; Arthur A. Hansen of California State College, Fullerton; Mrs. Barbara Guilliams; and Miss Kathleen Cronan. Two of my students had major roles in the book's preparation. Mrs. Thekla Hathaway, who has assisted me in various ways for a number of years, offered advice on the entire manuscript as it was in preparation, typed major portions of early drafts, and prepared the bibliography. I am keenly aware of and grateful for her many contributions to the way this book has been written. Miss Shirley Henderson aided in a section of the research, and typed the manuscript in its final form, making, in the process, far more than the usual typist's contributions to consistency of usage and other such difficult and elusive matters. Ashbel Green, managing editor of Alfred A. Knopf, Inc., has been kindness itself. Edward Johnson, copy editor at Knopf, provided gifted and painstaking assistance in the final stages of the manuscript's preparation.

I wish particularly to express my warm appreciation for the unfailing helpfulness and good humor of the Inter-Library Loan staff of the University of California, Santa Barbara, Library. For their thoughtful assistance during my visits, I wish to record my thanks to the staffs of the following libraries: those at the Los Angeles and Berkeley campuses of the University of California; Stanford University; the Library of Congress; the Public Archives of Canada, Ottawa; the Bodleian, Oxford; the British Museum; and the National Library of Scotland, Edinburgh. A summer fellowship received from the Humanities Institute of the University of California provided key assistance during a period of the manuscript's preparation.

Articles based on materials in portions of this book have appeared in *Victorian Studies, American Quarterly,* and *The Historian.*

R. K.
University of California, Santa Barbara
February 1968

CONTENTS

INTRODUCTION

This study began when for a number of reasons I decided
that a comparative study of the British and Canadian Liberals and the American Democrats in the time of William Gladstone and Woodrow Wilson might yield fresh insights into
the nature of politics and political thought in the Anglo-
American countries.[1] I chose these parties because I suspected that they were parts of a whole; that they were local
manifestations of a larger political persuasion that extended
throughout the Anglo-American community, and were therefore fit subjects for comparison.

I also felt that we were badly in need of a new understanding of the Liberals and the Democrats in the half-century between the American Civil War and the First World
War. The standard historical picture we had of them was
curiously void, lacking in purpose and content. This I found
strange and unaccountable. If anything has been revealed by
the work of intellectual historians in the past twenty years, it
is that every large human enterprise is inspired by some relatively coherent world view, some meaningful frame of reference or motivating social vision. The Democrats in particular,
and to only a lesser degree the Liberals, seemed to constitute
strange exceptions to this rule. Theirs was a story of apparently meaningless sound and fury. Historians generally did
not question, for example, Woodrow Wilson's verdict that the
Democrats and the Republicans before the turn of the century were as similar as two empty bottles, only their labels

[1] A study of the era of Woodrow Wilson will appear in a later volume.

being different. I decided to do what could be done by this method to recapture, in its own terms, a political point of view that had become lost to us.

I have also been moved by another consideration. In an important sense the purpose of this book has been to make a contribution toward giving us a new and much broader frame of reference for understanding the separate histories of Britain, the United States, and Canada. I have looked at these three countries together not simply for comparative reasons, but in order to illuminate the fact that they are part of a larger Anglo-American community whose history has gone largely unwritten. I have wanted to explore an assumption that the three countries have not simply a "common heritage" and a "special relationship," but actually constitute a continuing community with a common life and therefore a common history. The concept of European history, which includes nations that are remarkably different from one another, has had a long and useful career; the concept of Anglo-American history, comprising nations that are so demonstrably alike and interactive, should be at least as useful.

This study constitutes, then, an attempt to test the proposition that Anglo-American history can be written, and that, when written, it will provide us with a new and revealing framework for understanding many things within the separate countries. I hope that we will then see some old things differently, and some new things that have been obscured. Fortunately, there is now a growing literature on the Anglo-American *connection,* following the lead provided by J. B. Brebner's pioneering work in *The North Atlantic Triangle* (New Haven, 1945). What now needs illumination is the *common life* of the Anglo-American countries: the appearance of similar movements within the several countries, like the outcroppings of common strata, derived from shared intellectual and social influences. Frank Thistlethwaite has written what is perhaps the first book of this sort in his remarkable *America and the Atlantic Community: Anglo-American Aspects, 1790–1850* (New York, 1964).[2] It is as a con-

[2] Kenneth McNaught of the University of Toronto also has a major study underway of Anglo-American socialism. Stanley Nider Katz

tribution to this latter kind of Anglo-American history that I conceive the present book. In this sense, my study has two aspects. It is an essay both in comparative and in descriptive history.

In this kind of book, however, one is faced with a special problem. Few if any scholars, not to speak of the general reader, have a detailed knowledge of all three countries. The nature of the case has therefore required me, from time to time, to write with a bit more fullness than I might ordinarily use in order that the narrative might be fully understood. My objective has been to write this book so that someone inexpert in the history and politics of one or more of the countries might read it with complete ease of understanding.

As to the structure and method of the book, I have adopted the device of the group portrait, filling in at the same time an ample supply of context and setting. I am aware that in concentrating on key figures at the apex of the political pyramid one makes a severely limiting choice. John Vincent is quite correct in his recent book, *The Formation of the British Liberal Party* (New York, 1966), when he remarks that far too much political history is devoted to what is in reality a tiny subculture—the party politicians—which is mistakenly taken as reflecting in its ideas and nature the larger society of the nation as a whole. His own work demonstrates how exceptionally clarifying it is to consider instead the broad base of the political pyramid, the vastly complex world of local associations, provincial life, clubs, industries, farms, and other collectivities in the general population, which provide perhaps most of the reality of political life.

My field of consideration in this study is so wide, however, that the group-portrait technique is not only the most natural and attractive means of rendering the enterprise manageable, but the only means. And the subculture of party leaders is vitally important, for all its disproportion in size to the mass of the general population. Public conversations and public decisions are the product of an interactive dialogue

has just published *Newcastle's New York: Anglo-American Politics, 1732–1753* (Cambridge, Mass., 1968), another pioneering work in this new genre.

between leaders and populace, both providing inspiration and setting limits for the other. Elite studies have their own *raison d'être*. Biographical studies, furthermore, may also be used as points of departure for forays into many of the larger aspects of life in the Anglo-American countries. I have thought of the following chapters as essentially essays on this "life and times" model.

The plan for this book was to examine the thought of the men who led the Liberal and Democratic parties in the long Gladstonian era, beginning in the early years of the nineteenth century and coming to an end in the 1890's. I soon began to wonder, however, *what* I was studying. As I sought an answer to this question, I realized that there is not presently available any compact and reliable term for the political persuasion I was examining. The word "liberalism," for example, proved of little use. As in the similar case of the word "conservatism," so many divergent meanings have been stuffed into it and so many scholars have strongly personal commitments to one or another of these meanings that use of it led to frequent encounters in which it was insisted to me that a particular figure in the study was improperly included, for he was not "really" a liberal.

However, it was my specific purpose to avoid reading back into the past some current definition of liberalism and selecting men for examination because they met that a priori definition—a technique that explains, I believe, why we understand these men so little. We have insisted upon assessing them according to our own definitions of what is a genuinely liberal or conservative policy. My aim has been to study the men who actually led the Liberals and the Democrats and to see what in fact they believed—to take them on their own terms, not on ours. This led me to decide on the term "Liberal-Democratic" for its specifically historical, rather than philosophical, reference. Whether or not I am talking about "liberals" in this study readers will decide for themselves; my goal has been to discover and to describe the Liberal-Democratic mind—by which I mean its characteristic outlook on the world. I recognize that historians are traditionally resistant to new terminology, but since it is in any event an unusual undertaking to write a book that takes the whole Anglo-American community as its subject—and asserts that this is a unified topic—perhaps a new category in intellectual history will be regarded as a minor novelty.

———

By way of preparation, a few remarks on my own orientation may be useful. I have found the views of William James exceptionally helpful in this undertaking—as they are in so many other ways as well. "Any author is easy," he wrote, "if you can catch the centre of his vision." This seems to me the wisest maxim to follow in intellectual history. In this spirit, I have tried in these studies to discover each man's fundamental outlook on life; to find the spot, philosophically speaking, from which he looked out upon the world, and to see how the human enterprise looks from that location. With each of them I have found that certain conceptions, certain ways of thinking, were central to everything else. Once taken hold of, they make much that otherwise is disconnected fall into place as part of a coherent pattern. In trying to understand why a particular standpoint was chosen, I have been guided, too, by James's observation that an outlook upon life is "the expression of a man's intimate character."[3] I have been concerned, insofar as possible, with searching out configurations of personality. Hundreds of psychological studies in recent years have shown that what a man takes note of in his life, and elaborates in a world view, depends in good part on his perceptual readiness; that is, his sensitivity to particular things in his environment which arises from the special structure of his personality.[4]

On the other hand, public men also live and work within an inherited public tradition. Their views of politics spring not only from their own characters but also from a larger

---

[3] William James, *Essays in Radical Empiricism and a Pluralistic Universe* (New York, 1947), II, 20, 87.
[4] Cf. Gordon Allport, *Pattern and Growth in Personality* (New York, 1961), p. 263.

view of politics derived from admired figures and from the actual problems faced by their societies. I think of political world views as analogous to artistic and literary philosophies that are passed on from one generation to the next, recognizably different yet recognizably the same, giving a frame of reference and a sense of placement within a tradition to the individual artist or writer. In this sense I am concerned to get at not only the special attitudes of each man, but also the larger political world view that characterizes a whole movement as it passes across the generations.

Just as cultural traditions are found in the novels and paintings that form their public expression, so political persuasions are found in the public rhetoric of politicians. Recent books on the Jacksonians have shown how fruitful it is to pay close attention to what leading figures have actually said about what they were trying to do and why. The "dialogue of the parties," Marvin Meyers has remarked, is one of the principal conversations to be listened to in order to learn of "the fears and hopes, the passions and beliefs" that motivate an age.[5]

In this spirit, my work is of that fairly new genre in historical literature that finds its primary sources in the speeches and writings that were pored over and listened to and cheered in their own day, but have since gone largely ignored and unread. In this kind of work, original research consists in searching out the public utterances and writings of the men examined, in newspapers, pamphlets, printed collections, magazines, books, legislative reports, private papers, and wherever else they may be found, and in subjecting these documents to close analysis. From such research emerges the raw material for books of this nature: the images, the anxieties, the symbols, the enemies, the ways of thinking, the resonant words and concepts, and the dreams that are embodied in a political world view. One is searching, in short, for the ideas contained in the public conversations of great societies, hoping to find in them reflections of what it was

[5] Marvin Meyers, *The Jacksonian Persuasion: Politics and Belief* (New York, 1960), pp. v–ix.

that moved the Americans and the British and the Canadians to do what they did.

Close examination of political rhetoric produces the realization that world views in politics are essentially a special kind of dramatic vision. They are not only associated with the arts of gesture and political symbolism, they are themselves inherently dramatic images of conflict and possibility. The enemy is all-important, appearing over and over again in all his detestable and threatening forms. Who is the Tory? What is the Republican really like? Although such matters may sometimes have the appearance of a charade, I am convinced that the image of the enemy is the most serious and revealing element in a political persuasion, providing us with the best means for linking widely separated political movements. A shared vision of the enemy does more to bind men together than anything else. Tactics and programs and agendas for action may change, but the enemy remains the same. This essential element links Jeffersonians and Jacksonians and the Second New Deal—and, more than anything else, it makes the concept of the Liberal-Democratic mind a viable one. By and large, Liberal-Democrats marched to the same drummer; they looked out upon society and saw the same drama. They consequently responded to divergent problems in ways that were clearly stimulated by a common assessment of the order of battle.

In writing this book, it has been important to me also to explore the context within which the Liberal-Democrats acted. I have been much interested, for example, in working out the relations between religion and politics in that fervently religious age. G. Kitson Clark quite rightly speaks of the extraordinary religiosity of the Victorians. Only the struggles to establish democracy and to abolish aristocratic privilege, he observes, ranked with the great and continuing campaign that went on through much of the nineteenth century to reconvert England to the Christian faith. In his view, the dying away of religiosity is what actually marks the end of Victorian England.[6] It has been my feeling that this phe-

[6] G. Kitson Clark, *The Making of Victorian England* (Cambridge, Mass., 1962), pp. 147–205, 284–5.

nomenon must be fully explored. What did it mean for Gladstone's politics that he was an Evangelical Anglican? For Cleveland's that he was the son of a Presbyterian minister? I have considered the religious climate of the Liberal-Democrat in a search not for superstition, nor necessarily for the divine word, but for motivations and models, for archetypical world views.

I should perhaps here remark that I do not believe that in exploring these matters I have found the "causes" of the ideas examined. Few things are more elusive, as David Hume long ago established, than what causes something else. I agree with William Dray, rather, that knowing a man's religion, or his personality, or his setting gives us instead something else: a basis for understanding his actions as reasonable and appropriate. We secure from these considerations not a closed system of cause and effect, but rationales for understanding.[7]

Another principal objective in this study has been to explore sociological conditions and their relation to politics. I have been much struck by the fact that Liberal-Democratic politics had a special relationship to the minority groups. In a real sense, Liberal-Democratic politics and thought seemed to be the products of the habits of mind typical among outgroups. Occasionally I have been drawn to consider the ways of thinking created by position in society not only in the outgroups but in the dominant social classes. A great deal of Liberal-Democratic thought was concerned not with the formal categories we usually think of—the economy, the government, and the like—but simply and plainly with the fact of *arrogance*. As R. B. McCallum has observed to me, the Liberal thought of the Tory as a man of the *Ubermensch* mentality. In social relations, in imperial policy, in foreign relations, in domestic affairs, the Tory seemed in Liberal eyes always to be moved by St. Augustine's "lust to dominate." It was no chance remark when Gladstone said that Tories were bullies at heart. But I will discuss these matters fully in the

[7] Cf. William Dray, *Laws and Explanation in History* (London, 1957), Ch. v, "The Rationale of Actions," especially p. 124.

book, particularly in Chapter 10, where I undertake to pull them all together.

The key point of reference in this book is the remarkable figure of William Gladstone. During his extraordinary ascendancy, reaching from the 1850's into the 1890's, Samuel Tilden and Grover Cleveland were the principal figures in the Democratic Party in the United States, and—during much of this period—George Brown and Alexander Mackenzie were the leaders of the Liberal Party in Canada.[8] The essays on these five men are the core of the book, Part II.

In studying them, I learned what were in fact the intellectual sources upon which they drew, as distinguished from the sources traditionally assumed to have created, for example, British Liberalism. Despite the present assumption that Edmund Burke was the great Conservative, I was forced to think of him as the prophet of the Liberals, so venerated was he by Gladstone and others, and to read his writings and utterances from a new vantage point, finding them to embody things I had not earlier supposed were there. Similarly I found myself largely unconcerned with Jeremy Bentham, for despite his prominence in the textbooks and his undoubted influence among certain kinds of Liberals, he meant very little to Gladstone and to the kind of Liberal mentality he represented. In the same way, I began to get a new feeling for the long-maligned Adam Smith, who has only recently been the subject of fresh and penetrating work. For the

---

[8] Edward Blake and Sir Wilfrid Laurier present a special problem. They were also leading figures in Canadian Liberalism during the Gladstonian era, Blake from the late 1870's into the mid-1880's, and Laurier thereafter. Because Laurier's premiership began in 1896 and extended to 1911, and his leadership of the Party extended to his death in 1919, I shall include him in the next volume of this study. Blake's leadership was brief, little is known of it, and he was in any event linked far more with his successor, Laurier, than with his predecessor, Mackenzie. I have decided, therefore, that he falls more naturally in the second volume also.

Americans, the prominence of Thomas Jefferson was more to be expected, though here too recent studies have cast him in a new light. The essays on these three men constitute the bulk of Part I. In these chapters, I have looked also to see if influences in the larger social situation similar to those which proved so prominent in the nineteenth century might be found, and have explored them in some detail.

In addition to these formal intellectual inheritances from Smith, Burke, and Jefferson, Part I also examines the more generalized attitudes induced by the economic, social, and religious setting in which Liberal-Democratic politics took place.

Liberal-Democratic politics entered its second—and last —phase in the 1890's, when Gladstone and Cleveland left the scene and the next generation took over. This phase will be the subject of a later volume. Sir Wilfrid Laurier dominated all of this period in Canada; Lord Rosebery was followed by Sir Henry Campbell-Bannerman and H. H. Asquith in Britain; and in the United States, Woodrow Wilson followed William Jennings Bryan, carrying the Democrats to their greatest triumphs since the time of Andrew Jackson.

The end, when it came, arrived quickly. Asquith was ejected from the premiership in 1916, Laurier died in 1919, and Wilson was rendered permanently ill by his stroke in 1919. With these events, the Liberal-Democratic mind as a major force in public affairs passed from history (except, perhaps, in Canada). The Liberals completely collapsed in Britain, and when the Democrats were revived under Franklin Roosevelt, it was within an intellectual framework that, while clearly in the same line of descent, was in many ways so unlike the Liberal-Democratic point of view that it can be regarded as a different political mentality.

The First World War was what really brought an end to the Liberal-Democratic persuasion—as it did to so much else in the world. Liberal-Democracy was a political outlook that flourished in a world of relative stability and peace. It could not survive in the maelstrom of the war and its aftermath, for it was fundamentally unequipped to deal with such a changed and chaotic world. When Asquith as Prime Minister sat in silent grief in his office on August 4, 1914, waiting until midnight for the Germans to reply that they would not invade Belgium, and knowing he was waiting in vain, he was also waiting out, though he did not know it, the last hours of an era in the history of the Anglo-American mind.

PART I

PART 1

Chapter 1

THE SETTING:
ECONOMIC BOOM, MINORITY GROUPS,
AND RELIGIOSITY

The Democratic Party in the United States, and the Liberal parties in Britain and Canada, were born in the Age of Jackson and Peel. This is the period, comprising the decades from the 1820's to the 1850's, when throughout the Anglo-American world the first great surge of reform took place, and the outlines of subsequent politics began to appear. As the followers of Andrew Jackson formed the core of the emerging Democratic Party, so those inspired by Robert Peel became, somewhat later in the period, the leadership of the Liberal Party. These were the decades in which democracy fully emerged in the United States, and in which the struggle over the Reform Bill of 1832 ushered in middle-class voting in Britain and the power of public opinion over British governments. Humanitarian reforms in the prisons, the schools, and the factories were points of vigorous controversy, and two great domestic struggles—the Bank War in the United States and the Repeal of the Corn Laws in Britain—largely shaped the nature of politics for decades thereafter. Canada was similarly caught up in the beginning struggles over democratic reform in these years, highlighted by the Rebellion of 1837, which laid the basis for subsequent Canadian politics—despite the fact that this "first great democratic upheaval" in

Canada, as Frank Underhill has written, was a failure. What followed thereafter grew as much out of this failure as it would have out of success.[1]

All of this took place within a remarkably interactive Anglo-American community. Men and ideas passed back and forth across the Atlantic with notable facility as reformers of many persuasions drew inspiration from one another.[2] It also took place in the presence of a great economic boom after 1815, which persisted for many decades, despite periodic depressions. All relationships, institutions, and mental attitudes were reshaped as the rigid economic world inherited from the eighteenth century melted into the "fluid economics"—to use Vernon Parrington's term—of these years. The prospect of swift rises in wealth and status unknown to former ages opened out before almost everyone. Men could achieve rapidly what would formerly have taken generations to accomplish. A risk psychology, buoyed up by optimism, suffused formerly conservative communities. Romanticism flourished in this effervescent atmosphere, stimulating the idea that common men were equal to the aristocracy. The great boom was in fact what gave substance to the ideals originally uttered in the Declaration of Independence.

The boom began in the swift growth in cotton production in the United States that followed the invention of the cotton gin in 1792. An explosive expansion took place in the British textile industry when these supplies of cheap raw cotton became available, and the whole process was stimulated by the cumulative influence of the transportation revolution of canals, railroads, and Atlantic steam vessels. This interchange rapidly swelled into a gigantic volume of commerce, so that there emerged, in place of the two separate economies, one British and the other American, a single, transatlantic economy. Enormous flows of capital, labor, enterprise, and technology moved westward from Britain to North America. Perhaps a third of the mining population of Corn-

---

[1] Frank H. Underhill, "Some Reflections on the Liberal Tradition in Canada," in his *In Search of Canadian Liberalism* (Toronto, 1960), p. 12.
[2] Cf. Frank Thistlethwaite, *America and the Atlantic Community: Anglo-American Aspects, 1790–1850* (New York, 1951–64), *passim*.

wall, for example, emigrated to the United States to apply their legendary skills in hard-rock mining from Michigan to California and Arizona.

> When I came to Cornwall just after the war I was astonished and excited by . . . the fact that almost every Cornish family had relatives in America. Cornish students . . . would reveal quite casually some surprising information; one, who was a bus conductor, had worked in Detroit; another, a housewife, had been to school in Michigan; a third apologised for being absent for a term as she was returning to Idaho to see the silver camp where she was born; and a fourth claimed that he was the cousin of Deadwood Dick. To a Celt like myself from the other side of the border it was bewildering to live and work in a community that was half Cornish and half American in its outlook. One could talk to an old miner on a harbour wall and discover that he had never been to London but could describe quite clearly the streets and taverns of San Francisco. Some of the Cornish in the extreme west even spoke like Americans . . . [The Cornishmen had] pioneered the mining industry of America. No mine was ever without its Cornish captains and every mining company was keen to employ them, often to the disgust of their neighbouring Celts, the Irish . . . [In] every Cornish household for many years North America was an even more familiar name than England.[3]

For those people directly affected, the boom and the transportation revolution set the tone and shaped all the options of life, as shown in the experiences of William Gladstone, Samuel Tilden, and Alexander Mackenzie. Gladstone's father prospered in the rising commerce of Liverpool, which flourished in the American trade. He had emigrated to the town as a poor Scotsman, made his first wealth in risky ventures in the American trade, and with unending energy rose to become one of the richest entrepreneurs in England. As a boy in the 1820's, William Gladstone could look eastward a

[3] Arthur Cecil Todd, *The Cornish Miner in America* (Truro, Cornwall, and Glendale, California, 1967), pp. 9, 10, 19. See also Thistlethwaite, *America and the Atlantic Community*, p. 3; and George Rogers Taylor, *The Transportation Revolution: 1815–1860* (New York, 1951).

few miles from his father's great home on the long sandy beach running out from Liverpool and see the thin halo of smoke drifting over the city.[4] Soon the town was spreading, the Gladstone home was swallowed up by suburbs, and the thin wisp became a thick pall, joining the smoke rising from a thousand factory chimneys in Lancashire and the whole of the English North Country.[5] The cotton boom and the later wheat boom sent hundreds of boats crowding into the Liverpool anchorages to discharge their bales and grain, and to take on finished textiles, iron and steel products, pottery, and a multitude of other goods to carry back to the States.

Across the Atlantic, in upstate New York, Samuel Tilden was spending his boyhood in a small village through which ran an emigrant road leading westward from New England. "I well remember in my childhood," he later wrote, "seeing the endless procession of emigrants passing by day, and often encamping by night on the little green in front of the house where I was living." He was always captivated by the vivid picture this early experience gave him of the great migration from Europe and the eastern states, passing westward through the Mohawk Valley to spread out in the far interior on the network of waterways, canals, and railroads that linked everything together.[6] He was later to make millions in the railroad boom, rising to become perhaps the richest lawyer in the United States, and in the 1870's the wealthiest man to run for the presidency since George Washington.

Alexander Mackenzie, also a boy in the 1820's, grew up

[4] John Morley, *The Life of William Ewart Gladstone* (London, 1903), I, 9–21.
[5] The "North Country" is difficult to define precisely. It may generally be taken to include the six northern counties that run up to the Scottish border: Lancashire, Yorkshire, Westmorland, Cumberland, County Durham, and Northumberland. In another sense, the North Country is the industrial region that begins with Birmingham, the heart of the industrial Midlands, and runs northward.
[6] John Bigelow, *Life of Samuel J. Tilden* (New York, 1895), I, 356. See references to this theme in: Speech, New York Constitutional Convention, Sept. 11, 1867, in John Bigelow, ed., *The Writings and Speeches of Samuel J. Tilden* (New York, 1885), I, 350; Speech, Union Square, New York City, Sept. 17, 1866, ibid., I, 342; First Annual Message, Albany, Jan. 5, 1875, ibid., II, 37–8; Speech, Buffalo, Aug. 10, 1875, ibid., II 214–15; Second Annual Message, Albany, Jan. 4, 1876, ibid., II, 238; Speech, New York City, Nov. 8, 1877, ibid., 494.

almost within sight of the North Sea in a quiet Highland Scottish town. He left his home during the depression of the 1840's to find work building railroad bridges as a stonecutter in the busy west of Scotland—Glasgow and Liverpool shared much of the American trade—then took ship for Canada. He built stonework in the canals, and moved on with the tide to frontier western Ontario, where he prospered in the construction of public buildings in the new settlements.[7] When he became Canada's first Liberal Premier in the 1870's, the transportation revolution was still underway. He was immediately caught up in the endless railroad problems that afflicted the Canadian government in these decades, for the railroads, in fact, made Canada possible.

During the transatlantic boom, Britain and America became much alike in certain respects. The kind of atmosphere traditionally remarked upon in the United States came into existence in the English North Country as well. Together with the factories and the large urban conglomerates—Manchester, Leeds, Birmingham, Sheffield—regarded with alarm by the landed aristocrats who governed the nation, there arose new attitudes as well. The North Country was industrial, bustling, aggressive, and oriented to the future in a way strange to British culture. It was also egalitarian and democratic. Walter Bagehot remarked in distaste that while Lancashire was sometimes called "America-and-water," it was really "America and very little water. . . . [In] commerce, we question whether New York itself is more intensely eager than Liverpool—at any rate, it is difficult to conceive how it can be." England at large was still not a businessman's world, but in the North Country and in the west of Scotland the self-conscious new capitalist order of confident entrepreneurs was pushing itself forward. To the rural Tories, who disliked the new urban elements in British life, Manchester was almost an "alien colony, living on foreign produce, working up foreign materials, and exporting the produce of their labour to foreign parts." They detested John Bright, the voice of the North

---

[7] Dale C. Thomson, *Alexander Mackenzie: Clear Grit* (Toronto, 1960), pp. 1–25; William Buckingham and G. W. Ross, *The Hon. Alexander Mackenzie: His Life and Times* (Toronto, 1892), pp. 40–105.

Country. Looking to American equalitarianism in admiration
—he lauded what he described as its free churches, free
schools, free land, free votes, free careers open to all—and
caustically attacking the rooted aristocracies that dominated
British life, he was quite disrespectful of what Asa Briggs
calls "the traditional deference structure of English society."
Even in personal style, North Countrymen and Scots seemed
American. Justice Oliver Wendell Holmes met William Gladstone in 1866, and found him "to be . . . like an American. He
came out to meet you and had gusto . . ." Walter Bagehot
made the same point with disdain: "Underneath the scholastic polish of his Oxford education, [Mr. Gladstone] has the
speculative hardihood, the eager industry of a Lancashire
merchant."[8]

The similarity between the United States and Britain
went much beyond the introduction of a new openness and
egalitarianism in British culture. It extended to the whole
way of life. Long familiar has been Alexis de Tocqueville's
picture of the harried, terribly serious, rushing, dollar-conscious Jacksonian Americans with their inability to play, their
indifference to learning and culture, and their impatience
with anything that did not bear directly upon increasing
profits. Common too is the description of the American who
boasts about bigness, is in love with rising graphs, and forgets
quality in a delirium of quantity. Fatal to his peace of mind,
observers frequently have remarked, has been the American's
obsession with success.

But when the American intellectual, on his pilgrimage to
the shrine, visited Britain, he was shocked to find there the
same kind of world. The most recent researches into the life
of the Victorians reveal that they lived a dynamic, free-wheel-

[8] Asa Briggs, *Victorian People: A Reassessment of Persons and Themes,
1851–1867* (New York, 1963), pp. 197–9, 204–5; Walter Bagehot,
Bagehot's Historical Essays, ed., Norman St. John-Stevas (Garden
City, N.Y., 1965), pp. 241–2; Donald Read, *The English Provinces, c.
1760–1960: A Study in Influence* (New York, 1964), for the best discussion of the North Country; R. B. McDowell, *British Conservatism,
1832–1914* (London, 1959), p. 50; Mark De Wolfe Howe, *Holmes-
Laski Letters: The Correspondence of Mr. Justice Holmes and Harold
J. Laski, 1916–1935* (New York, 1963), II, 127.

ing life.[9] A constant Victorian complaint was to remark
wearily upon the ever increasing pace of things. The speed of
transport and communication meant greater competition,
more worry at missed opportunities. "If you want to see life,"
one of Benjamin Disraeli's characters in his novels remarks,
"go to Staley-bridge or Bolton. There's high pressure." Only
the Manchester bank, he said, had kept pace. "That's a noble
institution, full of commercial enterprises; understands the
age, sire; high-pressure to the backbone."

Victorians took great pride in themselves and in their
material improvements. They had a simple delight in bigness
and quantity—more people, longer railroads, more coal.
There was a grueling pressure of work, pushed on not just by
the opportunities of the boom but by a set of values that
idealized work almost above all other virtues. People were
grim, driven by care in the working classes, by a fear of
failure in the business world. "The *summum bonum* for everyone not born into the aristocracy was success. To win the
race of life, to outdistance your competitors, to reach the top
and hold a position in which *you* gave the orders that others
executed—this was the crowning glory."[1]

In such an atmosphere, intellectual appetites, as in the
United States, were dulled. Businessmen were proudly indifferent to education, advising their sons against going to
Oxford or Cambridge and wasting their time. Speculation of
any kind in matters not severely practical was frowned
upon. Concrete action, the development of enterprise, pragmatic solutions to practical problems—this was the dominating frame of the British mind.[2]

John Stuart Mill and Matthew Arnold, the chief critics of
British culture in the mid-century, often attacked philistinism
as the besetting evil of the new order. Arnold, indeed, was

[9] The following discussion is drawn from Walter E. Houghton's remarkable *The Victorian Frame of Mind, 1830–1870* (Yale, 1957), *passim*. On the American intellectual's response to British conditions,
see Richard L. Rapson, "The British Traveler in America, 1860–1935"
(Ph.D. dissertation, Columbia University, 1965; soon to be published
by the University of Washington Press), p. 63 *n*.
[1] Houghton, *Victorian Frame of Mind*, p. 191.
[2] Ibid., pp. 111–16.

the first to use the word as a synonym for smug, narrow, and conventional tastes, characteristic of his fellow Victorians and their indifference to cultural and aesthetic values. "Your middle-class man," he acidly observed, "thinks it the highest pitch of development and civilization when his letters are carried twelve times a day from Islington to Camberwell, and from Camberwell to Islington. . . . He thinks it nothing that the trains only carry him from an illiberal, dismal life at Islington to an illiberal, dismal life at Camberwell . . ."[3] The pervasiveness of such values, urged on by a booming economy, led to their being almost as common among the landed aristocracy as among the businessmen. Artists and literary men were equally concerned with the money nexus.[4]

For this reason, both Arnold and Mill tended to see the United States as simply Britain with some qualities missing, and others exaggerated. Did the Americans as a whole, Mill asked in 1840, "both in their good qualities and in their defects, resemble anything so much as an exaggeration of our own middle class?" Twenty-five years later Arnold complained that "to be too much with the Americans is like living with somebody who has all one's own bad habits and tendencies . . ." Mill argued that de Tocqueville's complaint that the Americans lacked respect for intelligence could be made of the British as well. This same "characteristic abounded in England, where it resulted not from democracy [as de Tocqueville had hypothesized of America] but from 'the habit of energetic action, without a proportional development of the taste for speculation.' "[5] "What stirs the hope or moves the aspiration of our Englishman?" John Morley asked bitterly in 1874. Nothing but "doing a roaring trade."[6]

The British were not only like the Americans in their business spirit, their hectic life, and their lack of concern for culture, but also in their indifference to the European continent. Isolation from continental affairs had always been a

3 Edward Alexander, *Matthew Arnold and John Stuart Mill* (New York and London, 1965), p. 193.
4 Houghton, *Victorian Frame of Mind*, p. 184.
5 Alexander, *Arnold and Mill*, pp. 225, 201.
6 Quoted in Basil Willey, *More Nineteenth Century Studies: A Group of Honest Doubters* (London, 1956), p. 278.

British characteristic, but the intellectual and cultural gap had been made far wider by the French Revolution and the Napoleonic Wars. In this long and bitter struggle, in which the British stood out as the one power that defied conquest, they developed a lively distaste for everything French. When they thought of France, and indeed of the whole continent, they thought of licentious reason, frivolous morals, and apparently senseless rebellions. The British gloried in their assumed superiority to all this, taking pride in what they felt was their greater moral health and their deeper religious faith, as contrasted with French intellectuality and loose living. By the mid-century period, they smugly contrasted their Victorian calm and prosperity with the revolutions, disorder, and infidelity that seemed to run rampant across the Channel. Their pride in themselves, their complacency, and their insular prejudice against anything continental became deeply rooted national characteristics.[7] On both sides of the Atlantic, the inward-turning Anglo-American world was indifferent to European thought, listening, rather, to its own voices.

Arnold and Mill urged in vain that their countrymen should break out of their insularity. "Nothing more clearly and decisively set [them] apart from their contemporaries," observes Edward Alexander, "than their serious concern with the life and thought of Continental countries." They singled out mid-century Liberals for special criticism, repeatedly blaming "the disasters of English politics and the failures of English Liberalism upon ignorance of foreign thought and institutions."[8]

Few British thinkers, conversely, had much prestige on the continent. Thomas Carlyle's impassioned pleas for work and success made him in many respects the prophet of the age in Britain, but as John Morley observed, he was entirely outside the mainstream of European thought. Young American scholars studying in German universities found that the great idol of many Americans and Britons, Herbert Spencer, was on the continent looked upon as only a "local writer of

[7] Asa Briggs, *The Making of Modern England, 1783–1867: The Age of Improvement* (New York, 1965), pp. 172, 344–5.
[8] Alexander, *Arnold and Mill*, pp. 199–201.

the English-speaking tribes and as no Aristotle."[9] T. H. Green's persuasive appeals to politicians to think in terms of the whole people, the state, and collective action, made him extraordinarily influential among Liberals toward the end of the century, but as his biographer remarks, his reputation suffered from the fact that Britain was still isolated from the intellectual life of continental Europe. Only two influences went against the tide of Britain's contented isolationism: the interest of key groups and leaders—William Gladstone chief among them—in struggles for independence in other countries; and the urgings of political economists, who were interested in the expansion of trade.[1]

The North Atlantic boom not only set off soaring hopes and reshaped lives, it suffused the Anglo-American world with anxiety. Prosperity, for one thing, did not continue endlessly. There were violent swings in employment, in business activity, in inflation and deflation, in the fortunes of families and individuals, and in public alarm and public hopes. This sequence "was the primal experience of Jacksonian life . . . [fixing] the content, tone, and terms of politics for as long as Jacksonianism counted in America."[2] In the midst of the sweeping away of cherished landmarks, the instability of money, and the transforming of ways of life, men on both sides of the Atlantic searched for explanations. The Jacksonians found them in the United States Bank, which was to them the symbol and the source of the rotten insubstantiality that had apparently come to afflict American life. Invisible forces, set in motion by the bank, seemed to be at work behind the façade of everyday life, sending prices sky-

[9] Donald Fleming, "Social Darwinism," in Arthur M. Schlesinger, Jr., and Morton White, eds., *Paths of American Thought* (Boston, 1963), p. 134.
[1] Willey, *More Nineteenth Century Studies*, p. 299; Melvin Richter, *The Politics of Conscience: T. H. Green and His Age* (Cambridge, Mass., 1964), p. 158; Briggs, *Making of Modern England*, p. 345.
[2] Marvin Meyers, *The Jacksonian Persuasion: Politics and Belief* (New York, 1960), p. 103.

rocketing and then tumbling, the whole quaking structure being founded upon flimsy pyramids of paper money and corrupt relations between moneyed interests and the government. Jacksonians looked back in despair to an idealized republic-that-was, a simple, honest, frugal, and stable Eden that they believed had surrounded the nation's Founding Fathers. They ascribed all their troubles to the greed of a moneyed aristocracy that was given special privileges and incentives by the government and used them to exploit the people.[3]

The British, too, were anxious over the changes that were overturning their traditional life. Anthony Trollope's popular novels contained the same attacks against the world of finance that the Jacksonians made. Trollope bewailed the "infamous trade of stock-jobbing," with its senseless speculations, its dangerous bubbles, and its intrusions into politics, where it induced the collapse of old values. He warned constantly that it was easy for men to rise swiftly in so fluid a society, and then to fall.[4] His views were typical of a widespread concern over the cycle of "speculation, prosperity, over-production, glut, distress," especially after the serious depression of 1837–42 began. Thomas Carlyle attacked the "cash nexus," and Charles Dickens's novels exposed the "shams and inherent emptiness of the world of mid-Victorian finance." The railway boom of the 1840's, which became a kind of mania, produced two reactions, one of them pride in progress, the other a sense of alarm at the shattering of the old order.[5]

William Cobbett was not the only angry man who wanted "his old world back again, his memory—idealised like most men's early memories—of the England which he had known and loved before the great wars and the great factories came." Benjamin Disraeli in the 1840's attacked the age as one of "political materialism and infidelity, mean passions, petty thoughts, an age of movement but of confused purposes, seeking a safety-valve in bustle." Rural Tories looked

[3] Ibid., *passim*, especially pp. 3–32.
[4] Briggs, *Victorian People*, pp. 95–6.
[5] Briggs, *Making of Modern England*, pp. 296–312, 472–4, 385–400.

upon all the new things in economic and political life as creating not only "increased activity, enterprise, wealth and power; but on the other hand, greediness of gain, looseness of principle, wretchedness, disaffection, and political insecurity." As Walter E. Houghton observes, the fundamental ambivalence of modern Anglo-American life, torn by the hopes of progress and by the pain that comes with loss of the old, springs from this hopeful and yet anxious age. Not only is their optimism still ours, so as well is their despair and skepticism.[6]

These British fears, so like those of the Jacksonians, found similar expression in politics. Robert Peel's government in the 1840's took a view of the economy that remarkably resembled that of the Jacksonians, and like them they enacted reforms intended to dampen speculation, stabilize money, and remove special economic privileges. In fact, the Peelites, though they went under the name "Conservative," were in many ways the British counterparts of the Jacksonian Democrats.[7]

The most dramatic counterpart in Britain to Jacksonian events, however, was the years-long campaign of oratory, parades, pamphleteering, and mass agitation that led to the Repeal of the Corn Laws—the protective tariff on wheat—in 1846. So like the controversy over the United States Bank, it reflected the conviction of British reformers that the root cause of Britain's troubles was the greed of the landlords, "the bread-taxing oligarchy, unprincipled, unfeeling, rapacious and plundering."[8] Holding vast acreages, forcing most farmers to be tenants, and demanding high tariffs on wheat to exclude foreign competition, the landlords seemed to be taking from everyone, worker and employer alike, the fruits of their toil. The key point in the whole campaign against

---

[6] G. D. H. Cole, *Persons and Periods* (London, 1938), p. 157. See also G. D. H. and Margaret Cole, eds., *The Opinions of William Cobbett* (London, 1944); McDowell, *Conservatism*, p. 42; Briggs, *Making of Modern England*, p. 216; Houghton, *Victorian Frame of Mind*, pp. xiv, 165.

[7] See Chapter 6 for a full discussion of this point.

[8] Briggs, *Making of Modern England*, p. 314. See also R. B. McCallum, *The Liberal Party from Earl Grey to Asquith* (London, 1963), pp. 43–60.

them was the demand for cheap food, primarily for the worker, but for all consumers as well. Low food costs would admittedly help employers by reducing the pressure for higher wages, but they were vital for the laboring classes. Even more appealing, perhaps, was the symbolic value of Corn Law repeal as a defeat for the older aristocratic order and a victory for the new elements in British life.

The Corn Law struggle also suggests one of the major contrasts within the Anglo-American community: the differing images of the enemy held by British and American politicians. To Jacksonians, and for that matter to Democrats in general, the enemy has always been found among the businessmen. Arthur M. Schlesinger, Jr., made the oft-quoted observation that in the United States the "business community has been ordinarily the most powerful of [the competing groups in society], and liberalism in America has been ordinarily the movement on the part of the other sections of society to restrain the power of the business community. This was the tradition of Jefferson and Jackson, and it has been the basic meaning of American liberalism."[9] With the important qualification that for Democrats the enemy consisted of certain kinds of businessmen—a distinction to be more fully discussed later on—this is a highly suggestive assertion.

In Britain, however, the businessman did not occupy the apex of the social pyramid, as he virtually did in the United States. For all his wealth he could never become supreme either in power or prestige, for this was reserved to the landed aristocrat. This had the important effect of providing a different enemy for the British Liberals. Their enemy was not so much an aristocracy of the wealthy and powerful in the business community as it was an aristocracy of the wealthy and powerful among the landed, which in effect meant the traditional upper class. The animus of British Liberalism "was directed against the aristocracy of birth and rank . . . against the whole amalgam of upper-class society in Britain, rank, land, Church, services and varsity [the aristo-

[9] Arthur M. Schlesinger, Jr., *The Age of Jackson* (Boston, 1945), p. 505.

cratic graduates of Oxford and Cambridge]."[1] British Liberals drew upon pungent criticisms of businessmen in Adam Smith's writings, but much more prominent in their eyes and in their oratory were the structure and the symbols of social superiority in all of its aspects, particularly as embodied in the position and the prejudices of the landed aristocracy.

When the American Democrats conceived of their enemy, therefore, they saw men whose privileges were specifically economic; who erected mechanisms of exploitation based upon such special privileges as tariffs, bounties, control of the currency system, and "influence." Though British Liberals were also concerned with these matters—the whole drive to Free Trade consisted of a long assault against such devices—they were far more likely to think of their enemy as men whose privileges were predominantly social. The aristocracy's land was a prominent object of attack, but so were all the other badges and institutions of hierarchy. The Liberal attack was perhaps more than anything else an attack against the aristocratic *mentality*. The Tory, Liberals said, was a man who liked to dominate, who felt he had a divine right to rule, who doted on exclusiveness and badges of status, who regarded all others as inferior beings. It was this image of the Tory that filled Gladstone's speeches and writings after he became a great popular leader.

The presence of the landed aristocracy is what gives all of British politics in the nineteenth century a special character, setting it off in major ways from politics in North America. In the Lords, in Ireland, in the countryside, in Commons, most of all in the cabinets, the landed continued to exercise great social and political authority, as recent researches have shown, long after the Reform of 1832, which ostensibly ushered the middle classes into the place of power. Even the Liberal Party's cabinets did not become preponderantly middle-class until after 1906. Even then, it was not the business element in the middle class that contributed the minis-

---

[1] R. B. McCallum, "The Liberal Outlook," in Morris Ginsberg, ed., *Law and Opinion in England in the 20th Century* (Berkeley and Los Angeles, 1959), pp. 69–70.

ters—businessmen by then having largely gone over to the Tories, following Joseph Chamberlain—but primarily lawyers and professional men.[2]

The landed were also a major source of capital for industry, deriving their funds from agricultural investments, minerals, and other rights. The great estates they held were sometimes empires in themselves. The Duke of Sutherland possessed 1,385,000 acres in Scotland, and the Duke of Buccleuch some 460,000. The political leverage this landed power had upon British affairs at some of the most crucial junctures of the nineteenth century is exemplified in the mass defection of the Whigs—who were generally landed aristocrats—from Gladstone on the Irish question, thus leading to the failure of his hopes and the splitting of his party. The Whigs owned far too much of Ireland for them to stay with Gladstone all the way. Eleven who voted against him on the land bill in 1880 held more than 20,000 acres each in Ireland. By the 1886 Home Rule fight, in which Gladstone went down to defeat, Whiggery had become an almost solid phalanx against its former leader.[3]

The power of the landlord was intensified by his ascendancy over the British mind. In the important function of providing the most admired social model, the American businessman was largely unchallenged in his own country. His counterpart in Britain, however, was far below the landed aristocracy in social status. The ambition for almost everyone in Britain was to achieve gentility, which meant land, a country seat, and preferably a title.[4] The "English gentleman," as a concept and as a role, was extraordinarily pervasive in the Victorian mind and world. The introduction of civil service itself was in part designed to preserve the power of the gentleman in government before the rising wave of democracy

[2] W. L. Guttsman, *The British Political Elite* (London, 1963), Ch. iv: "The Changing Social Structure of the British Political Elite, 1886–1955."
[3] Briggs, *Making of Modern England*, pp. 406–9; W. L. Burn, *The Age of Equipoise: A Study of the Mid-Victorian Generation* (New York, 1965), p. 306; Donald Southgate, *The Passing of the Whigs, 1832–1886* (London, 1962), pp. 370–6.
[4] Houghton, *Victorian Frame of Mind*, pp. 184–8.

swept him out, in the American fashion, in favor of common talents.[5] So persistent has been this difference between the United States and Britain that one recent commentator on the present sociology of Anglo-American politics could observe that Britain—and Canada as well—believes "in a traditional elite restricting and guiding representative democracy . . . and therefore has less distrust of central government. The United States believes that the bourgeoise can govern society far better than any government . . ."[6]

In Britain, therefore, despite the views of many Liberals, a pattern of deference toward social superiors remained a potent influence upon thought and politics throughout the Victorian period, and into the present century. "The English, of all ranks and classes," wrote John Stuart Mill in 1858, "are at bottom, in all their feelings, aristocrats. They have the conception of liberty, and set some value on it, but the very idea of equality is strange and offensive to them."[7]

There was, of course, an aristocratic tradition in the United States as well, springing from the colonial period. It was expressed in the assumption widely held among the American upper classes early in the history of the new nation that they could expect deference from the common people, could confidently proceed on the assumption that the people should choose their rulers but not govern them, and could act as if the idea of a governing elite were permanently rooted in the American mind.[8] This all gave way, however, rather quickly after the turn of the century. It has often been remarked that the Whigs[9] of the age of Jackson jettisoned the aristocratic mystique of their Federalist forebears. They did not by any means do so completely, however. As will be later discussed, they held to important aristocratic habits of mind

[5] Ibid., p. 283; Burns, *Equipoise*, pp. 255–65.
[6] Robert R. Alford, *Party and Society: The Anglo-American Democracies* (Chicago, 1963), p. 5.
[7] Quoted in Houghton, *Victorian Frame of Mind*, p. 103.
[8] Cf. David H. Fischer, *The Revolution of American Conservatism: The Federalist Party in the Era of Jeffersonian Democracy* (New York, 1966).
[9] Not to be confused with the English Whigs. The American Whigs existed in the age of Jackson as Jackson's opposition; they derived from the Hamiltonian Federalists, and became the Republican Party in the 1850's.

in government, and in so important a state as New York an aristocracy flourished long past the time when democracy was supposed to have swept it out. The great boom created a new wealthy class with genuine social and economic, if not political and legal, advantages, and the clamor for status was intense. The prevalent idea was not for all to be the same, but for all to get ahead.[1]

This was a relative matter, however, and to the Britons who toured the United States in the nineteenth century and wrote their hundreds of books about the new world, the thing that fascinated them most of all was the extraordinary social, political, and economic equality that they observed in the United States. It obsessed them. It was a historical equality, lacking all the feudal inheritances of rank and class that burdened British life; a material equality, which approached the level of classlessness; an equality of opportunity; and an equality of manifestation, in manners, in institutions, and in all the diverse forms of culture.

> Above all, the commentators portrayed an equality of youth: idealistic, rarely satisfied simply with present achievements, nor with accumulated, uninvested wealth, nor with the cultivated sophistication of the leisured, nor even with millennial goals; but an equality which strove and yearned restlessly, unceasingly upwards, energetic, cocky, rough, and humane: an equality which rested its deepest dreams in its children and in their education.[2]

The British government, being directed by aristocrats, was traditionally a strong government with little reluctance to use its powers, as its savage repression of rioting in the 1820's and 1830's demonstrated. The weak and nerveless government of the *laissez faire* stereotype has in fact recently been shown to be largely a historical myth. It is now clear that the long-influential division of the Victorian age by A. V. Dicey into a mid-Victorian era of rigorous *laissez faire* individualism, followed by a late-Victorian turn to collectivism,

[1] Douglas T. Miller, *Jacksonian Aristocracy: Class and Democracy in New York 1830–1860* (New York, 1967).
[2] Rapson, "British Traveler," pp. 127–30, 337.

was fundamentally unsound. There was much talk about the need for *laissez faire,* and with regard to protective tariffs it was in fact established. But weak and inactive government was much more the American way than it was the British. Even in the United States, *laissez faire* as a ruling concept in historical understanding must be greatly qualified.[3]

As A. P. Thornton has recently pointed out at length, the whole of English history, domestic and foreign, is best understood when seen in the light of the fact that the English until recently have for centuries been a *ruling* people. They have what he calls the "habit of authority."[4] The psychology induced by habitual dominance is one in which the rightfulness of authority comes to be assumed as given. Strong government was not the primary point of attack in English domestic affairs, as it often was in the United States, but rather governments that abused their strength. Much more irritating than the use of authority, to the psychology of dominant people, is resistance to authority. Since there is apparently little allowance for or understanding of the relationship of equality—hierarchy of one sort or another being expected in all situations—resistance to authority would seem automatically to have been interpreted as an attempt to reverse roles, to make the master inferior to the one formerly dominated. "Is not everything English maddened in our bosoms," an Englishman exclaimed during the argument with the American colonists, "at the remotest tho't of crouching to the creatures of our formation? Have we erected Colonies to be our masters?"[5] Turbulence itself—as among the Irish, or the Chartists, or the labor unionists—was sufficient cause for condemnation, leading to the view that the complainants were morally deficient. Disloyalty, in a certain sense, was the

[3] Cf. Dicey, *Law and Public Opinion in England During the Nineteenth Century* (London, 1914). Burn, *Equipoise,* discusses the *laissez faire* myth extensively, as does also Briggs, *Making of Modern England.* See also Sidney Fine, *Laissez Faire and the General-Welfare State: A Study of Conflict in American Thought, 1865–1901* (Ann Arbor, 1956).
[4] A. P. Thornton, *The Habit of Authority: Paternalism in British History* (Toronto, 1964). For the classic exploration of the authoritarian cast of mind, see T. W. Adorno *et al., The Authoritarian Personality* (New York, 1950).
[5] John C. Miller, *Origins of the American Revolution* (Boston, 1943), p. 205.

cardinal sin. That the Irish and the Americans might interpret loyalty differently was beside the point.

The issue of loyalty was therefore very prominent in nineteenth-century British political controversy. Many Englishmen felt that Gladstone and the Irish were simply not to be understood on this issue. In Canada, the nation was so deeply divided between the British and the French that the loyalty issue was bitterly obtrusive. Canadian Liberals had constantly to fight accusations that they were disloyal. On both sides of the Atlantic, in short, there was no more constant Tory cry than the loyalty cry. All of British politics was colored with it.

———

In light of the foregoing, it may be understood why the anxieties so prominent in American and British politics in the nineteenth century were different in kind in Britain than they were in the United States. The American Democrats were obsessed primarily by ills in the economy and by threats to a democratic republic of simplicity and virtue. In Britain, the despairs associated with the changes in the economy were joined by a different kind of anxiety altogether. Men were disturbed by the attacks against the institutions of the hierarchical structure—the Crown, Parliament, the Church, the universities were all to some extent under siege—but they were outraged by attacks against the hierarchical structure itself. John Bright opposed the deference system and called for equality; William Gladstone described the Tories as natural bullies with an insatiable urge to dominate others. This campaign against the privileged position of the ruling circles tied together the many separate campaigns against established institutions, giving a fundamentally hierarchical people much cause for alarm.

The Liberals in effect were calling for the creation of a different kind of British nation. There were many arguments going on in Britain, but perhaps the fundamental argument was over what form the nation was to take. It had entered the nineteenth century with an institutional structure built around one assumption, an assumption that lay at the heart of the Tory party: the nation was to be Anglican, English, and aristocratic.[6] The offices of the Crown were to be held only by Anglicans, the universities were open only to Anglicans, the common schools were Anglican, Parliament was in effect Anglican, local government was by law carried out by Anglicans, the larger circles of power and society were Anglican, and the whole was sanctified by the Established Church —the Church of England—supported by taxes upon the whole English population.

There were many other groups and religious communities in the British Isles. By long tradition they were allowed indifferent toleration, but they were regarded as unfortunate and in a certain sense comic variations from the Anglican English norm.[7] The Scots, the Welsh, the Irish, the Roman Catholics, the Jews, and the Dissenters[8] were tacitly assumed to be in a kind of schism that someday they would leave behind, as they saw the error of their ways, in a grand assimilation to the majority. Even the North Country Englishmen, with their dialects and strange ways, were regarded as crude outlanders who should become more like the southern English to gain equality. Only recently, of course—that is, in the late eighteenth century—had the superiority of southern England in population and wealth over all the other parts of the United Kingdom combined begun to be challenged by growth in the new industrial regions of the north of England and in Scotland.

The dominant groups felt that in enforcing the supremacy of traditional institutions they were carrying out a sacred mission. They were preserving for all Britons what they believed to be the beneficent and manifestly superior English

6 The term "Anglican" refers to members of the Church of England.
7 I am grateful to R. B. McCallum, Master of Pembroke College, Oxford, for his illuminating remarks to me on this subject.
8 The term "Dissenters," like the term "Nonconformists," refers to English Protestants who are not Anglicans: Methodists, Baptists, Independents (Congregationalists), Unitarians, Quakers, and the like. They are generally assumed to have composed perhaps 40 per cent of the English population in the Victorian era, the rest being either actively or nominally Anglican.

institutions that the whole nation would eventually inherit. If the deviants refused to conform, then they had only themselves to blame for being excluded. This attitude is, of course, prominent in all societies with a large and dominant majority. It may be seen among Anglo-Saxon Protestants in the United States, among Anglo-Canadians toward French-Canadians, and, to go further afield, among Hindus toward Moslems in India.[9]

The Anglican English therefore found no difficulty in justifying the policy of forcing Roman Catholic Irishmen to pay taxes for the support of an established (Anglican) Church of Ireland. If the Irish objected, and the world outside England was scornful, the duty of the English was to redouble their missionary effort and continue the long struggle to convert the Irish to the true faith. At the same time, the Irish economy was to be similarly remade in the English image. It was to be transformed from its peasant subsistence-farming condition to a capitalist, commercial agricultural system integrated into the market economy, cleared of its peasantry, farmed by tenant farmers, and directed by English landowners.[1] Thus the assumption behind British rule in Ireland—when one does not find it simply in economic interest or fears for military security—was that it was necessary in order to remake the Irish in the English image, to rescue them from what was felt to be the blight of Popery and the squalor of un-English ways of life.

On all sides, however, a new demand was being voiced in Victorian Britain. Newly militant minority groups—the Welsh, the Dissenters, the Irish, and the many other groups traditionally outside of power—began to insist in their diverse ways that all social groups should be admitted into the life of the nation on a basis of equality. It was also being demanded that the aristocracy, which for centuries had comfortably governed in the belief that government was to be for, but not by, the people, should accept the new age and

[9] I am grateful to my colleague Stephen Hay for his comments relating to India.
[1] Cf. J. L. B. Hammond, *Gladstone and the Irish Nation* (London, 1938).

allow the emergence of a democratic nation. This was disturbing to those in power, for it would involve a new status for the dominant elements, that of being equal partners with despised people. When one of the first steps in this direction was taken in 1830—the appointment of a businessman to a post in the cabinet—he was treated to "mortifying sneers when, a plain merchant, he took his seat on the Government bench" in Commons.[2]

The long argument over the admission of various kinds of people to seats in Commons reflected much of this bitter controversy. The socially dominant wanted a Protestant Parliament, and failed when the Roman Catholics were admitted in 1829; at least a Christian Parliament, and failed when the Jews were admitted in 1858; and at the last, at least a Parliament that was God-fearing, and lost when an atheist was admitted in 1886.

A search through the materials bearing upon this long controversy makes clear that there was more involved in it than whether or not the Anglican English would remain privileged. It meant giving up an illusion: the myth of the homogeneous nation. The English in the United Kingdom—perhaps more accurately, the Tory English—wanted to think of the nation as *English*, not as *British*, a term that implied a pluralistic nation of Welshmen and Scotsmen and Irishmen as well as Englishmen. They wanted to think of it as *Anglican*, not as a nation of many churches and faiths. It did not matter that there were in reality many minority groups present within the nation. Illusions of this kind seem little affected by reality. Those devoted to Anglican English superiority persisted in thinking of the nation in their own image, and of the rest as extraneous elements.

The United States and Canada were by no means free from this controversy. The Anglo-Saxon Protestant American —who was more often than not Republican in his politics— thought of his own kind when he used the word "American," and to a considerable degree he still does. When challenged, he persisted in visualizing the nation in his own image. The

[2] Elie Halévy, *The Triumph of Reform, 1830–1841* (New York, 1961), p. 14.

argument is the more easily followed in Britain than in the United States since superior status in the British Isles was supported by many laws and institutions that had to be challenged—some are still being challenged. That it went on bitterly in the United States, however, is clearly revealed in the long nativist controversy—the attack against immigrants.[3]

At the heart of much of Anglo-American politics lay an argument over what image of the nation men should carry in their minds. Should they see it as pluralistic, should they take pleasure in its diversity, its many accents and hues and life styles, and accord equal dignity to all? The minority groups argued for this image. Or should men rather see the nation as homogeneous, strong in its superior ways and character, its purity, its wholeness, its unity? This was the demand of the socially dominant.

This is an exceptionally difficult argument to document by reference to a few sources. It was often not explicitly stated, but was expressed more in political choices, in symbolic action, and in the implications of ideology and appeal. Minority groups usually chose to vote for a particular party not because it planned to launch a specific program of legislation that would help them, but because it gave them the self-respect that comes with simple recognition and acceptance, usually in the form of nominations to office and patronage. Often, indeed, men simply wanted to know that their side had won. When the Whitby fishermen carried Gladstone's son victoriously about in the election of 1868, "what they were to gain from a Liberal ministry must be rather obscure, but at any rate their position in the town could never be the same again after ousting the Tory landlord from the Whitby seat. They had raised themselves, and that was the central thing."[4]

Group feeling also ebbed and flowed. In what has been called the age of confidence in the United States—the twenty years after the Civil War—a cosmopolitan image of the na-

[3] The nativist controversy is skillfully explored in John Higham, *Strangers in the Land: Patterns of American Nativism, 1860–1925* (New York, 1963).
[4] John Vincent, *The Formation of the British Liberal Party* (New York, 1966), p. xv.

tion, deeply rooted in its formal ideology, flourished grandly. It expressed itself in a conviction that "this new land would bring unity out of diversity as a matter of course . . . [creating] an inclusive nationality, at once diverse and homogeneous . . . a mixed, assimilating nationality . . ."[5] The argument over pluralism and homogeneity was therefore not always prominent in political discourse. Perhaps its best documentation, however, lies in the fact—as Scotsmen and Negroes and French Canadians will attest—that it still goes on.

It was the historic function of the Liberals, and the Whigs before them, to be the voice of the minority groups in British politics. It is revealing that practically the last problem they were struggling with before the First World War was perhaps the greatest single minority-group issue: local self-government for the Irish. The many efforts the Liberals made to meet the demands of the minority groups—to create a pluralistic nation in law as well as in fact—cost them heavily. The most punishing fights they ever undertook were over such issues as the treatment of the Irish and the Welsh, and yet the party kept coming back again and again—if sometimes reluctantly—to the campaigns for Home Rule and for disestablishment of the Church of England in Wales. This suggests a wider meaning to such matters.

It has often been observed that the nineteenth century was more than anything else the century of awakened nationalism. If British experience was typical, this awakening involved more than the new self-consciousness of such large national groups as the Italians and the Poles. It involved also the submerged nationalities, or subcultures, within the nations themselves. A newly conscious Welsh nationalism after the middle of the century, for example, constituted "a political and indeed a cultural renaissance, a rekindling of the flame of national consciousness after centuries of isolation and neglect," as the first historian to explore this phenomenon

[5] Higham, *Strangers in the Land*, pp. 18–21.

has recently remarked.[6] In the United States the "South" had not really existed before the age of Jackson. Men spoke of themselves as Virginians or as Georgians, not as Southerners. Southern nationalism emerged partly in the effort to protect Negro slavery, but one suspects it also received significant stimulus from the rise of nationalism worldwide.[7]

There was also the self-consciousness of English Dissent. A social world that was concentrated in but not limited to the North Country, it was a variant but distinct form of nationalism. The gulf that separated Dissenters from the Anglican world was deep and broad in English life. The non-Anglicans lived separate social, political, and economic lives. They had not only their separate churches—for which their preferred term was "chapel," a Churchman being understood to be an Anglican—but their separate newspapers, schools, social organizations, and living areas.[8] The fact that John Bright was a Dissenter kept him out of the Establishment world and the cabinet for many years after a politician of his elevated standing would ordinarily have been given a ministry. The extraordinary fact is that he not only had to wait for his ministry until 1868, when Gladstone brought him into the cabinet, but that he was the first Dissenter ever to be a member of a British cabinet, though Dissent had formed a major part of English life for almost two hundred years.

The Liberals were not only uniquely sensitive to these subnationalisms and served as their voice in political life, they were also the party most sensitive to the claims of national groups for self-government elsewhere, in Italy, the Balkans, and in the colonies. Perhaps the principal element in William Gladstone's leadership was his sensitivity to national feelings, his belief that they were the most powerful forces in

[6] Kenneth O. Morgan, *Wales in British Politics, 1868–1922* (Cardiff, 1963), p. iii.
[7] Cf. Jesse T. Carpenter, *The South as a Conscious Minority, 1789–1861* (New York, 1930); Avery O. Craven, *The Growth of Southern Nationalism, 1848–1861* (New York, 1953); W. J. Cash, *The Mind of the South* (New York, 1941).
[8] Cf. J. F. Glaser, "English Nonconformity and the Decline of Liberalism," *American Historical Review,* LXIII (1958), 352–63; McCallum, *Liberal Party,* pp. 14–17; Raymond G. Cowherd, *The Politics of English Dissent: The Religious Aspects of Liberal and Humanitarian Reform Movements from 1815 to 1848* (New York, 1956).

the modern world, and his conviction that the disorders afflicting such places as Ireland could only be ended by recognizing these national feelings and giving them expression in self-government. There was a realism in the Liberals' thought that told them that "to deny national right was to defy natural forces greater than any one nation or any one generation could recognize."[9] What this amounted to was a vision of the world community as inherently and ideally a pluralistic community composed of equal states, rather than one divided into a few monolithic imperial power blocs.

The Liberals, then, spoke for the outsiders, the ones who for ethnic and religious reasons were not of the dominating social circles in the nation.[1] Usually the Liberals played this role in connection with internal minority groups, but in some ways they acted most dramatically in connection with a specifically sectional problem.

Britain, Canada, and the United States each grappled for generations with a sectional problem of enormous importance to the nation. For the United States it was the South; for Canada it was Quebec; for Britain it was Ireland. The three sections, for all their differences, were in fact remarkably alike. They were economically the most backward in their nations, were morbidly sensitive to their inferior and threatened positions, were given to rigid and xenophobic religious patterns, suffered from deficiencies in education and industry, and expressed themselves in extremist political styles and imagery. The eventual result of the controversy, of course, was in each case different. The American solution of direct

[9] McCallum, *Liberal Party*, p. 99.
[1] This is not to ignore the fact that most of the Liberals who actually sat in Commons were Anglicans, as John Vincent has demonstrated. They were the *voice* of the outsiders in the same way that mid-twentieth-century Northern Democrats in Congress are whatever voice in that body the Negroes possess, even though they are overwhelmingly white. Few Liberals in Parliament were Dissenters, and few were Irish, yet such aid as the Dissenters and the Irish received came from Liberal hands, and they knew it.

conquest ended the threat sectionalism posed to the nation's further existence without ending its essential bipolarity; the Canadian solution of uncertain accommodation has left the country still in a precarious condition; and the United Kingdom failed utterly to hold together the nation with which it had entered the nineteenth century, for the Catholic Irish successfully seceded.

In each situation, the Democrats and the Liberals sought to serve as the protectors and spokesmen of the threatened section. And in each case the result for the party was similar. They received for their pains widespread contempt in the dominant sections for championing the cause of the detested Southerner, *Québecois*, or Irishman. When the Whigs in Britain, and their successors the Liberals, worked for Catholic Emancipation, for Irish land reform, for disestablishment of the (Anglican) Church of Ireland, and eventually for Home Rule, they excited the hatred of those who opposed all of this.

It is the depth of these feelings that requires further examination. The term "sectional" has been used above in referring to these controversies, for they have the obvious appearance of sectional struggles, and, most notably in the case of the American South, have been so explained. That is to say, the reliance has usually been upon some variant of the interpretive scheme developed by Frederick Jackson Turner. His sectionalism hypotheis was primarily an assertion that the sources of political action lay in the economic interests of geographic regions in the nation.[2] This approach is related, though somewhat distantly, to that of Charles Beard in American and G. D. H. Cole and H. J. Laski in British historiography, all of whose influential works cast historical events in another kind of economic mold, the interests of class. This had the great merit of directing historians' attentions to "real"

[2] Cf. Frederick Jackson Turner, *The Significance of Sections in American History* (New York, 1932); Wilbur R. Jacobs, ed., *Frederick Jackson Turner's Legacy: Unpublished Writings in American History* (San Marino, California, 1965), pp. 45–78; and Wilbur R. Jacobs, "Turner's Methodology: Multiple Working Hypothesis or Ruling Theory?", *The Journal of American History*, LIV (March 1968), 853–63. Professor Turner first began writing on sectionalism in 1907.

factors of very large and abiding importance in politics, influences that could be quantified and specifically described. This kind of economic interpretation, however, has come under criticism as fatally simplistic[3] and tending to provide a misleading one-factor understanding of politics.[4] The "economic man" of Frederick Jackson Turner and Charles Beard explains much—as did the economic man of the classical economists—but his psychology is much too thin.

It is perhaps more expressive of the facts to consider the relationship between the dissenting section and the rest of the nation—while clearly involving economic factors—as an emotional one, involving such feelings as inferiority-superiority and mutual prejudice. In inter-group relations, it is clear that the most powerful sources of action and idea lie in the deeper regions of irrational fears and xenophobia. The secession of the Southern states in 1860–1, for example, was clearly the outgrowth of irrational convictions concerning what "the Yankee" was going to do to race relations in the South—themselves founded upon inferiority-superiority—after the election of Lincoln. Objective economic factors played their role, but the speeches of the fire-eaters in the South and the performance of the Southern armies make it doubtful that economic considerations were the chief factor.[5]

What is to be seen in these long struggles, in the violent resistances they stirred up, the implacable hostilities, the shattering of parties and the bloodshed, is the acting out of group hatreds. Men regarded one another with fear and contempt for almost tribal reasons. As Gordon Allport has shown, prejudiced feelings toward out-groups, while not universal, are a primal fact of life, particularly among peoples under stress.[6] So powerful are such feelings, springing as they do from the deepest sources of the human personality, that

[3] This point will be further developed below.
[4] Cf. Lee Benson, *Turner and Beard* (Glencoe, Ill., 1960).
[5] Cf. The discussion of the Yankee complex in Cash, *Mind of the South*, pp. 113–94. It perhaps should go without saying that my assessment of the most important "cause" of Southern secession represents a personal judgment.
[6] Essential to any understanding of the psychological and sociological roots of this phenomenon is Gordon Allport, *The Nature of Prejudice* (Garden City, N.Y., 1958).

they must often be considered the major determinants of political behavior and attitudes. Lee Benson's study of the politics of the state of New York in the age of Jackson, for example, convincingly demonstrates that prejudiced attitudes between what he terms ethnocultural groups, as against economic influences, "tended to be *relatively* the most important sources of political differences."[7] Parties contained voters drawn to them by a multitude of influences, but most strikingly they appeared to contain large and rather evenly matched coalitions of mutually hostile ethnic and religious groups.

The nineteenth century was pre-eminently the time when, for millions of people in the Anglo-American world, consciousness of group membership entered into their own identities to a much greater degree than is the case among most members of today's mass societies. It was also a time in which prejudice was expressed in hostile action toward many kinds of disliked peoples much more so than is presently the case, except toward the more "indelible" minority groups such as Negroes, Mexican-Americans, and French Canadians. From the standpoint of Allport's scale of acted-out prejudice —ranging from hostile talk, through avoidance, discrimination, and physical attack, to extermination[8]—it would seem accurate to say that the twentieth century differs from the nineteenth in the Anglo-American community chiefly in the reduction that has taken place in the number of groups toward which most men feel prejudice, and the level at which this prejudice is acted out.

Such feelings have not disappeared, nor lost their influence on politics. Subcultures of dialect and local feeling (though rarely of religious feeling any longer) are a prominent fact of British life in the mid-twentieth century, as the election of Welsh and Scottish Nationalists in 1966 and 1967 demonstrated.[9]

[7] Lee Benson, *The Concept of Jacksonian Democracy: New York as a Test Case* (New York, 1964), p. 165.
[8] Allport, *Nature of Prejudice*, pp. 14–15.
[9] Cf. George S. Pryde, *Scotland from 1603 to the Present Day* (Edinburgh, 1962), pp. 285 ff.; and Maurice Lindsay, *By Yon Bonnie Banks: A Gallimaufry* (London, 1961), *passim*.

Furthermore, it has recently been shown that ethnic voting patterns in the United States remain remarkably persistent. Serious doubt has been cast on the long-standing "assimilation" theory, which holds that second- and third-generation immigrants lose a consciousness of their ethnic identity with increasing economic prosperity, and as they enter the middle class begin voting a different ticket. There is persuasive evidence that so long as ethnic groups remain in one location and are not broken up, rising wealth even intensifies a tendency to vote for a particular party, for the ethnic group can produce more men who by wealth and position can claim nominations. Once "mobilized" by such nominations to office, ethnic groups continue to vote for a given party long after the occasion for the original vote has passed. The fact that the Democrats were the most ready to make nominations from among minority groups like the Italians and the Poles has resulted in the dominance of the Democrats among such groups growing even stronger during the twentieth century, rather than declining as affluence has risen.[1]

Nathan Glazer and Daniel Patrick Moynihan, in their studies of the ethnic groups of New York City, have been led to conclude that the politics of that city are still primarily shaped by ethnic identity. "Ethnicity is more than an influence on events; it is commonly the source of events. Social and political institutions do not merely respond to ethnic interests; a great number of institutions exist for the specific purpose of serving ethnic interests."[2]

In Canada, group prejudice between Anglo-Canadians and French Canadians is still so powerful that it remains, with regionalism, much more influential than economic considerations in shaping voting patterns. Class differences exist, and they express themselves in politics, but they do not deflect voters from one party to another so much as does the influence of group prejudice. It has been suggested that Can-

[1] Raymond E. Wolfinger, "The Development and Persistence of Ethnic Voting," *American Political Science Review*, LIX (1965), 896–908.
[2] Nathan Glazer and Daniel Patrick Moynihan, *Beyond the Melting Pot: The Negroes, Puerto Ricans, Jews, Italians and Irish of New York City* (Cambridge, Mass., 1964), p. 310.

ada possesses, in comparison with Britain and the United
States, an almost purely non-class political system, for the
political parties are still "identified as representatives of re-
gional, religious, and ethnic groups rather than as representatives of national class interests."[3]

The Liberals and the Democrats were shaped by circumstances largely peculiar to the nineteenth century, circumstances which have steadily declined in force in the twentieth
century, either through removal of grievances, the dissipation
of religious feelings, the scattering of minorities, or the steady
development of a unified national culture. In the British Isles
and in the United States, the majority culture is unconsciously getting its way. A homogeneous society is in process
of being created. Maurice Lindsay, a deeply partisan Scot,
has recently lamented that English culture is reaching out so
strongly to transform the rest of Britain that soon his beloved
Scotland will lose its distinctiveness entirely and become
nothing more than North Britain.[4] Similarly, the outward
pressure of the cultural life generated in the American North-
east and Pacific Coast is increasingly homogenizing the cultural life of all of North America and extinguishing the special character of local regions, to the complaints of Canadians
and Southerners alike.

In Great Britain the importance of religious groups as
subcultures mediating between their members and the larger
community has to a large extent died away. The best assessment of the decline of the Liberal Party, in fact, links it to the
dissipation of religious zeal among the Dissenting sects.[5]
Although ethnic identities still retain some of their former
salience in politics, it is difficult to find in Britain the powerful source of strength for left-wing politics that once existed
in the self-conscious group feeling of Dissent. In the whole of
the North Country, Colne Valley, high up in the Pennines,
would seem to be the only constituency where any longer the

[3] Alford, *Party and Society*, p. 251. See also pp. 250–86, the whole of Ch.
ix, "Canada: Pure Non-Class Politics?"
[4] Cf. Lindsay, *By Yon Bonnie Banks, passim.*
[5] Glaser, "English Nonconformity and the Decline of Liberalism."

mark of Dissent upon a candidate swings the victory in his way.[6]

Jacksonian New York provides an excellent case study of these matters. In this situation, the Democrats were clearly the party of the outgroups.[7] So obvious was this that a Whig newspaper angrily attacked the Democrats after their victory in 1844 for reaping the harvest of an "avalanche of Germans, Irish, Swiss, Prussians, French, Russians, and Poles."[8] The Germans in particular voted heavily Democratic, to a point approaching unanimity. Half of them were Catholic and encountered the hostility of the Protestant majority, and all of them spoke a foreign tongue and had markedly foreign traits. The French Canadian *Québecois* moving down into New York also voted almost unanimously Democratic—about 95 per cent—and so did the French merchants in New York City.[9]

The most revealing situation of all, however, was that relating to the immigrants from the British Isles. They were divided among themselves originally by deeply rooted mutual hostilities. One powerful influence, however, soon drove the English, the Scots, and the Welsh into the Whig-Republican party: practically every Catholic Irishman voted the Democratic ticket, giving that party a pronouncedly Irish image in everyone's eyes. They voted Democratic whether they lived in the city or the country, whether they were laborers or farmers.[1] They voted Democratic, in short, as an expression of their identity. For decades thereafter in American politics—until well into the twentieth century—it is clear that not to vote Democratic would make an Irish-American an outcast in his own community. As John Bright said in a similar situation in England, he was a Quaker and therefore "I could not be otherwise than Liberal."[2] An abortive bolt of

[6] The point was discussed with Labour Party agents in Yorkshire and Lancashire in the summer of 1966.
[7] With the glaring exception of the free Negro, who was detested by the Democrats, and voted strongly Whig. This important problem is discussed at length in Chapter 7.
[8] Benson, *Concept of Jacksonian Democracy*, p. 175.
[9] Ibid., pp. 173–6.
[1] Ibid., pp. 171–3.
[2] Briggs, *Victorian People*, p. 202.

Irish radicals took place to the Republicans in the 1880's, in an attempt to discipline the Democrats and gain a position of greater leverage. The result, if anything, was to solidify further the Democratic voting pattern of the Irish, for the movement failed in its larger goals.[3]

Several influences probably converged to make the Irishmen choose the Democrats. Following Thomas Jefferson, they were the anti-British party, a stance most appealing to the Catholic Irish. The Irish, furthermore, clearly recognized that the Democrats were the American counterparts of their friends in Britain, the Liberals. In the 1830's, when Irish political loyalties were being established, there was an intimate link between Jacksonian radicals and British Liberals.[4] If this were not enough, the American Whigs were the voice of nativism. The result was that when the Democrats developed an efficient system for recruiting Irish voters after manhood suffrage began in 1827, they had great success.[5]

The Catholic Irish apparently played the same role in the British mind as the Negro in the American mind, for they seemed to excite a strikingly similar kind of distaste. It is revealing that when investigators asked Americans in the twentieth century to describe the attributes of Negroes, they used terminology like that used toward the Irish Catholic in nineteenth-century Anglo-America: inferior mentality, primitive morality, emotional instability, overassertiveness, laziness and boisterousness, religious fanaticism, fondness for gambling, gaudiness of dress, closeness to anthropoid ancestors, tendency toward crimes of violence with razors and knives, high birth rate, susceptibility to bribery by politicians, happy-go-lucky attitude, ignorance, and fondness for music.[6] Striking, too, is the fact that defending the Irish, as Gladstone did, meant braving the same public condemnation that abolitionists received in the United States before the Civil War

---

[3] Thomas N. Brown, *Irish-American Nationalism, 1870–1890* (Philadelphia and New York, 1966), pp. 133–82.
[4] Thistlethwaite, *America and the Atlantic Community*, pp. 39–75.
[5] Robert Ernst, *Immigrant Life in New York City, 1825–1863* (Port Washington, N.Y., 1965), p. 162.
[6] Allport, *Nature of Prejudice*, p. 192.

and that civil-rights workers receive in mid-twentieth-century America.[7]

In the English northwest, and in western Scotland, the Irish had settled in large, compact gatherings to provide unskilled labor in industry and on the docks. They were regarded with alarm by English and Scottish workingmen because of their competition, and with hatred for their differences, in a manner much like that of workingmen in the Northern states in their relation to free Negroes.[8] It was the presence of large numbers of Irish in and around Glasgow that eventually pushed significant numbers of Scots, normally determinedly Liberal, into the Conservative Party.[9] Hatred of the Irish in the early days of Robert Peel was enough in good times to swing English cities over to the Tory column, since Peel opposed the vote for Catholic Irishmen. He loathed them, felt an "honest despotic government" was the best thing for them since they were—in his eyes—semi-savages, largely because of their Roman Catholicism. Through his influence Catholic Emancipation was defeated in 1816 and 1817, and an approving Oxford University, the nucleus of hard-core Anglicanism, voted him thereafter the Oxford seat in Commons. In the 1820's, when the Irish issue almost dominated English politics, the masses clearly agreed with the Tories in their bitter anti-Catholicism and disagreed with the Whigs and Radicals who pleaded for admitting Catholics to the vote and to Parliament. Some Tories, of the Canningite persuasion, were pro-Catholic, but much more typical of the Tory mind were the "ultras" who worked closely with the Protestant Ascendancy forces in Ireland, supported missionary Bible campaigns among the Irish peasantry, and felt an almost visceral contempt for Catholicism.[1]

---

[7] Cf. Herman Ausubel, In Hard Times: Reformers Among the Late Victorians (New York, 1960), pp. 273–4.
[8] Halévy, Triumph of Reform, pp. 159–61; Joseph G. Rayback, "The American Workingman and the Antislavery Crusade," Journal of Economic History, III (1943), 152–64; Albon P. Man, Jr., "Labor Competition and the New York Draft Riots of 1863," Journal of Negro History, XXXVI (1951), 375–405; Williston H. Lofton, "Northern Labor and the Negro during the Civil War," ibid., XXXIV (1949), 251–73.
[9] J. G. Kellas, "The Liberal Party in Scotland, 1885–1895" (Ph.D. dissertation, University of London, 1961), pp. 25–7.
[1] Elie Halévy, The Liberal Awakening, 1815–1830 (New York, 1961),

To most Englishmen, the Irish seemed beyond salvaging. What was to be thought, they asked themselves, of

> peasants whose traditions and living conditions had hardly accustomed them to sustained industry or self-improvement, the cardinal virtues which the Victorians commended to the poor? . . . The middle classes despised a country without a respectable middle class; the professional men scorned a nation without an intelligentsia. And the character of the Irish M.P.s in the 'fifties confirmed British prejudices. "As silly, as broguey, as useless, as quarrelsome and as contemptible as ever," a Radical called them after the election of 1852. "Mr. Duffy, Mr. Moore and their little party have two Irish reforms to effect—first to make the Irish Catholic members honest, next to make them respectable."[2]

The uproar in British politics caused by the Irish problem in the second half of the century constantly exacerbated relations and attitudes. Those against Home Rule continually rolled out the familiar charges: the Catholic Irish were inferior; they were "fickle, impulsive, unstable, unreliable, violent; and they could not be trusted to govern themselves, much less the protestants in Ireland."[3] The Fenians in America may have been few in numbers and ineffectual, but they aroused alarm in England as they launched direct attacks not only against Canada but against England itself in wild attempts to bring about Irish independence. It was believed they might murder any public official in his bed or blow up any government building, for they had vowed war on any agency of the Queen wherever met. This heightened anti-Irish sentiments on both sides of the Atlantic in the 1860's.[4]

Tragically, people subject to widespread contempt and oppression tend to behave as if their popular image is accurate. They display the traits of victimization. Constant reiteration of what is expected of a person tends to become a self-

---

pp. 138–42; Halévy, *Triumph of Reform*, pp. 180–2; G. I. T. Machin, *The Catholic Question in English Politics, 1820 to 1830* (Oxford, 1964), *passim*.
[2] Southgate, *Passing of the Whigs*, pp. 186–7.
[3] Ausubel, *In Hard Times*, p. 302.
[4] Ibid., pp. 270–3.

fulfilling prophecy. It is not uncommon for members of such groups to defend themselves by adopting suspicious, cunning, aggressive, and rebellious traits, or conversely—as in the case of the Negro, both slave and free—to curry favor by the pathetic clowning and self-deprecating behavior of the Sambo type. It was the cruel fate of many Irish in the United States to be either a bitterly angry person who created fear and distrust in the general populace or the comic Irishman who projected an impression of limited capacities.[5] In either case, the prejudices of other people were confirmed, righteous indignation could be joined by a sense of superiority, and the status of the Irish as an outgroup was intensified.[6]

Fused by their common distaste for the Catholic Irish, the Welsh, English, and Scottish immigrants formed a solid bloc of Whig, and later Republican, votes. They had not carried with them a sense of being "British" when they emigrated, but in a classic demonstration of what has been called negative reference group behavior,[7] they discovered their common identity when they found here their common enemy cutting such a great figure in American politics. Particularly after the middle of the century, when the Fenian uproar and

[5] Allport, Nature of Prejudice, pp. 138–57; Stanley M. Elkins, Slavery: A Problem in American Institutional and Intellectual Life (New York, 1964); Brown, Irish-American Nationalism, pp. 178–82.
[6] It may be necessary here to note that, despite my name, these remarks do not spring from any particular awareness of ethnic identity nor from residual bitterness toward the English. For one thing, my forebears' emigration to this country is so remote in time as to be lost to family memory. No family traditions remain of English oppression. For another, my ancestry is apparently Ulster-Irish (Protestant), or what is in this country called Scotch-Irish. As a native Californian I did not even become aware of the problem of prejudice against Irishmen, Catholic or Protestant, until I read of it in historical literature. My sympathies clearly lie with the Catholic Irish in this account, but Anglophobism is not an attitude in which I was bred. Membership in the Episcopal Church might even indicate an opposite tendency. In any event, Anglophobia, long a virulent force in American politics, has all but dissipated in America; it is largely unheard of in my generation and region. A recent Gallup poll (reported in the Los Angeles Times, Dec. 14, 1967) reports 36 per cent of the American population as "highly favorable" to England, only 3 per cent registering their views as "highly unfavorable."
[7] Robert K. Merton, Social Theory and Social Structure (Glencoe, Ill., 1957), pp. 300–4; Tamotsu Shibutani, "Reference Groups and Social Control," in Arnold M. Rose, ed., Human Behavior and Social Processes: An Interactionist Approach (Boston, 1962), pp. 128–47.

the controversies over Irish Home Rule kept loyalties ablaze, British immigrants joined together in active hostility to the Irish, demanding discrimination in jobs, in housing, and in political preference. They were fearful that the Irish might grow so politically powerful, through the Democratic Party, that they would actually gain control of the federal government and launch an American war against Britain to secure Irish independence. Working against this eventuality, they voted faithfully for the Republican ticket.[8] Cornish miners in the United States usually disturbed the peace only "at election time when they voted Republican to keep out the Roman Catholic influence of their Irish rivals." Even British Canadians, who emigrated into the United States in large numbers, carried this anti-Irish prejudice with them and voted in the same way.[9]

In the late 1880's, when the Irish in Boston violently protested a local celebration of Queen Victoria's Golden Jubilee, a British-American Association sprang to life throughout the nation, supplanting such separate English, Welsh, and Scottish groups as still existed. In the 1890's, the B.A.A. led a national assault upon Irish Catholics, condemning them in lurid "exposés," publishing stories about alleged papal conspiracies, immorality in nunneries, and the danger of parochial schools. The American Protective Association joined in, the Loyal Orange Institution—representing the Scotch-Irish —expanded rapidly, and a hysteria broke out over the "Catholic menace."[1]

The British immigrant was not alone in his rabid anti-Irish prejudice. He was joined by the self-consciously "native" American, often of English extraction and proudly Anglophile. In both the United States and in Canada, Anglophilism usually meant a warm admiration for, and indeed envy of, traditional Tory England: the England of titles, of gentility,

---

[8] The fear of an Irish-induced war between the United States and Britain did not dissipate until the First World War, which seemed to cement a permanently friendly Anglo-American relationship.
[9] Todd, *Cornish Miner in America*, p. 101; Rowland Tappan Berthoff, *British Immigrants in Industrial America, 1790–1950* (Cambridge, Mass., 1953), pp. 166–210.
[1] Ibid.

of venerable lineage, and of ancient institutions. It seemed to include also an adoption of Tory England's distaste for the Irish, the ancestral embodiment of all that was not English.

> The recoil of fashionable Boston [against the Irish] took the form of an Anglophilism that would have warmed the Federalist heart of Fisher Ames . . . The descendants of the generation that had led the nation in the public school movement chose to educate their own progeny at St. Paul's and Groton, where British names, sports, and methods of instruction were aped. The Back Bay resembled fashionable England, and, to make sure of the intended identity, its inhabitants gave its streets, hotels, and apartments such names as Clarendon, Exeter, Wellington, Hereford . . . Julia Ward Howe . . . complained: "English manners are affected by those among us who mistake the aristocracy of position for the aristocracy of character."[2]

From the nativist uproar of the 1850's, when the Irish immigrant flood created such paranoia over an alleged papal invasion and a feared destruction of all that was denominated as truly American, the right-wing parties in American politics attacked the Irish Catholic. The Whigs and the American Party led the assault upon the Irish and all other "strange" immigrants, and the Republican Party into which they merged in the 1850's carried on the tradition. "As the Irish influence over one party grew (New York, Boston, and other cities got their first Irish mayors in the eighties), the Democratic candidate for mayor of Chicago was opposed by every general English-language newspaper (except one that he owned), but supported by virtually the entire immigrant press and elected by a large majority."[3] When the restrictionist campaign to halt the "wrong" kind of immigration got underway in the 1890's,

> From the outset the Republican party provided the main vehicle for restrictionist sentiment. It never monopolized or committed itself wholly to the movement, but it supplied the principal leaders, most of the energy, and most of the

[2] Arthur Mann, *Yankee Reformers in the Urban Age: Social Reform in Boston, 1880–1900* (New York, 1966), pp. 7–11.
[3] Higham, *Strangers in the Land*, p. 60, and *passim*.

votes. Throughout the North and West the party tended to attract those who thought of themselves as "the better sort." It seemed the guardian of respectability, morality, and standing. In those regions the party appealed to most of the people alarmed at the growth of class antagonisms: middle-class reformers, Brahmin intelligentsia, the more substantial workingmen (to whom it offered restriction as a supplement to tariff protection), and the great bulk of white-collar folk conscious of status and tradition.[4]

It was altogether fitting that it was the Democratic President Grover Cleveland who struck down, with his veto, one of the first restrictionist enactments to get through Congress, a literacy test for immigrants.

As the Democrats in the United States were the party of the Irish Catholic, so in time the Canadian Liberals became the party of the French Canadian. This was not the case in the early years of Canadian history. The skill of Sir John A. Macdonald in building bridges to the *Québecois* kept them voting Conservative for many years, as did the firm convictions of the Roman Catholic Quebec hierarchy, to whose fervently ultramontanist ears in mid-century the word "liberal" was an abomination. Church-state issues also kept the Conservatives and the French Canadians together for some time.

But the Orange Order, composed of Protestant Irish, was a major force in the Conservative Party in Canada, and its rabid anti-Catholicism, together with the Anglophilism natural to Conservatism, were too strong to allow this *rapprochement* to continue. In time it was to be the Liberals who built such enduring bridges as exist between Anglo-Canadian and French Canadian. Edward Blake began this process in the 1880's as Liberal leader, denouncing Protestant bigotry and appealing to universalist and equalitarian symbols typical of Gladstonian and Jeffersonian thought.[5] He called upon Anglo-Canada to forget its prejudice and make Canada a genuine nation. His successor, Sir Wilfrid Laurier, embodied all these ideas in his own luminous personality and

[4] Ibid., p. 98.
[5] He was also a leading spokesman for the Irish, even sitting in the British Parliament for an Irish constituency in the 1890's.

eloquent oratory. It still remains true that when Canada has a Liberal government, French Canadians will form much of the cabinet and may even hold the premiership—as at present. When Canada has a Conservative government, French Canada, to all intents and purposes expelled from the ministry, must turn in upon itself.

More than any other minority in the Anglo-American world, the French Canadians have been an encapsulated group with a fortress mentality. They keep fresh and vivid within their historical memories a consciousness of having been conquered by force of arms by the people now represented in the majority culture that surrounds them. The Plains of Abraham and 1763 are remembered in Quebec as Gettysburg and 1865 are remembered in the American South. By historical circumstance, furthermore, they are the only minority group in the Anglo-American community equipped in quite the same way with the apparatus of self-government, including a chief executive in the person of the premier of the Province of Quebec. Faced with a far more powerful obstacle to equal treatment than the Irish—their different language— it is remarkable that they have been willing to remain within the Dominion. As Marius Tallard muses bitterly to himself in MacLennan's novel *Two Solitudes*, why does the French Canadian hate the English?

> The English lessened him . . . that was it. Merely by their existence, they lessened a man. You could become great and powerful only if your people were also great and powerful. But what could his people do when the English constantly choked them? What could the French do, alone against an entire continent, except breed children and hope? . . . You had to imitate the English or they refused to look at you. You had to do things their way. If you were different, they automatically regarded you as second-rate. If you wanted different ends they called you backward . . . And all the time the English took what they wanted. They had the big business. They had the army, the railroads, the banks, they had everything. What was left to a man like himself but the Church, medicine, or the laws?[6]

[6] Hugh MacLennan, *Two Solitudes* (New York, 1945), pp. 172–3.

The political links between Quebec and the rest of Canada are of critical importance to the continued existence of the nation in its present form. It remains one of the more lasting and important inheritances from the nineteenth-century Liberal-Democratic world that there exists in Canada a political party still committed, by its ideology and character, to be the voice of the minority groups and to bring into being a pluralistic society. For much of the Canadian population to "think British" denominates the Conservative, while to "think Canadian"—that is, to recognize a unique multi-ethnic national identity including the *Québecois*—denominates the Liberal, as the recent long debate over a national flag demonstrated.[7]

———

This discussion differs from the views of R. B. McCallum, who writes that the Liberal Party was "the party of the middle class,"[8] with the support of the industrial workers. The difference is largely a matter of emphasis. McCallum makes room in his account for the minority groups, though his frame of reference is different from mine, and it would be an ill-advised tactic to ignore the middle class, which in fact I do not. I am persuaded, however, that the drive toward equality of status and the existence of group prejudices must be given a considerably more central place in the analysis than has traditionally been the case. This is, in fact, perhaps

[7] It is relevant to remark here that the current status of the French Canadian outside his province—or even in cosmopolitan Montreal—is like that of the Mexican-American in the American Southwest (who votes strongly Democratic). The French Canadian performs the menial work and is denied entrance to the higher posts in government and business. The American who visits eastern Canada finds that while to him the French language signifies cultivation and learning, to many Anglo-Canadians it carries the stigma of an inferior caste, with associated implications of crudeness, poverty, parochialism, and ignorance—exactly the stereotypes applied to the Spanish language in the American Southwest (taken as including California). "I hate to visit Quebec," an Anglo-Canadian woman of Conservative sympathies remarked to the author in the impartial and apparently uninhibiting atmosphere of Edinburgh. "It's so French it makes you sick."

[8] McCallum, *Liberal Party*, p. 63.

the principal fruit of the comparative approach herein relied upon. The recurrence of this pattern consistently in the three countries made clear its central role.

Norman Gash's recent assessment of the age of Peel confirms the view of a relatively monolithic English, Anglican, and landed party on the one hand (the Tories) and a heterogeneous party on the other (the Liberals), composed in important degree of non-English and urban (Dissenter) elements.[9] Equally relevant are the recently published discoveries of J. R. Vincent, whose study of Victorian pollbooks—as well as his larger work on the Liberal Party[1]—reveals that explanations of voting patterns that rely upon the concept of economic class in the Marxian sense of employer and employee, or of class in the conventional sense of a stratum in society, are highly misleading.

Gross understandings of politics on the traditional order, Vincent makes clear, remain generally true. The rich and the poor would seem generally to have voted for different candidates. The world of the landed, and its hangers-on, was predominantly Tory, as were the professions and the Anglican clergy. Dissenting ministers were determinedly Liberal, "a sort of Communist hard core to the Popular Front." Those who were in their nature essentially urban, who expressed in their occupations the very heart of town or city life—the craftsmen, shopkeepers, local businessmen—tended to be Liberal, while conversely those in town or countryside whose way of life and mental outlook were linked to traditional rural ways of life tended to be Tory. The vast range of occupations and life styles that began above poverty and ended somewhere below great wealth tended toward the Liberal side.

So many qualifications must be made, however, that these generalizations can no longer be counted upon confidently as solid categories. Butchers voted Tory; shoemakers Liberal. Dockworkers on the northeastern coast voted Tory; the carpenters in the same towns voted Liberal. Town labor-

[9] Norman Gash, *Reaction and Reconstruction in English Politics, 1832–1852* (Oxford, 1965), pp. 133–8, 164–5.
[1] Cf. his *Formation of the British Liberal Party.*

ers often voted Tory, but so did wine merchants, in contrast to grocers. Ironfounders were Tory, woolstaplers Liberal. Where is that great phalanx of industrialists and large employers that as tradition would have it was supposed to be voting *en bloc* Liberal, and forcing its workers to do likewise? What happens to the view that Liberalism, with its "crude and callous" *laissez faire*, was the philosophy of the businessmen? "The business community," Vincent reports, "was not a coherent entity, and it was not especially committed to middle-class liberalism." The fact is that Tories and Liberals were strong in all classes. "In many cases," for that matter, "the rich or the employers in a town were fairly evenly divided . . ."[2]

Quite similar discoveries have recently been made in American historiography as well, in addition to Lee Benson's work on the Jacksonians. In the process of criticizing Charles Beard's oversimplified economic analysis of post-Civil War politics in the United States—an analysis based upon the assumed existence of specific classes voting *en bloc*—Robert P. Sharkey and Irwin Unger have provided a new and more sophisticated understanding of the operation of economic motives in politics. As they make clear, it is the kind of businessman that matters; it is in what kinds of enterprises that bankers have invested that matters; it is in what kind of industry the worker labors that matters. Classes are divided within themselves and against themselves as to economic interest. Textile-mill owners in New England thought of foreign trade, wanted low tariffs and sound money, and voted Democratic. Iron producers in Pennsylvania thought of the internal market, needed huge supplies of capital to get their industry going, wanted protective tariffs and inflation, and voted Republican. When men voted in the Reconstruction Era, and when economic factors provided the motives, they voted in accordance with their specific needs, not simply according to economic class membership.

Economic interpretations, properly framed, are most revealing, and are not necessarily to be cast aside. It is possi-

[2] J. R. Vincent, *Pollbooks: How Victorians Voted* (Cambridge, 1967), pp. 1–33.

ble to elucidate from a properly framed economic inquiry some insights into political behavior that agree with the view that emotional factors play a powerful role, perhaps even a dominating one, in politics. Vincent proposes a provocative explanation of the Victorian Liberal voter's social psychology. He suggests that the economic information in the pollbooks—ethnic and religious information was apparently not included in them—makes it appear that Liberal voters were generally the kind of men who worked alone, or with a few employees. They were small producers, individual farmers, retailers, men who practiced a craft, who rented a floor in a factory and ran a few machines with some helpers—a surprisingly common practice—or had corner shops where they cobbled or sold groceries. They had not the emotional camaraderie or the sources of self-respect and support that come from working in large gangs—in factories, on capitalist farms, in the mines, on the docks. They were usually in circumstances where they were at the mercy of forces largely beyond their control. These forces appeared to be generated by the "great folk," the world of the landowner, the Anglican hierarchy, the lawyer and banker, the speculative stockjobber, all of whom seemed in one way or another to be fattening upon privilege. In the midst of all this, the small man, truly an outsider, worked on quite alone, surrounded by privilege, hauteur, and sloth.[3]

The only collectivity that such men of small property belonged to was their political party (unless it was their Dissenting chapel, which would simply heighten the influence of these factors), and its principal function for them was to cry out a radical demand for a change in the structure of the nation at large. Forced to be "nice" in their businesses, they were violent in their politics.

[3] The Liberal voter Vincent here describes reminds me of a certain kind of Jacksonian Democrat, who also seems to have been a man of small property, angry with the privileged world of the wealthy that was symbolized by the United States Bank and dismayed at the constant booms and busts that sent his personal fortunes in wild gyrations over which he had no control. I suspect it was this kind of man in both countries who supported the measures enacted by Jacksonians and Peelites—to be later discussed—that aimed at stabilization of the economy through currency reform and the damping down of speculation.

The only way for them to assert that they were as good as the holders of authority and of the means of enjoyment, was through national politics, and in national politics the really interesting thing would be the transfer of power from "them" to "us," and generally any symbolic reform which commuted the individual helplessness of the Radical voter into a sense of power over his betters.

This is what Liberalism was for, so far as the people were concerned, to enable them to have nationally, the satisfaction daily and local life denied to them. It was therefore not necessary that Liberal measures should benefit them; so long as they vexed the mighty, this was a sufficient reason for enthusiasm. What Gladstone was offering was emotional subsistence . . . —the possibility of participation, antagonism, struggle, commitment, eventual victory, a sense of power and domination—to people normally entirely subject to circumstances and to other people.

The permanent issue behind Midlothian and Reform and Home Rule was what kind of people should have power, in whose name, and in accordance with whose ideas. Gladstone offered the psychic satisfaction of ruling to the ruled—not ruling over themselves, but ruling and overruling the traditional holders of authority . . .[4]

In this sense, Vincent insists, Liberalism was more radical than Labour. The latter wanted improved social welfare. Liberalism hoped to transform the power structure of the nation itself and cast down its traditional hierarchies. Labour's demands were immediate, limited, and describable in terms of pounds and pence. Liberalism's demands were deeper. They reached to the inner man, to the rooted feeling in the Tory mind that it was ruling because it was superior. Superiority-inferiority was the issue, and this was what gave such violence to a political world that to a later generation seemed to be fighting over trifles.

It is clear, then, if Vincent's assessment is accepted, that the concept of politics as public drama must be given closer attention.[5] What the people wanted was emotional satisfac-

[4] Vincent, *Pollbooks*, pp. 44–5.
[5] The "Radical voter . . . found great vicarious excitement in identifying himself with an attack on authority, conducted as a public spectacle

tion, a victory of the downtrodden over the haughty. Irish Catholics in America voted Democratic not because they expected a specific return, but because they wanted supremacy over those who poured scorn upon them. Who held the power in the state, their friends or their enemies? That was the key question. The emotional facts of the nineteenth century—far more than the present one a century of hierarchy and prejudice—fueled its politics fully as much as did its economic facts.

In religion, as in the sociology of politics, the British and the Americans also shared a common pattern. Through the long operation of religious toleration, the Anglo-American community, in contrast to the continental pattern of one or two great national churches, was religiously pluralistic. In contrast again to the continent patterns, the Anglo-American community was characterized by remarkable religiosity.

Political exiles from the continent after 1848 in England were struck by this aspect of English political life. They had come from a Europe in which priest and radical were at swords' points; in which to be a reformer meant by definition to be antireligious. But in Britain, Dissenting ministers and even Anglican priests had prominent roles in reform politics. It has become a commonplace to remark that the Labour Party owes more to the Methodist Church than it does to Karl Marx. Church and chapel—especially chapel—were familiar meeting places for reform politics. William Gladstone was simply the most prominent among those who justified their political actions by semi-theological discourses. Not even the workers were anticlerical, for there were too many churches for them to consider religion a tool of the ruling classes.

---

at national level. Gladstone created a national theatre for England as Verdi did for nineteenth-century Italy . . . The people went to the conflict like Greeks went to the play." (Ibid., p. 47.) Richard Hofstadter makes persuasive observations about this trait in the mass political mind in his Introduction to *The Paranoid Style in American Politics* (New York, 1966).

Friedrich Engels wrote that "what struck every cultivated foreigner who set up his residence in England was what he was then bound to consider the religious bigotry and stupidity of the English respectable middle class." European radicals were generally freethinkers, and they were astonished to see "that almost all educated people in England [believed] all sorts of impossible miracles."[6] Until well past mid-century, to be a freethinker in England was to be a social outcast. Skepticism in religious matters was more than a matter of opinion; it often had serious consequences for one's employment and career.[7]

A pervading religiosity was also a characteristic of nineteenth-century America. Genuine devotion and churchgoing, indeed, seemed to be more widespread in the United States than in England. British observers often questioned the depth of American religious commitments, but they had to note that religion was popular in the same sense that the schools and all the other egalitarian institutions in America were popular.

Nowhere else had religion ever been so exclusively addressed to this world, so accessible, so awe-uninspiring, so common-sensical, so unmysterious, so simple, so sympathetic to ordinary every-day human needs. Nowhere else had beliefs in Christianity, certainly not in England, been so voluntary, nor had the Christian churches so readily accepted equality as their *modus vivendi,* as their operating principle. The British could, only with the greatest difficulty, recover from their astonishment when they were compelled to admit that the United States had achieved a more perfect harmony between her religious beliefs and her national aspirations than had any nation with an established church.[8]

The last words in this observation point up the great difference that did exist in religious matters between the United States and Britain. The Americans had separated what

6 Richter, *Politics of Conscience,* p. 300.
7 Burn, *Equipoise,* pp. 276–7.
8 Richard Rapson, "The Religious Feelings of the American People, 1845–1935: A British View," *Church History,* XXXV (1966), 19.

was joined in Britain: church and state. Largely under Thomas Jefferson's inspiration, they had erected a secular governmental system. Nowhere in evidence were the intimate links that existed between the established church in Britain and every aspect of government: the Crown, the Lords (in which bishops sat), the schools, the universities, and the whole structure of local life and government. The very Prayer Book of the Church of England could be changed only by Parliamentary enactment.

No other contrast, therefore, caused such strong reactions among visiting Britons as this most extraordinary break with not only British but also all of European tradition.[9] Of "all the differences between the Old World and the New," James Bryce remarked, this one was "perhaps the most salient." They recognized it as a genuine innovation, one that they found difficult to understand. The idea that religion was entirely a matter between each man and his God, the state having nothing whatever to do with it, was an astonishing one. To establish the schools, and yet to disestablish the church! The reversal of the British situation excited their constant remark.[1]

In this, as in so many things, Canada occupied a halfway house between the British and American systems. After the early Canadian years, in which there were bitter controversies over the role of the Anglican Church in Canada, there was no longer an elaborate system of Church establishment and authority at all levels outside Quebec. This, at least, had been eliminated in the reform movements in Canada. But there was not, on the other hand, any legal separation between church and state. Public funds could be provided to support parochial schools, and religious instruction was legal in the public schools. There were many controversies over proper arrangements. Secularity, total and complete, remains one of the fundamental differences between the United States and the rest of the Anglo-American world.

It soon became clear to the British observer, however, that the churches nonetheless played a prominent role—in

[9] These observers were clearly predominantly Anglican.
[1] Rapson, "Religious Feelings of the American People," pp. 3–4.

some ways the most prominent role of any institution until the rise of the business corporation—in nineteenth-century American politics. Jacksonian and mid-century politics rang with ministerial pronouncements and church-inspired reform movements.[2] The clerical mind in the United States had not yet fully adjusted to the separation between church and state. In most of New England, and in the South, churches had paralleled the governments, and the free-church idea established itself only slowly after the Revolution. Many clerics tended to think automatically of using the power of the state to achieve what they wished to see in society. In such campaigns as the fight against drink, lewd habits, and slavery, "again and again they reverted to the old custom of using government or tax monies to support church work."[3]

This was particularly true of New England Puritanism, which for generations had existed as the state-supported and state-connected Congregational Church. It was still fired by the theocratic ideal, by the mission of Christianizing the state by coercion if necessary. Wherever Puritanism went in the United States, in the great swarming that carried New Englanders into New York State and the Middle West, it carried a righteous and confident urge to reach out for the power of the secular government to gain its goals.[4]

In the United States, as in Britain, self-conscious religious groups identified themselves by their voting behavior. Catholicism as a factor was practically impossible to separate from being Irish or being German, but clear distinctions may be made between different kinds of Protestants. In general, the Whigs, in Jacksonian politics, tended to be the party of the aggressively religious who liked to mount church-oriented campaigns in politics. The Whig theory of government, fashioned in good part from the British model of a strong government run by an aristocracy, stressed the need for a positive

[2] Cf. Whitney R. Cross, *The Burned-Over District: The Social and Intellectual History of Enthusiastic Religion in Western New York, 1800–1850* (New York, 1965); and Timothy L. Smith, *Revivalism and Social Reform: American Protestantism on the Eve of the Civil War* (New York, 1965).
[3] Franklin Hamlin Littell, *From State Church to Pluralism: A Protestant Interpretation of Religion in American History* (New York, 1962), p. 47.
[4] Ibid., pp. 1–47.

state continuously intervening in the economy to create conditions presumed favorable to the entrepreneur and national
growth. They inherited from Alexander Hamilton and the
Federalists a preference for a government that had a maximal
scope of action, giving large latitude to a governing elite.
They were necessarily the allies of those whose religious beliefs sprang from the old state-church tradition in Puritanism.
So prominent was this phenomenon that the Whigs were
called the "religious party" and the Democrats the "free-
thought party."[5]

The Democrats were generally identified with agnosti-
cism and anticlericalism. They were hostile to moralistic reforms, resisted any intrusion of a "Christian party in politics,"
and attempted to prevent the passage of Sunday laws. On
these matters, "party differences were distinct, passionate,
and enduring."[6] This came not only from the Democrats'
Jeffersonian heritage, but also from the long colonial opposition to the establishment of an Anglican bishop in the colonies.[7] In consequence, the Democrats in the nineteenth century, having attracted those elements that were generally
anticlerical and irreligious, were accused of favoring infidelity
and the devil, a charge that gained force from the "popery"
of their Irish adherents.

This is one of the major contrasts between the British
Liberals and the American Democrats. The Liberals, with the
devout William Gladstone at their head and the equally faith-
centered Dissenters in their ranks, could hardly be regarded
as the agnostic, anticlerical party. However, the contrast was
not a polar difference. The Liberal Party was always the
home of those who were freethinkers and agnostics on the
John Morley pattern. Most of all, it was the party of the
Dissenters, who argued endlessly for an end to state and
church ties, and for secular schools. Even Gladstone's Anglicanism was of a special kind. In due time he became leader
of the demand that England could no longer be kept exclu-

[5] Benson, *Concept of Jacksonian Democracy*, pp. 104–9, 193. These
matters are discussed at length in Chapter 7.
[6] Ibid., p. 196. Cf. also Cross, *Burned-Over District*, pp. 168, 270; and
Schlesinger, *Age of Jackson*, pp. 136–9, 350.
[7] Discussed in Chapter 4.

sively in law an Anglican country; he fought against his own Church leaders for freedom of speech and faith, to the point of arguing insistently for the admission of Jews and atheists to Parliament; and he was almost constantly in trouble, in his mature years, with the hard-shell High Churchmen of the bishop's bench. He was even ready to create completely secular schools.

The Canadian analogue confirms the similarity of Liberal and Democratic secularism. In Canadian politics, the Liberals constantly had to fight off the charge of infidelity and of irreligion. George Brown and Alexander Mackenzie were devout men, yet they struggled for secular schools and a separation between church and state in the 1840's and 1850's. Later on, Sir Wilfrid Laurier, though he was a French Canadian Catholic, has no more persistent aim or enterprise than terminating the direct interventions of the Roman Catholic hierarchy into Canadian politics. He was angrily attacked as an enemy of the Church, for he was a major figure in the long effort undertaken by Liberals to secularize Canadian politics.

———————

It has been traditional to speak of political parties as expressions of forces generated within the economy. This chapter has not rejected this traditional approach, but takes the position that party behavior and attitudes spring perhaps as much from irrational, fundamentally emotional origins as from calculations of economic interest. The Liberals and the Democrats may have had their true *raison d'être* more in the emotional facts of nineteenth-century life than in its economics. At the least, sociological and cultural influences must be considered to understand the full political role of the Liberal-Democrats in the age of Gladstone.

On both sides of the Atlantic there was a struggle going on between majority and minority cultures; between those speaking for the minority groups, who demanded pluralism, and those speaking for the majority culture, who demanded homogeneity. Social prejudice in all its forms was and is one of the great engines that impart force and passion and shaping motion to Anglo-American political life. There was also— most prominently in Britain, though one suspects it was not absent in the States—a rigidly hierarchical social arrangement, expressed in key institutions, that degraded those on the middle and lower end of the ladder. The habit of authority, objectified in the hauteur and panache of a rooted aristocracy, created ways of command and styles of life that stirred up an unquenchable bitterness among men of small property. John Bright was their voice; William Gladstone was their hero.

Intimately related was the role of religious attitudes and religious prejudice. The strange Liberal-Democratic coalition of agnostics and freethinkers and devout Dissenters and Gladstonians was driven together by a shared hostility toward a common enemy, the aggressively religious state-church mentality that wished to maintain discrimination against other faiths, took religious homogeneity as a goal, and believed its superior knowledge of the will of God justified state action against social practices condemned by their faith. For Liberal-Democrats the ideal of the secular state was not a merely philosophical position derived from the calm reflections of eighteenth-century philosophy, it was an immediate necessity to remove a clear and present danger. Religious prejudice, as well as social prejudice, goes far to explain the existence of the Liberal-Democrats and to make their historical role seem valid and understandable.

A large part of the Liberal-Democratic world was composed of men who responded to all three influences—ethnic identity, economic loneliness, and religious dissent. There was wide consensus, therefore, upon the nature of the enemy: superiority and special privilege; prejudice and dominating power; wealth and the habit of authority; economic exploitation and insulting airs; religious arrogance; a calm assumption that the nation was coterminous with themselves and that only they were "loyal." These qualities constituted the Liberal-Democratic conception of the enemy, and the bitterness of this conception gave force, passion, and reality to nineteenth-century Anglo-American politics.

Chapter 2

THE INHERITED WORLD VIEW:
ADAM SMITH AND THE
DYNAMIC ECONOMY

The distinctive characteristic of the Liberal-Democratic mind was a remarkably persistent view of the nature of politics and the economy. Drawn from many sources, it came most of all from the works of three eighteenth-century figures: Adam Smith, Edmund Burke, and Thomas Jefferson.

Of these men, Adam Smith had the widest influence on the Liberal-Democratic mind. The British paid little attention to Thomas Jefferson, and the Americans—until Woodrow Wilson—were similarly indifferent to Edmund Burke. But on both sides of the Atlantic, Adam Smith was the Liberal-Democratic prophet in economic matters. "All Liberals," R. B. McCallum has written, "believed themselves to have read and learned Adam Smith's *The Wealth of Nations.*"[1] The American Democrats looked to him with equal admiration. Samuel Tilden read him carefully and relied upon him throughout his career, and he would appear also to have been the principal influence on Woodrow Wilson's economic thinking.[2]

[1] McCallum, "Liberal Outlook," in Ginsberg, *Law and Opinion*, p. 66.
[2] Cf. Schlesinger, *Age of Jackson*, pp. 314–17; and William Diamond, *The Economic Thought of Woodrow Wilson* (Baltimore, 1943), pp. 28, 30–1, 51–2.

Adam Smith's reputation has long suffered from the stereotyped view that he was the father of a crude *laissez faire* in which the government only maintained law and order, and a glorified businessman, his greedy instincts sanctified, was free to riot as he would.[3] For this reason it may be an unaccustomed experience to think of Smith as a left-wing thinker.[4] Happily, recent studies have made it much easier to gain a fresh understanding of the economic world view that he created for generations of Liberals and Democrats.

Adam Smith was born in 1723, the son of a Scottish collector of customs. He became a well-known Glasgow University professor of philosophy, joining that faculty in 1751.[5] A warm, enthusiastic, much-loved, and amusingly absent-minded man, he attracted students from many countries. He was known as the professor who walked along the Glasgow streets pausing with each step as he argued with himself some abstruse matter; who brewed a cup of bread and butter and pronounced it awful tea. He formed warm friendships— with David Hume, with Edmund Burke, and with his colleagues—but he was also a recluse capable of withdrawing from the world for ten years to produce his masterpiece, *The Wealth of Nations* (1776).

His initial work, however, was in philosophy.[6] In 1759

[3] Even Max Lerner's introduction to the Modern Library edition of *The Wealth of Nations*, the most widely used version, purveys the same image. Cf. Adam Smith, *An Inquiry into the Nature and Causes of the Wealth of Nations*, ed., Edwin Cannan (New York: Modern Library; 1937).

[4] As Arthur M. Schlesinger, Jr., has remarked, "Believers in the myth of Adam Smith, as expounded by present-day publicists both of the right and of the left, may find [it] singular . . . [that] the real Adam Smith was rich in ammunition for the Jacksonians . . . " *Age of Jackson*, p. 314.

[5] Personal information concerning Smith may be found in W. R. Scott, *Adam Smith as Student and Professor* (Glasgow, 1937).

[6] The following discussion is drawn from Joseph Cropsey, *Polity and Economy: An Interpretation of the Principles of Adam Smith* (The Hague, 1957). This brilliant analysis is practically the only interpretation available of the whole range of Smith's thought.

he published a work, *The Theory of the Moral Sentiments,* which made him a considerable reputation throughout Europe. It was a penetrating analysis of the human personality in which he developed conceptions that lie at the heart of his later *The Wealth of Nations.* Like David Hume, he was convinced that the eighteenth-century Enlightenment had developed false hopes concerning the nature of man's mental powers. It was a serious misconception, he believed, to erect vast systems of ideas on the assumption that man's reasoning powers were practically unlimited, and that what "causes" this or that may be found out by reason and the scientific method. The Enlightenment thirsted after an understanding of the ultimate concerns in human existence, but the very nature of the mind, Smith believed, hid them from us. It was a vain illusion to believe that by carefully compiling the information our senses gave us, and ruminating logically upon these "data," we could understand the deepest matters of human and cosmic affairs.

It was an illusion if nothing else because the very senses that Enlightenment philosophers relied upon give us distorted information. The faculty that they most trusted—that of sight—is helpful to us only in understanding the externals and the outer relationships of things, not their inner natures. Indeed, even in these functions the power of sight helps us only to see what is near. Whatever is more remote grows vague and indistinct. By our nature we are limited to perceptions of that which immediately surrounds us. Our real concerns, therefore, should not be with the airy concerns of contemplative philosophy, but with the life of action in the here and now.

The first step in this direction should be to understand clearly and realistically the actual nature of man. We are fundamentally passionate creatures, Smith insisted, moved primarily by an instinct for self-preservation. We also possess an in-built capacity for projecting ourselves into the situation another person occupies. Feeling his pain when he suffers, we grow solicitous for his welfare. This behavior is in its deepest nature an instinctive, emotional, irrational phenomenon. It is *sympathy* that makes us good to others, not a rational assessment of what is good or bad.[7] Most of all, what we want is the approbation of our fellows, which speaks to us through our conscience, or as Smith described it, the man within our breast. The contempt or disregard of those around us is intolerable to us. Happiness above all "arises from the consciousness of being beloved."

The best things for society may be seen, therefore, to have arisen from influences traceable not to reason, but to passion. Men cannot be made good by teaching them some rational understanding of the ends of society, but by so arranging public policy that it flows out of their real psychological nature, giving their instinctual drives full play in socially creative ways. It is not possible for *philosophes* at the center to direct affairs in detail all over the nation, for the task is beyond them. It is not a bad idea in itself to seek to do this, it is simply impossible to do it, because of the inherent limitations of our reasoning powers. This is why supposedly benevolent autocratic governments create only chaos and stultify national economies. For this reason it is difficult to base jurisprudence on the concept of "duties" rather than "rights." Men always know what is best for themselves, and they may be trusted to understand clearly and to apply successfully their "rights." But "duties" apply to others, who are often remote and in strange situations, and therefore they will always be vague and indistinct. Societies may be based on justice, conceived of as a protection of individual rights, but not on benevolence, conceived of as an understanding of duties to others. Benevolence can ornament a society, but not maintain it.[8]

[7] Unfortunately, Smith said, all types of passions can communicate themselves from one person to another, including such destructive ones as selfishness and anger.

[8] It is an irresistible temptation to point to the remarkable resemblances between these ideas and those of such twentieth-century thinkers as Sigmund Freud and Graham Wallas. Both advised that governments become alive to the fundamentally passionate nature of man and arrange their policies in accordance with this reality. Wallas insisted in his *Human Nature in Politics* (London, 1908, and many subsequent editions), which had wide influence among Anglo-American political thinkers, that governments must shape their actions so as to satisfy the psychological needs of the population.

One is reminded, too, of the atmosphere that came to suffuse

When Adam Smith after 1759 began to consider the booming economic life of eighteenth-century Great Britain, it was therefore as a philosopher with the widest concerns about the human condition that he did so. It is in good part this breadth of understanding that gives *The Wealth of Nations* such extraordinary appeal. But there is another element: its often astringent and biting tone. Smith's work was such a lasting inspiration for the political left wing in good part because he pointed at malefactors and acidly criticized the existing economic system.

The harshness and authority of the book's criticisms must be understood against the circumstances of Adam Smith's life. His father was a customs collector, a profession that provided a close, yet detached and critical vantage point on the business world. Though he died shortly before Adam's birth, it has been suggested that his experiences probably created enduring family traditions.[9] Furthermore, as an academic man in Glasgow, Smith also had an excellent opportunity to observe the new commercial world of the eighteenth century in one of its most explosive locations from the standpoint of the professional scholar.

It is important to note, however, that he was a Scottish intellectual observing a predominantly English economic system. The Scots were still newcomers to the English world in Smith's lifetime. The Union of 1707, creating the United Kingdom out of the formerly separate kingdoms of England and Scotland—and the term "British," which implied a joint nationality, and took so long to be accepted—was yet a relatively recent event. The common citizenship that Scots could claim with Englishmen in an encompassing Great Britain remained a fresh and unfamiliar new status. For centuries be-

---

F.D.R.'s Second New Deal, as described by Arthur M. Schlesinger, Jr., an atmosphere with a new sense of human limitations. The N.R.A., New Deal leaders came to realize, had failed not because it was a bad idea to think of directing the economy in detail from a centralized location, but because it was simply a task beyond human capacities. As they moved in the direction of reviving competition and relying once more on the market to discipline the economy, men of the Second New Deal returned to classic Smithian concepts.

[9] Cf. Bruce Mazlish's Introduction to his edition of *The Wealth of Nations* (Indianapolis and New York, 1961).

fore 1707 the Scots had been foreigners in English eyes, an alien people, traditional enemies, despised as turbulent and self-seeking inferiors who lived in a remote country, "the back of beyond."[1] In the eighteenth century, the English were contemptuous of them, scoffing at their crudity and their supposedly uncouth speech. They were commonly regarded as greedy men come to fish in the richer waters of England. They had an "evil name as servile, miserly, treacherous and corrupt." In London, mobs jeered and taunted them and attacked prominent Scotsmen's coaches in the streets.[2] When George III, after his accession in 1760, made such extensive use of Scotsmen, "it was put about that the King was using the barbarians from beyond the border to destroy the liberties of Englishmen. It was not Bute only, nor the Scottish members of Parliament, that were pilloried. Scotsmen of every sort or station—Chief Justice Mansfield for example—were reprobated or ridiculed for being Scotsmen."[3]

Scots encountered harsh prejudice, in fact, throughout the Anglo-American world. After 1707, when the colonies were opened to them, they began to appear in America in significant numbers, where they were much disliked. English soldiers in the colonies sometimes protested against being placed under the command of Scottish officers. Highland Scots who settled in the colonies attracted particular attention for their peculiar dress, their Gaelic language, and their clannishness. They were also conspicuous for their fervent loyalty to the Crown, traditionally their protector against the Lowlanders in Scotland, whom they hated. Lowland Scots immigrants who were farmers, however, seem to have dispersed as individuals through the population and were little noted.

[1] Cf. Wallace Notestein, *The Scot in History: A Study of the Interplay of Character and History* (New Haven, 1947).
[2] Cf. Lindsay, *By Yon Bonnie Banks*, pp. 104–5, and Pryde, *Scotland*, p. 117. It is difficult to realize the way in which Scotland was looked at before the age of her great philosophers, and especially before Sir Walter Scott's novels transformed Scotland into a land of romance and noble adventure. The best analogy might be with parts of America's Appalachia, or with the Kansas of William Allen White's day, looked at from New York.
[3] Reginald Coupland, *Welsh and Scottish Nationalism: A Study* (London, 1954), p. 147.

The most visible of all the Scots in the colonies were the merchants from Glasgow. Living in Norfolk and other towns, they largely monopolized the Southern tobacco trade with Britain. This was a major reason for Glasgow's sudden swift growth out of obscurity in the eighteenth century. The Scottish merchants in America stayed to themselves as a separate people and were bitterly disliked for the debts owed to them. English and Scots openly opposed one another in political contests in Southern towns, flying their own colors and running their own candidates. Scottish merchants were the chief target of mob riots in Norfolk in 1769, leading a prominent Scot to protest to the governor that "the people they were pleased to call foreigners had as a good claim to protection and justice as if their ancestors had first settled this Coloney."[4]

It is clear, in short, that the Scots in eighteenth-century America, as in eighteenth-century England, served the classic "scapegoat" function traditionally associated with Jews in other societies.[5] Scottish merchants were often described as mean, miserly, and scheming in ways reminiscent of the Jewish-merchant stereotype. When many Scottish merchants —together with practically all the Highlanders—proved to be Loyalist in the Revolution, the whole Scottish population suffered the usual experience of scapegoat minority groups by being lumped together in the popular mind. They were subjected to vigilante activity, mass deportations, and proscriptive legislation. There were many Scots on the patriotic side, some of them of great prominence, but it was necessary to protest the patriotism of the Scots in the face of the widespread conviction that all Scots were Tories.[6]

[4] William M. Dabney, "Letters from Norfolk: Scottish Merchants View the Revolutionary Crisis," in Darrett B. Rutman, *The Old Dominion: Essays for Thomas Perkins Abernethy* (Charlottesville, Va., 1964), pp. 110–11; Ian Charles Cargill Graham, *Colonists from Scotland: Emigration to North America, 1707–1783* (Ithaca, N.Y., 1956), *passim*.
[5] See Allport, *Nature of Prejudice*, pp. 235–49, for a discussion of this phenomenon.
[6] Graham, *Colonists from Scotland, passim*. These remarks do not apply to the Scotch-Irish, the Protestant immigrants from Ulster who settled in Pennsylvania and back-country Maryland, Virginia, and the Carolinas. The Scots and the Scotch-Irish had become almost two separate nationalities by the eighteenth century, so long had the immigrant

Scottish intellectuals in Britain were similarly made sharply aware of their minority status. Adam Smith came home from his six years as a student at Oxford, spent at Balliol College, smarting from the prejudice he had there encountered. Dr. Samuel Johnson had a legendary contempt for Scots, loudly and frequently expressed, and it is hardly surprising that he and Smith argued bitterly. Even so great a Scottish luminary as the philosopher-historian David Hume "was at times painfully and apologetically conscious of his un-Englishness . . ."[7]

What Adam Smith and his countrymen confronted must be borne in mind when seeking to look at such work as *The Wealth of Nations* in its most revealing perspective. It seems at the least worth noting that the first full-scale criticism of the English economic system came from a Scottish academic.

Smith benefited from the convergence upon his world of several intellectual influences. As he entered mature life in mid-century, Scotland was just beginning its legendary "Athenian Age," the decades glorified in Scottish history when Scotland's universities were brilliant, her philosophers supreme, her scientists and technicians at the forefront of the

Scots been settled in Ulster. They did not like each other, settled in separate regions—New Jersey was the center of the Scottish population and its spiritual homeland, focused on Princeton University (then known as the College of New Jersey)—and in many cases took opposite sides in the Revolution. The Scotch-Irish, who had left Ulster with burning grievances against the English, were ardent rebels in the Revolution; so much so that many English called the Revolution a Presbyterian war. Patrick Henry was Scotch-Irish, and may be taken as symbolic of the whole group. Cf. James G. Leyburn, *The Scotch-Irish: A Social History* (Chapel Hill, N.C., 1962), *passim*.

[7] Ian Finlay, *Scotland* (London, 1945), pp. 100–1. This awareness of secondary status in an English-dominated United Kingdom is a constant theme in the history of Scottish political attitudes. Maurice Lindsay speaks for it in the mid-twentieth century as he explains his return to Scotland after spending the years of the Second World War in London: "Fond as I am of London, I have never ceased to feel an alien in its streets. The leisured assurance of the Southern English upper classes; the easy superiority of a people who have never been conquered and who harbour the instinctive assumption that the Scots and the Welsh, who submitted, are unimportant and slightly comic, while the Irish, who did not, are odd and troublesome—these things, constantly implied in attitudes if rarely consciously formulated, made it impossible for one perhaps over-sensitive Scot ever to be unaware that in England he could never really enjoy the sense of belonging." *By Yon Bonnie Banks*, p. 19.

age, and her arts flowering in the poetry of Robert Burns and the novels of Sir Walter Scott. An uprush of wealth in Glasgow, derived from the booming colonial tobacco trade, spread prosperity throughout the Scottish Lowlands. Edinburgh, Scotland's political, social, and cultural capital, was at the peak of its fame. Americans came to study in the famous university, and one of them, Dr. Benjamin Rush, wrote home that he wished his beloved Philadelphia could become the "Edinburgh of America." Intellectuals of many kinds "gravitated to the congenial setting of 'Auld Reekie,' with its *salons,* its learned societies, its convivial inns and genteel coffee-houses."[8]

Scottish intellectual life was enriched by the cultural ties maintained for centuries with France, growing out of the shared hostility to England. French influence ranged from the ridiculous to the sublime. Slops and household filth were thrown into Edinburgh's streets after the traditional warning cry "Gardyloo" (*Gardez l'eau*),[9] and Scottish scholars studied when they could in Paris. Voltaire was important to both David Hume and Adam Smith. In short, the Scots were open to influences that were anathema to many Englishmen, especially to the criticisms of mercantilism being made by the Physiocrats.

———

The state of economic thought by the middle of the eighteenth century was analogous to that of biological thought a hundred years later, and to work in the physical sciences half a century after that. Darwin and Einstein were able to do their work because decades of labors by earlier workers had reached the point where a synthesis was possible. Similarly, by the middle of the eighteenth century the science of economics, which had been emerging out of the crudities of its seventeenth-century beginnings, was in a state in which only

[8] Pryde, *Scotland,* pp. 74–5, 144–6, 162–8. Cf. also C. R. Fay, *Adam Smith and the Scotland of His Day* (Cambridge, England, 1956), Ch. i.
[9] Ibid., p. 84.

a brilliant synthesizing mind was required for it to become established as a matured discipline.[1] That Smith fulfilled this office with consummate success is attested to in the words of the twentieth-century economist Joseph A. Schumpeter, who remarked that *The Wealth of Nations* was "the most successful, not only of all books on economics, but, with the possible exception of Darwin's *Origin of Species*, of all scientific books that have appeared to this day."[2]

On March 9, 1776, not quite four months before the writing of the American Declaration of Independence, *An Inquiry into the Nature and Causes of the Wealth of Nations* appeared, in two volumes quarto, running to just short of 1,100 pages. It was before long a great success, was translated into many languages, and went through edition after edition. Smith was thereafter to enjoy the benign delights of being, like Sir Isaac Newton, Charles Darwin, and Albert Einstein, a legend in his own day. In a famous incident, the Prime Minister of Great Britain himself, William Pitt the Younger, rose in his honor upon his entrance into a London drawing room. It must have seemed a pleasantly long way for a Scottish intellectual to come from the scalding prejudice of Dr. Johnson.[3]

The fundamental problem that Smith dealt with in *The Wealth of Nations* was the sweeping transformation then taking place in the age-old character of the British economy and in British life. The apparent stability of the ages had given way. The industrial revolution was beginning, a booming commercial activity was remaking British life, and great fortunes were beginning to accumulate. Tragically, however, masses of degraded poor were beginning to gather in the new cities. What could be done, men asked themselves, about this

[1] Cf. William Letwin, *The Origins of Scientific Economics* (New York, 1965), pp. 238–46.
[2] Joseph A. Schumpeter, *History of Economic Analysis* (Oxford, 1954), p. 181.
[3] Edwin Cannan, "Editor's Introduction" to his 1904 edition of *The Wealth of Nations* (New York: Modern Library; 1937); J. Bronowski and Bruce Mazlish, *The Western Intellectual Tradition from Leonardo to Hegel* (New York, 1960); Robert L. Heilbroner, *The Worldly Philosophers: The Lives, Times and Ideas of the Great Economic Thinkers* (New York, 1961).

terrible new phenomenon, the urban poor? They were drunken, diseased, given to riotous disorders; a stolid, ignorant, and almost dehumanized world of faceless men. How could matters be arranged so that all could share in the new wealth that seemed to go only to the few? How was it that so shocking a maldistribution of the riches of the new economy had taken place? *The Wealth of Nations* provided the first full-scale analysis of these grinding disorders, and pointed the way out of the dilemma.[4]

Adam Smith was convinced that the root cause of Britain's difficulties lay in the crude and stultifying mercantilist economic system that the British government had built over the previous century. A "benevolent" system, it was founded upon the assumption that Whitehall in its aristocratic wisdom knew best how to direct the operations of the national economy so as to produce a strong and prosperous Britain. The result was an almost infinitely confused and complicated system of tariffs, bounties, privileged monopolies, navigation laws, and other such devices, each of them established in different times and particular situations, none harmonized with the others, and all hopefully engaged in producing a greater Britain.

In actual fact, Smith wrote, all these devices had their true origin in the greed and monopolizing spirit of the merchants and manufacturers. They had skillfully played upon the fears and prejudices of the landowning aristocrats, who lacked much understanding of these matters, and convinced them that privileges were necessary to the building of a strong and efficient Great Empire. What they asked for and received, in essence, was a vast program of governmental aid to commerce and industry. Without it, they insisted they would go bankrupt. The empire would be dependent upon France and other enemies, the laboring class would be thrown out of work, and England's miseries would grow

---

[4] The foregoing and following discussions are drawn principally from two books: the compact distillation of Smith's argument in Eli Ginzberg, *The House of Adam Smith* (New York, 1934); and the analysis of this argument in Cropsey, *Polity and Economy.* Useful too have been the insightful essays on Smith in Bronowski and Mazlish, *Western Intellectual Tradition,* and Heilbroner, *Worldly Philosophers.*

worse. Without support for industry and trade, the farmers
would lack the markets they needed at home, and the landed
aristocracy would find their rent revenues sadly shrunken.

No raw materials, according to the businessmen, should
be allowed to leave the country. They should instead be
turned into manufactured goods by home industry created
for the purpose. Practically all foreign goods should be excluded, especially cloth goods. In Adam Smith's day, in consequence of this appeal, tariffs were levied on 1,200 items.
Most commodities could not be imported at all, at least
legally. Meanwhile, native industries received subsidies and
rebates upon taxes. Other concerns received special subsidies
for exporting their goods and capturing foreign markets, the
linen manufacturers being the chief among these. Furthermore, when they imported flax, they received a bounty.
Bounties were similarly granted for the import of naval
stores, indigo, hemp, raw silk, barrel staves, and a wide variety of other goods.

Smith attacked all of this as corrupt, absurd, and coun-
ter-productive. Real prosperity would only arrive, he said,
when Britain threw off all the shackles on her trade; when
she traded her goods freely with all other nations and bought
from them what she could not make so well herself. Britain,
he warned, could not manufacture everything. To try to do so
by supporting industries not natural to Britain simply meant
the excessive investment of capital that could be more pro-
ductively used in other pursuits. Wine could be made in Scotland, he observed, but only at about thirty times the cost it
took to procure the same commodity from France. Why,
then, divert unnecessarily that much capital? Each country
was equipped by climate, skills, and resources to manufacture
different things. All would grow richer if they relied on an
international division of labor.

The key factor in creating prosperity, he said, was the
size of the market—as Scotsmen had found after the Union
with England in 1707 had thrown open to them the English
market and the whole trade of the American colonies. The
United Kingdom was hurting itself by its restraints on trade,
for they hindered the fundamental process that must be en-

couraged, which was an increasingly efficient division of labor.

In effect, the whole system of bounties, tariffs, subsidies, and the like was an attempt by the government to direct the flow of capital investment into the channels where it would produce the best result. At the source of this effort, Smith warned, there lay the false assumption that such a program was within the range of man's intellectual capacity. Governments must dispense with the comforting but misleading illusion that good intentions carried with them the equipment to do the job. They must humbly recognize the limits to their knowledge and capacity. Parliaments should instead ground their policy on natural facts and allow the appearance of a "system of natural liberty" (he never used the terms "capitalism" or *"laissez faire"*).

An economy grounded on natural facts, Smith considered, would first take in view the fundamental nature of mankind. Men were moved most of all by a passion for self-preservation. They instinctively did the things that best meet this goal. While it was not within their capacities to frame large national economic plans in detail, individual men in their immediate situations would always be able to act better in their own interests than a distant government acting upon supposedly virtuous principles but ignorant of local conditions. It was impossible to create a productive society by teaching people virtue, but it was possible to have one if their desire for self-preservation and improvement was released and allowed to flourish.

Legislative bodies must therefore cease meddling with industry and trade. The sole result of such activities, he said, however laudable and objective, was the creation of an unholy alliance between business and government in which shrewd men, by bribery and other means, got what they wanted to their own profit and to society's loss. Release the economy, and its natural tendency to dynamic growth would take hold.

> The natural effort of every individual to better his own condition, when suffered to exert itself with freedom and

> security, is so powerful a principle, that it is alone, and
> without any assistance, not only capable of carrying on the
> society to wealth and prosperity, but of surmounting a hun-
> dred impertinent obstructions with which the folly of
> human law too often incumbers its operation . . ."[5]

One of the continuing dangers that threatened society,
however, was the incorrigible determination of businessmen
to rig the market. They constantly sought to erect artificial
controls on the flow of goods, keeping prices high by collu-
sion and monopoly. Businessmen—as Smith was to observe
repeatedly in *The Wealth of Nations*—were the only element
in economic society (labor and land constituting the other
two elements) the interest of which was inherently and always "in some respects different from, and even opposite to,
that of the public." The public wanted prices as low as possible and goods as abundantly available as necessary, but businessmen always wanted to cut off competition, keep prices
high, and maintain scarcity. By this means they were able in
effect "to levy, for their own benefit, an absurd tax upon the
rest of their fellow-citizens." For this reason, every proposal
for legislation that came from businessmen must be examined with the greatest suspicion. They were

> an order of men, whose interest is never exactly the same
> with that of the public, who have generally an interest to
> deceive and even to oppress the public, and who accord-
> ingly have, upon many occasions, both deceived and op-
> pressed it.[6]

While Smith distrusted the mercantile classes, he viewed
farmers as fundamentally kindly and good-natured, and remarkably skilled in a wide variety of ways. To keep a nation
healthy, he said, a good proportion of its people should be on
the land. The aristocratic landowner, however, was another
matter. He had fastened a monopoly upon the honest tillers
of the soil, getting in the form of rents the profits of the land,
while doing nothing himself to earn it. The fact that one

[5] Smith, *Wealth of Nations*, p. 508.
[6] Ibid., pp. 249–50.

quarter of Scotland was under entail, making the sale and distribution of such land impossible, was monstrous. The land must be more equitably distributed. Far too much of it was locked up in hunting preserves; high rents extorted by noblemen living luxurious lives in London prevented farmers from making necessary improvements; and the basic price of food for everyone was elevated, not only through high rents but by the protective tariffs that landowners had long ago gotten Parliament to put up against foreign wheat.

The laboring poor were the special object of Smith's concern. In his time they were generally regarded simply as fodder for different kinds of aristocratic projects, such as wars and industrial developments. They were to work hard, pay high taxes, and behave themselves. When some of them in the eighteenth century began to drink tea and enjoy a few other simple amenities such as wheat bread and candles, there was a great outcry at the moral degradation of the working classes, and taxes were immediately placed on these new objects of consumption.

Smith wanted to encourage those few reformers who were beginning to worry about the sufferings of the poor. His signal intellectual achievement in this direction was his theory, much relied upon thereafter by reformers from trade unionists to Karl Marx, that all wealth was fundamentally derived from labor. The mercantilist had tended to think of wealth as a passive, fixed commodity expressed in gold and silver. The French Physiocrats had developed an innovation in their more dynamic view that wealth was generated in agriculture, whence it circulated through society—a conception that has been termed the first "flow sheet" model of the economy in modern thought.[7] Smith, though much influenced by the inherently dynamic view of the Physiocrats, located the true origin of wealth in labor, and specifically in the division of labor.

[7] Bronowski and Mazlish, *Western Intellectual Tradition*, pp. 339–40.

This conception, in fact, is the opening statement of *The Wealth of Nations*.

> The annual labour of every nation is the fund which originally supplies it with all the necessaries and conveniences of life which it annually consumes, and which consist always either in the immediate produce of that labour, or in what is purchased with that produce from other nations.[8]

It was not trade that enriched the country, as the merchants contended, nor was it the production of land, as landowners insisted. It was, according to Smith, the status of labor and the development of the industrial arts.

Everything, therefore, was dependent on the skill and dexterity of the workingman. Anything that affected these qualities should be of the greatest concern to governments, since the wealth of the nation was directly involved. The seven-year apprenticeship system must be abolished, for example, because it held men largely idle for years, and allowed older men to monopolize certain trades. The poor laws were cruelly restrictive, for a man could get relief when out of work only in his own parish. This hobbled an essential element in the economy, the mobility of labor. Men should be free to seek both employment and the best use of their talents wherever they could find them.

How ironic it was, Smith remarked, that workmen were savagely punished when they sought to combine together to raise wages, yet employers were never hindered in their efforts to conspire together to keep them down.

> We rarely hear, it has been said, of the combinations of masters, though frequently of those of workmen. But whoever imagines, upon this account, that masters rarely combine, is as ignorant of the world as of the subject. Masters are always and every where in a sort of tacit, but constant and uniform combination, not to raise the wages of labour above their actual rate . . . [and sometimes] to sink the wages of labour even below this rate.

[8] Smith, *Wealth of Nations*, p. lvii.

Angry workmen, stung to outrage and folly, brought on the repressive actions of the government, while the masters, whose whole procedure was carried forward in "the utmost silence and secrecy," emerged always the winners.[9]

Were the state to act without concern for class interests, it would punish the businessmen for their conspiracies too. But unfortunately, Smith remarked acidly, government was always class government. The upper classes, callous in their luxury, took delight in oppressing the poor. They complained frequently of high wages, never of high profits. It was absurd, he warned, to fear high wages, for if one class grew wealthier, the whole community would benefit. Poverty was not an instructive and helpful condition for the laborers, it was actually a great social liability. "No society can surely be flourishing and happy," Smith observed, "of which the far greater part of the members are poor and miserable." Well-paid workmen were active, diligent, and stable; poorly paid workmen were riotous and bitter, reaching always for some form of release.[1]

Smith found the same false spirit of monopoly and privileged enrichment in imperial policy. Colonists were burdened with all manner of restraints, under the governing illusion that forcing them to trade only with Britain made the British richer and other nations poorer. The result was the enrichment of a few merchants, the diversion of too much capital to colonial trade, and the exploitation of hundreds of thousands of people.

The colonies, in fact, were not profitable for Britain, he said. Empires were an economic drain, not a gain. There might conceivably be colonial possessions that provided greater military or financial strength to the mother country, but the American colonies did neither. Much more profitable was the trade that Britain had with other nations.

[9] Ibid., pp. 66–7.
[1] Ibid., p. 79.

Yet even in this sphere the old restrictionist ideas prevailed. Since time out of mind foreign trade had been regarded as a field open only to those chosen by the Crown. Charters were necessary, and they gave monopolistic privileges in various parts of the globe to favored individuals. The result was constant abuse of monopolies, as in the case of the East India Company, which grievously exploited the people of India. Once subjected to fair competition, such corrupt and self-seeking arrangements would quickly collapse. But the merchants clung to the system, which so typically ran at cross purposes to the interests of the nation at large. Since they got their income from profits, which were always highest in the most backward countries, there was a scramble in London for monopolies in foreign trade and constant pressure for government aid to foreign activities.

Smith considered monopolies the principal obstacle in the path of national progress. The real hope for the country lay in sweeping away all these special privileges, which simply enriched the already wealthy, and in creating competitive conditions in as wide a sphere as possible. There was no part of the economy in which this rule should not be allowed to operate. Even the banking system should be made competitive. With only a few large banks, their power over fluctuations in the value of money was very great. Rising and falling prices could be stimulated by unscrupulous men who, in secret, could profit therefrom. If there were many banks, their power would be scattered, and the failure of one or two would have little harmful effect. Furthermore, small businessmen would find capital easier to get, thus putting an end to the arrogance of central bankers.

The banking business, in fact, was so important to Smith that he regarded it as an area in which the government should not be reluctant to meddle. The state, he said, had a perfect right, indeed a duty, to control banks. They were too critical in the national economy, their operations were much too central to be ignored. It was always justifiable, he said, "to limit the natural liberty of a few individuals which might endanger the security of the whole society."[2] There should be

2 Ibid., p. 308.

little worry about limiting the freedom of the rich and powerful who directed banks. They had sufficient strength to care
for themselves.[3]

Smith applied the same conceptions to the whole problem of the business corporation. The power of incorporation
was not open to everyone, but was rather handed out only to
specific groups of individuals by charter. Corporations were
few, compared to modern times, but they had chartered
monopolies over whole trades and skills. These creatures,
Smith warned, with their exclusive privileges and monopolies, were a severely limiting influence on the economy.
Workmen were forced to deal with a single employer if they
intended to work in a particular line of activity, and they
were subject thereafter to the power of that corporation over
their income, since alternative employers were not available.
The general effect of corporation policy was to keep prices
high and to force the economy to advance at a crawl, rather
than with the buoyancy it would display if restraints and
privileges were ended.

What of education? In Smith's day, the ignorance of the
poor was much praised on the ground that it kept them from
getting appetites they could not satisfy. Smith took the view,
however, that widespread education would help everyone by
giving the common laborer an opportunity to gain new skills
and to grow more productive, and thus more prosperous.
Education almost alone, he insisted, made the difference between a philosopher and a common street porter. Native abilities were stunted or stifled by environmental deficiencies.
Uneducated laborers could not further their own interests.

They were, in truth, threatened through lack of education with "almost entire corruption and degeneracy." The rea-

---

[3] These observations upon the banking system provided the direct inspiration and rationale for the Jacksonian war against the U.S. Bank
and for the Jacksonians' own banking system, as will later be made
clear.

son for this lay in the new industrial order, which gave workmen severely limited tasks to labor at, day after day. This
stultified the laboring man's mind, so that he became "as
stupid and ignorant as it is possible for a human being to
become."[4] Workmen lost not only the power of rational conversation, but also the capacity for harboring generous,
noble, or tender sentiments. This fatally injured their powers
of judgment in their ordinary lives and in their public responsibilities. But if provided with schools—as laboring men were
in Scotland, in a glaring contrast to England that was a constant source of pride to Scots—then men would be better
fitted for life, and a natural aristocracy that could help to run
the country intelligently and industriously would begin to rise
from the laboring classes.

A free society, in short, needed education, for the general
population in a free society must know how to take care of
itself. Furthermore, with growing industrialization, workmen
with more and more skills were needed. All of this meant that
the state should begin providing—indeed, imposing, if necessary—the essentials of learning. In the process, the cur-
riculum must be modernized. Children going into carpenter-
ing or the iron trade should learn physics and geometry, not
the higher mysteries of Latin verbs. Science was vitally important in the new age, yet the incredibly backward schools
of the day, Smith complained, left their students in ignorance
of it.

———————

It is clear that the Adam Smith of reality does not very
closely resemble the Adam Smith of the *laissez faire* stereotype. He would have the government regulate the banks,
support schools, ensure competitive conditions by eliminating
special privileges—he did not think of the next step, positive
measures to break up monopolies—watch businessmen with
great care and be suspicious of their proposals, and do much

4 Ibid., p. 734.

else besides. The danger of fanaticism in the professions should be guarded against by frequent examinations establishing rational competency and intellectual stability. Interest rates should be regulated, highways and canals should be maintained, and lighting and water supplies should be supervised. By state action there should be provided public diversions of "frequency and gaity." The people, who lived such grim lives that they periodically broke out in shocking violence and fanaticisms, should be amused and diverted by "painting, poetry, music, dancing; by all sorts of dramatic representations and exhibitions, [which] would easily dissipate . . . that melancholy and gloomy humour which is almost always the nurse of popular superstition and enthusiasm."[5]

The beginning and the end of Adam Smith's *laissez faire*, in fact, related to just one governmental function: its attempts to control the flow of capital investment. The state must give up its efforts at deflecting the flow of capital into favored industries and depend upon the market for this central function. In a free market there would operate Smith's famous "invisible hand."

> As every individual . . . endeavours as much as he can both to employ his capital in the support of domestic industry, and so to direct that industry that its produce may be of the greatest value; every individual necessarily labours to render the annual revenue of the society as great as he can. He generally, indeed, neither intends to promote the public interest, nor knows how much he is promoting it. . . . [He] intends only his own gain, and he is in this . . . led by an invisible hand to promote an end which was no part of his intention.[6]

Competition, if allowed to operate freely, would establish just prices, and much else besides. In a free market, scarcity induces higher prices, and leads men to produce more of what is needed. Competition, therefore, makes certain that society will have what is essential to it. This influ-

[5] Ibid., p. 748.
[6] Ibid., p. 423.

ence will also control quality, ensure distribution generally, and create a steadily rising level of commercial activity. This, in turn, would bring about a massive upward movement of the entire economy. A dynamic economy would appear, an economy in which wealth would be created, not just hoarded. Based primarily upon a free market and the progressive division of labor, the economy would steadily progress toward opulence, an opulence which all would equitably share. The continual increase in wealth in an open and progressive society, he said, was what raised wages. That is to say, not the richest but the most thriving nations had the highest wages.

As workmen grew wealthier, they would be able to care better for their children, thus ensuring that they would live through the dangerous years of childhood into maturity. Population would grow, providing more hands for labor, and more competition for work, driving wages downward once again, but—and this was critically important—not all the way. In short, the progress toward opulence would take place in stair-step fashion. In this way, the grave problem facing the whole nation—its hordes of degraded poor—would ultimately be solved.

Smith had "constructed for society a giant endless chain. As regularly and as inevitably as a series of interlocked mathematical propositions, society is started on an upward march." It was not a cycle, but "a long-term process, a secular evolution. And it is wonderfully certain."[7] If the government would only ensure that the market was free of grasping monopolists, that labor was mobile, and that the law was impartial, then everyone would rise to prosperity.

Such a reordering of national policy would carry with it, however, a profound shift in social arrangements, and Smith was aware of this. It would mean that a new order of men should take over the direction of the state, and direct its policies. Who should they be? Smith was positive that they should not be composed merely of the common people. In their actual condition of degradation and poverty, he distrusted the capacity of the poor to direct governments. He was also completely opposed to the direction of society by

[7] Heilbroner, *Worldly Philosophers*, pp. 50–1.

businessmen. Their "mean rapacity and monopolizing spirit"
fatally disabled them from being the rulers of mankind.
Trader and sovereign were inconsistent roles for anyone to
play, especially when businessmen were daily exposed to the
irresistible moral temptations of their occupations. Smith
acidly observed,

> People of the same trade seldom meet together, even for
> merriment and diversion, but the conversation ends in a
> conspiracy against the public, or in some contrivance to
> raise prices. It is impossible indeed to prevent such meet-
> ings, by any law which either could be executed, or would
> be consistent with liberty and justice. But though the law
> cannot hinder people of the same trade from sometimes
> assembling together, it ought to do nothing to facilitate such
> assemblies; much less to render them necessary.[8]

It was equally dangerous to allow the aristocracy to rule.
Their vice was different from that of the businessman. They
were in search simply of "honor." This meant not simply the
luxury of profligate lives, it meant the prestige of office and
patronage to dispense. Aristocrats surrounded themselves
with retainers and sycophants. Aristocratic governments were
therefore corrupt governments, given to luxurious and func-
tionless offices, oppressive taxes, and wasteful expenditure.

The result was to sap an essential foundation for a prosperous economic system, which was the confidence among
men that they might keep the property that they had earned.
Aristocratic government led to capricious taxation, swollen
far beyond the essential needs of government. The array of
sinecures and empty offices that characterized eighteenth-
century governments, providing rulers with many devices for
corrupting legislators, must be swept away. Ruminating on
the fact that absolute rulers could tax their subjects as whim-
sically as they wished, Smith even made guarded references
to republicanism as the best system of government, pointing
to the Dutch republican austerity as responsible in large part
for Dutch prosperity. He vigorously condemned tyranny,

[8] Smith, *Wealth of Nations*, p. 128.

stressing the need for separation of powers to maintain freedom.

Who, then, should rule? A natural aristocracy of men that would spring from the middle and lower ranks of life once the economy was freed of its restrictions. These men would have lifted themselves from poverty by their "own industry and abilities." They would be best suited to run the government, not through their natural virtue—always a quality of doubtful constancy, in Smith's view—but through their ambition, their passion to rise, and their determination to hold on to the places they have claimed. Their very drive toward eminence meant that, as they drew nearer the summit, they would balance one another, preventing tyranny.

Smith therefore considered no distinct order in society—labor, landed gentry, merchants and manufacturers, the nobility, the clergy—fitted to rule, for their particular class interests contradicted the interests of the whole society. Rather, there should be at the head of the state a heterogeneous collection of talented individuals who by their own efforts would have emerged from all of the orders. He was calling, in short, for the pluralistic and entrepreneurial state.[9]

———

The Wealth of Nations, in sum, is a vast, complex, and subtle book, containing a far more penetrating commentary on social man, and a far more pungent and biting economic analysis, than has been generally realized among twentieth-century scholars. It was in fact not a dry economic treatise, but a political program. It was crammed with all the materials needed by a political movement looking for both a sweeping assessment and a comprehensive agenda. Its myriad concrete details about cordwainers in Glasgow, glass makers in London, tobacco raising in America, market conditions in Buenos Aires, the price of salted hides in varying circumstances, the specific ways in which pins were made; about the

[9] This discussion of the proper leadership of the state has been drawn from Cropsey, *Polity and Economy*, pp. 66–70.

conditions of childbearing in the Highlands, of fisheries in the offshore islands, of landholding in Pennsylvania; about the devices used by bankers to manipulate money, by governments to issue regulations, by merchants to establish monopolies—these and thousands of alternately homely and sophisticated details made the book a rich store of wisdom and practical information for decades of politicians.

What should be the party's banking policy? It was in Smith, carefully explained. What taxes should be placed upon farmers? *The Wealth of Nations* describes them. How do we bring about steadily rising wealth? What should be our commercial policy toward other nations? Who is the social enemy? For all of these and more, *The Wealth of Nations*, with its enormous store of facts and analysis, provided the answers. In economic policy, Smith was the teacher of the Liberal-Democratic world for a century.

Perhaps his most important gift to the Liberals and the Democrats was a sense of confidence. With Smith's immense authority behind them, they could be certain they were right. They could be alternately outraged or contemptuous when confronted by those who benightedly proposed an alternate course. He had given them the grand vision they needed: the regular and inevitable progress of the whole society toward wealth, if only certain fundamental requirements were fulfilled. He had given them a vision that for a great many years to come would make the Liberal-Democratic mind confident that it could answer the intractable problem of mass poverty posed by the new economic order. With Adam Smith as their teacher, they could have the confidence of true believers. The Ark of the Covenant was in their hands. The road to abundance for all was open and clear.

Chapter 3

THE INHERITED WORLD VIEW:
EDMUND BURKE AND THE ARGUMENT
FROM CIRCUMSTANCES

The mid-twentieth century has come to look upon Edmund
Burke in a special way. He was admired by Liberals and
Conservatives in the nineteenth century, both of whom drew
inspiration from him. William Gladstone spoke of Burke as
his greatest teacher, and yet Benjamin Disraeli so admired
Burke that he took the name of his earldom, Beaconsfield,
from Burke's country home near London. Burke's *Reflections
on the Revolution in France* (1790) became the Bible of the
Tories, and yet John Morley, perhaps the archetype of the
Liberal genus, could call him the "largest master of civil wisdom in our language," and claim him for the Liberals.[1]

　　Present-day scholarly opinion, however, usually sees
Burke as simply the father of Conservatism. Some may explain this on the ground that both Liberals and Conservatives
in the nineteenth century were "conservative." A better assessment, however, would seem to lie in the circumstance that
Burke is at present generally known only as he presents himself in one book, his *Reflections on the Revolution in France*,

[1] John Morley, *Edmund Burke: A Historical Study* (London, 1866). Cf.
also Peter J. Stanlis, ed., *The Relevance of Edmund Burke* (New York,
1964, p. 27.

which he wrote in the last few years of his life. The riddle of why William Gladstone and John Morley claimed him for the Liberals, therefore, is perhaps best answered by considering the whole of his career and his utterances. Thus examined, he takes on a new appearance.

In 1751, the young Irishman Edmund Burke arrived in London. Fifteen years later, after having become a literary figure of some note, he entered Parliament as the principal intellectual of the Rockingham Whigs. For the next thirty years his fertile intellect, his compassion for suffering, his gifted pen, and his talent for Parliamentary oratory were to make him one of the major figures in the politics of the British Empire, though he held office only briefly.

His long relationship with the Marquis of Rockingham was of considerable importance in the history of British politics. It represented, for one thing, perhaps the earliest link between the English North Country and Ireland, for as Burke was an Irishman, so the Marquis was the head of Yorkshire politics.[2] It is interesting to note that these two men, who came from regions marginal to the main center of British life, showed a concern when they were briefly in power in 1765–6 for the opinions and interests of groups that had traditionally been outside the circles of influence. Burke laid particular stress on carefully maintaining the support of public opinion outside the walls of Parliament, through the media of newspapers established for the purpose, public gatherings, and pamphleteering. To the outraged aristocracy, this violated the basic maxim that government was a mystery committed by design only to their hands. To Burke, these steps simply expressed one of the more daring maxims in his political beliefs, the need for governments to begin paying close attention to public opinion.

He also took pride in the fact that the Rockingham min-

[2] G. H. Guttridge, *The Early Career of Lord Rockingham, 1730–1765* (Berkeley and Los Angeles, 1952).

istry of 1765–6 was the first to establish direct relationships with the ordinary merchants of London, who were pleading for an end to the many restrictive regulations that governed imperial trade. He was much influenced by Adam Smith—"outsiders" both, they were apparently personal friends—and talked often of the need for freer trade policies. He also shared with Smith the basic assumption underlying Smith's philosophy, the conviction that human reason was a far weaker tool, and human passion a stronger force, than the Enlightenment believed. He was therefore willing to listen sympathetically when the merchants complained that economic regulations like the Stamp Act, which were designed for political purposes, or the similarly motivated requirement that all West Indies trade had to flow through one port, were actually harmful to the nation's economy. Such arrangements, they charged, only enriched a few great men to the harm of all others. The Rockingham ministry accordingly responded by greatly easing the conditions of the West Indies trade, and, most dramatically of all, by repealing the Stamp Act.

By these policies, the Rockingham ministry began a transition of high importance in the history of British economic policy. The steps they took were in effect a recognition that Britain should begin moving away from the idea that economic policy was to serve political policy, and toward its reverse. Trade and general prosperity, the new voices argued, should be paramount. The nation should dismantle its mechanisms of economic warfare, by which it was perpetually in rivalry with all other nations, and follow the peaceful routes of open international trade. The link between the Liberals and the economic interests flourishing on free trade that characterized nineteenth-century politics may be seen, in sum, to have taken shape first under the eager ministrations of Edmund Burke.[3]

As the years went by, the Rockingham Whigs gradually took form as perhaps the first distinct political party in British history. More than anything else, they survived because Edmund Burke held them all together and gave them their polit-

[3] L. Stuart Sutherland, "Edmund Burke and the First Rockingham Ministry," *English Historical Review*, XLVII (1932), 46–72.

ical *raison d'être*. From 1766 to 1782—the year of the Marquis's death—Burke

> prepared, with scrupulous care, scores of speeches; worked
> up unnumbered drafts for the heads of the party; wrote
> three large pamphlets; published three speech-pamphlets;
> kept up a voluminous party correspondence; drafted peti-
> tions to King and Parliament for men who knew not how to
> do that; wrote to the newspapers, and composed all the
> great protests that his friends in the House of Lords entered
> upon the journal—all the while attending Parliament regu-
> larly, speaking often from carefully prepared notes and
> running to town, or to Newmarket, or to Yorkshire, when-
> ever his chief summoned.[4]

In this process, he was in effect creating the very idea of a political party as something distinct from a conspiratorial cabal. In the eighteenth century and well into the nineteenth, it was common to condemn parties harshly as "factions" that divided the nation, violated the idea of loyalty to the monarch, and disrupted the life of the nation. In this circumstance, the Rockingham Whigs persisted in thinking of themselves—though not in modern terms—as a party with stated principles, rather than as an organized group of hungry placemen looking for office at any opportunity. In their two brief periods of power, in 1765 and 1782, they gave England, as Carl B. Cone has remarked, its first experience with party government.[5]

Viewed from the twentieth century, the principles they embodied seem hardly exciting. In the context of the eighteenth century, however, they were bold departures for which the Rockinghamites paid a heavy price in years of exile from preferment. They believed that the king should appoint men to office in accordance with the public interest and public opinion, rather than on the basis of his own personal likes and dislikes; that the corrupt mechanism of sinecures and

[4] Ross J. S. Hoffman, "Edmund Burke as a Practical Politician," in Stanlis, *Relevance of Edmund Burke*, p. 126.
[5] Carl B. Cone, *Burke and the Nature of Politics: The Age of the American Revolution* (Lexington, Ky., 1957), pp. xiv–xv.

bribes by which the king bought votes in Parliament should be swept away; and that the desires and needs of the nation, rather than the prejudices of the Crown, should shape legislation.[6]

The cause for which Edmund Burke labored the longest —his "old man of the sea," as it has been called[7]—was the cause of Roman Catholic Ireland. He had himself brought from Ireland a rich Irish brogue. All his career he had to fight the contemptuous charge that he was an "Irish adventurer" come to trade on his wits in the wealthy purlieus of official London. He had every reason to know intimately what it meant to be an Irishman in the British Empire. Though he was a devout Anglican, having inherited this faith from his father, his mother and sisters and his closest relatives were Roman Catholic, and he had to suffer the constant charge that he was a Jesuit in disguise. In truth, he was almost as devoted to the Catholic faith as to his own. He never shared the religious bigotry that so disfigured British politics until well into the twentieth century. He maintained an open, universalist attitude toward faiths other than his own. Salvation, he believed, was open to all regardless of denomination.[8] That most distinguishing mark of the classic Tory, an anti-Catholicism that identified the nation with the Anglican Church, was never his.

Ireland, he said, was the most oppressively exploited nation in Europe. Not only was the great mass of the population—the Catholic Irish—denied the vote, so that the Irish Parliament was a purely Protestant body, they were also de-

[6] Cf. ibid., pp. 62, 65; Ross J. S. Hoffman, "Edmund Burke as a Practical Politician," in Stanlis, Relevance of Edmund Burke, pp. 122, 127; Peter J. Stanlis, ed., Edmund Burke: Selected Writings and Speeches (Garden City, N.Y., 1963), p. 102.
[7] Thomas Mahoney, Edmund Burke and Ireland (Cambridge, Mass., 1960), p. ix.
[8] Mahoney, Burke and Ireland, pp. 6, 29, 312, 316; Cone, Burke and the Nature of Politics, p. 36.

nied entrance to the professions, denied the right to own
land, even denied the right to education. So wide was the
abyss between Protestant and Catholic in Ireland that it was
even possible, he said, for thousands of Protestant Irishmen
to achieve the incredible distinction of never having even
conversed with a Catholic Irishman, though the latter surrounded them in the millions.[9] The whole purpose of English
policy, he insisted, was so to degrade the common Irishman
that he would be submissive to slavery. The most contempti-
ble aspect of the whole system was its denial of education to
the Roman Catholic priesthood.[1]

The Protestant ascendancy in Ireland excited his condemnation. It was "a machine of wise and elaborate con-
trivance . . . fitted for the oppression, impoverishment, and
degradation of a people, and the debasement, in them, of
human nature itself . . ."[2] It created a monstrous arrangement
in which one set of people in Ireland thought of themselves
as the only citizens of the commonwealth, and kept dominion
over all the rest by naked military power. Meanwhile, they
divided the wealth of Ireland, produced by all, as military
booty among themselves.[3]

Why, he asked, was this insane policy maintained? How
could Englishmen really believe that narrowing the foundation was the best way to build a building?[4] The argument
that it was necessary in order to protect the nation from
millions of Roman Catholics was fallacious, he said, for the
only real danger to the nation would arise from making its
subjects discontented. There was in fact a greater danger, he
said, that threatened everyone. Since the British constitution
was not made for "great, general, and proscriptive exclusions

[9] "A Letter to Sir Hercules Langrishe, Bart., M.P., on the Subject of the
Roman Catholics of Ireland . . . ," Stanlis, *Selected Writings and
Speeches*, pp. 259–60. Mahoney, *Burke and Ireland*, includes the Penal
Laws in its appendix.
[1] "A Letter to a Peer of Ireland on the Penal Laws against Irish Catholics . . . ," Feb. 21, 1782, in Stanlis, *Selected Writings and Speeches*,
p. 233.
[2] "A Letter to Sir Hercules Langrishe . . . ," ibid., p. 265.
[3] "A Letter to Richard Burke, Esq., on the Protestant Ascendancy in
Ireland, 1793," ibid., p. 267.
[4] "A Letter to Sir Hercules Langrishe . . . ," ibid., p. 260.

. . ." increasingly oppressive measures would have to be introduced to maintain them, and eventually the whole governing system would be corrupted.[5]

He appealed to the English to base their Irish policy not on prejudice and hatred, but on the fundamental requirements of civilized society—and in outlining these "fundamental requirements," he became the first eighteenth-century British politician to appeal to a broad framework of political philosophy. The only policy that the Empire should be based on, he said, was in fact the only policy that could hold it together: namely, a recognition that all men must enjoy the common advantages of society. A healthy Empire could not subsist on reluctant ties, but only on the existence of a happy Ireland. If mutual interest were created, then equality and a sense of affection would keep the Irish joined to the English.[6] It was madness to try to convert the Catholics to Anglicanism by making the Catholic faith so odious a burden that it would be discarded; by sacrificing the civil prosperity of Ireland in the vain hope that this would lead to its religious improvement.[7] What was needed, instead, was a generous system of home rule, in which an autonomous and fully reformed legislature in Ireland would handle domestic matters, leaving imperial affairs to the London Parliament.[8]

When as a result of his long labors Ireland secured commercial relief in the legislation of 1778–80, legislative independence in 1782, and the franchise for Roman Catholics in 1793, he felt his work was largely completed. Tragically, the threat of Irish rebellion during the long Napoleonic wars after his death led to a reimposition of the former system in all its harshness.

---

[5] Ibid., pp. 245–6; "Fragments of a Tract Relative to the Laws against Popery in Ireland (1765)," ibid., p. 226.
[6] Ibid., p. 220; Mahoney, Burke and Ireland, p. 313.
[7] "A Letter to a Peer of Ireland on the Penal Laws against Irish Catholics . . . ," in Stanlis, Selected Writings and Speeches, p. 236.
[8] Mahoney, Burke and Ireland, pp. 311–14.

Ireland was not his only concern. He spent many years of his life attacking the oppressive and exploitive rule in India of the East India Company, looking upon himself as perhaps the only defender in a callous and profligate London of the poverty-stricken Indian peasant. He also condemned from its inception the whole policy of the British government toward the American colonists after 1763. In this long controversy, he returned again and again to one of his most fundamental beliefs, which was that it was imperative for the government to unbend from its aristocratic hauteur and listen to public opinion. The English, he said, were insufferably arrogant. "I know," he said in 1777, "and have long felt . . . the unwieldly haughtiness of a great ruling nation, habituated to command, pampered by enormous wealth, and confident from a long course of prosperity and victory . . ."[9]

It was wholly wrong, he argued, to govern on the arrogant assumption that simply promulgating a law made it binding. The consent of the people was ultimately necessary in order to make law valid. The "true end of legislature," he said, was to "follow, not to force the public inclination; to give a direction, a form, a technical dress, and a specific sanction to the general sense of the community." Three years later, as the American argument grew hotter, he warned that there could be no such thing as governing a whole people against their inclinations.[1] Relying upon coercion in America, he said, was hopeless, for it always creates unity and strength in the people coerced. To those who demanded that, come what may, Britain's power to do what she chose must be vindicated and her dignity protected, he scoffed that empty pretensions of power were folly. The only principle that should be followed was dispassionately to consider the facts of the situation, and to adopt the policy that was most expedient, leaving aside

[9] "A Letter to John Farr and John Harris, Esquires, Sheriffs of Bristol, on the Affairs of America, April 1777," in Elliott Robert Barkan, ed., *Edmund Burke on the American Revolution: Selected Speeches and Letters* (New York, 1966), p. 195.
[1] "Fragments of a Tract Relative to the Laws against Popery in Ireland," in Stanlis, *Selected Writings and Speeches*, p. 212; Speech, Commons, Nov. 18, 1768, in Barkan, *Edmund Burke on the American Revolution*, p. 3; Sir Leslie Stephen, *English Thought in the Eighteenth Century* (New York and Burlingame, 1962 reissue of 1876 ed.), II, 204–5.

emotion and the itch to assert a "rightful" power. "The question with me is," he said in 1775, "not whether you have a right to render your people miserable, but whether it is not in your interest to make them happy."[2] To those who argued that the colonists were committing a criminal act in being rebellious, he made the famous reply, "I do not know the method of drawing up an indictment against a whole people." And when others began by tortuous legal argument to prove that Britain was right in what she was doing, he replied, "An Englishman is the unfittest person on earth to argue another Englishman into slavery."[3]

What Burke was trying to do, in short, was to teach his generation the concepts that were to become the fundamental basis for nineteenth-century Liberalism. They were strange, indeed infuriating, ideas to the eighteenth-century oligarchy, but he kept at it. They must learn, he said, that a governing power could only proceed in its work by moving in accordance with the spirit that motivated the mass of the people. They must pay attention to "the general character and situation of a people [to] determine what sort of government is fitted for them. That point nothing else can or ought to determine."[4] No nation, particularly one that loved freedom, could ever be perpetually governed by force. Whatever was oppressive to the minds of the people had to be removed. Otherwise, the government would inevitably pay the mandatory price of failure, for this price was always exacted whenever ruling authorities tried to defy the general feeling of great communities.[5]

Local freedom, he said, would not lead inevitably to license and anarchy, as so many said it would. England had had constant difficulty with the Welsh and with the people of Chester and Durham, he pointed out, when these outlying regions had been kept under grim military rule and given no share in the general government. But when they were given a

[2] Speech, Commons, May 9, 1770, in Barkan, Edmund Burke on the American Revolution, pp. 16–17; Speech, Commons, Apr. 19, 1774, ibid., pp. 30–3; Speech, Commons, Mar. 22, 1775, ibid., p. 96.
[3] Ibid., pp. 91, 93; cf. also Speech, Commons, Apr. 19, 1774, ibid., p. 65.
[4] Speech, Commons, Apr. 19, 1774, ibid., p. 44.
[5] Ibid., pp. 81, 96; "An Address to the King," 1777, ibid., p. 151.

full share in the rights of government accorded the rest of England, then they became tranquil. These examples showed conclusively that "freedom, and not servitude, is the cure of anarchy . . ." How could they possibly ignore the lessons of history? The English must *admit the people of our colonies into an interest in the constitution.*[6]

What Burke was doing was not only formulating the idea that public opinion was the ultimate arbiter of national policy and that the habit of authority must be discarded in these matters, he was also laying the basis for what was to become the characteristically Liberal idea of empire. There was one great solution for Britain's imperial difficulties, he said: home rule. The whole Empire could be organized on this basis. It could be extended almost endlessly, to scores of colonies, without danger to anyone. Giving the same rights to colonists that Englishmen enjoyed in the home country would preserve the Empire.

Every practical consideration, and everything in English history, he said, pointed to this solution. America simply could not be governed in London. The English, furthermore, had taught the colonists by their own example to love liberty, to regard the taxing power as the most critical for freedom, and to react angrily to threats against that freedom. The Americans were composed of active Dissenting Protestants, the most prickly of all religions where rights were concerned, and of slave-owning aristocrats sensitive to their dignity. They studied law actively, had popular assemblies, and sniffed tyranny at the slightest hint on the breeze. Most importantly of all, they were three thousand miles across the ocean. For the love of the Empire, he pleaded, consider these facts—for it is facts alone that govern the situation, not the imaginings of power-mad politicians in London, or abstract ideas of legal right.[7]

The key to the whole problem, he said, was for the English to give up their lust for domination. They must divest

---

[6] Speech, Commons, Mar. 22, 1775, ibid., pp. 96, 1–2.
[7] Speech, Commons, May 9, 1770, ibid., p. 9; Speech, Commons, April 19, 1774, ibid., p. 67; Speech, Commons, Mar. 22, 1775, ibid., pp. 75, 81–86, 113–14.

themselves of the habit of looking down possessively and arrogantly on everyone else. There were too many men in England, he said bitterly, whose whole idea of freedom was composed of "pride, perverseness, and insolence." They feel "in a state of thralldom . . . their souls are cooped and cabined in, unless they have some man or some body of men dependent on their mercy." They must constantly speak of "*Our* subjects in America; *our* colonies; *our* dependents. This lust of . . . power is the liberty they hunger and thirst for . . ." They must learn not to regard it as unmanly to listen to the colonists' side of the argument, and magnanimously to respond to their complaints, for the colonists were speaking out of a profound knowledge of the truth. Even the most ignorant people, he warned on another occasion with regard to the Irish, were good judges of the existence of oppression.[8]

This was the Burke whom the Liberals venerated, the Burke of compassion, the Burke who attacked the habit of authority and the love of domination, who pleaded for the revolutionary idea that public opinion must be listened to, that the people's will was what made a law valid. It was this Burke whom Gladstone read daily for instruction on how to deal with the Irish question; who taught the English what John Locke never considered, the proper way to rule over subject peoples. It was Burke more than anyone else, perhaps, who created the idea that an opposition party, listening to the public and not necessarily to the king, was not a disloyal faction but a legitimate part of the constitution.

But there was of course much more to Edmund Burke. There was the Burke who detested democracy and railed at radical eighteenth-century reformers who wanted to establish equal electoral districts, mass voting, and triennial parliaments. This Burke was a confirmed believer in rule for the people by the aristocracy—though in truth an aristocracy distinguished not just by birth and wealth, but by independence, enlightened views, and a strong sense of the national

[8] Speech, Bristol, Sept. 6, 1780, ibid., p. 209; "A Letter to Sir Hercules Langrishe . . . ," Jan. 3, 1792, in Stanlis, *Selected Writings and Speeches*, p. 257.

interest.[9] Though the people, he said, could accurately judge that they were oppressed, they lacked the settled wisdom and ripe experience to decide the remedies to that oppression. The poor, illiterate, and uninformed people "ought never to be called into council."[1]

There was also the Burke who, in the *Reflections*, could sob over the death of Marie Antoinette and could utter the classic phrase, "The age of chivalry is gone"; could reject the reasons advanced for the Revolution and scorn the intellectual reformers who had brought it on; and could utter imperishable paeans in praise of crowned heads, traditional institutions, respect for one's betters, and landed wealth as the ballast of the state. Liberals like John Morley had always to wince at these views and to explain them away as consistent with Burke's long-held horror of hasty and sweeping change and his compassion for suffering, wherever it took place.

There was much food for Liberals in the *Reflections*, however. Few of them, in any event, had much interest in or liking for French intellectuals, and they would not be upset with Burke's criticism of such men. They were British liberals, not Continental liberals, and the differences were profound. As earlier observed, across most of the spectrum of British opinion there was a veneration for the past, for the crown, for religion, for the rule of settled law, as well as a faith in what was felt to be accumulated wisdom. These were the great forces that Burke praised, not autocratic misrule. He believed that the essential nature of a healthy society lay in a familial attachment between its members and its great institutions. Love must bind together the commonwealth, affection and awe of the monarch paralleling love and awe of the father in a healthy family. The existing institutions of society, in his view, bore an erotic charge, an emotional significance that was rooted in our tendency to love all the things that are nearest and dearest to us as being part of the

[9] See the analysis of his aristocratic whiggism in Stephen, *History of English Thought in the Eighteenth Century*, II, 197.
[1] "A Letter to Sir Hercules Langrishe . . . ," in Stanlis, *Selected Writings and Speeches*, p. 257.

moral universe in which we live. Like the family, the state trains us as moral tutor and presents us with an inheritable estate. Without the family, we are psychically naked; without the traditional state, rooted in ancestral memories, we are similarly bereft of dignity and of the means of self-respect. Sheer force is the only thing that can take the place of unforced love as the binding element in a familial society.[2]

These were the virtues that Burke celebrated in his attacks on the French Revolution, and he celebrated them within a framework that was profoundly satisfying to the ordinary Gladstonian Liberal. As a long and acrimonious debate in the 1962-4 issues of *The Journal of British Studies* demonstrates, almost any view of the deeper structure of Edmund Burke's thought is certain to attract dissent. The remarkable outburst of Burke scholarship since the opening of his papers a generation ago has been intensely partisan, in both a scholarly and a political sense. One steps gingerly on ground so heavily mined. Looking upon Burke from the standpoint of the men in this study, however, one is forced to take the view that the much-maligned position of Peter J. Stanlis, even though it may be distrusted by some because it speaks from departments of English and outspokenly conservative political precincts, had correctly perceived in Burke a fundamental concern for law that was later to be equally fundamental in the world view of William Gladstone.[3] Whatever the validity of the Stanlis view that Burke's thought was grounded in the Natural Law, he accurately and tellingly delineates a love for *statute* law as perhaps Burke's most continous intellectual concern.

Burke's father was a lawyer, he studied law in London for a time, he always read much thereafter in legal history, and he often larded his speeches with impressive displays of legal history going back many centuries to the Romans. He was editor, for some years, of a law journal, and even en-

[2] I am grateful to Larry L. Adams for his perceptive observations on this subject.
[3] This position was originally laid out in Peter J. Stanlis, *Edmund Burke and the Natural Law* (Ann Arbor, 1958), which included an adulatory introduction by Russell Kirk. Much better is the compact and penetrating essay with which Stanlis later introduced his *Edmund Burke: Selected Writings and Speeches* (1963).

gaged in some writing on the history of English law. He frequently reviewed books on law, including Sir William Blackstone's *Discourses on the Study of Law* (1759), and regularly studied ancient treatises. "I have studied," he said in Parliament in 1773, "God knows: hard have I studied, even to the making dog-ears of almost every statute book in the kingdom . . . the letter as well as the spirit of the laws, the liberties, and the constitution of this country."[4]

He was also, it must be observed, a devout member of the Church of England, an institution that is rooted in Richard Hooker's *Laws of Ecclesiastical Polity* (1594–7). Concern for law as a central obsession has usually been ascribed only to Puritans, but it is a deeply Anglican tradition as well. Richard Hooker described in his book a grand and awesome process through the ages in which man's reason, ordained of God, limited in capacity, but vitally essential, built up in growing majesty the great body of laws that organize the commonwealth.[5]

Edmund Burke had the same vision of the past, and of the legal system. That is to say, he perceived it as the tangible product of countless historical occasions on which men made specific decisions based upon concrete, particular facts, these decisions forming jointly a compacted mass of ordered wisdom, growing through the ages. He had a firm belief that mankind must rely upon this heritage of law, must always work within it, and must look upon it as the principal protection from oppression, whatever the source. Gladstone and Woodrow Wilson, in their later fervent appeals for a worldwide rule of law, were speaking directly out of the tradition that led Burke to utter his elaborate attack against the French Revolution as a wild and dangerous thing. "Burke looked upon the Revolution," Leslie Stephen observed, "with that kind of shudder with which man acknowledges the presence of a being believed to be supernatural. All ordinary rules seemed to be suspended. The earth trembled, and the strongest barriers gave way."[6]

---

[4] Stanlis, *Selected Writings and Speeches*, p. 5.
[5] Peter Munz, *The Place of Hooker in the History of Thought* (London, 1952).
[6] Stephen, *English Thought in the Eighteenth Century*, II, 206.

There was of course a lively consciousness of law in the eighteenth-century Enlightenment. It was common for writers to discourse upon the laws of nature as holding the universe together in the orderly system embodied in the Newtonian vision of the cosmos. This was a predominantly rationalist and scientific view of law, however, and Burke's outlook was fundamentally different. He conceived of the law humanistically. It must be remembered that Burke's original career in London—and, in a sense, his whole career—was as a literary man. His friends were Dr. Samuel Johnson and David Garrick and Sir Joshua Reynolds. The club that with them he helped to found contained a different perspective on the world from that of the scientists who were meeting elsewhere in London. Their vision of life was not rational and mechanical, but poetical and humanistic. One emerges from reading Burke—especially from his *Reflections*—with a realization that his world view was essentially dramatic, personal, and historical. It abounded in visual images. Burke saw mankind as living in the specific confines of history, with its multitudinous concrete and varied details, each of which defies scientific abstraction. As Burke might say and as Reinhold Niebuhr has observed, history and personality are alike in that they are both essentially indescribable, mystical, and elusive, refusing to submit to formulas and patterns. "A [personal] character," as Burke said, "is too complex a thing to be drawn into a definition."

He venerated history, therefore, as a theater in which personality and fact commingled in an almost mystical process, producing, as their highest achievement, civil society. History was complex, multiform, and rich in the swarming of personal detail, yet it displayed also—one hears overtones of Richard Hooker here—the operation of the reason God has given man for dealing with the specific tasks of life. Burke always deplored the rationalism of the skeptic and the scientifically minded philosopher, but he was convinced at the same time that man possesses a powerful intellectual capacity. Individuals are foolish, but mankind is wise. In its arduous process of problem-solving, mankind has built institutions that must be venerated, and are tampered with at heavy cost.

They must be dealt with in the full light of the humbling knowledge that, as his admired friend David Hume had said, reason, like sight, is limited in nature, and is at its best when dealing with things close at hand.

The history of European civilization, therefore, was to Burke a long evolutionary process whose highest product has been systems of law. Concrete, specific, solid, and venerable, law holds together the world of civil man, saving him from the weakness of his intellect and the torrent of his passions. Being without law was being disorderly, and Burke had, as John Morley called it, a "passionate enthusiasm for Order."[7] He remarked at the outset of his *Reflections* that a wild, free, and lawless outbreaking of liberty was all that worried him, for "I love a manly, moral, regulated liberty as well as any gentleman."[8] The sovereign consideration to bear in mind, he said, was the nature of the *circumstances*, for liberty, like everything else, could not be properly assessed as a strictly abstract proposition. No force in human society, no civil phenomenon, no idea could be judged

> stripped of every relation, in all the nakedness and solitude of metaphysical abstraction. Circumstances (which with some gentlemen pass for nothing) give in reality to every political principle its distinguishing color and discriminating effect. The circumstances are what render every civil and political scheme beneficial or noxious to mankind.[9]

This was perhaps Burke's most characteristic idea. In every dispute of his career, and in practically all of his writings, Burke insisted that circumstances must be the basis for the making of policy. It was folly, he said during the American controversy in 1777, to ignore circumstances. Intelligent rulers, he insisted in 1782, must *"take the state in the condi-*

[7] John Morley, *Edmund Burke: An Historical Study* (New York, 1924 edn. of the 1866 work), p. 38.
[8] Edmund Burke, *Reflections on the Revolution in France*, ed. Thomas H. D. Mahoney (Indianapolis and New York, 1955), p. 8. This edition is skillfully divided into headings and subheadings, breaking up the oppressive length of the original letter form.
[9] Ibid.

tion in which it is found, and . . . improve it *in that state . . ."*[1]

The argument from circumstances is one that fits ill with conservatism (defined as love for the *status quo*), for it disarms dogma. By emphasizing circumstances and social evolution—both deeply Burkeian concepts—nineteenth-century reformers could slide around the barriers put up by entrenched ideas, not so much by directly refuting them as by making them irrelevant. No more dramatic demonstration of the remarkably dissolvent and reformist potentialities of the combined arguments from circumstances and evolution can be found than in William Gladstone's open and unashamed use of the Burkeian formula in 1847 to explain to his angry Oxford constituents why he had voted for the admission of Jews to Parliament.[2] Richard M. Weaver, in fact, has recently pointed out that the argument from circumstances has limitless reformist potentialities, and has warned conservatives that Burke might be an enemy to their cause, rather than a friend. By taking circumstances rather than theory or definition as his guide, Burke seriously weakened such typically conservative positions as the rights of property or the fundamental limitations upon legislative attempts to enact social legislation.[3]

It was Burke's emphasis upon the argument from circumstances, repeated over and over again, that led John Morley to praise him fulsomely as the prophet of Liberalism.[4] Leslie Stephen, another Liberal intellectual of the Gladstonian era, insisted that for this reason Burke was at heart a utilitarian. The argument from circumstances, Stephen remarked, is the "true method" of enlightened politics.

[1] "A Letter to John Farr and John Harris, Esquires . . . ," in Barkan, *Burke on the American Revolution,* p. 193; "A Letter to a Peer of Ireland . . . ," Feb. 21, 1782, in Stanlis, *Selected Writings and Speeches,* p. 236.
[2] W. E. Gladstone, *Substance of a Speech on the Motion of Lord John Russell for a Committee of the Whole House, with a View to the Removal of the Remaining Jewish Disabilities,* Commons, Dec. 16, 1847 (pamphlet; London, 1848).
[3] "Edmund Burke and the Argument from Circumstances," *The Ethics of Rhetoric* (Chicago, 1953), quoted in Donald C. Bryant, "Edmund Burke: A Generation of Scholarship and Discovery," *The Journal of British Studies,* II (1962), 110.
[4] Morley, *Burke,* pp. 16–20.

Even Burke's conception of the state as a living organism growing out of the past, usually acclaimed as a conservative principle, was in fact utilitarian in Stephen's mind, for it was based on the presumption that "every existing social arrangement has been developed by certain needs . . ."[5]

Burke, firm evolutionist that he was, regarded change as the most powerful natural law in human society. The statesman's task, he said, was not to resist change, but to ensure that changes were not violent, and proceeded by insensible degrees.[6] "A state without the means of some change," he asserted in the *Reflections*, "is without the means of its conservation."[7]

He believed that it was unwise, however, to proceed on the basis of abstract theorizing. It was far preferable, because safer, to build from inherited rights, specifically stated, won in particular historical situations, and cherished through the centuries alike for their excellence and their venerable age. Men are moved perhaps most of all by passion, he would say with Adam Smith, and their attachments to things of value are more emotional than rational. Speculative rights are easily "torn to pieces by every wild, litigious spirit," while inherited rights constitute an estate for all the people that need not constantly be defended by arguments that fly over most heads, certainly over those of the common people.[8]

Burke sanctified in this way the mode of reform that was to be typical of the British Liberal mind. One searches in vain in most Liberal speeches for arguments based on broad theories about the good society. They were predominantly factual and specific, with copious references to historical precedent. They were legal, moderate, and remarkably pragmatic. Gladstone's speeches, which showed all these characteristics, were made in a style of argumentation especially suited to a society dominated by a powerful aristocracy that could only be offended at peril to the project at issue.[9] It was ever the aim

[5] Stephen, *English Thought in the Eighteenth Century*, II, 185–95.
[6] "A Letter to a Peer of Ireland . . . ," Feb. 21, 1782, in Stanlis, *Selected Writings and Speeches*, p. 263.
[7] Burke, *Reflections*, p. 24.
[8] Ibid., pp. 35–8, 196–7.
[9] In the mid-1870's, as will later be discussed, Gladstone's speeches suddenly became pungently anti-aristocratic.

of the Liberal to demonstrate how close his project flew to the ground, how well it flowed from what had gone before, how conservative, in fact, it really was. At the same time, the arguments were implacable, continuous, and cumulative, holding always before society the view that change was not the option, but the necessity.

Burke's political outlook also embodied the deep religiosity that later characterized Gladstonian Liberalism, for Burke was a devout man who took a fundamentally Christian view of the state. Shocked by the attacks on the Church in France, he lengthily condemned the spoliations in the *Reflections*. He gloried in the fact that the British, in their simplicity and what he saw as their fundamental soundness, knew that "religion is the basis of civil society and the source of all good and of all comfort." They were not misled by the unhallowed fire of atheism, which in his eyes so detestably disfigured France. "We know, and it is our pride to know that man is by his constitution a religious animal . . ." The English therefore clung to their religious establishment not out of superstition, he said, but out of a profound and extensive wisdom. They knew that selfish passion, licentiousness, and faithless indifference to social duties could only be checked, transformed, and civilized by religion.[1]

The whole state, in Burke's view, was an indirect emanation of God's power and goodness. It rested upon divine law. The church, furthermore, performed a far broader social function than simply the "consecration of the state." It had lifted the whole of European civilization upward from barbarism.

> Christianity was the spiritual equivalent of Burke's conception of a worldly "Commonwealth of Europe." In the eighteen centuries of its existence, through historical continuity and legal prescription, it had added immeasurably to the richness and stability of European civilization . . . In the struggle to subdue the barbarians, the Church had preserved, transcribed, and spread the learning, literature, science, laws, and manners of the ancient world . . . [after

[1] Burke, *Reflections*, pp. 102–3.

Rome withdrew from Britain], the Church [infused] the arts and civil manners through the spiritual nature of man.[2]

The image of Burke in the Gladstonian Liberal mind, therefore, was a many-sided and deeply attractive one. He was a devout man and an intellectual at the same time, the inspiration of the reforming Whigs whose powerful writings and speeches had validated the deepest concerns of the Liberal mind. He elevated compassion as the fundamental spirit in political society, a compassion that listened with sensitivity and concern to the wishes of the public, not simply to the private desires of the monarch and his coterie of sycophants. It was a pragmatic compassion that concerned itself with actual circumstances, not with remote and prescriptive theories. It was a compassion that warned governments not to be too concerned with their own dignity, nor too greatly offended by apparent ingratitude. The chief concern of governments should not be the jealous maintenance of prerogatives, but the creation of a tranquil society, which meant ministering to grievances rather than callously ignoring them.

The constricting hand of government should be lifted from trade. A sense of mutual economic interest and affection should be the only tie binding together the various parts of the empire. An authoritarian empire in which ruling circles simply fed their own love of power and domination would not be conserved but destroyed. Religious prejudice must be rigorously shunned; the special privileges of Anglicans in Ireland must be swept away. Christianity in its highest teachings and functions should pervade the life of the nation, which could in no sense be free of the searching criticism and the categorical imperatives of the moral law.

The ruling principle in the empire at large should be local self-government, in which freedom and liberty would be cherished as the true sources of stability and prosperity. The rights won in the hallowed struggles enshrined in British history would be sedulously maintained, within the protecting

[2] Stanlis, *Burke and the Natural Law,* pp. 36, 195–7. Cf. also Burke, *Reflections,* p. 105.

embrace of law, received institutions, and history. Corruption in government, perhaps the most basic evil of all, must be expunged by rooting out the tendency of governments to buy support. There must be an end to the issuance of sinecures, special posts and honors, and lucrative offices. The "economical reform" for which Burke agitated would establish the ideal of an austere, honest, and effective government in which the needs of society could be properly examined and ministered to in an atmosphere of objective concern for the facts.

There was also, of course, much in Burke's vision that was anathema to nineteenth-century reformers, and particularly to the Americans. His veneration of the past, his distrust of philosophy, his refusal to deal in mass symbols, his glorification of traditional European society, and his deeply religious commitment to a union between church and state were in sharp contrast to the thought of the American Democrats, and particularly to that of their presiding genius, Thomas Jefferson.

Chapter 4

THE INHERITED WORLD VIEW:
THOMAS JEFFERSON AND THE
IDEOLOGY OF CONFLICT

Thomas Jefferson mesmerized the Democratic Party for a hundred years. The record of his career and influence is extraordinary. For forty years, from 1769 to 1809, he was a towering figure in American politics, passing through the offices of Virginia legislator, representative to the Continental Congress, governor of his state, ambassador to France, Secretary of State, Vice-President, and finally, from 1801 to 1809, President of the United States. For sixteen more years his close associates James Madison and James Monroe occupied the White House. Thereafter the Jacksonians idolized him, and then Samuel Tilden, Grover Cleveland, and William Jennings Bryan continued to worship at the Jefferson shrine as they led the Democratic party during the half century after the Civil War. Only in the Wilsonian era did the party turn in any serious way to voices other than that of the Messiah. Even this represented, however, only a moderate dimming of the image. Jefferson would seem still to have only Abraham Lincoln as his rival in the American political heart, though Alexander Hamilton may have had an equally great effect on actual economic and political practices in the United States.

The Jeffersonian inheritance was many-sided and oftentimes contradictory. In this respect, as in others, Edmund Burke and Thomas Jefferson are counterpart figures in Anglo-American politics. Both were complex men who were in politics for a long time, who wrote a great deal, and who left behind such a vast corpus of political utterance that it seemed to contain somewhere in its many coves and recesses a home for politicians of almost any persuasion. As both Liberals and Conservatives claimed Burke, so there were times when both Democrats and their enemies scrambled for the Jeffersonian mantle.[1]

In appearance, Jefferson was a tall man, graceful in a loose and informal way; in manner, he was reserved in public, yet in private given to an unceasing flow of frank and open talk on an astonishing range of topics. Jefferson "sits in a lounging manner," Senator William Maclay recorded in his *Journal* (1890) after visiting him while he was Secretary of State in the early 1790's, "on one hip commonly, and with one of his shoulders elevated much above the other; his face has a sunny aspect; his whole figure has a loose, shackling air . . . I looked for gravity, but a laxity of manner seemed shed about him. He spoke almost without ceasing. It was loose and rambling, and yet he scattered information wherever he went, and some brilliant sentiments sparkled from him." He seems never to have given a speech, explaining his reluctance on the ground that he felt few men were persuaded by oratory, but rather by private talk, reading, and reflection. He was a sensitive man, almost morbidly reactive to criticism, shy, and probably lonely. Yet he could form warm friendships, was always tender in his concern for the welfare of others, lavished his hospitality, and had the quality of attracting intense devotion.

He was, of course, quite beyond any of his contemporaries—Franklin perhaps excepted—in the breadth of his interests, his studies, and his skills. He learned many languages, built one of the great eighteenth-century libraries, and was warmly claimed by French intellectuals as a fellow *philosophe*. James Parton, commenting on Jefferson in middle life,

---

[1] Cf. Merrill D. Peterson, *The Jefferson Image in the American Mind* (New York, 1962).

has left the classic picture of him as "a gentleman of thirty-two who could calculate an eclipse, survey an estate, tie an artery, plan an edifice, try a cause, break a horse, dance a minuet, and play a violin."[2] There is little wonder that it was later felt almost impious to question the ideas of so awesome a man.

Born a British subject in Virginia in 1743, Thomas Jefferson grew up in a situation which, for all of its American differences, was remarkably like that encountered by similar young men reared in other outlying provinces of the British Empire, such as Scotland or Ireland. Certainly the central focus of politics was the same. Until independence turned the Americans' gaze to Washington, D.C., they too looked to London as the center of their world. As Benjamin Franklin observed, before the revolutionary troubles began the colonies actually felt closer to Britain than they did to one another.[3]

The relationship that England had with the provinces was always peculiarly mixed and ambivalent, compounded in varying measure of admiration and distaste. England was so rich, so powerful, and—compared to the provinces—so sophisticated that admiration was unavoidable. In some, it reached the point of discipleship. The Anglicized Scot, or New Englander or Virginian—or, at a later date, Canadian—was a common phenomenon, one that flourished in times of little friction with England. Certainly there was no question about Virginia's loyalty to the Crown before the troubles began in 1763. The model of the English aristocrat was universally aspired to by the planters, who often liked to think of themselves as descendants of seventeenth-century Cavaliers.

But the Virginians, like the Scots and the Irish, also felt

[2] Quoted in Peterson, *Jefferson Image*, p. 234.
[3] H. Trevor Colbourn, *The Lamp of Experience: Whig History and the Intellectual Origins of the American Revolution* (Chapel Hill, N.C., 1965), p. 3.

they were an exploited satellite much looked down upon by the arrogant English. After the Stamp Act controversy in 1765, these latent attitudes became dominant—aided, it must be observed, by supercilious oratory in the House of Commons. The English always treated the colonies, George Mason of Virginia complained, in "the authoritative style of a master to a schoolboy."[4] The rooted English belief that they were superior to the Americans led Benjamin Franklin finally to despair of reconciliation. It seemed a common opinion in England to speak of "the American colonists as little more than a Set of Slaves, at work for us, in distant Plantations one Degree only above the Negroes that we carry to them." As an English newspaper put the matter, "Mr. Hancock may be a very good Englishman amongst Bostonians, but he is no more an Englishman amongst Englishmen, than General Gage is a King amongst Sovereigns."[5]

Jefferson reciprocated these feelings heartily. He was, in fact, representative of the British provincial who, when he looked at England and Englishmen, saw an insufferable arrogance. When he wrote his first major political utterance—his *Summary View of the Rights of British America* (1774), which catapulted him from obscurity to international notoriety—it was clear that he wrote it as a provincial smarting at the arrogance of the metropolis. His constant theme was to assert the complete equality of the colonials with the English. Two years later, when he wrote the Declaration of Independence, he expanded the principle of equality into a grand and sonorous universal principle, an assertion generally regarded as having its roots in the Enlightenment philosophy to which he was devoted. It is common, however, for outgroups quickly to translate their demands for specific recognition into values claimed to have universal validity. Of these, the most cherished is the ideal of the equality of all men, for it is hoped that as the ideal grows in acceptance, the specific degradations inflicted by arrogant majorities and power groups will decline. Seen in this framework, it is not surpris-

[4] John C. Miller, *Origins of the American Revolution* (Boston, 1943), p. 205.
[5] Ibid., pp. 204, 206.

ing that an intramural argument within the British Empire between American provincials and the metropolis began with assertions of equality within the empire, and then issued forth in the magisterial utterance "all men are created equal." Whatever its roots in the Enlightenment, one suspects that Jefferson's assertion was in a sense simply another passage in his long polemic against English pretensions of superiority.

Throughout his life, Anglophobia was to be one of the organizing principles in his political world view. His love for the classical style in architecture, the revival of which in America he seems to have instigated, arose out of his distaste for the English styles that then dominated colonial architecture. As governor of Virginia during the Revolution, he was kindly to captured Hessians, but he stayed on strictly formal terms with the British, for "their arrogance, even as prisoners, repelled him."[6] After a brief visit to England in 1786, he was clearly projecting his own feelings when he wrote to a friend, "That nation hates us, their ministers hate us, and their King more than all other men."[7]

His whole career, in a certain sense, was devoted to resisting the imposition upon America of anything that smacked of England, and particularly of Tory England. His bitterest attacks on Alexander Hamilton were accusations that Hamilton was trying to remake America in the British image, an image to Jefferson monarchical, corrupt, plutocratic, industrial, and squalidly urban, implying a degradation of the masses and a slavish relationship between social classes.

The fact that his early teachers were also provincials— one a Scot and the other an Anglican priest of Irish descent —may have had its part in making the young Jefferson an Anglophobe. There was in fact an interesting repetition of Scottish influences in his intellectual life, in his preferences, and in his images.[8] He disliked the Scottish merchants who kept Virginia planters in debt, but he admired Scottish cul-

[6] Nathan Schachner, *Thomas Jefferson: A Biography* (New York, 1951), I, 64.
[7] Jefferson to John Page, May 4, 1886, in Paul Leicester Ford, ed., *The Works of Thomas Jefferson* (New York and London, 1904), V, 100.
[8] Jefferson himself claimed remote Welsh descent.

ture. He was well read in the Scottish philosophers of the "Athenian Age," and as a lawyer particularly admired the Scottish jurist and philosopher Lord Kames (Henry Home, 1696–1782), whose legal philosophy was based on the concepts of natural rights and morality. He was devoted to the legendary Scottish bard Ossian, whose alleged poetry, richly romantic and Scottish in scene, enchanted him. Like the Scots, too, Jefferson was to establish and maintain a firm attachment to the French and to their ideas.[9]

Of special importance among these influences was that of his beloved professor at William and Mary, an extraordinary Scotsman named Dr. William Small. Jefferson observed in later years that this man of "enlarged and liberal mind . . . fixed the destinies of my life."[1] Small was a freethinking intellectual imbued with Enlightenment attitudes in the sciences and in philosophy. He served on the William and Mary faculty in consequence of a brief overthrow of Anglican authority there. For two years, in fact, he was practically the entire faculty, and Jefferson in these years became his disciple. Small brought Jefferson into the regular company of the intellectual Governor Francis Fauquier, and got him well launched in his legal career. It seems safe to assume that in his months with Small, the intellectual and heterodox Scotsman, Jefferson heard relatively little of the glories of Englishmen.[2]

---

[9] Schachner, *Jefferson*, I, 36, 48–9; Dumas Malone, *Jefferson the Virginian* (Boston, 1948), p. 392.

[1] Jefferson, *Autobiography*, in Ford, *Works*, I, 506.

[2] Thereafter, Small returned to England, where he became part of a brilliant intellectual circle. His influence helped to create the Lunar Society in Birmingham. Erasmus Darwin, Joseph Priestley, James Watt, Josiah Wedgwood, and Matthew Boulton were leading figures in the society, representing in their persons the juncture of science, rational religion, technology, and entrepreneurism that was to characterize the coming era in the English North Country and in Scotland. Cf. Herbert L. Ganter, "William Small, Jefferson's Beloved Teacher," *William and Mary Quarterly* (1947), pp. 505–11; and Robert E. Schofield, *The Lunar Society of Birmingham: A Social History of Provincial Science and Industry in Eighteenth-Century England* (Oxford, 1963).

Virginia, as a province in the empire, experienced many of the same controversies that shaped political life in the home country in the eighteenth century. There were the same religious struggles, the same problems arising from ethnic differences, and similar intellectual controversies. Virginia was like England in being Anglican in law and in institutions, and in experiencing an American version of the Anglican-Dissenter conflict. Each county in Virginia was divided into parishes governed by vestries, in which taxes were raised for the support of resident Anglican clergy. Each priest had his church—or churches—his glebe land, and his rectory. All Virginians were required by law to attend his services. The one college in the province, William and Mary, founded in the provincial capital, Williamsburg, in 1693, was an Anglican institution designed in good part for the training of priests. The ceremonies of marriage and burial could be conducted only by Anglican priests.[3]

The Old Dominion, settled originally almost entirely by Englishmen, ruled as a Crown colony and fashioned in its customs after an idealized image of the rural English gentry, was apparently an ideal location for the Church to carry out its mission. In actuality, the position of the Church grew steadily more tenuous in the eighteenth century. Scotch-Irish Presbyterians and German Lutherans and Calvinists began moving down into Virginia from Pennsylvania in the 1730's, settling in the broad Shenandoah Valley west of the Blue Ridge. By the time of the Revolutionary troubles, this new element in Virginia life constituted half or more of the population and objected to the position of Anglican superiority.[4]

The campaign against the Anglicans in Virginia that Jefferson directly witnessed and figured in was but a part of a

[3] The best source on the Church of England in Virginia and its successor, the Protestant Episcopal Church, to 1814 is George Maclaren Brydon, *Virginia's Mother Church: And the Political Conditions Under Which It Grew* (Philadelphia, 1948, 1952), 2 vols.

[4] It is interesting that Jefferson lived close to the Scotch-Irish. Even today, Augusta and Rockbridge counties, abutting Jefferson's Albemarle County on the west, are the most heavily Scotch-Irish in the nation. The influence their hatred of the English had on Jefferson can only be conjectural, but it seems likely that it was not inconsiderable. Cf. Leyburn, *Scotch-Irish*, pp. 200–21; Thomas Jefferson, *Notes on the State of Virginia* (New York, 1964), pp. 150–2.

struggle that had been going on in all the American colonies for many years. Throughout most of the eighteenth century the Church of England attempted to Anglicize the colonies. The dispute grew increasingly harsh in the years of Jefferson's youth, and reached its climax in the pre-Revolutionary period, in good part helping to bring on the Revolution itself.[5]

To the Anglican hierarchy in England, the Northern colonies constituted an irresistible challenge. They consisted almost wholly of Dissenters, presenting to the grieving Anglican eye a vast range of assured and confident Dissent at the same time that Dissent in England seemed steadily on the decline, through the cumulative effect of discriminatory legislation and the decline of religious zeal. From Virginia southward, the Church of England was the established body. North of the Mason and Dixon line, however, there was the heterogeneous and pluralistic religious world that foreshadowed modern society, presenting a spectacle offensive to those devoted to the ideal of a unified Christian commonwealth. From the Congregationalists of New England to the Quakers in Pennsylvania, therefore, Dissent in America came under a long and determined attack from England. "For eighty-five years, church and state was the greatest and most familiar issue before the colonial public."[6]

The Anglicans sent missionaries to the Northern colonies after 1699. By the 1720's, they began to achieve major victories in Connecticut and Massachusetts, winning spectacular conversions, establishing churches, and gaining a significant foothold at Yale College. The religious Great Awakening, a revival movement that shook the entire colonial world in the 1720's and 1730's, allowed the Anglicans to reap an abundant harvest among those who detested enthusiastic religion. They showed their strength, too, in preventing the Presbyterians from gaining the right of incorporation in New York and in

---

[5] This conflict was first described in Arthur Lyon Cross, *The Anglican Episcopate and the American Colonies* (New York, 1902). Building upon this classic account is Carl Bridenbaugh, *Mitre and Sceptre: Transatlantic Faiths, Ideas, Personalities, and Politics: 1689–1775* (New York, 1962). The following discussion of the controversy is drawn from the latter, *passim*.
[6] *Ibid.*, p. xiii.

winning control of most of the colonial colleges. Only the Presbyterian College of New Jersey (Princeton) and Congregational Harvard, of the early collegiate institutions in the colonies, remained outside Anglican influence. By the middle of the century, furthermore, the colonial aristocracy was beginning to move in the Anglican direction, perhaps perceiving the advantages of such membership where royal governments were wholly Anglican. Anglican membership was also acquiring snob appeal.

In mid-century, the Anglican authorities began to urge the reluctant British government—which disliked stirring up the colonists further—to create an Anglican bishop in America. The Anglican churches in the colonies were within the diocese of the Bishop of London, requiring all who desired priest's orders to make the dangerous journey across the Atlantic for ordination, thus sharply reducing the number of possible candidates. The Anglicans were convinced, too, that their cause in the colonies would be much advanced by a resident bishop, who, as a member of the House of Lords, would outrank every governor in the colonies. As it was, even in such colonies as Virginia, the absence of a bishop meant that the Anglican clergy were hired and fired by local vestrymen in a strange kind of congregational arrangement. After 1763, when the British government began its fateful program of unifying and centralizing the Empire, the demand for an Anglican episcopate in America grew even more pressing.

This caused violent alarm among American Dissenters. To all of them, bishops represented nothing more or less than tyranny. All the chords of memory, all the persecutions enshrined in their histories and kept alive by constant ministerial references, told them that the advent of a bishop in America would be the beginning of the end of their religious liberty. So deeply disturbed were they by this campaign that they began to construct a broad theory of conspiracy to explain such devilish machinations. They attributed the whole program of the British government after 1763 to an Anglican plot. They were convinced that the real purpose of the Stamp Act was to raise a revenue outside of local control that would support an Anglican bishop, his expensive court, and a vastly expanded Anglican clergy. A fine house built by the Church in 1761 in Cambridge, Massachusetts, in bold proximity to Harvard, was widely rumored to be the prospective seat of the first American bishop. After the Stamp Act controversy, therefore, which energized the whole colonial world, "Religion and politics could never again be distinguished one from another . . ."[7]

Giving the whole controversy a specially manic twist was a conviction in the hypersuggestive American mind that the Anglican Church in England was actually swinging rapidly to Roman Catholicism. All of its moves, therefore, were seen as subtle strategems in an insidious conspiracy directed from Rome to Romanize the colonies. "We may live to see our churches converted to mass houses, and lands plundered of tythes for the support of a Popish clergy," patriots warned; "the Inquisition may erect her standard in Pennsylvania and the city of Philadelphia may yet experience the carnage of a St. Bartholomew's day."[8] After the Quebec Act of 1774, which approved and established Roman Catholicism in that province, these paranoid fears were believed to be confirmed. Alexander Hamilton warned of millions of Papists storming the colonies, pointing to the Quebec Act as proof that "a superstitious, bigotted Canadian Papist . . . is now esteemed a better subject to our Gracious Sovereign George the Third, than a liberal, enlightened New England Dissenter, though ever so virtuous."[9]

Intimately linked to this conviction that there was an Anglican conspiracy to subvert colonial religion was an equally pervasive belief throughout the colonial world that there was a carefully laid Tory plot afoot to subvert political freedom throughout the empire. The Americans became convinced by the steps the British government took after 1763 that a comprehensive assault "against liberty throughout the English-speaking world" was underway. As Bernard Bailyn writes, it was thought to be "a conspiracy believed to have

[7] Ibid., p. 260.
[8] Miller, *Origins of the American Revolution*, p. 373.
[9] Ibid., p. 374.

been nourished in corruption, and of which, it was felt, oppression in America was only the most immediately visible part . . ."[1]

This view took into consideration the fact that the remarkably open and libertarian English constitution was relatively new, having only been completed in 1688. It was known that many, primarily of the Tory persuasion, still preferred the older, more Royal and less Parliamentary, constitution. These men, it was believed, had launched an organized effort both in Britain and in the colonies to destroy Parliamentary government and restore an unlimited monarchy. Thomas Jefferson and the other colonials who used words like "slavery" and "conspiracy" in their pamphlets were expressing real fears. They came to believe, as Burke did, that the central evil in the system of government as it had developed in mid-eighteenth-century Britain was the system of corruption by which the King bought support. They looked upon the swarming world of royal ministers and hangers-on holding useless offices and sinecures, and drawing unearned pensions, as a new element in the British constitution designed for nothing less than the destruction of liberty. This corruption, furthermore, was to colonial eyes only a part of the sickness that extended itself in profligacy and licentiousness throughout the English population. Burke's attacks on corruption were in "language . . . largely interchangeable with that of innumerable Revolutionary pamphleteers . . ." Furthermore, all manner of specific incidents, such as the prosecution in England of John Wilkes, the political reformer, in the 1760's, gave credence to the Tory plot theory.[2]

Frightened, the American Dissenters began to mobilize for defense. They created an intercolonial network of correspondence committees and organizations that reached across the Atlantic to join forces in common self-defense with organized Dissent in England. Moved by their sense of common danger, they began for the first time to extoll the virtues

[1] Cf. Bernard Bailyn, *Pamphlets of the American Revolution, 1750–1776* (Cambridge, Mass., 1965), Introduction, p. ix. See also Bailyn, *The Ideological Origins of the American Revolution* (Cambridge, Mass., 1967), a larger work.
[2] Ibid., pp. 60–87.

of religious pluralism. Ezra Stiles couched his widely influential plea in 1761 for a Christian Union in these terms, calling for an end to sectarian rivalries and a positive affirmation of pluralism. Such a union, he said, would provide a firm barrier against the encroachments of the Anglicans.

English Dissenters, on their side, considered the American struggle as their own. They gave their American counterparts continuous support and counsel and derived great psychological strength from their membership in a revitalized transatlantic world of Dissent. It has been accurately observed that the American Revolution was a calamity for English Dissent, since it left them alone, thereafter, in an Anglican England.[3]

The issue in Virginia in the years of Jefferson's youth around which all these attitudes gathered was the "Parson's Cause," a controversy in which Virginia experienced its first major conflict with the imperial authorities. Virginians were at best unenthusiastically Anglican.[4] The colony had not been founded as a religious undertaking, but as a business enterprise. New England embodied a religious ideal, but Virginia was created and sustained by the search for wealth. Virginia planters were businessmen, not devout souls. They were primarily concerned, it would seem, that the reverends stay in their place. They were quite in sympathy with the essentially Erastian arrangement whereby the vestry, composed of the local gentry, hired and fired the local priest. In the western regions of Virginia, the predominant influence of Dissent gave support to these attitudes. The Scotch-Irish Presbyterians flourished in the Shenandoah Valley, and the

---

[3] To an extraordinary degree, however, the Dissenting churches and their counterparts in the United States—the Methodists, Quakers, Congregationalists, Unitarians, Presbyterians, and Baptists—kept in being after the Revolution a remarkable Anglo-American community of shared thought, feeling, and action. They visited one another, intermarried, maintained extensive correspondence, founded great circles of transatlantic families, and launched into reform movements in church and secular society together. They constituted, as Frank Thistlethwaite observes, "a genuine Atlantic community." Cf. Thistlethwaite, *America and the Atlantic Community*, pp. 77–8, 87.

[4] H. G. G. Herklots, *The Church of England and the American Episcopal Church, from the First Voyages of Discovery to the First Lambeth Conference* (London, 1966), pp. 35–7.

provincial authorities accorded them complete freedom. The Anglican cause, as they saw it, was not theirs to implement.[5]

By mid-century, in fact, the Virginia legislature (the General Assembly) was passing legislation directly prejudicial to the Church. This inspired militant clerics, led by William and Mary professors who wanted to make the Church as majestic as it was in England, to launch a counteroffensive. They chose the Parson's Cause as the issue upon which to fight.[6]

The controversy arose from a Virginia law that sharply reduced the salary of the Anglican clergy by commuting their statutory tobacco payment to a money salary, computed at a fixed low ratio of twopence for each pound of tobacco. The clerical militants appealed to London, and in 1759 the law was disallowed, to the great anger of the colony, particularly since the circumstances of the disallowance required heavy back payments. A war of pamphleteering blew up, in the course of which the Bishop of London accused the General Assembly of Virginia of treason.

It was in these circumstances that Thomas Jefferson's Anglican tutor, the Rev. James Maury, brought suit for back payment, providing Patrick Henry his opportunity to make his sudden eruption into notoriety. Scotch-Irish and a Dissenter, Henry as attorney for the defense used the case to launch a violent assault on England and the Anglican clergy, giving the western Virginia jury heart to award the luckless clergyman total damages of one penny.[7]

Jefferson's lifelong anticlericalism, and his lengthy struggle to disestablish the Church in Virginia and achieve religious liberty, thus sprang from one of the most fundamental issues of his time. He not only watched these proceedings, he early took sides. The issue of religious liberty had in fact fused with the issue of political liberty. The two were aspects of the same problem. The Church, furthermore, was the physical embodiment of all that England stood for, and to an

[5] Bridenbaugh, *Mitre and Sceptre*, p. 131; Leyburn, *Scotch-Irish*, pp. 208–9.
[6] Brydon, *Virginia's Mother Church*, pp. 295–301.
[7] Ibid., pp. 309–20; Malone, *Jefferson the Virginian*, pp. 43–4, 89–91.

Anglophobe it was doubtless an irresistible object of attack.

Jefferson's anticlericalism was not, however, simply a political stance. It was consistent with his most basic beliefs. Shortly before Jefferson began studying at William and Mary with Dr. Small, Viscount Bolingbroke (Henry St. John), the stormy petrel of British politics, published his Voltairean *Letters on the Study of History* (1752). This book, doubtless recommended by Small, had a profound influence on Jefferson. He copied out long sections from it in his commonplace book, particularly Bolingbroke's attack upon traditional, received, orthodox religion as fundamentally unhistorical.[8] The documentary underpinnings of all religious faiths, Bolingbroke felt, should be subjected to the sternest tests of historical criticism. He explained at length how difficult it is to know definitely the truth or falsity of even the smallest historical "fact," and he held up to scorn the efforts of orthodox Christians to get others to believe in events alleged to have taken place by men who were not there, in documents alleged to be copies of the originals, long since lost. These alleged historical events, Bolingbroke said, were all the proof there was for the revelation being preached with such calm authority.

The whole Christian message, he insisted, should be held up to the test of reason and logic. Did it contain anything contradictory to the natural laws that since Newton and Galileo had become accepted as established truth? If so, then belief must be withheld, for men should accept no allegation if even a single phenomenon knowable to them through their senses "stands in direct opposition to it." Far preferable to Christian superstitions was "natural religion"; that is, a simple faith in God as he reveals himself in nature. The "missionary of natural religion," Bolingbroke observed, was freed of the embarrassments that faced the orthodox, for he could "appeal at all times, and everywhere, to present and immediate evidence, to the testimony of sense and intellect, for the truth of

[8] Cf. Gilbert Chinard, *The Literary Bible of Thomas Jefferson: His Commonplace Book of Philosophers and Poets* (Baltimore and Paris, 1928), pp. 40–71.

those miracles which he brings in proof . . ."⁹

Look to the actual conditions of life, Bolingbroke wrote, for the proof that orthodoxies were parochial and tyrannous. "Who are reputed good Christians," he asked.

> Go to Rome, they are papists. Go to Geneva, they are Calvinists. Go to the north of Germany, they are Lutherans. Come to London, they are none of these. Orthodoxy is a mode. It is one thing at one time and in one place. It is something else at another time, and in another place, or even in the same place: for in this religious country of ours, without seekings [sic] proofs in any other, men have been burned under one reign, for the very same doctrines they were obliged to profess in another. You damn all those who differ from you. We doubt much about your salvation.¹

Religious institutions, then, were like political institutions in that they were made to fit particular times and circumstances. Absolutes were rare indeed. There was doubtless a God, for all the beauties and regularities and laws of nature proclaimed him. There was doubtless a universal religious faith at the heart of every religion, including that of the Jews. But to go beyond "natural religion," Bolingbroke warned, was to insist upon conformity to rituals and dogmas and to deny men the incontestable evidence of their senses and the use of their critical reason.

Moved by these diverse influences, Jefferson became in his early maturity the leading American apostle of anticlericalism, fixing an aggressive secularism in the Democratic mind for a hundred years to come.² Jefferson led the assault on the Church of England in Virginia as soon as the colony declared its independence in 1776. It was a long and difficult experience for him. Late in life he looked back on all the

⁹ Adrienne Koch, *The Philosophy of Thomas Jefferson* (Chicago, 1964), Ch. ii, "Jefferson and Bolingbroke."
¹ Chinard, *Literary Bible*, p. 60.
² Jefferson's anticlericalism was joined by that of Adam Smith as well. In his *The Wealth of Nations*, Smith was critical of orthodox religions and of churches in politics. He classed them with what he deplored above all, "superstition" and "fanaticism."

controversies in which he had figured and said that the religious battles in Virginia were "the severest contests in which I have ever been engaged."[3] Most of the legislators were Anglican—as was Jefferson himself, at least nominally—and there were many who were hostile to the reform. Some of the Dissenters complicated the situation further by asking not for disestablishment but for establishment for all sects, so that tax income would simply be distributed equitably, not terminated. The church-state mentality died a lingering death.

His efforts had therefore to take the form of a gradual campaign in which the whole apparatus of state involvement in religion was progressively dismantled. One of the major steps in this direction was taken by Jefferson as governor of the state during wartime, when he completely ended Anglican control at William and Mary and terminated its use as a divinity school for Anglicans studying for the priesthood. Thereafter the college became, to Anglican distaste, a center of liberal and deistic thought.[4]

After ten years of agitation and piecemeal victories, the battle was finally won, not long after Jefferson had gone to France as American minister. When James Madison wrote him that the Act for Religious Freedom (1786) was finally carried, Jefferson wrote home in jubilation:

> The Virginia act for religious freedom has been received with infinite approbation in Europe and propagated with enthusiasm. I do not mean by the governments, but by the individuals which compose them. It has been translated into French and Italian, has been sent to most of the courts of Europe, and has been the best evidence of the falsehood of those reports which stated us to be in anarchy . . . In fact it is comfortable to see the standard of reason at length erected, after so many ages during which the human mind has been held in vassalage by kings, priests and nobles: and it is honorable for us to have produced the first legislature who had the courage to declare that the reason of man may be trusted with the formation of his own opinions.[5]

[3] Jefferson, *Autobiography*, in Ford, *Works*, I, 62.
[4] Brydon, *Mother Church*, pp. 430–2.
[5] Malone, *Jefferson the Virginian*, p. 279.

At about the same time, he developed his conceptions of religious liberty in his *Notes on the State of Virginia,* which appeared in the 1780's and was widely circulated as a radical document in America and Europe. It was a contemptuous business, he said, to seek to control the thoughts in people's minds. We "are answerable [only to] our God" for our religious opinions. Unless they result in harm to others, religious views should be no concern of governments whatever. It "does me no injury for my neighbor to say there are twenty gods, or no God. It neither picks my pocket nor breaks my leg."

The only safeguards against error, he said, were reason and free inquiry. Coercion simply ensured the vigor and growth of error, for people proudly clung to that which others said they must disavow. "It is error alone which needs the support of government. Truth can stand by itself." Who, indeed, would judge what is right, Jefferson asked, if governments took the power of censorship upon themselves? "Fallible men; men governed by bad passions, by private as well as public reasons." It was, after all, a pitifully shallow view of life to want uniformity of belief. Was not nature infinitely multiform? Did we lop off taller men, and stretch out shorter men, to make them all of a size? Welcome diversity, then. Competition among the sects would be a salutary influence, providing healthy checks upon the pretensions of each, and a wider choice for the faithful.

Above all, meditate upon the results of the age-old efforts that had been made at religious coercion. "Millions of innocent men, women, and children, since the introduction of Christianity, have been burnt, tortured, fined, imprisoned; yet we have not advanced one inch towards uniformity. What has been the effect of coercion? To make one half the world fools, and the other half hypocrites. To support roguery and error all over the earth." No two nations had established the same religion. Truth, claimed so confidently by authority, would seem to be variable, at least insofar as man can understand it.

Fly instead to freedom, Jefferson urged. Pennsylvania and New York had long done so, he pointed out, and they "flourish infinitely." Religion in its various kinds was well supported; peace and order were preserved; good sense was listened to; and there seemed to be no more crime than in Virginia. "They have made the happy discovery, that the way to silence religious disputes, is to take no notice of them. Let us give this experiment fair play, and get rid, while we may, of those tyrannical laws."[6]

There was in all these matters, of course, the sharpest possible contrast between Jefferson and Edmund Burke. The latter had achieved his first literary reputation by a slashing attack on Bolingbroke, Jefferson's inspiration. Critical rationalism was Burke's *bête noire*. No more profound difference may be pointed to between the two men than the determined anticlericalism of the one and the fervent love for the Church of the other. Burke regarded the Church as the divine civilizing agent in history and clung to the idea of a Christian commonwealth formed by the intimate union of church and state; Jefferson detested established churches as corrupt and bigoted conspiracies.

Their differences, however, should be clearly understood. They did not occupy opposite poles. Rather, the contrast between them was typically Anglo-American, not one that might be seen between a continental thinker and an American or an Englishman. They lived within a common culture and operated within its range of possibilities. Jefferson was not an atheist, as he might have been had he been a Frenchman. He was, rather, a deist for a long time, and eventually a Unitarian. He was in fact primarily a moralist, not a rationalist. He was devoted to one of the most prominent British philosophical ideas in the eighteenth century, the belief that God had placed in every man a "moral sense" as real as all the other senses. Each person, so this view ran, was equipped by his moral sense to discern intuitively right from wrong.[7] The common people reacted with the most sureness in these matters, for their moral sense had not been corrupted by the temptations of power.

The moral sense gave men pleasure when they did some-

[6] Jefferson, *Notes on Virginia*, pp. 150–4.
[7] Jefferson, *Notes on Virginia*, p. 90.

thing good for others, thereby making human society possible. It might be developed further by education and experience, thus providing philosophical justification for Jefferson's faith in education as the means by which the masses might grow steadily in their competence and capacity to direct a democratic society. Common men, therefore, were fundamentally trustworthy and genuinely good through the goodness of God.[8]

As he searched for a viable moral system, one that could help to create the good society, Jefferson, the freethinker, found himself growing increasingly devoted to the teachings of Jesus Christ. In this his mentor was Joseph Priestley, the English Dissenter, member of the Lunar Society, and North Countryman who laid the basis for modern chemistry and founded Unitarianism. Jefferson maintained a correspondence with Priestley, read his writings carefully, and proclaimed himself a Unitarian. While he was President, he even went to the extraordinary length of putting together a small volume of Christ's moral teachings, the famous Jefferson "Bible."[9]

Jefferson, in brief, was a religious man, even if his faith was not orthodox. He believed in one God, and in Jesus as a supremely inspired man. He believed that Christ was the greatest of all moral teachers because he was the first to teach that morality did not simply consist of following formal rules. Christ was inspired, Jefferson believed, because he insisted that our moral behavior must spring from a genuinely sincere inward motive and intention, one that flowed from a love of our fellows that extended to all the vast brotherhood of mankind. The classical moralists had written only of individual morality, Jefferson observed, while Christ alone had created for man an encompassing social morality. It was not strange, therefore, that while Jefferson believed that making Jesus into a God was only a cleric's trick to get people into churches, he nevertheless developed a genuine loyalty to

---

[8] Koch, *Philosophy of Thomas Jefferson*, pp. 15–22.
[9] The best edition of this long-unpublished work is O. I. A. Roche, ed., *The Jefferson Bible, with Annotated Commentaries on Religion of Thomas Jefferson* (New York, 1964).

Christ that was in effect a personal religion.[1]

He shared with Adam Smith and David Hume an impatience with those intellectual fundamentalists who believed that all problems could be solved by man's unaided reason; that there were no ultimate mysteries hidden to the human intellect. Jefferson had the characteristically Anglo-American opinion that man's reasoning power is limited to the things of this world.[2] He was quite consistent, therefore, in detesting Plato and the whole cast of mind that dwelt in abstract realms where ultimate truths were believed to lie. Jefferson shared with Burke, in short, a fundamentally antimetaphysical bias. The facts of this world, and not fixed dogmas, were the proper objects of man's attention.

As to our knowledge of the deity, Jefferson felt men could know no more about God than that He exists, and has established an orderly, reasonable universe. His guide in these matters, he said, was Christ himself, who only described God as good and perfect and let the matter remain there. "I am," he said, "therefore of his theology, believing that we have neither words nor ideas adequate to that definition. And if we could all, after this example, leave the subject as indefinable, we should all be of one sect, doers of good, and eschewers of evil." How, then, to know whether or not a religion was a valid one? By its results for man. Utility, he said, was the test of virtue. If a faith, a political institution, or an idea contributed to the happiness of others, then it must be accepted as good and true.[3]

Burke and Jefferson were similar not only in their fundamental religious and philosophical attitudes, but in their shared attitudes toward history. Where the Enlightenment, in its continental expression, is usually regarded as indifferent, indeed hostile, to history, Jefferson—like Burke—looked to the past for instruction. It is true that he made the much-

[1] Koch, *Philosophy of Thomas Jefferson*, pp. 23–9.
[2] This view may be said to have begun with William of Ockham in the fourteenth century, and to have become thereafter the dominant tradition in British and, subsequently, American thought, being expressed in the views of such diverse major figures as John Locke and William James.
[3] Ibid., pp. 38, 40–3.

discussed assertion that the earth belongs to the living, not to the dead—thus helping to set off a famous Edmund Burke–Thomas Paine debate[4]—and his most quoted words on natural rights from the Declaration of Independence have an antihistorical ring to them. But fundamental to the Declaration, as to the *Summary View* that preceded it, was a detailed historical recounting of the way in which the colonies were founded, where they derived their rights—reaching back to the Saxons—and what specific acts had been undertaken by the British that justified American rebellion. As H. Trevor Colbourn has shown, the American rebels were serious students of Whig history, they knew in detail the historical development of English rights, and they appealed constantly to their common heritage with the Whigs.[5] Jefferson was a leading worker in this vineyard. Drawing copiously upon the "True Whig" tradition, he lauded the democratic Saxons, condemned the tyrannical Normans, and sought to prove from history that the ancient liberties the Americans claimed were all rooted in English history.[6]

Indeed, as Merrill Peterson has insightfully remarked, this essentially historical rather than philosophical mode of thought was to be characteristic of the Democratic mind. "The history of the parties," he observes, "was the common American substitute for political theory."[7] Nineteenth-century Democrats insisted on viewing the struggles they faced as if they were re-enactments of the legendary conflicts between Jefferson and Hamilton, and they persistently used the original Jeffersonian images and rhetoric. As well read in Jeffersonian history as Jefferson himself was in Whig history, they doggedly recategorized and selected from their experiences so that the same dogmas could be applied.

This had important results. For the American Democrats, the historical mode of thought led to an increasing obsolescence of vision and program, for they adhered to the

[4] Adrienne Koch, *Jefferson and Madison: The Great Collaboration* (New York, 1953), pp. 62–96.
[5] Colbourn, *Lamp of Experience, passim.*
[6] See ibid., Ch. viii, "Thomas Jefferson and the Rights of Expatriated Men," pp. 158–84.
[7] Peterson, *Jefferson Image*, p. 73.

Jeffersonian agenda. The Democrats appealed to history not in order to move forward, but to keep what had been: the idealized golden age of the Old Republic, the Jeffersonian nation of honest and simple democracy. The events to which they looked back were not, as in Britain, disposed in time down through the centuries. They were instead concentrated in the dramatic and to them awesome years in which the nation was formed. In the hands of the British Liberals, however, the argument from history, linked to the argument from circumstances, was a force for innovation, because it could present desired reforms as simply new chapters in a long and beneficent evolutionary process.

The preceding discussion has been intended to demonstrate that for all the apparent ways in which Burke and Jefferson contrasted, they shared certain fundamental assumptions, certain basic ways of looking at the world, that reveal their common membership in a distinctive Anglo-American culture. They were not so unlike one another as it at first appears.

There is no question, however, that there was a hotter dimension in Jefferson's thought than there was in Burke's. Burke was passionate, but he spoke largely in generalized terms of oppression and exploitation. Jefferson was pungently specific. He described the enemy for his political posterity in language of biting clarity. Perhaps this was because he was concerned with domestic as well as with foreign affairs, while Burke was primarily involved with external matters: America, Ireland, and India. Whatever the reasons, Jefferson's nature, for all his geniality and compassion, contained an unforgiving side. He was capable of hatred. He nourished his prejudice against Englishmen, he detested Tories, he was obsessed with what were in his eyes the evil designs of the Federalists—the party of Alexander Hamilton—and he developed a sweeping theory of conspiratorial forces at work to destroy the new nation.

Jefferson believed, in short, that there are among us, always and everywhere, dishonest men who seek constantly to subvert the proper social order and exploit their fellow men. It was in this fundamental view of society that Jefferson gave to his posterity what has been called his ideology of conflict, his belief that there is an inherent struggle going on constantly in society between the masses and those who would exploit them.[8] After religious freedom had been established in Virginia, and the independence of the nation assured, this aspect of Jefferson's world view grew dominant in his work and writings. All governments, he said in the *Notes on Virginia* (1785), are misshapen by human weakness. They all contain some germ of corruption from which cunning men will profit. For this reason he severely criticized the great powers lodged in the General Assembly of Virginia as certain to corrupt its members, and called for a separation of powers.[9] In the early 1790's, he served as Secretary of State in the new federal government of the United States and soon found himself involved in his legendary political struggle with Alexander Hamilton. After these controversies had been underway for some time, he wrote to an old friend:

I do not believe with the Rochefoucaulds and Montaignes, that fourteen out of fifteen men are rogues . . . [but] I have always found that rogues would be uppermost, and I do not know that the proportion is too strong for the higher orders, and for those who, rising above the swinish multitude, always contrive to nestle themselves into the places of power and profit. These rogues set out with stealing the people's good opinion, and then steal from them the right of withdrawing it, by contriving laws and associations against the power of the people themselves.[1]

He believed political divisions were rooted in the very nature of man. Tories, he said, were a coalition of the rich and corrupt with the weak and nerveless, both of whom de-

[8] Peterson, *Jefferson Image*, p. 74.
[9] *Notes on Virginia*, pp. 113–20, 142.
[1] To Mann Page, August 30, 1795, in Koch, *Philosophy of Thomas Jefferson*, p. 119.

lighted in a strong government that could be accessible to the greedy and protective to the timid. Whigs, on the other hand, were in his view composed of those men who were healthy, firm, virtuous, confident in their physical and moral resources, "willing to part with only so much power as is necessary for their good government; and, therefore, to retain the rest in the hands of the many . . ." By 1793, his attacks upon those seeking special economic privileges from the government made him so politically resonant a figure that he told President Washington that the aristocrats, the merchants connected with England, and the men wealthy on paper fortunes—in brief, the greedy and the corrupt—were combined in their hatred of him.[2]

In Jefferson's eyes, the evil spirit behind all the machinations underway to corrupt the new nation was Alexander Hamilton. He became Jefferson's grand obsession. For that matter, Hamilton induced an extraordinary fascination apparently in all Democrats whose memories reached back into this era. There was no more devoted Jeffersonian in the nineteenth century than Martin Van Buren, for example, but it is curiously not Jefferson but the giant figure of Hamilton, the fallen angel, who dominates the scene in Van Buren's autobiography. Hamilton was so brilliant, so personally charming, yet so utterly evil—to Jeffersonian eyes—that Van Buren's fascinated gaze could hardly move away from him.[3] In Jefferson's *Autobiography*, likewise, and in *The Anas*—both of which were virtually memorized by devoted Democrats— the figure of Hamilton is constantly in view, a threatening, devious, and implacably malign figure whose aim was fatally to disfigure the brave American experiment in simple and democratic republican government.

It was true that Hamilton did seek to fashion the nation after the contemporary British model. As the first Secretary of the Treasury, he seems to have thought of himself as filling the same role played by the British Prime Minister, who is

[2] Jefferson, *The Anas*, in Ford, *Works*, I, 311.
[3] Martin Van Buren, "The Autobiography of Martin Van Buren," John C. Fitzpatrick, ed., *Annual Report of the American Historical Association for the Year 1918*, II; and *Inquiry into the Origin and Course of Political Parties in the United States* (New York, 1867).

technically First Lord of the Treasury. In a series of bold and successful strokes, he imparted remarkable vigor to the new government, building into it in significant measure the basic institutional structure that characterized the existing British system. He believed firmly in aristocratic rule, but his efforts at establishing this kind of system were inevitably doomed, given the nature of the country.

He was much more successful, however, in building an essentially British economic system in the United States. Its basic feature was a belief that there should be an intimate partnership between the government and the business community. Far from acting on a sense of distrust of businessmen, or from a belief that its task was to guard the community at large from the excesses of selfishness and profit-making, the government, Hamilton clearly believed, should look upon men of property as benefactors, as inherently superior men suited by their talents and large views to advise the government and to direct the economy in conjunction with those who directed the political institutions of the nation. The government's interest should be in national power; the distribution of wealth should be left to the great men of business. The goal should be, therefore, a mercantilist state on the current British model—the model deplored by Adam Smith—in which the government provided such aids as businessmen said they needed in order to build a strong and self-sufficient economy.

Hamilton created, therefore—in a struggle with the Jeffersonians—a federally chartered Bank of the United States, modeled on the Bank of England. It would receive the government's revenues, regulate the currency issued by private banks, and serve as a great pool of capital to be invested in selected industries under the direction of the nation's leading financiers. He also secured the assumption by the new federal government of the moribund state debts and the debts of the Confederacy. By these two devices he sought at a stroke to restore the credit of the new nation, attach firmly to the federal government the loyalties and the interests of the financiers, and deflect the flow of investment capital from commerce and land to industry. Warning the nation of the mercantilist policies of other powers, and urging Americans themselves to build a powerful mercantilist state in self-protection, he urged in his *Report on Manufactures* (1791)—as it turned out, vainly—that tariffs be erected to protect infant industries and that bounties and other devices be provided to stimulate their appearance.[4]

By this time, the brilliant young Secretary of the Treasury had become the darling of the age, and especially of the Federalists. The nation was booming upward out of the depression in which it had wallowed during the short and unhappy years of the Confederation, and it seemed that Hamilton was responsible.

> With the establishment of the Bank of the United States, Hamilton reached the pinnacle of his influence and—such as it was—his popularity. He had carried everything before him . . . and the businessmen of the country hailed him as their benefactor. In Boston, among the "better sort," those who could claim an acquaintance with Colonel Hamilton were besieged with questions concerning this remarkable young man; and his portrait, painted by John Trumbull for the citizens of New York, was hung in the City Hall. All the wise, the rich and good delighted to do him homage . . .
>
> Elsewhere, and particularly in Virginia, Hamilton had succeeded in arraying against himself a roster of enemies of which, said Gouverneur Morris, any self-respecting Federalist ought to be proud. For sheer unpopularity, no other member of the administration could compete with the Secretary of the Treasury: his political theories, his financial policies and his objectives all made him anathema to those who did not share his vision of the American future. "Seldom," said John Marshall, "has any minister excited in a higher or more extensive degree than Colonel Hamilton, the opposite passions of love and hate" . . .[5]

The leader of his enemies soon became Thomas Jefferson, who spoke for the instinctive American distrust of any-

[4] John C. Miller, *The Federalist Era, 1789–1801* (New York, 1960), pp. 55–69.
[5] John C. Miller, *Alexander Hamilton and the Growth of the New Nation* (New York, 1964), pp. 278–80.

thing British. He spoke too for everything in agrarian America that distrusted financiers, city merchants, and sweeping visions of commercial empire directed from Philadelphia and New York. All of Hamilton's schemes, Jefferson said, were aimed at puzzling the people with intricate arrangements, while at the same time linking the sordid interests in the country to the government and corrupting those who sat in Congress. Hamilton's funding of the national and state debts, Jefferson said, had accomplished nothing more than to set off a scramble for plunder by those who were given inside knowledge. There had been a raid on the public treasury that only enriched the unscrupulous at the cost of the poor. He accused Hamilton of being a monarchist at heart who believed with British Tories that the government must use corruption as its lubricant. Hamilton's real object was the destruction of the republican system of government, and its replacement with a grand monarchy on the British Tory model. As he wrote in later life, Hamilton

> was indeed a singular character. Of acute understanding, disinterested, honest, and honorable in all private transactions, amiable in society, and duly valuing virtue in private life, yet so bewitched and perverted by the British example, as to be under thro' [sic] conviction that corruption was essential to the government of a nation.[6]

Hamilton's schemes held an even greater danger for the nation, Jefferson believed. They would not only corrupt the government, they would corrupt the whole American people by drawing them off into speculative and destructive pursuits. Hamilton's paper-money schemes, Jefferson warned Washington in 1791, stimulated people into frenzies of risky profiteering and distracted them from their true pursuits of honest commerce and farming. They "occupy themselves and their capitals in a species of gambling, destructive of morality, and which had introduced it's poison into the government itself."[7] In the difficult times of 1798, Jefferson and President

[6] Jefferson, *The Anas,* in Ford, *Works,* I, 171–80.
[7] Ibid., p. 196.

Adams condemned the banks, agreeing that the depression from which the nation was suffering arose chiefly from "the floods of bank paper now afloat."[8] The center of it all, Jefferson and his followers were convinced, lay in Hamilton's Bank of the United States, which to them was the radiating focus of his web of "speculating and monarchical influence."[9]

Hamilton's *Report on Manufactures* aroused Jefferson's determined resistance. It was unconstitutional, he insisted, for Congress to enact tariffs and other mercantilist devices, even under the general welfare clause of the Constitution. A firm believer in the doctrines of Adam Smith—he wrote his son-in-law in 1790 that Smith was the best authority on political economy—he insisted that the new nation should "throw open the doors of commerce, and . . . knock off all its shackles, giving perfect freedom to all persons for the vent of whatever they may chose [sic] to bring into our ports, and asking the same in theirs."[1]

Jefferson believed that the true pursuit of the nation lay in agriculture, as much for its moral as for its economic results. "Those who labor in the earth," he wrote, "are the chosen people of God, if ever He had a chosen people, whose breasts He had made His peculiar deposit for substantial and genuine virtue." Before the exigencies of his presidency forced him to recognize that industry might be valuable to the nation, he was fond of saying that America's workshops should remain in Europe. The principal result of industry, he said—speaking out of his distaste for what he saw in England—was to create cities crowded with ignorant mobs.[2] He opposed any program that would make America an urban, industrial, and bank-dominated nation. This distaste lay behind the pained words he wrote to Du Pont de Nemours soon after he began his presidency in 1801:

> When this government was first established, it was possible to have kept it going on true principles, but the contracted,

8 Ibid., p. 341.
9 Miller, *Alexander Hamilton*, p. 328.
1 Schachner, *Jefferson*, I, 391; Jefferson, *The Anas*, in Ford, *Works*, I, 197; Koch, *Philosophy of Thomas Jefferson*, pp. 170–85; Jefferson, *Notes on Virginia*, pp. 164–5.
2 Jefferson, *Notes on Virginia*, pp. 157–8.

English, half-lettered ideas of Hamilton destroyed that hope in the bud. We can pay off his debts in 15 years: but we can never get rid of his financial system. It mortifies me to be strengthening principles which I deem radically vicious, but his vice is entailed on us by the first error. In other parts of our government I hope we shall be able by degrees to introduce sound principles and make them habitual. What is practicable must often control what is pure theory.[3]

He opposed Alexander Hamilton not only because he detested the thought of an industrial society, and the opportunities for corruption and aristocratic rule that a government-business partnership would create, but because he had a different vision of the actual structure of the nation. He opposed anything that would give greater power to the federal government, for he was firmly devoted to localism.

This attitude was doubtless in part emotional in origin, for Jefferson loved his native countryside. Hamilton was a rootless man. Born in the West Indies, he left them early for the greater stage of the North American colonies, and attached his loyalties to the nation as a whole. Jefferson, in one sense, never left home. His feeling for his beloved Virginia seemed to be part of his very being. He always spoke of Virginia as "my country." It was his fervent wish to retire to Monticello and enjoy its bucolic pleasures. The better part of his lifetime was spent in deep involvements in the life of Virginia, rearranging its government, its religious system, its educational arrangements, even, in a certain sense, its technology and agriculture.

Jefferson was thus closer to the inner heart of American life than Hamilton. It was to be a long time indeed before Americans in general lost a sense of primary affiliation to their states. Hamilton spoke from New York City, with its dreams of a great national economy for which it would be both entrepôt and financier. The men he led thought in national terms. Jefferson and his political tradition spoke instead for those whose horizons were still essentially local, whose

[3] Quoted in Richard Hofstadter, *The American Political Tradition and the Men Who Made It* (New York, 1949), p. 34.

affections were yet in many ways—like those of most Europeans—firmly rooted in village, hillside, and surrounding country. Even in post-Gold Rush California, the classic example of rootlessness, it was common for newspapers to be primarily concerned with Californian, rather than with national, affairs.

In this sense, "states' rights" as a constitutional doctrine arose not simply from the Southern concern for slavery, but from the social psychology of Americans everywhere. Distrust of Washington came naturally to a people who had long been trained in distrusting London. Pride in one's state, indeed a sense of primary identification with one's locale, was a rooted characteristic. It was no accident that most army units in the Civil War fought under the names of their states, as the countless monuments at Gettysburg eloquently testify.

Jefferson's localism was also a product of his distrust of government *per se*. In his view the people stand always in danger of their governors. It was therefore essential that they have the government as close to them as possible so that they might the more easily watch over it. Very small societies, he wrote, were the most moral ones, as the small communities of the Indians he had observed in Virginia demonstrated.[4] He wanted to divide every county into hundreds—taking this term from his admired early Saxons in England—in which most of the functions of government would take place. Later calling these units "wards," he explained the principle as "dividing and subdividing these republics from the great National one down thro' all its subordinations, until it ends in the administration of every man's farm and affairs by himself; by placing under every one what his own eye may superintend, that all will be done for the best."[5]

The issue of localism versus centralism, which has traditionally been regarded as solely an American problem, has in fact been found to have much concerned nineteenth-century Britons as well. W. L. Burn, who has done much to end the myth that the great controversy in Victorian Britain was be-

[4] Jefferson, *Notes on Virginia*, p. 90.
[5] Jefferson to Joseph Cabell, Feb. 2, 1816, quoted in Koch, *Philosophy of Thomas Jefferson*, p. 163.

tween individualism and collectivism, writes that contemporaries "were perhaps more concerned with the struggle between localism and centralization." Localism meant more than simply a love for geographical locale. It meant also a reliance upon

> local authorities, from vestries upwards . . . [and] included a wide range of bodies, whether incorporated or not, from the Oxford and Cambridge colleges and the chapters of Cathedrals down to the trustees of the most obscure and poverty-stricken of endowed schools.[6]

The Victorian was generally suspicious of the state and of centralization. He clung to the belief that "individual energy, initiative and philanthropy would . . . given time, accomplish all that had to be accomplished."[7] Jefferson spoke out of the same attitudes in his First Inaugural Address (1801) when he called for

> a wise and frugal government, which shall restrain men from injuring one another, which shall leave them otherwise free to regulate their own pursuits of industry and improvement, and shall not take from the mouth of labor the bread it has earned. This is the sum of good government, and this is necessary to close the circle of our felicities.

When Jefferson visualized the political structure of the United States, therefore, it is clear that he saw something like the British Empire before 1763. In this arrangement, the central government would be limited almost solely to foreign affairs, leaving practically everything else to largely self-governing states and local agencies. The sum of Jefferson's desire, in effect, was simply to transfer London to Washington, and to let it go at that. It was not his hope to see created in America some strong unitary system where a vigorous federal government would set about busying itself with all manner of things, hammering and pummeling scattered communities into a unified collectivity.

[6] Burn, *Equipoise*, pp. 167, 222.
[7] Ibid., p. 226.

The key question in his mind, therefore, was whether the new central government would be largely limited to the conduct of foreign affairs, or whether a central and single government over all would emerge.[8] What was later to be called "states' rights" was therefore only another version of the "home rule" empire that Burke and Jefferson had both called for in the eighteenth-century Irish and American troubles. This concern motivated Jefferson's authorship of the Kentucky Resolutions in 1798, in which he took the view that the Constitution was merely a compact between the sovereign states. The latter were to be, in some ultimate sense, the judges of whether or not a federal law was valid and need be obeyed.[9]

Behind all of this lay Jefferson's generous faith in the majority of the people. As Richard Hofstadter succinctly stated the issue, the Federalists "feared, above all, power lodged in the majority. Jefferson feared power lodged anywhere else."[1] This was what led him to scoff at the wild fears set off by Shay's Rebellion in Massachusetts in 1786–7. A little rebelliousness, he observed, is a good thing. The people must not be held down. Their errors are not so bad as the errors of those in power. When the people become inattentive to government, then "you and I," he wrote to Edward Carrington, "and Congress and Assemblies, judges and governors shall all become wolves."[2] As he said in another famous utterance, "The tree of liberty must be refreshed from time to time with the blood of patriots and tyrants. It is its natural manure."[3]

These were the statements, and others like them, that permanently enshrined Thomas Jefferson as the prophet of radical democracy—and set him off so sharply and distinctly in historical memory from Edmund Burke. To the British mind, Burke provided in his *Reflections on the Revolution in France* a justification for a traditional, aristocratic society. But to the Americans, who needed a champion for the idea that ordinary people did not need a titled aristocracy and an established monarchy to govern them, Jefferson's voice was

[8] Jefferson, *The Anas*, in Ford, *Works*, I, 167–8.
[9] Miller, *Federalist Era*, pp. 239–41.
[1] Hofstadter, *American Political Tradition*, p. 26.
[2] Letter, Jan. 16, 1787, quoted in Schachner, *Jefferson*, I, 343.
[3] Jefferson to Wm. S. Smith, Nov. 13, 1787, ibid., I, 343.

endlessly appealing. It has often been observed, of course, that he was no populist democrat totally devoted to equalitarianism. There are many remarks in his writings which show his disdain for the crude masses, for the "rubbish." But this disdain was primarily for the unlearned and the incompetent. He was firmly convinced of the need for an aristocracy to rule the country, but like Adam Smith he believed that it should consist of men risen from the common people, aided only by the benefits of public education.

Jefferson was the original prophet of the American faith in popular education. Education would not only ensure the success of a democratic government, it would equip men to utilize their talents and open the way for the rise of what in another connection he called "an aristocracy of virtue and talent, which nature has wisely provided."[4]

Jefferson spent his presidency trying vainly to disassemble Hamilton's system, primarily by practicing rigorous austerity and economy. He could do little about the Bank of the United States, though in 1811, two years after he left the presidency, his followers let the Bank's charter lapse at the end of its twenty-year term. But the facts of life refused to fit very comfortably into his expectations. He followed, accordingly, a pragmatic course. What was "practicable must often control what is pure theory." The great achievement of his presidency, the Louisiana Purchase, had to be undertaken with eyes averted from his favorite theories about strict interpretation of the Constitution. His various measures to deal with the dangers posed by the Napoleonic Wars led to the founding of the American industrial system, since his embargoes diverted capital from commerce to factories. In time, he was moved to express himself in terms that were no longer hostile to workshops and towns.

But his distaste for a strong central government and his distrust of the moneyed who seek special privileges remained with him to the end. In the last years of his life he watched in growing anger as what he saw as a rebirth of Hamiltonian Federalist doctrines took place among the younger politicians

[4] Jefferson, *Autobiography*, in Ford, *Works*, I, 58; Jefferson, *Notes on Virginia*, pp. 139–43.

who moved into positions of leadership as the old Jeffersonians died away. The changing of the guard took place in
1825, when John Quincy Adams assumed the presidency at
the end of the twenty-four years in which Jefferson and his
direct political legatees, James Madison and James Monroe,
occupied the White House. Adams called for a wide variety
of federal programs to stimulate the economy and the cultural life of the nation, including a university and scientific
surveys.

Jefferson's reaction was in the form of a dramatic public
statement in 1826 that the Adams men were Federalists in
new dress, though they claimed Jeffersonian inheritance.
They had defected from the true democratic faith, looking
back "to a single and splendid government of an aristocracy,
founded on banking institutions, moneyed incorporations
under the guise and cloak of their favored branches of manufacture, commerce and navigation, riding and ruling over the
plundered plowman and beggared yeomanry."[5] The "mass of
mankind," he wrote in a public letter a few days before his
death in 1826, were not predestined to permanent subserviency, as many seemed to believe. Paraphrasing an early
English Whig, he insisted that the common people had "not
been born with saddles on their backs, nor a favored few
booted and spurred ready to ride them legitimately by the
grace of God."[6]

Jefferson had brought to life once more the old controversies, warning the nation that the conspiracies of the rich
still flourished. In a real sense, the beginning of the age of
Jacksonian controversy may be dated to Jefferson's outbursts
in 1826. He then bequeathed in his *Memoirs*—which appeared posthumously in 1829—an explosive diatribe against
all his old enemies. Containing his *Autobiography, The Anas,*
and a rich store of letters, the *Memoirs* caused a national
sensation. They revived all the old party feelings that had
grown quiescent during the long reign of the Jeffersonians
and the so-called Era of Good Feelings.

[5] Peterson, *Jefferson Image*, pp. 18–20.
[6] Colbourn, *Lamp of Experience*, pp. 182–3.

The publication of the *Memoirs* . . . opened to public view for the first time not only the history of Jefferson's character and opinions but also a revelation of the momentous era in which he was a principal actor. Whether regarded from a historical or a political standpoint, it was, as reviewers on both sides of the Atlantic attested, "one of the most important publications ever presented to the world" . . . No sooner had it appeared than the leading Jackson organ in the West declared that the *Memoirs* "must emphatically become the text-book . . . [of the Jacksonians]." But the Library Company of Philadelphia refused to place the volumes on its shelves; and a New York editor found their impiety and radicalism so shocking that he warned his readers away from them. Few, if any, publications of the period had a greater impact or importance than Jefferson's *Memoirs*. Men of letters tasted it, politicians swallowed it, historians digested it—or tried to.[7]

He ended, therefore, as he began, bitterly attacking the social enemy. But he left behind a contradictory and fundamentally ambivalent legacy.

He authored the nation's birthright, but he also wrote the Kentucky Resolutions of "nullification." He was the friend of Washington, but the enemy of his administration. Americans remembered his Presidency for the achievement of the Louisiana Purchase and the disaster of the Embargo. None of the ordinary categories of the hero—lawgiver, chieftain, prophet—sufficed for Jefferson. As his character was somewhat labyrinthian, so his mind was bewildering in its range and complexity. Later generations comprehended his thought only in fragments, crossing and colliding with each other, until it seemed that the protean figure, if ever he had genuine historical existence, must never be rediscovered.[8]

Which Jefferson did his successors see? Was it the passionate democrat who called for the rule of the majority, demanded that the people's will be sovereign in all matters, and that frequent revolutions be allowed to clear the air and

[7] Peterson, *Jefferson Image*, p. 29.
[8] Ibid., p. 9.

sweep out the rubbish of the cautious past? Or was it the Jefferson who distrusted centralized power, preached states' rights, and advocated strict adherence to Constitutional limitations on the federal government—presumably the instrument of the people's will? Was it the Jefferson who venerated law in an almost Burkeian way, or was it the Jefferson who prefaced the Declaration of Independence with assertions of overriding natural rights in the French manner? Was he the secularist who scorned the churches and clerics, or the moral and kindly man who looked for an encompassing social ethic in the words of Jesus Christ, and spent quiet evenings in the White House carefully putting together the Jefferson Bible? The key, of course, was liberty, but liberty in what sense?

> One derived from the English legal heritage: the Whiggish liberty of individual rights. The other partook strongly of American and French revolutionary ideology; the democratic liberty of popular rule. Was Jefferson the conservative guardian of the law or the flaming prophet of democracy?[9]

One liberty entailed a careful, cautious legalism that scrupulously guarded individual rights as vested in law and restricted governments to measured steps within constitutional limitations. The other liberty meant impatience with restrictions and emphasis on the will of the people having its way, by whatever means could be found.

Jefferson embodies the essential ambivalence, the "irresoluble ambiguity," built into the American system. He could quite properly be visualized in both dimensions, for he said and did contradictory things. "Repeatedly in his posthumous history he was to be caught up in the dilemma of a nation committed both to a system of constituted rights and to the sovereignty of the people."[1]

But in his social, as apart from his constitutional, message, Jefferson was powerfully and pungently unequivocal. He gave to his inheritors a clear picture of the chief danger to

[9] Ibid., p. 10.
[1] Ibid.

the Republic: it lay in a corrupt alliance between business
and government. The image he gave the Democrats of the
fundamental American problem was that of "the mass of toiling producers battling their exploiters in commerce, finance,
and other speculative enterprises dependent upon the resources and favors of government."[2] The wealthy and the
arrogant will always be struggling to use their sovereign
weapon, political corruption, to twist the government to their
desires and to gain special privileges that will let them fatten
from the toil of everyone else. It was this danger that made
the idea of strong government anathema to Jeffersonians, for
strong governments always and everywhere had apparently
existed only for the purpose of exploiting the poor and en-
riching the already wealthy. The wealthy and arrogant will
also corrupt the body of the people by launching speculative
frenzies, based on central banking institutions, in which the
clever ones on the inside can profit in both boom and bust.
Meanwhile, the common people lose their moral purity, forsake the pursuits of simple toil for dreams of wealth, and
then suffer in the inevitable collapse. Speculation, corruption,
strong governments, and mass degradation, to Jeffersonians,
were the four evils that inevitably went together to destroy the
tranquillity that had been bequeathed to Americans in their
new land.

———

Liberal-Democracy received from Adam Smith, Edmund
Burke, and Thomas Jefferson a coherent political and economic world view. All of these men pointed to arrogance, to
the English love of authority, to the pride that makes men pre-
tentious and prejudiced. Freedom, Burke said, was the cure of
anarchy, not coercion, and this was certainly the Jeffersonian
spirit as well. People must be allowed to govern themselves,
and those in power must make public action responsive to
public opinion. Promulgating laws was not enough to make

[2] Ibid., p. 84.

them valid. When public resistance to a law or a system became serious, the proper answer was not righteous anger and condign punishment, but a simple recognition of the facts and appropriate changes in public policy.

As these men saw the matter, the great danger for the public lay in the fact that aristocracies had more subtle weapons than their opponents. With their wealth they could buy off the opposition, could indeed recruit them. This was what made "corruption" perhaps the most resonant of all issues, an obsession for Democrats and Liberals alike. The business community, too, with its inveterate efforts to gain monopoly, was a principal enemy to social health. Business acquisitiveness would lead to efforts to influence those who governed—who, in turn, would listen complacently to the businessman because they enjoyed having the power and the profit that strong government placed in the hands of the governors. Strong governments and exploitive economies went inevitably together; destroying the one meant eliminating the other.

In the background, wherever there was corruption and misrule, Smith and Jefferson felt there was always a self-seeking clerical influence that led the masses into superstition and hysteria by feeding them myths and panics. Established churches constantly conspired with autocrats, with the arrogant wealthy who were their natural allies, to prevent freedom of thought and to extort land, income, and special privilege. Therefore, Smith and Jefferson both believed, public affairs should be completely secularized.

From Jefferson and Burke alike came a cautious and conservative emphasis on the restrictions of established law and vested rights. Just as Jefferson condemned the large new programs of Alexander Hamilton, so Burke protested against the innovations of the French Revolution. Too much, in fact, has been made of the differences between Jefferson and Burke with regard to the French Revolution, the former being depicted as urging it on from his official residence as the American minister in Paris, and the latter uttering his dark prophecies in Britain. Jefferson was indeed favorable to the early stages of the Revolution, but he was soon shocked at its excesses, and felt that it went much too far. He always believed that the French should have done no more than to establish a constitutional monarchy, with guarantees of civil rights and a representative legislature. "They thought otherwise, however," he later observed in his *Autobiography*, "and events have proved their lamentable error."[3] In a real sense, Jefferson was just as historically conscious as Burke, just as distrustful of unusual schemes—and just as worried about what was being done to the common people under the weight of autocratic and callous aristocratic governments. Both, in short, were working within a common Anglo-American culture, and they shared the fundamental assumptions provided by that *weltanschauung* for those who thought of themselves as political reformers.

But they lived and worked in the two poles of the Anglo-American world, and this affected their political performance and their political styles in important ways. Jefferson spoke out of a situation in which Dissent was victorious; it had secured the religiously impartial state that it wanted. In the course of this argument, strong philosophical positions were taken. What came down to Jefferson's posterity was not so much a positive feeling about having many kinds of churches, but a philosophically rooted anticlericalism that exalted secularism and was implacably hostile to religious influences. Democrats inherited a distrust of the Christian-in-politics from Jefferson. Freethinkers, agnostics, and the religiously indifferent found their home in the Democratic Party not simply in the nineteenth century, but it would appear, in the twentieth as well. Jefferson's freethinking, radical even in the twentieth century, has given the Democrats a distinctive coloration never lost. The strongly Christian reformer, therefore, tended to find his political base of operations among the Republicans—as in the case of abolitionism—or nowhere at all. Not until the advent of William Jennings Bryan in the 1890's did the American Democrats acquire leadership that was unashamedly Christian, calling upon religious symbols and values for political inspiration.

Burke's influence, however, helped to create in Britain a

[3] Ford, *Works*, I, 139.

climate in which the Liberal party could attract and hold the devout, like William Gladstone and many others. One possible effect was to place the Liberals in contact with influences that worked against the more callous aspects of *laissez faire* long before the American Democrats began seriously to consider them—though this is a problematical suggestion.

More important, however, was the fact that Burke's placement in a predominantly aristocratic society, whose values in good part he shared, muted the style in which he could express his reformist ideas. Unlike Jefferson, he was either unable or unwilling to point directly at social enemies. He deplored autocratic habits of mind, not specific institutional arrangements. He was faced, for that matter, by a severe tactical problem. Whatever he secured would have to be won from the aristocrats themselves, for they possessed practically all power. He was therefore forced to develop an oratorical style that justified piecemeal reform to an entrenched aristocracy without offending it, a posture that imposes certain limitations. Pragmatic, nonideological, fact-oriented, concentrating upon small steps forward, appealing all the while to the idea that evolutionary change was simply inevitable, his style of reform oratory and appeal was perhaps the only variety that could have had any success at all in a social environment as resistant to change as that which existed in eighteenth- and nineteenth-century Britain.

Jefferson, after all, did little more—on the national scene —than talk, or rather write. The Federalist Fisher Ames might complain that he would soon smell "the loathsome steam of human victims offered in sacrifice" when the reputedly radical Jefferson was elected president in 1800, but the aftermath hardly fulfilled the prophecy.[4] The Jefferson presidency was conciliatory and moderate, confining itself to modest steps at paring down the Hamiltonian system. The Jeffersonians, it has been observed, were excellent critics, but they had little to offer in the way of program.[5] Like Burke, Jefferson believed in pragmatism and a close attention to

[4] Ames quotation drawn from Hofstadter, *American Political Tradition*, p. 32.
[5] Ibid., p. 36.

circumstances. It would have been disruptive to apply his ideas to the letter, and he therefore compromised. And why not? With Burke, he believed that change was the ceaseless habit of nature; that in time, given proper directions, the good society would appear.[6] Both were evolutionists content to give utterance to the values that would shape the future, and to help nature when circumstances allowed.

But the fact remains that Burke left the Liberals—to the extent that they were Burkeian—without an essential core of social radicalism. As a party, of course, they were not limited to Edmund Burke for their inspiration. Radicalism was abundantly available to them in nineteenth-century Britain, and many Liberals, John Bright most notably, made use of it. It is significant, however, that Edmund Burke, the man most admired by the leading Liberals—the William Gladstones, the John Morleys—gave them not ideology but pragmatism. They were passionate about the things he was passionate about—corruption, Ireland, and tyranny in foreign policy— and they found in his numerous concerns much food for a concerned and dedicated reformism. But they did not find a caustic social analysis there, as the Democrats did in Jefferson's thought. Reading Jefferson is reading an angry man who makes harsh charges; reading Burke is reading a passionate man aroused by injustice who makes reasonable proposals. This may, for that matter, have had some bearing on the eventual displacement of the Liberals by Labour. Gladstone became a vigorously Jeffersonian figure in his attacks upon the aristocracy in the latter stages of his career, but after the establishment of free trade he paid the businessman little heed. When the kind of Jeffersonianism developed in the new democracy of late Victorian Britain that saw the business community as the principal enemy, it had to find its outlet in a new political party.

[6] Ibid., p. 42.

PART II

PART II

Chapter 5

WILLIAM GLADSTONE:
BACKGROUND TO LIBERALISM

Of all the great Victorian careers, William Gladstone's was the most remarkable. Born in 1809, he was in Parliament by 1833 and remained a member of that body for sixty-two years. In that long span of time, during which several political generations matured in power and fell away, he was four times Prime Minister of the United Kingdom. As Premier and as Chancellor of the Exchequer, he lived twenty-four years of his life on Downing Street.

He dominated Liberal politics for so long that by "the end of his long life he had almost made [the Liberal Party] in his own image."[1] A charismatic political figure, he was hated and loved with equal fervor. J. D. Coleridge called him "the greatest, noblest, purest and sincerest public man" of the century.[2] A Tory, however, could seriously report that he had listened to "thieves, pickpockets, dynamiters and Socialists talking [in Trafalgar Square] and praising Mr. Gladstone, who relied upon their support and because he relied upon them he was afraid to condemn their evil work."[3]

Gladstone was more than just a British politician. He became the first Anglo-American political leader, in the sense that his example inspired politicians in all three countries to

[1] McCallum, "Liberal Outlook," p. 65.
[2] Quoted in Southgate, *Passing of the Whigs*, p. 355.
[3] Ausubel, *In Hard Times*, p. 166.

the point of discipleship. The three men who were leading the Liberals and the Democrats in Britain, Canada, and the United States when the First World War broke out—H. H. Asquith, Sir Wilfrid Laurier, and Woodrow Wilson—were all devoted Gladstonians.

In appearance he was a slim, upright figure of medium height, attractive in youth as a black-haired and intense man with snapping eyes, and in age as a stern-faced, eternally active patriarch. Shifting constantly about in his place as he listened to Commons debates, turning this way and that to fix his eye first upon this speaker and then upon that, rising swiftly to his feet to make an interjection or an astonishingly complex and overpowering oration, Gladstone simply dominated the House of Commons. The mobile countenance, the nervous pacing, the pointing finger, above all the rich and penetrating voice, a "remarkable organ"—these combined to strike his hearers with extraordinary force. From his first speech in the Oxford Union as a young man to his famous Midlothian orations at the age of seventy and beyond, Gladstone transfixed his audiences. In a political system peculiarly built on the spoken word, he was the archetypical orator. In a democratic society just being born, he was the first voice of the newly awakened masses.

Gladstone's character was complex. He had incredible stores of energy and through self-discipline he could keep them focused on the tasks in front of him. When asked, he would say that his master secret was *"Concentration."*[4] He detested empty minds, worked constantly to make use of the time, took up a book and plunged into it when he had five minutes to spare, deplored his inability to read in lurching carriages, and urged his children to organize their lives carefully.[5] His arguments were usually masterpieces of controlled, monumental, and highly articulated oratory. He particularly delighted in making knowledge quantitative, for he

[4] Morley, *Gladstone*, I, 186.
[5] Philip M. Magnus, *Gladstone, a Biography* (New York, 1954), p. 50; Morley, *Gladstone*, I, 186, 205–6; William E. Gladstone, *Correspondence on Church and Religion of William Ewart Gladstone*, selected and arranged by D. C. Lathbury (London, 1910), II, 149–96, hereafter cited as Lathbury, *Correspondence on Church and Religion*.

doted on facts. His capacity for dealing with incredible volumes of statistics in his memorable budget speeches made men marvel as they would at a natural wonder.

This careful, organized, disciplined, and factual personality was also, however, an emotional one. Driven by an urgent sense of duty, his nervous constitution made him "combative, passionate, and excitable."[6] His energies found release in campaigns of unceasing oratory, particularly after the midpoint of his career. He liked to feel that passion itself ennobled a cause. "Good ends," he observed during the Bulgarian agitation in the 1870's, "can rarely be attained in politics without passion . . ."[7]

Gladstone in this was much like Edmund Burke. Atmosphere meant much to him, for, like Burke, "he worked at a high temperature." Jeremy Bentham might be patient with years of work spent piling up small details of fact into a great reform, but men like Burke and Gladstone reacted instead to large and generous impulses set off by a terrible wrong that aroused their consciences or imaginations.

[Gladstone] did not set out on any large reform [J. L. Hammond observed] until his imagination had been excited, and his imagination was not excited unless he saw some hope of exciting the imagination of others. He took naturally an imaginative view of politics, but his imagination would brood sadly and aloof [as it did for many years on the Irish problem] until he saw the moment for making others feel what he felt.[8]

Though he came to be loved by millions, he was lonely among politicians. His contemporaries in Commons hardly knew what to make of him, other than that he was extraordinary. They often found his excitable manners and his brooding moods provoking, and they resented his refusal to sit in the Commons tearoom and exude bonhomie. Because he be-

[6] J. L. Hammond, *Gladstone and the Irish Nation* (London, 1964), p. 142.
[7] R. T. Shannon, *Gladstone and the Bulgarian Agitation 1876* (London, 1963), p. 107.
[8] Hammond, *Gladstone and the Irish Nation*, pp. 77–8.

lieved in the moral rightness of his positions, he usually enraged those who took the other side. Fundamentally a
scholar, the interests of his mind separated him from the
great majority of politicians and made him happiest when he
was in the company of intellectuals like Lord Acton and John
Morley, who liked to talk of things that only mystified the
ordinary M.P.[9]

Though complex, he was at the same time a guileless and
remarkably innocent man. He was idolized within his own
family circle and among his intimate friends for his natural-
ness and his almost childlike qualities. He could hardly understand stories that even remotely impinged upon sex, and
he was disgusted by irony and cynicism. Unless they were
unusually disliked political enemies, he trusted in the fundamental goodness of other men. "Whether Mr. Gladstone ever
became what is called a good judge of men it would be hard
to say," John Morley tactfully observed. "Like Lord Aberdeen, he had a marked habit of believing people; it was part
of his simplicity."[1]

He was not, on the other hand, an innocent while in
government. In his long possession of power he acquired a
shrewd, robust, and mildly cynical attitude about the methods
politicians followed to get ahead. He had no illusions about
the appetite for power that most men possess and was usually
much less surprised or upset than those around him by the
things men did in cabinets.[2] But his limited ability to understand motivations led him to mismanage personal questions,
which were almost intolerably painful for him. He bungled
such key relationships as those with the young Lord Rosebery, whom he practically announced as his successor, and
Joseph Chamberlain, who might have remained a Liberal
had Gladstone handled him differently. He once said, in despair, that of all the men he had served with in cabinets, he
only understood Lord Aberdeen, the open and uncompli-

[9] Ibid., pp. 74–6, 707–8.
[1] Morley, *Gladstone*, I, 197.
[2] G. T. Garratt, *The Two Mr. Gladstones* (London, 1936), p. 6; Morley, *Gladstone*, I, 554.

cated Scottish Presbyterian Premier under whom he served in 1852–4.[3]

He possessed that most distinguishing mark of the Liberal mind, a fundamental optimism about life in its larger aspects. His supreme optimism allowed him to bear the innumerable disappointments that came his way. To him the nineteenth century clearly demonstrated that the processes of history tended inevitably and progressively to free the individual. Like Jefferson he believed in social evolution to some consummation, though in his case to a pre-eminently Christian one. Even after his defeat on Irish Home Rule in 1886, he disagreed with Alfred Tennyson's bleak ruminations on the modern world, insisting that it had grown gentler, more tender in public conscience, in the years since he had first entered public life.[4]

Gladstone made the rare journey from vigorous conservatism to vigorous liberalism. The son of a rich Tory entrepreneur, he began his political career as a young man whose seat in the Commons was given to him by a duke. He execrated the Reform Bill of 1832, saying it foretold the collapse of Britain into weakness and anarchy—in sharp contrast to his later optimism. In despair he wrote to a friend: "The day of our greatness and stability is no more . . . the chill and damp of death are already creeping over England's glory."[5] In his first years in Parliament he opposed practically every reform that came before it. The Toryism of his youth was never more arrogantly put than in his 1836 campaign for re-election when he said, of Ireland, "The protestant faith is held good for us, and *what is good for us is also good for the population of Ireland.*"[6]

Of primary importance among the influences that led him to Liberalism was his placement in the ethnic geography

[3] Hammond, *Gladstone and the Irish Nation*, p. 708; Morley, *Gladstone*, II, 462; Robert Rhodes James, *Rosebery: A Biography of Archibald Philip, Fifth Earl of Rosebery* (New York, 1964).
[4] Morley, *Gladstone*, I, 207; II, 178–9; III, 354; Magnus, *Gladstone*, pp. 356–66.
[5] Morley, *Gladstone*, I, 70–1.
[6] Ibid., I, 129.

of the British Isles. He was a Scot who spoke with a burr all his life. His father, John Gladstone, had emigrated to Liverpool from Edinburgh in the 1780's and had risen to great wealth, first as a dealer in American grain, then in trade with the West Indies and India. When William Gladstone was twenty, the family returned to Scotland and he became an habitué of Edinburgh. As a politician, therefore, he was one of a number of Scots who in the nineteenth and twentieth centuries rose to prominence in British political life, especially within the Liberal Party. Not only was Gladstone a Scot, so also was his successor as leader of the Liberal party, Lord Rosebery, and his successor in turn, Sir Henry Campbell-Bannerman. This was a significant fact in the history of the United Kingdom. Since the most talented Scottish politicians had the highest posts open to them, Scottish nationalism did not incline toward secession, as did Irish nationalism. Scottish politicians were attracted to national rather than to provincial politics. No Irishmen, conversely, were ever taken into the British cabinet. This had much to do with their decision to form their own Nationalist Party and in time to withdraw violently from the United Kingdom.[7]

Scotland in the nineteenth century—indeed, until the First World War—was determinedly Liberal. The Toryism that the American colonists had suspected in them was largely a misconception. They seemed so because the tiny Scottish electorate was firmly controlled, through corruption,

[7] Gladstone discussed this fact in *The Home Rule Bill*, Speech, Commons, February 13, 1893 (pamphlet; London, 1893), pp. 1–9. This was not to be an isolated event in British politics. Not long after the Irish veered away from the Liberals, organized labor did the same. Largely denied nominations to Commons seats by class-conscious local Liberal organizations, they similarly formed their own organization, the Labour Party. Liberal openness to the outgroups had its limits, and this insensitivity was eventually to prove to be the party's downfall. Cf. L. D. Epstein, "British Class Consciousness and the Labour Party," *The Journal of British Studies*, I (1962), 136–50. Raymond E. Wolfinger has discussed the larger aspects of this phenomenon. Appointment to political office, he observes, is one of the critical steps in "mobilizing" a new minority group. It is one of the key symbolic acts open to political parties. Such recognition is not simply part of the expressive drama of politics, an essential act in the symbolic demonstrations that accord equal status to the outgroups, it is the principal way to gain loyalty. The Scots were mobilized; the Irish were not. Cf. Wolfinger, "The Development and Persistence of Ethnic Voting," *passim.*

by the Tories, and its representatives were therefore George III's men. Prejudiced against Scots anyway, as were the English in general, in the heat of the revolutionary times the Americans magnified their Toryism and counted them enemies. The exceptional visibility of the Gaelic-speaking Highlanders, who were in fact loyalist, served to make American suspicions more credible.

The Scottish population in general, however, was firmly Whig, though denied the power to express these sentiments until the Reform Bill of 1832 by the limitation on suffrage. Toryism, to the Scots, was synonymous with England. It represented Anglicanism, rule from London, and class distinctions that were anathema to the remarkably equalitarian Scots. Those who voted Conservative in Scottish elections were in a sense proclaiming their loyalty to and admiration of England. They were often Anglicized aristocrats who were members of the Anglican branch in Scotland, the Episcopal Church.

The ideas of Liberalism, indeed, were largely Scottish in origin. Not only was Adam Smith a Scot, so were such seminal thinkers as James and John Stuart Mill. This reflects the real cultural differences between the two countries. Scotland's intellectual style was not like England's. Rationality was prized. It is a commonplace to say that Scotsmen *reason*, while Englishmen *feel*. Too much cannot be made of this aphorism, but it is at least suggestive. At a time when most Englishmen were illiterate, education in Scotland was more widespread than anywhere else in Europe; and the lower and middle classes attended the same schools, went to the same universities, and acquired from this a notable sense of social unity. The Presbyterianism of the Church of Scotland, in true Calvinist fashion, dwelt upon a carefully reasoned sermon as the central experience in divine observance. Deductive reasoning in Scottish universities had made many brilliant successes in the eighteenth century, and the same tradition continued in the nineteenth century in science, philosophy, medicine, and economics. French ideas, especially the "Rights of Man," had deeply influenced Scottish thought, and when young English Whig noblemen studied in Scottish universities in the nineteenth century—as many of them did—they were surrounded by the ideas of Scottish rational Liberalism, as expressed in such great organs as the *Edinburgh Review*, the voice of Whiggery. Even "the poems of Robert Burns," J. G. Kellas observes, "are a high-point in the fusion of religious and secular deductive rationalism in a popular form, and their lasting political effect for the Scottish population (even to this day) must be counted a striking instance of literary influence in politics."[8] It is not happenstance that a disproportionate amount of modern British philosophy springs from north of the Scottish border.

There were other reasons why Scotland was archetypically Liberal. The representative system of government within its Church, hard-won in the Reformation, and the stubborn individualism that Calvinism inculcated in its members were both of the essence of Liberalism. Scots liked to contrast their Kirk with the Church of England, which they said was not the "people's church." Where hierarchy infused Anglicanism, in this reflecting English society, equality between minister and congregation characterized the Auld Kirk, reflecting again the notably equalitarian social relationships that existed between classes in Scottish society.

Scotland, furthermore, had become—especially in the Lowlands—a markedly business-oriented and entrepreneurial world of individualists pushing their own way upward. With education readily available, there seemed to be few barriers for the ambitious. The "lad o' pairts" could even count on university training regardless of his social origin. Perhaps a fifth of the university students in Scotland came from the lower classes. Furthermore, the dynamic economy that Adam Smith said would emerge if all restraints were removed seemed to come into being in his own homeland. The Glasgow industrial boom energized all of Scotland, sending population soaring. The nation that had roughly 1.5 million people in 1800 had almost 3 million by 1850 and by 1900 had grown more populous than Ireland, reaching 4.5 million. Beatrice Webb looked in vain in Scotland in 1892 for any counter-tendencies to its aggressive individualism. "The Scottish na-

8 Kellas, "The Liberal Party in Scotland," pp. 16–17.

tion," she said, "does not lend itself to combination; the strong men seek to rise and push for themselves and not to serve others."[9]

Added to all of this was the impact of William Gladstone upon the Scottish political mind. He was their *beau ideal,* by far the most eminent public man that Scotland had produced in British politics. Though he was an Anglican, he was an Anglican of an Evangelical cast—blending rational analysis with a fervent moralism—which made his appeals exactly of the kind that would excite the equally Evangelical Free Kirk mentality that infused Scottish Liberalism from the 1840's on.[1] "Gladstone came to represent," J. G. Kellas writes, "most of what the Scots themselves thought Scottish—a strong morality, expounded publicly by sermonising; a belief in the desirability of the freedom of the individual as justified by his essential rationality; the doctrine of self-help, to be achieved by thrift and hard work; and in politics, equality through the extension of the franchise."[2]

When in 1832 the minuscule 5,000-vote electorate in Scotland was expanded to 60,000 by the Whig Reform Bill of 1832, Scottish feelings expressed themselves immediately by giving the Whigs in the next election a four-to-one majority north of the border. Great majorities in Scotland were often thereafter the margin by which the Liberal Party won national victories and took office. In spite of its small size, Liberal Scotland played a major role in deciding who took over Downing Street[3]—just as the Democratic South in the United States often ensured Democratic majorities in Congress and Democratic Presidents in the White House.

Gladstone's North Country and Scottish antecedents may be part of the explanation, therefore, for his eventual drift leftward to join the Liberals. The fact that first needs explain-

9 David C. Elliott, "The Liberal Party, in Scotland from the Midlothian Election to the First World War" (Ph.D. dissertation, Harvard University, 1950), p. 5.
1 Evangelicalism and the Free Kirk will be discussed later.
2 "The Liberal Party in Scotland," p. 30. All of the foregoing has been drawn from Kellas, pp. 1–30, and Elliott, "The Liberal Party in Scotland," pp. 1–30.
3 Pryde, *Scotland,* pp. 194–9, 209; Norman Gash, *Politics in the Age of Peel: A Study in the Techniques of Parliamentary Representation 1830–1850* (London, New York, and Toronto, 1953), p. 36.

ing, however, is that about the time of William Gladstone's birth his family gave up their Whiggism and their Presbyterianism—to the dismay of their Scottish friends in Liverpool—and became Tory and Anglican.

Their behavior was perhaps no more than typical of the traditional *nouveau riche* desire to acquire greater social prestige. On the other hand, when they shifted their allegiances the Gladstones would seem to have been clearly reacting to major changes taking place in both the Church of England and the Tory Party in the early years of the nineteenth century. Since these changes go far to explain the politician that Gladstone became, they require examination at some length.

William Pitt the Younger, during his long premiership from 1783 to 1801, made the Tory Party the principal medium by which the "new men" of business and industry might rise to influence. The Whigs, a closed caste of country gentlemen and nobility, were devoted in their somewhat languid fashion to political reform, but despite Burke's entreaties they were contemptuous of businessmen and showed little interest in the ideas of Adam Smith.[4] Pitt, however, found in the new men of trade and industry an excellent new source of power to balance against the Whigs. He also had an economist's cast of mind, greatly admired the ideas of Adam Smith, and began reforming the taxing structure in accordance with his doctrines. At the same time, he shared with the businessmen a distaste for revolutionary France, where anti-property ideas and democracy seemed to go hand in hand. Pittite businessmen therefore rejected the proposals that sometimes came from advanced Whigs that Parliament be reformed in ways that would make it more representative of the populace. The Tory position on Parliamentary reform was that the oligarchical Whigs wanted Parliament to be stronger in order to bend it to their own aristocratic will, while they, the Tories, had the true key to the nation's welfare: a powerful and independent Crown that would rule through its ministers in the interest of all. Skillfully using the patronage of the Crown to bind together the new economic order and the Tory Party, Pitt created a powerful party that—as the Ameri-

4 Southgate, *Passing of the Whigs*, pp. 76–7.

can Alexander Hamilton doubtless admiringly observed—linked together executive vigor, the interests of the business community, and a loyal if not wholly enthusiastic rank-and-file following in the squirearchy.[5]

By 1815, therefore, the young and active men in the House of Commons were Tories. Being young and in power, they attracted the support of reformers, intellectuals, and political economists, especially after they were joined by the Burkeian Whigs, who supported the war with France. With the rise of George Canning after 1812, the Tory leadership—as distinct from its squirearchy following—became even more firmly committed to rational and liberal internationalist policies in economics and foreign affairs. Soon they began applying similar attitudes in domestic affairs. It was the ostensibly Tory governments under Lord Liverpool in the 1820's that began what has traditionally been called the Age of Reform in British history.

It was in these circumstances that John Gladstone became a Tory, as Canning, the representative of the newer ideas, pulled him away from the Whigs after 1812. John Gladstone, in fact, became Canning's political sponsor in Liverpool, and his son later wrote:

> I was bred under the shadow of the great name of Canning; every influence connected with that name governed the politics of my childhood and of my youth; with Canning, I rejoiced in the removal of religious disabilities, and in the character which he gave to our policy abroad; with Canning, I rejoiced in the opening he made towards the establishment of free commercial interchanges between nations; with Canning, and under the shadow of the yet more venerable name of Burke, my youthful mind and imagination were impressed.[6]

With the Whig Party moribund, and Toryism attractively Canningite, John Gladstone's change of party looks like rather more than simple social climbing.

[5] The foregoing and the following discussion of Pitt and the Tories is drawn from Elie Halévy, *England in 1815* (New York, 1961), pp. 9–11, 25–6, 191–3, 197–9.
[6] Morley, *Gladstone*, I, 25.

The Tories were also attractive to the Gladstones for religious reasons. Within the Church of England, a movement warmly appealing to the Gladstones—the Evangelical movement—began in the late eighteenth century. William Pitt was sympathetic to the Evangelicals and gave them much encouragement, through the influence of his intimate friend William Wilberforce, the prominent reformer and Evangelical.

The Evangelicals were part of a growing national revolt against the eighteenth century, a revolt that in many ways explains the British nineteenth century. Men as widely apart as Cardinal Newman and Thomas Carlyle could agree that the eighteenth century was an age of "decay of religion, licentiousness of morals, public corruption, profaneness of language . . . an age whose poetry was without romance, whose [rationalist] philosophy was without insight, and whose public men were without character."[7]

The Church of England in the eighteenth century had fallen on particularly dry times. Gladstone in a Commons speech in 1847 deplored its relaxation of discipline, its separation between hierarchy and people, its gross and notorious scandals. The Church, he said, was then "a skeleton of dry bones, without life, or heat, or movement; there were no warm and living bonds of love and of duty such as ought to connect a Christian people with their ministry."[8]

The Evangelicals were Anglican priests who preached a return to what they called "vital religion," which meant a religion centered upon the radiant, divine, and all-forgiving person of Jesus Christ. "It was common, in my early days," Gladstone wrote in 1879, "for morality to be taught without direct derivation from, or reference to, the Person of Christ."[9] It was against this solely rationalist approach that the Evangelicals directed their most vehement attacks.

---

[7] Willey, *More Nineteenth Century Studies*, p. 151, quoting Mark Pattison.
[8] *Hansard*, Third Series, XCV (Dec. 16, 1847), 1301–2.
[9] "The Evangelical Movement; Its Parentage, Progress, and Issue," in W. E. Gladstone, *Gleanings of Past Years, 1843–78* (New York, 1878), VII, 222.

They wanted above all to bring personal purity and sincerity back into private and public life. They wished to do it, however, not by appealing to a philosophically respectable set of moral laws, but by creating in their hearers a cataclysmic sense of their own personal depravity. Only when men were aghast at their own individual barbarism, and convinced thereby of their inevitable destiny in hell, could they begin properly to realize what Evangelicals described as the sweet gifts opened out to them by the forgiving love and sacrifice of Jesus Christ. His life and teachings would then take their proper role in men's consciousness, a role far more appealing than would be the pale ruminations of reason. Vitality, fervent personal commitments, passion, despair and release —these were of the pith and marrow of Evangelicalism.[1]

All this was classically stated in the Evangelical "bible," William Wilberforce's *A Practical View of the Prevailing Religious System* . . . (1797). The age in which they were living, he said, knew not how corrupt mankind really was. It had laid to its heart the soothing illusion that men were fundamentally amiable and kind, with just an imperfection here and there; that God, knowing their good intentions, pardoned all freely if they but made a reasonable effort at a blameless life. "Far different," he wrote, "is the humiliating language of christianity."

> From it we learn that man is an apostate creature, fallen from his high original, degraded in his nature, and depraved in his faculties; indisposed to good, and disposed to evil; prone to vice, it is natural and easy to him; disinclined to virtue, it is difficult and laborious; that he is tainted with sin, not slightly and superficially, but radically and to the very core.[2]

---

[1] This and the following discussion is largely drawn from the following: Horton Davies, *Worship and Theology in England: From Watts and Wesley to Maurice, 1690–1850* (Princeton, 1961), Ch. ix, "Anglican Evangelicalism: The Spirit and the Liturgy," III, 210–40; William Wilberforce, *A Practical View of the Prevailing Religious System of Professed Christians, in the Higher and Middle Classes in this Country, Contrasted with Real Christianity* (London, 1797); and Gladstone's excellent essay, cited above.

[2] Wilberforce, *A Practical View* (London, 1851 [?] edn.), p. 14.

We must always be struggling, Wilberforce insisted, with the evil spirit, who is here in this world. Thus embattled, by both our fallen nature and the Evil One, we face a Judge whose power is irresistible, who knows everything we do, "not our actions only, but our most secret cogitations . . . " He exacts vengeance, for he is angry with our transgressions. We must, therefore, take a "due sense of the malignity of our disease, and of its dreadful issue," if we are to be enabled to take the radical steps necessary for our protection. We must "shake off that lethargy which is so apt to creep upon us!"[3]

It is for this that we must turn to Christ. We must acquire a lively sense of his "unspeakable mercies . . . mercies so dearly bought, so freely bestowed—a deliverance from eternal misery—the gift of 'a crown of glory, that fadeth not away.'" We must love him truly, which meant eagerly and with whole heart, not simply with the mild respect accorded to a fine teacher. "True love is an ardent and active principle: a cold, a dormant, a phlegmatic gratitude, are contradictions in terms."[4]

We must allow the passions to come into religion, for only they could give us the capacity to open our minds to our true condition, and elevate our souls to the full love of him who alone could save us.

> Love, zeal, gratitude, joy, hope, trust, are each of them specified [in scriptures]; and are not allowed to us as weaknesses, but enjoined on us as our bounden duty, and commended to us as our acceptable worship . . . Lukewarmness is stated to be the object of God's disgust and aversion; zeal and love, of his favour and delight; and the taking away of the heart of stone, and the implanting of a warmer and more tender nature in its stead, is specifically promised as the effect of his returning favour, and the work of his renewing grace.[5]

Mere knowledge by itself, though lauded by eighteenth-century philosophers, was much too weak to do the work in us

[3] Ibid., pp. 24–7, 30.
[4] Ibid., p. 43.
[5] Ibid., p. 51.

that was required. "The affections alone remain to supply the deficiency." When we were thus moved, then the divine assistance that alone could save us from ourselves would be granted.[6]

So moved, too, the Christian would take up his true vocation in this world, which was to battle sin in every form. "Christians," Wilberforce insisted, "are become the sworn enemies of sin; they will allow it in no shape, they will admit it to no composition; the war they have denounced against it, is universal, irreconcilable."[7] In this great struggle, everything they have is God's. "God will not accept of a *divided* affection," Wilberforce warned, "a single heart and a single eye are in express terms declared to be indispensably required of us."[8]

No man had a right to be idle. He must work ceaselessly to turn his life to good account, recoiling from the flaccid emptiness that characterized so many lives. "Watering-places, the sports of the field, cards! never-failing cards! the assembly, the . . . amusements multiplied, and combined, and varied, 'to fill up the void of a listless and languid life' . . . in which, with all imaginable decency, year after year wears away in unprofitable vacancy." We must be always in active service, fulfilling our duties to ourselves and to our fellow creatures, shunning display, spurning the appetite for public adulation, taking the "lowly, modest, unassuming carriage of the true christian." Religion was a totally encompassing demand, "a principle of universal application and command." It was not merely a compilation of statutes of behavior; it was an inner principle that vitalized a whole life.[9]

Wilberforce addressed his book to the middle and upper classes because "the poor have the advantage" in living the Christian life.[1] They were not subject to all the temptations of affluence, of power, and of high standing so corrupting to the personality. The higher classes all displayed far looser morals than did the lower, in good part because they gath-

[6] Ibid., pp. 57, 59.
[7] Ibid., p. 97.
[8] Ibid.
[9] Ibid., pp. 104–5, 107, 112, 115.
[1] Ibid., p. 265.

ered for diversion and pleasure in the great new cities of the land where the "splendid and luxurious" life tended to "accelerate the discontinuance of the religious habits of a purer age, and to accomplish the substitution of a more relaxed morality."[2]

The nation needed "vital christianity" to regain its wholeness. All true Christians must be bold to assert the "cause of Christ in an age when so many, who bear the name of christians, are ashamed of Him . . . " Perhaps this did not require a "busy interference in politics," Wilberforce said, for politics was always an uncertain career. Rather, it called for an infusion of the public mind with true Christianity by other means.[3] But the need for action was imperative.

Out of such injunctions there developed an Evangelical tradition of powerful preaching. This is not to say that Evangelicals ignored the sacraments. They were in fact responsible for elevating Communion far above its former status in the Church, for it put them in direct contact with the person of the beloved Christ. But more than anything else Evangelicals were preachers. Charles Simeon, the patriarch of Evangelical priests, devoted himself wholly to teaching priests how to preach, leaving behind an incredible work that ran to more than twenty volumes and contained the outlines of more than two thousand sermons. Preaching always Christ and the Cross, eagerly seeking to convert their hearers to true Christianity by the spoken word, Evangelical priests laid open the universal sinfulness of nature, the darkness of the mind, and the utterly fallen nature of man. As an early Evangelical had urged the young Simeon,

> When your Hearers have been well harrowed, and the clumps begin to fall, (which is seen by their hanging down the head) then bring out your CHRIST, and bring him out from the heart, thro' the lips, and tasting of his Grace while you publish it. Now lay open the Savior's Almighty Power to soften the heart, and give it true repentence: to bring Pardon to the broken-heart, and the Spirit of Prayer to the

[2] Ibid., p. 243.
[3] Ibid., pp. 317–19.

prayerless heart; Holiness to the filthy heart; and Faith to the unbelieving heart.[4]

Evangelicalism expressed its deeply personalist viewpoint in many ways. Its hymns, above all its trademark hymn, "Rock of Ages," were hymns of personal experience. In its sermons, the message was always of an immediate confrontation with Christ, not of the religious community and the historical Church. Holiness was their concern, not catholicity or the apostolic succession.[5] If not antihistorical, certainly Evangelicalism was historically indifferent in its mode of thought. It knew nothing of the history of the Church, and certainly little of the Reformation.[6]

It was also relatively indifferent to the concerns of this world, despite Wilberforce's urgings to consider one's duty to one's fellow creatures. His own career—his long campaign against slavery—represented "*almost* purely an individual case," Gladstone later wrote. "Speaking generally, I am sorry to say," he went on, "the Evangelicals of that day were not abolitionists. They left that honour to the Nonconformists, most of all to the Quakers. Their Toryism obstructed them, as it does now."[7] Evangelicalism harmonized excellently with the business spirit, as Gladstone observed elsewhere, and aside from the luminous social-reform career of Lord Shaftesbury, it spawned no sweeping movement of legislative agitation after Wilberforce's abolition campaign.

Evangelicalism was actually quite Tory in its political characteristics. Even Wilberforce opposed the Reform Bill of 1832. Evangelical priests did not care for laymen to take much role in the governing of the Church. This was a principal reason why they remained Churchmen instead of becoming Methodists. They disliked lay preaching as it developed in the other evangelical movements, and stressed the concept of loyalty to the Crown.[8] It was wholly in conform-

---

[4] Quoted in Davies, *Worship and Theology*, pp. 229–30.
[5] Ibid., pp. 234–9.
[6] Gladstone to R. H. Hutton, Nov. 6, 1890, in Lathbury, *Correspondence on Church and Religion*, I, 406.
[7] Gladstone to the Rev. Dr. Fairbairn, Oct. 15, 1893, ibid., II, 333.
[8] Davies, *Worship and Theology*, p. 215.

ance to their personalist view of life that they should stress loyalty to the person of the monarch, for it was a secular version of their message of personal loyalty to the Savior. As Gladstone grew increasingly Liberal, the Evangelicals became some of his severest enemies within the Church.

He was, of course, eventually to find Evangelicalism too narrow and constricting. In his own view, Evangelicalism made a critically important contribution to the British religious mind by reintroducing as the center of all religious thought the glorious figure of Christ. But it also created spiritual appetites, he said, which it could not satisfy. It "filled men so full with the wine of spiritual life, that larger and better vessels were required to hold it." Lacking any real theology, "it raises questions to which it can furnish no replies." In attempts to answer these cosmic questions, therefore, spiritual men later moved out in all directions, many of them to Roman Catholicism, including, ironically, two of Wilberforce's sons.[9]

It seems inescapably true, however, that Gladstone was in every sense an Evangelical in his life style, in some of his key attitudes, and in his public character. Through the influence of his family and through personal contacts with Charles Simeon—Wilberforce even stayed briefly in their home—he was steeped in Evangelicalism.[1] Always of an ardent nature, he was extravagantly Evangelical as a young man. He was convinced that all unbelievers and Unitarians were damned, and that most Roman Catholics and Dissenters had little chance of salvation.[2] At age twenty-one, while at Oxford, he entered in his diary: "In practice the great end is that the love of God may become the *habit* of my soul, and particularly these things are to be sought: —1. The spirit of love. 2. Of self-sacrifice. 3. Of purity. 4. Of energy."[3] Deeply torn as to his choice of vocation—a tension he was to carry all his life—he agonized over whether he should become an Anglican priest or go into public life. The world was lost, he wrote his father; it was alienated, apostate. We could not save our-

[9] Gladstone, "The Evangelical Movement," *Gleanings*, VII, 232–5.
[1] Morley, *Gladstone*, I, 11–14, 32.
[2] Magnus, *Gladstone*, p. 8.
[3] Diary entry, Apr. 25, 1830, in Morley, *Gladstone*, I, 52.

selves by our own exertions; God alone could make the world glorious. God was infinitely loving to have given Christ to atone for our miserableness. For unregenerate sinners, there awaited only the doom of fire and torture and eternal punishment. We are constantly driven by passions we can never fully satisfy.[4] "Twenty-four years have I lived," he entered grievingly in his diary in 1833. "Where is the *continuous* work which ought to fill up the life of a Christian without intermission?"[5]

Gladstone in these years—and in a certain sense for a long time thereafter—was experiencing in all its painfulness the identity crisis of which Erik H. Erikson has written; the challenge that

> occurs in that period of the life cycle when each youth must forge for himself some central perspective and direction, some working unity, out of the effective remnants of his childhood and the hopes of his anticipated adulthood; he must detect some meaningful resemblance between what he has come to see in himself and what his sharpened awareness tells him others judge and expect him to be.
>
> In some young people . . . this crisis will be minimal; in other people . . . the crisis will be clearly marked off as a critical period, a kind of "second birth . . ." Some young individuals will succumb to this crisis in all manner of neurotic, psychotic, or delinquent behavior; others will resolve it through participation in ideological movements passionately concerned with religion or politics, nature or art.[6]

Gladstone, in his search for the existential justification of which Erikson speaks, went through the miseries of indecision. He felt the classic shame over what he was, and the doubt over what he was to become. He yearned to enter the priesthood, yet his father wanted him to choose politics, the unholy arena that in truth fascinated Gladstone. When he

[4] Gladstone to his father, Aug. 29, 1830, and to his brother, Dec. 30, 1830, in Lathbury, *Correspondence on Church and Religion*, II, 223–8.
[5] Morley, *Gladstone*, I, 108–9.
[6] Erik H. Erikson, *Young Man Luther: A Study in Psychoanalysis and History* (New York, 1962), p. 14. See also Erikson, *Childhood and Society*, 2d edn. (New York, 1963), Ch. vii, "Eight Stages of Man," pp. 247–274.

finally entered public life, he continued to be torn by a feeling he had chosen the wrong vocation.

He resolved the crisis in one way by the force with which he threw himself into the various causes of his political career, infusing them in his mind with religious significance. More directly, he embarked on a kind of personal missionary program. In 1845, he began a program of searching out prostitutes along the river in London and seeking to induce them to take up a more wholesome life. He founded a home for regenerate ex-prostitutes, and expended large sums in their support.

> He had experienced a call to enter the Church, and he had not responded to it. [This was his penance.] . . . No consideration on earth could have induced him to abandon it until old age had enfeebled him. All his life, in a spirit of simple and unaffected humility, he did his best to reconcile a nineteenth-century political career with the Gospel and example of his Savior.[7]

There were other ways in which Gladstone's fundamental Evangelicalism showed through. The distinguishing mark of an Evangelical household was family Bible-reading and prayer, and Gladstone engaged assiduously in these devotions every day, throughout life, writing more than two hundred sermons for use in the church on his estate. He shared Wilberforce's conviction that God knows our every act and thought, and was constantly uncertain of his ability to meet the divine injunctions.[8] He was positive that God had given him special missions to perform, most notably the solution of the Irish problem and the task of awakening and keeping alive "an English conscience on the . . . [foreign relations] of the British people.[9]

As the Evangelicals were pre-eminently preachers, so was Gladstone pre-eminently an orator who sought to arouse men's passions and thereby gain their adherence to great public causes. His whole career embodied the Evangelical's

[7] Magnus, *Gladstone*, p. 110.
[8] Lathbury, *Correspondence on Church and Religion*, II, 149–96.
[9] Hammond, *Gladstone and the Irish Nation*, p. 164.

passionate appeal to the heart. Firmly imbedded in his political outlook was a conviction that politics is a constant struggle with sin, with evil men—Benjamin Disraeli chief among them—and with the tendency of mankind to listen to dark counsels. After the midpoint in his career he repeatedly echoed Wilberforce's dictum that the upper classes were peculiarly untrustworthy, through having been corrupted by power and wealth, while the common people, in their simplicity, were fundamentally sound.

Most central to his Evangelicalism was his devotion to the person of Christ as the beginning and the end of true religion—a loyalty he shared, revealingly, with Thomas Jefferson. He insisted to Lord Acton that belief in the divine nature of Christ was the soul, substance, and creative force of the Christian religion, and the primary source of much of the good that the Church had been able to accomplish.[1] For this reason he was always devoted to the Communion service. "My mind is quite made up," he wrote the Earl of Aberdeen in 1856, "that if belief in the Eucharist as a reality is proscribed by law in the Church of England, everything that I hold dear in life shall be given and devoted to the oversetting and tearing in pieces such law, whatever consequences, of whatever kind, may follow."[2]

Gladstone's adherence to the person of Christ suggests an explanation for the reverence he always displayed for persons in high position, such as Queen Victoria or the various Prime Ministers under whom he served. Cardinal Newman spoke of conservatism as being fundamentally characterized by loyalty to persons. In this sense, Gladstone remained conservative throughout life. Like Burke he revered not only the institutions of the nation, but also the great personages who symbolized them. For both men, these attitudes were congruent with a basic orientation to life that conceived of it in essentially dramatic and personal terms.

Gladstone did not have what is generally regarded as a

---

[1] Morley, *Gladstone*, III, 360. See also Gladstone, "On the Functions of Laymen in the Church," in *Gleanings*, VI, 25; Gladstone to Mr. Darbishire [*sic*], Dec. 21, 1862, in Morley, *Gladstone*, II, 136.
[2] Letter, Aug. 13, 1856, in Lathbury, *Correspondence on Church and Religion*, I, 373.

sophisticated or a penetrating mind, but rather one with an extraordinary capacity for holding a wide range of materials in view. At Oxford—like Robert Peel many years before—he took a rare double first; that is, he was brilliant both in classical literature and in mathematics, itself a demonstration of unusual comprehensiveness of intellect. As Prime Ministers, in fact, he and Peel towered above all other nineteenth-century Premiers in sheer intellectual capacity. Among other legendary accomplishments of a similar nature,

> Gladstone's drafting of the Irish Land Bill of 1870 . . . was to be one of the most remarkable feats of the century, beyond the powers of Russell, Derby, Aberdeen, Palmerston or Disraeli: compared in this respect with him, the others, even Palmerston, were like poor swimmers, content to cling to a floating plank without much attention to spare for the direction it was carrying them in.[3]

Gladstone possessed, as Charles Francis Adams observed in 1866, "the most extraordinary facility of conversation on almost any topic, with a great command of literary resources . . ."[4] The only way, indeed, that he could establish close relationships with public men was through a shared concern with intellectual and cultural matters. He could thus be intimate with the agnostic John Morley and the Roman Catholic Lord Acton alike. He read constantly, obsessively, critically, with deep concern, dashing off many quick essays and critiques to record his reactions, delving and digging in almost every imaginable kind of literature. He was writing, writing, all the time, pouring out all his life an amazing stream of articles and books, even while Premier. He committed a great deal of poetry—especially Wordsworth's—to memory.

His reading, together with his experience, worked on his mind steadily. He was usually aware of the latest intellectual currents and reacted to such new ideas as Darwinism with more liberality than is credited to his image as the archetypical Victorian. It was not that he liked to change his mind; he

[3] Burn, *Equipoise*, p. 220.
[4] Morley, *Gladstone*, II, 212.

was simply compelled to it because his intellect was open to persuasion by information. In Norwich in 1890, at the age of eighty-one—and on the verge of endorsing the new Liberalism of the Newcastle Programme—he described his own mind accurately and honestly:

> I have been a learner all my life, and I am a learner still . . . I do not like changes for their own sake, I only like a change when it is needful to alter something bad into something good, or . . . better. I have a great reverence for antiquity . . . There are those who have been so happy that they have been born with a creed that they can usefully maintain to the last. For my own part, as I have been a learner all my life, a learner I must continue to be.[5]

He did not, of course, accept everything that was new. He never warmed, for example, to socialism. But he displayed such flexibility that great numbers of Victorians distrusted him completely, for the Victorian age was a time when men held fixedly, almost desperately, to their opinions.

Openness of mind such as Gladstone's is a puzzling phenomenon. Gordon Allport has pointed out that little is actually known about those kinds of men whose minds are flexible, who show the marks of what he calls, for want of a better term, the "tolerant personality." We seem still to know no more than that such personalities tend to come from unusually permissive households like the one in which William Gladstone was reared. He later liked to call his own home Liberty Hall, reproducing it in the open and joyous atmosphere he experienced in his father's house. Like his father, he encouraged his many children to express themselves at dinner on every imaginable subject, challenging them to catch him out if they could. There were times when "grave and earnest visitors were . . . disconcerted to hear some chance remark of the great man greeted with childish shouts of, 'A lie! A lie!' "[6] Children from such homes, Allport remarks, lack the threat orientation that is so often a promi-

---

[5] Morley, *Gladstone*, II, 178–9.
[6] Magnus, *Gladstone*, p. 128.

nent feature in the background of prejudiced persons—that is, persons addicted to fixed ideas.[7]

Men like Gladstone, in short, display characteristics that seem to run together. They have positive feelings toward minority groups, believing in the equality of all men. They can tolerate ambiguity. They deplore exclusiveness, and preach the classic message of the loving brotherhood of all mankind. Some of them are so concerned with equality that they become militants in its cause, and are in danger—as Gladstone was in later life—of dividing all men into good and evil groups, displaying an inverse prejudice of their own. They seem, however, whether militant or peaceful in their manner, to be reformist in their politics. Clear correlations have been found between prejudice, as a social attitude, and those who may be called conservative by reason of the fact that they are firmly committed to the *status quo*.

The Oxford that the young Gladstone attended at first confirmed him in all his Tory and Anglican prejudices, for Oxford was the fort and symbol of Anglican, Tory, and aristocratic England. Oxford feared liberty, anathematized the Reform Bill of 1832, execrated radicalism, praised the Corn Laws, and idolized all venerable British institutions.[8] But it also gave young men like Gladstone complete freedom to read widely and to discuss what they would, doubtless confident that no good Oxford student could go wrong. Gladstone founded an Essay Club at Oxford in 1829, with something more than a dozen members, and they ranged widely through such fields as poetry, philosophy, phrenology, modern drama, and psychology.[9]

In his vast reading, Gladstone was captivated by Burke and thereafter regarded him as his principal guide within the

---

[7] This discussion draws upon Allport, *Nature of Prejudice*, "The Tolerant Personality," pp. 398–412.
[8] Cf. Gladstone's description in Morley, *Gladstone*, I, 60, 84–5.
[9] Ibid., I, 59–60.

realm of politics. He took lifelong pleasure in the Waverley novels of Sir Walter Scott. To his romantic mind, always moved by a historical consciousness in which great men worked at great deeds, Scott's panorama was rich with beauty, lofty thoughts, and ideal men and women. He was also himself a Scot, of course, and since the Waverley novels rescued Scotland from its obscurity and elevated it into a land of romance, daring, and largeness of soul, like many other Scots Gladstone believed Sir Walter Scott to be the greatest of his countrymen.[1]

It is not surprising, therefore, to find that Gladstone, the inveterate romantic, believed that contempt for John Locke was the beginning of knowledge. Locke's dry and rational discourses and his vague religious faith were doubtless repellent to Gladstone. More than this, Locke thought that man was fundamentally good before government was instituted, while Gladstone believed rather that only in civil society, ordained of God, was man saved from himself.[2] He similarly detested Benthamism, regarding it as a philosophy that mechanized the soul and treated human needs and motives as something one could add up like any ordinary sum. It was pernicious to elevate enlightened self-interest into the guiding force for civilization. This would impoverish men's spiritual faculties, he believed, and destroy "the sense of obligation and the Christian spirit of fellowship in which he found the ties that unite men and keep societies together." Of course, he was both unequipped for and uninterested in metaphysical or highly abstract discussions.[3]

Like Thomas Jefferson, he was fundamentally a moralist, a fact symbolized by their shared devotion to Christ and his teachings. They also shared a dislike for the Platonic cast of mind, the readiness to spend one's day examining abstractions and mistaking them for the real world.

There were four men whom he called the doctors of his mind: St. Augustine, Aristotle, Bishop Butler, and Dante. St.

[1] Ibid., III, 424.
[2] Ibid., III, 476–7; J. L. Hammond and M. R. D. Foot, *Gladstone and Liberalism* (London, 1952), pp. 40–1.
[3] Morley, *Gladstone*, I, 209; J. L. Hammond and M. R. D. Foot, *Gladstone and Liberalism*, 2d edn. (New York, 1966), pp. 19–20.

Augustine, in so many ways the John Calvin of the early Fathers, was understandably absorbing to so devoted an Evangelical as Gladstone, with his sense of being torn between the city of God and the city of man. Even more important to him, if the themes that ran constantly through his later orations on foreign affairs are any indication, was Augustine's conviction that the lust to dominate infects every human act. Year after year, decade after decade, this was to be the burden of Gladstone's criticisms of British foreign policy—and, indeed, the burden of his whole attack on Toryism, both domestic and foreign.

Aristotle may be taken in two modes. One is as the guide to the life of contemplation, and this is the role apparently given him by most of Gladstone's generation at Oxford. The other is as the thinker who was absorbedly interested in gathering the facts of the real world, who loved to classify and use them according to their exact character, and who urged the use of such knowledge in the making of the better life. Aristotle saw the universe, in both its human and physical aspects, as dynamic, growing, always seeking to achieve its "nature," its true potential—a conception reinforced for Gladstone, doubtless, by Burke's image of the evolutionary political state. The awareness of growth that infuses all Aristotle's work must have encouraged and supported a reformer forced to justify change to himself and to a resistant aristocracy whose emotional conservatism he could not help but share. Gladstone's love for facts, his delight in making knowledge quantitative, was doubtless nourished by Aristotle, as was also his preference for history—that is to say, the "real" world —over philosophy. Aristotle's generous humanity, his insistence on the importance of continual moral development, his dictum that law is the true sovereign in the state, and his justification of the right of the people to take a major role in the state—all these were spiritual food to Gladstone.

Bishop Joseph Butler, the eighteenth-century Anglican divine and philosopher, captured him completely. He wrote much on Butler's thought, eventually preparing a major work on the subject. "I cannot say," Gladstone observed in 1860, "what value I attach to Bishop Butler's works."[4] He was delighted by the way in which Butler established the intellectual validity of religious faith. Men need not be disturbed, Butler wrote, by their inability to prove their faith scientifically, for in religion, as in everything else in life, man's ultimate reliance must be on the law of probability. Nothing is certain. Religion is not alone in being a matter that must be taken on faith. We take the honesty of business partners, of our wives, even the belief that tomorrow will come, on faith —that is, on the ground that all experience shows it to be probable. To Gladstone, this position—so like that of William James at the end of the nineteenth century—became the rock upon which he could found his faith in an age when all religion was under intellectual assault.[5]

Gladstone's devotion to Dante, whose works he read again and again, reveals the larger path that his political thoughts were beginning to take. He got from Dante not only a confirmation of his Evangelical belief that life may be made good in God's sight only by a constant struggle with our passions, but also a sense of membership in a larger European community.[6] The key fact about Gladstone's intellectual development was the way in which his mind instinctively reached for wider frames of reference than those provided simply by Evangelicalism, the Church of England, or even Britain itself. Whatever was limited in scope could never satisfy him; universalism was always the keynote. His mind, as earlier observed, was not penetrating, it was capacious; its impetus was centrifugal, not inward-turning.

He was therefore to be pre-eminently characterized in his political attitudes, as has been persuasively argued, by a "European sense." He came to feel that Britain and its problems must be regarded from the vantage point of Europe as a

[4] Gladstone to W. H. Gladstone, Aug. 1, 1860, in Lathbury, *Correspondence on Church and Religion*, II, 163–4.
[5] Cf. Bishop Joseph Butler, *The Analogy of Religion, Natural and Revealed, to the Constitution and Course of Nature* (1736); Gladstone, "The Law of Probable Evidence and Its Relation to Conduct," in *Gleanings*, VII, 153–99; Gladstone, *Studies Subsidiary to the Works of Bishop Butler* (New York, 1896).
[6] Cf. Morley, *Gladstone*, I, 202.

whole, not simply by reference to Britain's own parochial prejudices. Only this allowed him to take the large and liberal view of Ireland that was required in order to break away from the inveterate prejudices of an insular and culture-bound people.[7]

One of the first symptoms of this widening of perspectives was the dissolution in his mind of all that was narrow and restricting in his Evangelicalism. The initial blow to a framework that from the beginning had been too small for him came from the mother of an Oxford friend, who gently pointed out to him that salvation might be open to all true Christians, regardless of the faults of their opinions. This otherwise ordinary remark had a profound effect on him.[8] Shortly after, he made his first trip to the continent, and returned from it a changed young man. He stopped to visit the Vaudois, the Waldensians in the Cottian Alps southwest of Turin who were looked to by Evangelicals as the true saints of the Middle Ages. Gospel preachers who, like the Evangelicals, were devoted to purity of life, the Waldensians' brave resistance to persecution had inspired a famous poem by Milton and enshrined them in Evangelical hearts as the true and still-pure repository of primitive Christianity. The visit was most disenchanting. Gladstone found them to be hardly the saints of legend. He underwent "a chill of disappointment at finding them . . . [not] ideal Christians [but] much like other men." The Waldensian pastor he met was "without the smallest sign of . . . vital religion."[9]

His Evangelicalism thus lowered in temperature, he went on to Rome, where, upon entering St. Peter's, he was seized by a vision of the fundamental unity of the universal Christian Church, Catholic and non-Catholic. He began to feel "the pain and shame of the schism which separates us from Rome—whose guilt surely rests not upon the venerable fathers of the English Reformed Church [then his preferred

[7] Cf. Hammond, *Gladstone and the Irish Nation*, Ch. v, "Gladstone's European Sense," pp. 49–66.
[8] Morley, *Gladstone*, I, p. 8.
[9] Magnus, *Gladstone*, p. 12.

term for the Church of England] but upon Rome itself
. . ."[1]

Later on, in Naples, he chanced to fall upon examining
the occasional offices of the Church of England as contained
in the Book of Common Prayer, and another sensation flowed
in upon him. He had always lacked—as was typical of the
Evangelical—any sense of the Church as a collectivity, as a
great organism linked to God, passing through history, and
bearing with it a divine teaching mission. He had taken his
Christianity from the Bible, but "now the figure of the
Church arose before me as a teacher too, and I gradually
found in how incomplete and fragmentary a manner I had
drawn divine truth from the sacred volume, as indeed I had
also missed in the thirty nine articles [the stated creed of the
Church of England] some things which ought to have taught
me better." He developed an abiding belief in the Church as
a historical entity, a great community passing through time,
as he described it,

> its ministry of symbols, its channels of grace, its unending
> line of teachers joining from the Head: a sublime construc-
> tion, based throughout upon historic fact, uplifting the idea
> of the community in which we live, and of the access which
> it enjoys through the new and living way to the presence of
> the Most High.[2]

Gladstone's loyalty to the Prayer Book was most revealing. It is primarily in the Prayer Book that there is expressed
the original spirit of Thomas Cranmer, the creator, if anyone
was, of the Church of England. Cranmer, first Archbishop of
the new Church under Henry VIII, was a gentle and scholarly man, a true Christian humanist. He was of the temperament that prefers by conscious choice not to drive definitions to their logical extremes, but to find that which unifies,
that which holds together, that language which breathes
brotherhood despite differences, unity despite diversity. He

[1] Morley, *Gladstone*, I, 87.
[2] Morley, *Gladstone*, I, 87–8.

was ready, indeed, to leave paradoxes unresolved if resolution meant division. He wanted more than anything else to create an encompassing Church in which all could feel theologically at home. He sought to create in the Prayer Book, and in the Articles, a broad and subtle and inclusive spiritual tradition. It was his belief that Englishmen were agreed in the true fundamentals of Christianity; that forms were all that separated men, especially when they tried to choose language that was too precise. The spirit of the Church, he believed, should be genuinely catholic—that is, universal.

The spirit of the Book of Common Prayer became the spirit of Gladstone's Anglicanism. Universalist, loving, and nontheological in its general nature, the Prayer Book gave Gladstone the foundation of his Churchmanship. He was called a High Churchman, but he always protested with considerable justice that he belonged to no sect in the Church at all. In the long ritualist controversies led by High Churchmen that racked the Church from the 1860's to the 1890's, involving prosecutions, expulsions from livings, jailings, and the like, he not only kept his distance, he was contemptuous of it all. As he had asked Manning long before, in 1845, "Who can *restore* spiritual life by ceremonial? Now, if I must choose *between* the two, give me a reverent clergyman, whose voice, countenance, manner, movement, tell me incessantly of the presence of God, and I will give you all the rest."[3]

To his friends in the Church he deplored the tendency many of them displayed of giving doctrinal significance to what Gladstone insisted were simply forms of expression. Coercion was no remedy. The time had come, he said, to rely simply on the moral influence of the Church. Only its capacity to influence the inner life, he felt, could save it.[4]

His distaste for coercion in religious matters was akin to his feeling that men should not suffer political disabilities because of their beliefs. Despite protests from Oxford constituents, he advocated admission of Jews to Parliament as early as 1847. In the midst of the wild anti-Catholic outburst

3 Gladstone to Manning, Oct. 20, 1845, in Lathbury, *Correspondence on Church and Religion*, I, 348–50.
4 Lathbury, *Correspondence on Church and Religion*, I, 374–401.

of 1851, he opposed repressive legislation and, speaking "to a House practically almost solid against him," he called for an open and unforced toleration of Catholics.[5] A generation later he surmounted his personal distaste for atheism to make one of the greatest orations of his career in support of Charles Bradlaugh's admission to Commons. There must be, he insisted, "a total divorce between the question of religious differences and the question of civil privilege and power . . ." Religious liberty, he said, was not something to "deal out . . . by halves, quarters, and fractions, but to deal . . . out entire, and make no distinctions between man and man on the ground of religious difference from one end of the land to the other." In one of the ironies of the British nineteenth century, the Irish Catholics in Commons strongly dissented, and succeeded in keeping Bradlaugh out of the House of Commons for a number of years.[6]

Disagreeing so profoundly with those prelates in the Church who insisted on punishing other clerics for matters of belief, Gladstone in time came to assume that public distaste for Anglican squabbles would eventually lead to disestablishment. Though such an idea had put him into panics when he was young, by middle age he had come to feel that disestablishment might indeed aid the Church, for it would free it from the influences that flowed from its determined efforts to keep the state connection. He observed that too many of the Church's bishops and clerics cared more for gold than they did for purity of doctrine; that they were willing to accept any indignity from the state so long as the Church could hold on to its property. The Gorham Judgment of 1851 was to him the crowning example of this tendency, for in it a secular court defined baptism, and the bishops meekly accepted the judgment. By the 1850's he was reading much in the writings of Father Félicité Robert de Lamennais, the *enfant terrible* of

---

[5] Morley, *Gladstone*, I, 375–7, 410–12; *Substance of a Speech on the Motion of Lord John Russell for a Committee of the Whole House, with a View to the Removal of the Remaining Jewish Disabilities*, Commons, Dec. 16, 1847 (pamphlet; London, 1848).
[6] Speech, Commons, April 26, 1883, *Hansard*, CCLXXVIII, 1,174–98; Walter L. Arnstein, *The Bradlaugh Case: A Study in Late Victorian Opinion and Politics* (Oxford, 1965), pp. 186–225.

the Catholic priesthood in France. Lamennais, like Gladstone, stressed the *sensus communis*—the universal testimony of the human race—as the basis to faith. He also demanded that the Church in France totally separate from the state in order to purify itself for its holy work.[7]

By 1865, Gladstone could write to his son that if he, Gladstone, had lived to any purpose at all, it was largely for the purpose of reconciling the Church to the modern age by urging the bishops to relent judiciously and prudently on matters that affected only the things of this world. It had become clear, he said, that the Church must give up its delusion that through laws awarding it special privileges, it could convert the whole nation into Churchmen. Only by relinquishing its use of state power could the Church ever reinstate itself again in the hearts of the people and take up once more its divine mission.[8]

During this long process, Gladstone came to look upon himself not simply as a member of the Church of England, but as a member of a universal Church of Christ, with its symbols and its teachers leading all the way back to the Savior himself, and including all Christian communions.[9] "I am entirely convinced," he wrote a friend in 1839, "that the movement termed Evangelical, and that which is falsely termed Popish, are parts of one great beneficent design of God, and that, in their substance, they will harmonize and cooperate."[1] He saw in the Roman Catholic Church "the very best and the very worst of all the Churches of Christ"; the very best in its deposit of true Christian faith, the very worst in its oppressive policies abroad, by which he felt it drove men away from Christianity.[2] He was always devoted to the Catholic principle, which to him meant that all men were

[7] Lathbury, *Correspondence on Church and Religion*, I, 374–401; Gladstone, "The Church of England and Ritualism," in *Gleanings*, V, 108–89; Morley, *Gladstone*, I, 457; Philip Spencer, *The Politics of Belief in Nineteenth-Century France—Lacordaire: Michon: Veuillat* (London, 1964), pp. 39–41.
[8] Gladstone to W. H. Gladstone, Apr. 16, 1865, in Lathbury, *Correspondence on Church and Religion*, II, 168–72.
[9] Magnus, *Gladstone*, pp. 12–13.
[1] Ibid., p. 35.
[2] Gladstone to J. R. Hope, May 15, 1845, in Lathbury, *Correspondence on Church and Religion*, I, 335–42.

bound together through the sacred link provided in the Communion service.[3]

Perhaps the most revealing of Gladstone's intellectual activities was his long love affair with the Homeric Greeks. His contemporaries idolized fifth-century-B.C. Athens, the Athens of Plato, but he much preferred the wider, earthier, and more democratic world of Homer, who wrote some time before 700 B.C. Gladstone saw in the Homeric age the source of all that was enlightened in government and true and lasting in religion. In his view, God had used the Homeric Greeks to teach us how to act toward one another, just as he had used the Hebrews to teach us how to act toward Himself. The Homeric Greeks and the Jews were both God's agents in preparing us to understand and to accept the divine Christian Revelation when it came. Apollo, in his mind, embodied the Christ role; the Virgin was foreshadowed by Latona and Satan by Ate; and the Trinity appeared in a combination of Zeus, Poseidon, and Hades.[4]

The importance of the Homeric deities in the evolution of our religious ideas, he believed, lay in the fact that they were not animals or natural elements. Rather, Homer had in them created a religion wholly unlike the lustful, animal-worshipping religions of the East; a religion in which, as in the Christianity to come, the gods represented an intimate union of the divine and the human. For all their foibles and frolicking, they embodied also a concern for righteousness. They reverenced human life and nature; they were moral; they elevated the status of women; and they put mankind at the center of their philosophy. Like Christianity, Gladstone said, the religion of the Homeric Greeks struck a middle ground between sensuality and its opposite, a hatred of material things and the human body.

He came to feel that true religious teaching was not limited in its resources to the Bible and to the traditions of the Church, but included all the art and literature and all the

---

[3] Gladstone to the *Times*, Jan. 31, 1842, in Lathbury, *Correspondence on Church and Religion*, I, 277.
[4] This and the following discussion is largely drawn from Hammond, *Gladstone and the Irish Nation*, pp. 53–6, 698–705; and Magnus, *Gladstone*, pp. 34, 122–4, 220.

politics and government that had come down to us from the Greeks. In Gladstone's view the Greek mind was the secular counterpart to the Gospel. Greek civilization was the thing salted by the salt of Christianity, when in the fullness of time it was vouchsafed to man. The Greeks "have their place in the Providential order," he told the students at Edinburgh University, "aye, and in the Evangelical Preparation, as truly and really as the children of Abraham themselves."[5]

These concerns had interested him from the beginnings of his career. As early as 1837 he was arguing with friends that the pagan gods foreshadowed some of the teachings of the Gospels, and in the next twenty years he began working out this thesis in widely ranging researches. From 1858 on there were eighteen years in each of which he published a book or an article on Homer. He read the *Iliad* and *Odyssey* dozens of times, searching for the civil and ethical and religious sources that had shaped European civilization. The Homeric Greeks, he came to believe, had been the first to develop publicity and discussion as the essential arts of government. Only when the orator had gained in Homeric Greece his great role, Gladstone believed, and persuasive wisdom had come to rival in renown the feats of warriors, was it possible to create a free society.

Gladstone's studies and writings in Homeric history were designed to give Europe two things: a new sense of its fundamental unity; and a widened understanding of what in fact constituted divine revelation. He was convinced that, if he could persuade the world of the truth of his speculations, a new age of faith would replace the existing age of skepticism. Men would see that true religion was not limited to the Bible. They would come to realize that the entire cultural matrix of European civilization was the loving and beneficent work of God. Not only would faith re-enter the life of nations, but there would develop a newly righteous and ethical mode of conduct within and between nations, for it would be seen to be the will of God. Imaginative culture, the education of the intellect, the direction of civilized politics, the "law of Na-

[5] Address, "Place of Ancient Greece in the Providential Order," Edinburgh University, 1865, in *Gleanings*, VII, 31–96.

tions"—all would gain new strength when seen to be part of the providential order.

He longed to spend more time in his Homeric studies, for he hoped in this way to give to men the same grand vision of their common history, universal in scope, that he had. Feelings of unity and a love of peace would grow, moderating the passions induced in a world of aggressive and wildly flourishing nationalisms, bequeathing to mankind a soothing realization of the love and care of God.

The background to Gladstone's Liberalism, then, lay essentially in a spiritual and intellectual pilgrim's progress that drove him unceasingly to the acquisition of ever more universalist frames of reference. In politics these took the form of what J. L. Hammond calls his "European sense." In religion they expressed themselves in his Prayer Book Anglicanism, his open and tolerant view that all Christians, whatever their sect, belonged with him to a universal Church of Christ.

In this process, he acquired a new sense of membership. His long identity crisis expressed itself not only in his anguished search for a profession, but also in his search for a world in which he could feel at home. He developed a sense of membership in a vast and cosmopolitan human community reaching back in time to the Homeric Greeks, and outward in space to include all of European civilization. If Toryism in the nineteenth century essentially meant exclusiveness, rigidity, and narrowness, Gladstone's expansive nature was destined, sooner or later, to break out of it.

Chapter 6

WILLIAM GLADSTONE:
APOSTLE OF LIBERALISM

To a remarkable degree, British and American politics resembled each other in the 1820's. In both countries one political party had been so long in power that the party system had practically disintegrated—if it had ever, indeed, existed in anything like its modern form. Jefferson and his followers had been in the White House since 1800, the Federalists had collapsed, and the Jeffersonians themselves had become so numerous that there were factions within factions, each of them claiming to be the true believers. Not until the Bank Veto of 1832 was American political life clarified, the followers of Andrew Jackson thereafter calling themselves Democrats, and their opponents coalescing as Whigs in opposition to the "executive tyranny" of Jackson.

Also in British politics all traditional party lines were confused in the 1820's. It is in fact not really useful, in Norman Gash's view, to analyze British politics in that decade in terms of Whig and Tory party groupings, for by that time the nominally Tory government had been in power for so many years that it had simply become the government of the country. Open to many influences, its leadership was even reluctant to use the name "Tory." Not until after the Reform Bill of 1832 does it seem possible to look seriously for the emergence of modern political parties, and even then they were not firmly entrenched in men's minds as primary identities until after the Repeal of the Corn Laws in 1846.[1]

The resemblance between the two countries goes yet further. Robert Peel did indeed begin to organize the Conservative Party—which name he chose to replace "Tory"—in the 1830's, and the Democrats did begin to emerge as a fairly coherent body in the same years. However, in both countries the following decades were to see more kaleidoscopic changes and regroupings. The Corn Law issue was to create a long period of instability in British politics after the Repeal in 1846, and the slavery issue was to do the same in the United States, beginning with the Wilmot Proviso controversy of the same year. The 1850's in Britain saw an almost continual dance of the factions in progress, and the same decade in the United States witnessed a shattering of the political system so severe that four parties entered candidates in the presidential election of 1860. The Civil War, of course, was the ultimate stage of this disintegration.

The establishment of a relatively firm two-party system came to Britain in 1859, when several factions on the left coalesced, forming the Liberal Party in Parliament and thus beginning the classic Liberal-Conservative rivalry of the high Victorian years. And in the United States, the Civil War polarized the political situation so strongly that the Republican-Democratic confrontation was established as the fundamental pattern in American politics thereafter.

The reasons why Anglo-American politics, after decades of fragmentation, suddenly stabilized in two-party systems in the mid-century period are interesting matters for speculation. The American situation presents the readily available explanation that a great war inevitably polarizes politics, but the British experience requires a more subtle analysis. John Vincent has recently suggested that the important factor was not the coalescence of the left-wing factions in Parliament, but rather a final coming together at the base of the social pyramid, most notably in countless local milieus in the provinces, of the popular forces that were to provide the solid

[1] Gash, *Reaction and Reconstruction in English Politics*, pp. 119–28.

foundation for Gladstonian Liberalism. It was the people at large who captured and made the Liberal party.

> There were no orders from above to create a party. Community of sentiment had to exist before organization could be possible: where such community existed, not much organization was necessary. The real units of opinion and organization remained the mill, union, pub, street, high street, estate, farmers' ordinaries, and so on . . . It was from outside Parliament, and from the world outside the World . . . that the Liberal Movement drew its social strength and social meaning.
>
> After 1865 the Liberals, without important changes in the Parliamentary personnel, came to represent great and dynamic social forces in the country, by reason of their vitalizing connection with their rank and file. The representative of that connection was Gladstone.[2]

Something like half of William Gladstone's political career was spent in the confusion that existed before the 1860's. He spent his first decade in Parliament, after his entrance there in 1832, as an implacable opponent of political reform, and—most of all—as a passionately devoted Anglican who conceived it his primary task to fight off all attacks on the church-state tie. He was known to be unusually bright and possessed of an astonishing gift of oratory, but he was put down as fundamentally a curious kind of Anglican Jesuit absorbed in speeches and writings that tortuously piled up argumentation for the idea of a state church.

From 1841 to 1846, Robert Peel led one of the most remarkable reform governments of the century, and he brought William Gladstone into it, thus completely changing the course of his career. A torrent of legislation on mines, on factories, and on many other matters was enacted by Peel in these years. Gladstone's specific task was to be Peel's chief

[2] Vincent, *Formation of the Liberal Party*, pp. xxxi–xxxiii.

associate in carrying through the progressive reductions of
the tariff structure that culminated in 1846 in the Repeal of
the Corn Laws. It seemed at first a curious appointment.
Gladstone was not only ignorant of trade matters, he was
indifferent to them. He disliked the idea of dealing with par-
cels and packages. There were some who even thought his
appointment a satirical gesture on Peel's part, designed to
show his contempt for economic reforms.

Peel simply recognized latent talent and put it to use. In
extraordinary labors of concentrated study, and in mounting
excitement, Gladstone became the first man within memory
to work his way through the maze of the archaic tariff structure. His aptitude for understanding incredible bodies of
facts came into its first flowering, and it was never thereafter
to leave him. He saw how severely the tariff system hobbled
Britain's economy and hampered its recovery from the severe
depression that had struck both Britain and America in 1837.
His rank-and-file Tory protectionism melted away, and he
became an enthusiastic convert to the ideas of Adam Smith,
who held out the vision of an unleashed and dynamic economy. When challenged on the issue by Lord Howick, who
taunted him for his change of front, he retorted that "Burke
had said that the statesman who refused to take circumstance
into his view and consideration is not merely in error—he is
mad! Stark mad! Metaphysically mad!"[3]

With all the zeal of the new disciple, he published his
views in the *Foreign and Colonial Quarterly Review*. Wealth
among all the nations of the world, he said, was what would
make Britain wealthy. The beggar-thy-neighbor approach
and its concomitant policy of concentrating on a protected
home market were totally misinformed. The "several families
of the human race" all gained by exchanging the things they
were best suited to produce. A sense of mutual interest and
advantage would be created by free interchanges, which
would in fact go far to ensure another objective, world peace.
Britain's great mission in the world, therefore, was to stimu-

[3] Magnus, *Gladstone*, p. 64.

late a worldwide reduction of trade barriers by wholesale reductions in her own tariffs.[4]

Though these opinions were those of a Conservative minister, they amounted to exactly what the Cobdenite Radicals of the North Country were saying. This important fact bears further exploration, for it reveals much about the true nature of Anglo-American politics. It demonstrates that the Peelites and the North Country Radicals, taken together, constitute the British counterpart to the Jacksonian Democrats in the United States.[5]

Robert Peel and Andrew Jackson would hardly be classed together if looked at superficially, for one was a polished British Premier and the other a rough American President from frontier Tennessee. Appearances, however, are in this case misleading. Both came from outside the traditional centers of social prestige, Jackson from the trans-Allegheny and Peel from the world of commerce. Both, furthermore, were strong executives in political systems ordinarily directed by aristocratic oligarchies that preferred to share power and to exert leadership primarily through the vehicle of committees. Both the American and the British Whigs vigorously disliked the idea of a strong executive. Rule by a collection of notables was their ideal. In contrast, where Whig Premiers administered, Peel governed. Peel has been called "essentially an authoritarian."[6] Similarly, no issue reflected American political life more deeply than the Whig attack on Jackson's "executive tyranny."

Gladstone was to inherit the Peelite tradition. It was common in the nineteenth century to associate Gladstone with William Pitt the Younger and with Robert Peel as forming the great triumvirate of rarely talented Premiers who were cast from the same mold. All became Smithians in their economic policies, seeking to stimulate economic growth

[4] Morley, *Gladstone*, I, 249–50; W. E. Gladstone, "Course of Commercial Policy at Home and Abroad," *Foreign and Colonial Quarterly Review*, January 1843 (reprinted London, 1919). See also F. W. Hirst, *Gladstone as Financier and Economist* (London, 1931), p. 73.
[5] The relationship between the Radicals and the Jacksonians will be further discussed in the next chapter.
[6] Gash, *Reaction and Reconstruction in English Politics*, p. 150. On these matters, see also Southgate, *Passing of the Whigs*, pp. 211–12.

through free trade; all worked hard to make the sluggish British government austere and efficient; and all were powerful Premiers, easily the masters of their governments. Where the Whigs liked to think of Parliament as supreme in the government of the country—a conception perhaps congenial to the oligarchical temperament—Gladstone, even though he was a great House of Commons man, always believed that the power of the executive should be increased rather than diminished. As party leader, furthermore, he was like Peel in being little inclined to take his followers into his confidence, preferring to ruminate upon the challenges of the day and then to deliver himself of pronouncements as to future party directions.[7]

This is not a wholly uncomplicated matter. The Whigs' preference for a weak executive did not mean they also preferred a weak government. Neither party in Britain desired the passive government of the *laissez faire* myth. It was firmly believed that the government, thought of as a total institution, should be a present force at all times in the life of the nation, especially when faced by mobs and agitation, or by heartless employers.

It is in this sense that Walter Houghton speaks of the strong streak of authoritarianism in the British mind. This temper translated itself in politics into a determined conviction that authority is needed in public life. Norman Gash refers to this hunger for authority as the "great taproot of Conservatism" that pre-existed the formation of any visible political Tory party.[8] The Church, the Crown, the venerable corporations at Oxford and Cambridge, the local magnate, the courts, and all the rest of the multitudinous authorities that directed British life should be obeyed implicitly because they were *authorities*. It was wild and revolutionary to bring them into doubt on the grounds that they were nonutilitarian.

Underlying all of this was the hero worship to which the Victorian mind was so given. The age was one of swift and

[7] Magnus, *Gladstone*, p. 272; Southgate, *Passing of the Whigs*, p. 212; Gladstone to S. E. Gladstone, May 26, 1868, in Lathbury, *Correspondence on Church and Religion*, II, 179.
[8] Houghton, *Victorian Frame of Mind*, pp. 325–7; Gash, *Reaction and Reconstruction in English Politics*, pp. 130–3.

unsettling transitions, and men looked for saviors. Thomas Carlyle urged his readers to find their hero and to follow him. Give your hero, he urged, *"infinite* admiration." His appeals were repeated by others in an extraordinary spate of books with titles like *Lectures on Great Men* and *The Red Book of Heroes.* Heroic literature on past lords and ladies was very popular, especially in Tory circles. The Victorians wanted intensely to believe, to satisfy the intellectual and spiritual hungers that formed as the Bible and other traditional under-pinnings to the "world taken for granted" were pulled away.[9]

The resemblance between the Jacksonians and the Peel-ites was much more than simply a shared belief in strong leadership. They also had remarkably similar assessments of what needed to be done to reform the economy. Peel became convinced that the government's first concern should be the condition of the poor—in itself a new conception. The best thing that could be done for them, he believed, aside from creating jobs by making the economy dynamic, was to make England a cheap country to live in; that is, to keep the cost of food and other necessaries at the lowest possible level.[1] Fur-thermore, the Peelites felt it imperative to strike at the boom and bust cycle, which was apparently brought on by specula-tion, seemingly the fundamental sickness of the new econ-omy. The Jacksonians also considered speculation a great evil and looked about for means of curbing it. Doubtless J. R. Vincent's man of small property working alone found the economy's gyrations a particularly cruel and infuriating bur-den. Gladstone, sharing this antipathy, said in his 1843 essay that the distress of the 1840's was caused primarily by the speculation, based on loose money and easy credit, that pre-ceded the crash of 1837.

Reformers on both sides of the Atlantic fastened on un-controlled issuances of paper money as the fundamental cause of the widespread suffering that afflicted Britain and the United States. Paper money appeared to cause high

[9] Houghton, *Victorian Frame of Mind,* p. 332. For all the foregoing, see pp. 306–40.
[1] For Peel's economic policies, see Briggs, *Making of Modern England,* pp. 294–344.

prices, which struck the laboring and urban consuming classes cruelly, and to bring on frequent panics and depressions, which caused unemployment. The more radical Jacksonians even wanted hard money—that is, a limitation of the circulating medium to gold coin alone. They echoed what William Cobbett had said in England in 1819 when he had attacked "rag money" as the bane of the poor. For reasons to be discussed in the following chapter, this led in America to an attack on the Bank of the United States and its eventual collapse.

The debate over currency in England had been going on since the economic turmoil that followed the end of the Napoleonic Wars in 1815. It then featured a debate between the supporters of Thomas Attwood, who argued for no restrictions on credit or the size of the money supply on the ground that inflation and rising prices would help farmers and industrial producers, and those of David Ricardo, the economist who supported sound money, a linking of the currency supply to gold, and stable prices.[2] The upshot of that debate was Peel's establishment of specie payment in 1819, thus grounding the money supply in the gold standard and laying the basis for a sound-money system and stable prices.

As in America, this did not end the controversy in Britain. It was endlessly argued through the next decades of rapid economic development. Many demanded closer controls on the money supply on the ground that loose money was the root cause of the speculative frenzies that seemed to afflict the economy. The Manchester Radicals, led by Richard Cobden, saw that inflation and high tariffs were connected, being the policies not only of the farmers, who wanted a protected home market in which there would be high food prices, but also of the metal-goods producers of Birmingham.

In 1844, all these influences converged in Peel's Bank Charter Act, which so reformed the banking system—particularly the Bank of England—that the issuance of currency was placed under stringent controls. With strong Radical support, Peel carried through his act in a kind of triumphal progress,

[2] These matters will be explained in greater detail in Chapter 7.

all his opponents having been swept aside by events and by the arguments of the political economists.[3]

At the same time, Gladstone dealt with another source of speculative pressures within the economy by his Companies Act of 1844, which sought to end the uncontrolled creation of joint stock companies and the lavish issuance of their securities. All companies were required to register and to publish prospectuses and balance sheets.[4] He went on to propose regulatory legislation to bring some order out of the railroad scramble then going on. He arranged for the permanent provision of cheap trains for the masses, and a declaration that the state had the right to intervene in the affairs of the railroad companies. Unfortunately, his initiatives in this direction were not followed up in the succeeding years.[5]

The Peelites and the Jacksonians were not, however, mirror images of one another. They operated within significantly different contexts. Peelites—like most British political factions—disliked democracy. They tended to be devoted to a church-and-state connection, while Jacksonians were violently opposed. Peelites certainly did not use Jeffersonian imagery about social enemies and the aristocracy. They were Burkeian evolutionists who spoke in the reasonable language of pragmatism, working within a powerful aristocratic society. The two movements faced economies at quite different stages of development, and their prescriptions on how to achieve sound money and low food costs for the poor, or how to break corporate power, were different. The Americans were certainly a long way from establishing laws on working conditions: Martin Van Buren as president (1837–41) was much criticized for decreeing a ten-hour work day at all federal public works.[6]

[3] Briggs, *Making of Modern England,* pp. 201–5, 338–9; Elie Halévy, *The Liberal Awakening, 1815–1830* (New York, 1961), pp. 196–202; and Elie Halévy, *Victorian Years, 1841–1895* (New York, 1961), pp. 97–9, 206–11.
[4] The Jacksonians had a similar fear of corporations, but as in the Bank controversy, they caught the problem at a different stage and attacked it in a different way. Not until Cleveland's day did they begin calling for Gladstone-type controls. See Chapters 7 and 8.
[5] Briggs, *Making of Modern England,* pp. 339–40; Morley, *Gladstone,* I, 269; Magnus, *Gladstone,* p. 67; Burn, *Equipoise,* pp. 162–4.
[6] Schlesinger, *Age of Jackson,* pp. 265–6.

But the similarities between the Peelites and the Jacksonians are simply too striking to ignore. It is revealing that Martin Van Buren himself praised Peel, finding in him and in his following kindred spirits to Jackson and the Jacksonians.[7] Both Peelites and Jacksonians admired Adam Smith. They perceived the same enemies, had the same goals, and aroused the same angers. They had by far the greater proportion of the intellectuals on their side, many, of course, in advance of them and eagerly trying to pull them on. And they created in the idea of the strong executive exactly what their opponents feared, a model of leadership that could grow into the vitalizing role of tribune of the people. This kind of leadership, finding its power base in the electorate at large, would be free of the numbing limitations imposed by oligarchies, whether in Parliament or in Congress. It was to be the kind of leadership peculiarly necessary to democratic societies if major periods of reform were to be inaugurated and carried through.

Were not the British Whigs better counterparts to the Jacksonians? Donald Southgate, in *The Passing of the Whigs,* has recently given us a highly detailed and persuasive picture of the Whigs that makes it difficult to characterize them other than as a closed caste of aristocrats who enjoyed power. "Whig" is defined not by presenting a set of principles, but by describing a social position. Whigs believed in all manner of things. They were certainly not democrats. They looked upon the Reform Bill of 1832—which they took up not from principle but as a means of gaining office—as a final step, leaving the mass of the population, other than the middle class, entirely out of the franchise. Lord John Russell's persistent efforts to broaden the franchise after 1832 were considered a tiresome personal hobbyhorse, allowable in a great magnate. They had almost no knowledge of or interest in political economy. They were more "squeezable," as Southgate uses the word, than their aristocratic colleagues on the other side of the House when demands arose for various kinds of political reforms. Perhaps this was so because they were generally larger landholders than the Tory squirearchy, more urban-

[7] See below, Chapter 7.

ized, intellectual, and cosmopolitan in their habits, and possessed of wider sources of income, and therefore not nearly so concerned about such things as repeals of Corn Laws and currency matters.

They were, in short, that relatively small part of the aristocracy that was politicized, in the sense that by reason of their high social rank they could expect to hold office if the party won. The Tories used talented commoners as their leaders—Pitt, Canning, and Peel—but not the Whigs. They were the nineteenth-century embodiment of the ancient desire of the aristocratic magnate for noneconomic forms of social income, notably the prestige and power that come with office and the patronage it provides.

Traditionally, they represented the idea that Parliament should be supreme over the executive, which suited their oligarchical and generally passive style of governing. From Charles Fox and Edmund Burke they inherited a formal sympathy with self-governing regimes abroad and a hostility to aggressive foreign policies. In this sense—and it is an important one—they were in the eighteenth century, especially in the hands of Burke, the ancestors of the Liberals. A minority themselves, in the nineteenth century they acquired the arts of being the political spokesmen for the heterogeneous outgroups in British life—the Irish, the Scots, and, briefly, the Dissenters—that populated the left wing in British politics. Often generous and kindly, and sometimes highly intelligent, they were also, as Burke had found to his exasperation in the previous century, languid men, made so by wealth and position and an elaborate social life. The principles they traditionally represented were a habit, not in any sense a burning and present concern, nor were they in any sense definitions of Whiggery. A Whig was a member of a specific social circle, not somone who held certain views. A Whig worker or a Whig businessman would be a contradiction in terms, and they did not exist.

Their urbanity and their secularist outlook on life led most of them to find Gladstone incomprehensible. One Whig *grande dame* is reported to have said, "In short, he is not frivolous enough for me. If he were soaked in boiling water and rinsed until he were twisted into a rope, I do not suppose a drop of fun would ooze out."[8] Lord Hartington, with whom Gladstone had to work on the closest terms in the 1870's and 1880's, insisted that he could not understand what Gladstone said even in private conversation.

Thus as Donald Southgate has clearly shown, the Whigs have very little in the way of an American counterpart. They were an aristocratic anachronism in an increasingly democratic age, and they were inevitably destined to begin leaving Gladstone as he grew more radical. When in the 1880's he began reforming the land situation in Ireland, they defected to the Tories *en masse*.

The climactic events of Peel's government began in 1846, when the potato famine struck Ireland. The Corn Laws of the United Kingdom, which still stood despite the many reductions Gladstone had already made in other tariff schedules, were now thrown into the glare of pitiless publicity, for they kept food costs high in a time of desperate need. They remained in existence because Peel had not advanced as far as Gladstone in his free-trade ideas as yet, and he had resisted taking the ultimate step.

Meanwhile, through all of the years since 1838, an extensive agitation against the Corn Laws had been underway. Launched by Richard Cobden in the center of Dissent and the new commerce—the North Country, and more particularly in Manchester—it was a campaign in which Biblical rhetoric, economic theory, and social jealousy flowed together in a tirade against the "titled felons" of the landed aristocracy. The whole country was in turmoil, and in March 1845, "the whip was cracked near at hand. After listening to a long factual speech by Cobden, Peel crumpled up his notes and said to his colleague, Sidney Herbert, who was sitting next to him, '*You* must answer this for *I* cannot.' "[9]

There followed then those dramatic months in which

[8] Magnus, *Gladstone*, p. 142.
[9] Briggs, *Making of Modern England*, p. 316, and *Victorian People*, pp. 207–8; Halévy, *Victorian Years*, pp. 122–36.

Peel drove through the Repeal of the Corn Laws. Supported by the leader of the Whigs, Lord John Russell, who alone among the Whigs seemed to understand what it was all about, by Richard Cobden and the Radicals, and by his immediate following within the Conservative Party, as well as by a kind of dumb readiness to follow the man who had become the giant of the day, he won his great victory. It was impossible to deny him, though Cobden himself estimated that two thirds of the Commons disliked the idea. Mortally angered, however, the Tory squirearchy—led by Benjamin Disraeli, the man whose brilliance now became indispensable to them—threw Peel out of office as soon as possible. The Conservative Party was irrevocably sundered.

The circumstances of Peel's departure confirmed, if confirmation were necessary, the relationship that had come into being between the Peelites and the Radicals. In Peel's last address to the House as Premier, he took pains, in reviewing the accomplishments of his ministry, to say that the name that should be at the head of the Corn Law success should not be his own, but that of Richard Cobden. "Many in his audience were shocked by this panegyric of the great middle-class demagogue who for the last ten years had dragged the British aristocracy in the mud, depicting it as engaged in a deliberate design to enrich itself by impoverishing the lower classes."[1] But it was a comment that recognized the Peelite-Radical relationship that had become perhaps the key feature in British politics—and was later on to make up the core of the Liberal Party in Parliament. Peel had, in fact, just received a letter from Cobden appealing to him not to resign the premiership, but to found a new party on the ruins of the existing system, a Peelite-Radical Party that could lead the country openly instead of, as before, informally. Peel had himself become Cobden's pupil. And Cobden, recognizing the pre-eminence of Peel in the country, told him, "You represent the *idea* of the age, and it has no other representative amongst statesmen." Peel was not ready to launch out on so hazardous a course as a remaking of the parties, and he was

[1] Halévy, *Victorian Years,* p. 147.

soon to meet with his tragic death. But the die had been cast.[2]

The Tory squirearchy, behind Disraeli, had many grievances. In their eyes the Repeal of the Corn Laws was a shattering blow to the solid core, the center of gravity, of British life: the landed aristocracy. But this was not their only grievance. They condemned Peel's currency policies as well, for they had wanted a looser money supply, in the classic belief of farmers everywhere—the parallel with the Kansas Populists is ironic—that loose money would lead to higher grain prices. Lowering the living costs of workers and urban consumers had few appeals for them. In 1857, Disraeli even went so far as to call for an unlimited issue of bank notes.

The squirearchy also had an almost visceral contempt for Irishmen and for Catholics generally, and they saw in Peel and in his close associates a disgusting toleration and indeed compassion for such creatures. They similarly regarded with unconcealed distaste the North Country Radicals, led by Cobden and Bright, who rallied around Peel. They considered all these people practically aliens, for they were Dissenters, they spoke with crude North Country accents, and as businessmen they worked up materials bought and sold abroad.

The Tories were nationalists in the same way that the American Whigs and Republicans were nationalists. The Whig-Republicans urged the development of a protected internal market, with tariffs to protect industry. The British Tories of the anti-Peel variety talked similarly of the internal British market for grains, and the need for tariffs to protect that market. They could not understand the economic internationalism of the North Country businessmen, whose eyes were directed not inward, to the English market, but outward, to the world. The internationalism of their free-trade doctrines, to the Tory mind, was simply a lack of patriotism.

Tories were also, like their Whig-Republican counterparts in the United States, hostile to strange, "un-English" peoples. That is to say, in both countries, these political movements were the expression of nativism, one of the more

[2] Ibid., pp. 147–50, 209.

virulent forms of nationalism. In Britain, however, being properly native to the country, being a true Englishman, carried both an ethnic and a religious connotation.[3]

The average Tory instinctively recoiled from the aura of intellect that seemed to surround Peel and his advisers. From the 1820's, when the Lord Liverpool government began listening to intellectual reformers, the Tory squirearchy had deplored as madness the "March of Mind." As *Gentleman's Magazine* put the matter, "Philosophical or speculative theorists, and political economists have been so long experimentalizing and administering empirical nostrums to the naturally robust constitution of John Bull, that he is rapidly sinking from his once vigorous condition to weakness and decrepitude."[4]

About eighty Peelites in Commons—Gladstone among them—rallied around Peel after his fall, forming a separate group within the Conservative Party. Their political role was now highly unsettled. It has been observed that they could have served in either party, for they occupied the center where Whigs and Tories overlapped.[5] They were Conservative in that, like Peel himself, they were devoted to maintaining the traditional institutions of British life, especially the Church of England. This kept them apart from egalitarian Dissenting Radicals like John Bright and from the latitudinarian Whigs, who were traditionally secularist and freethinking in religious matters. The Peelites sprang from Tory Oxford, had aristocratic connections, and moved in the charmed circle of dukes, bishops, and wealthy families. Yet they were linked to the world of commerce and industry by sympathies and by family ties, were firmly committed to free trade, and were open to the new currents of thought in political economy, literature, and philosophy. In power of mind they were far above their contemporaries in the House—and showed that they knew it. Proud of the prestige that surrounded them as Peel's disciples, they maintained for a number of years

[3] The British aspect of the above discussion has been drawn from McDowell, *British Conservatism, 1832–1914*, pp. 1–50.
[4] Briggs, *Making of Modern England*, pp. 214, 221–2, 225, 327.
[5] Gash, *Reaction and Reconstruction in English Politics*, p. 155.

their separate identity. The direction they would take in the future—whether back to the Conservatives or over to the Radicals—was one of the key factors that waited to be resolved before the confusion of mid-century politics could be clarified.

It took years for Gladstone to resolve this dilemma in his own mind. Everything romantic and traditional in his nature made him cleave as long as possible to the party of his father, of Pitt, Canning, and Peel, and of the Church that he loved. Crucial issues in foreign policy, however, eventually drove him over to the other benches.

He had inherited the Canningite tradition of sympathy for self-governing regimes abroad. To this inherited sympathy he added a special concern of his own, one clearly shown in the words he wrote in his diary during the British Opium Wars in China, which he had harshly attacked: "I am in dread of the judgment of God upon England for our national iniquity towards China."[6] Foreign policy to him was not simply a secular and practical matter. It was charged with the highest religious significance. For this reason he was to be capable of sharp dissociations in his own mind between what his national government was doing and what seemed right by reference to a system of values larger and more universal in scope than those related simply to national advantage. What he was above all concerned to combat was the "lust to dominate."

Gladstone was quite content with Peel's foreign policies in the 1840's, for they were peaceful, nonaggressive, and internationalist.[7] But he was thoroughly angered by Lord Palmerston's bellicose and insouciant nationalism as Whig Foreign Secretary after 1846. In the Don Pacifico affair in 1850, when Palmerston justified a show of force with the claim that a British subject, like a citizen of ancient Rome, was entitled

6 Morley, *Gladstone*, I, 226–7.
7 Halévy, *Victorian Years, 1841–1895*, pp. 44–59.

to privileged treatment wherever he was in the world, Gladstone made his first great oration on foreign affairs. In the face of a hostile House he condemned the whole proceeding as callous and arrogant. Forcing the Greeks to a humiliating defeat over a trivial matter revealed Britain's arrogant pride, which Gladstone said was her "besetting fault and weakness." The British people, he said, must cease trumpeting their superiority to all the world in impossibly offensive speeches in Commons, speeches praising the "unapproachable greatness" of Great Britain and asserting British rights above all others. "It is this insular temper," Gladstone warned, "and this self-glorifying tendency, which the policy of the noble Lord, and the doctrines of his supporters, tend so much to foment . . ."

No nation should claim rights it does not accord to others. It should indulge in intervention only in the rarest and most demanding circumstances, not at every pretext, as seemed to be Palmerston's habit. They should instead rely upon the "law of nations" for settling their disputes. With all the fervency of a Burkeian, Gladstone praised the law of nations as

> a great and noble monument of human wisdom, founded on the combined dictates of reason and experience—a precious inheritance bequeathed to us by the generations that have gone before us, and a firm foundation on which we must . . . build . . . if, indeed, we wish to maintain and to consolidate the brotherhood of nations.

Everything depended on a frank recognition of "the equality of the weak with the strong; the principles of brotherhood among nations, and of their sacred independence."[8]

Soon after, during a visit to Naples in 1851, Gladstone discovered the Neapolitan government's shocking mistreatment of political prisoners. Worse yet, these practices were apparently condoned by his own Conservative Party, to which he still nominally belonged. The Conservatives supported the Neapolitan government against those who would

[8] W. E. Gladstone, *Substance of the Speech of the Right Hon. W. E. Gladstone, the Affairs of Greece, and the Foreign Policy of the Administration*, Commons, June 27, 1850 (pamphlet; London, 1850).

liberalize the regime. Determined to take dramatic action, he published two sensational pamphlets in which he execrated the butchery that was going on in Naples and characteristically appealed to "the bar of general opinion—of that opinion which circulates throughout Europe with . . . facility and force . . . and which . . . is . . . impregnated with the spirit of the Gospel . . . "⁹

Though it did no immediate good for the prisoners, this attack on an established government by a Conservative produced a sensation throughout Europe. It was translated into various tongues, attained a huge circulation, and made Gladstone an object of affection among Italian patriots. Odes were composed to him, the newspaper press took it up warmly, "and for the first time Mr. Gladstone found himself vehemently applauded in liberal prints." He became a national hero and a moral force in Europe.¹

Soon he was internationally famous for his economic skill as well. In the mid-1850's, in his first service as Chancellor of the Exchequer, he carried through the famous budgets that, after the final steps he took in 1860, brought to a close Britain's transition to complete free trade. In a series of brilliant performances that have acquired a legendary air, he completely reorganized the nation's revenue system, shifting the government's reliance almost entirely to the income tax and away from tariffs.²

By these measures, Smithian economics reached their final triumph in Britain. *Laissez faire*—conceived of in the properly Smithian sense as a *complete termination of the government's attempts to deflect the flow of investment capital,* encouraging this industry or that by such devices as tariffs —had been achieved. With the disappearance of practically all tariffs, raw materials were freed from taxation and the whole economic system, as Smith had foretold, seemed to receive an enormous stimulation. A flexible taxation system

⁹ W. E. Gladstone, *Two Letters to the Earl of Aberdeen on the State Prosecutions of the Neapolitan Government* (pamphlet; New York, 1851).
¹ Morley, *Gladstone*, I, 396–7; Magnus, *Gladstone*, p. 100.
² Cf. his speech, Commons, April 18, 1853, *Hansard*, Third Series, CXXV, 1350–428.

had replaced one that was rigid and regressive. Furthermore, the demands of business interests were finally divorced from the revenue system, thereby accomplishing the separation of business and government that was perhaps the key item in the Liberal-Democratic economic agenda.

The booming prosperity of the 1850's, and the extraordinary rise in real income for all classes that Gladstone delightedly described in the annual budget messages he gave with flair to packed Houses of Commons thereafter, seemed to demonstrate beyond question that Adam Smith had been a genius and that Gladstone was his legitimate prophet. As the revolutionary troubles of the 1840's receded into memory and the prosperous and confident Victorian era dawned, Gladstone achieved an enormous reputation throughout Europe as the statesman who had solved the problems of the new economy. He became the sign and symbol of the triumph of the new economics.

Gladstone remained content thereafter with Smithian economics and never warmed to socialism. The events of his own life and time seemed to confirm that all that was necessary was to release the economy, and everyone's standard of living would rise; that the economic problem, in effect, had been solved. Not only did prosperity follow his completion of free trade, it was peculiarly his fortune to have good times coincide generally with his premierships. The depression of the 1870's and the hard times in the late 1880's took place when the Tories were in power, and he could blame them on "unsettling" Tory policies abroad.

After all, it had only been in the 1840's and 1850's that the victories for Smithian economics had been won. It was quite understandable that in the generation following, Gladstone's confidence in free trade as the solution of the economic problem remained unshaken. Like Jefferson, he so mesmerized his successors in the party that it took them a long time to begin questioning the dogmas he had sanctified.[3]

---

[3] A useful analogy might be found in Labour's faith in nationalization. The history of that idea practically mirrors that of free trade. Smith's *The Wealth of Nations* appeared in the 1770's, and was finally victor-

Another characteristic of Gladstone's policies in the mid-century years and after was his obsession with economy in government. His political generation had direct knowledge of the results of eighteenth-century political corruption. It shared Burke's and the American colonials' conviction that corruption threatened everything else in free government. Sinecures, unnecessary offices, pensions, lavish spending on local projects—all combined in their view to create both heavy tax burdens that drained the economy of its capital, and devices by which governments could purchase support from legislators. Gladstone's inauguration of civil service in the 1850's sought to eliminate one source of this venality, and the corrupt-practices legislation he later enacted in the 1880's aimed at eliminating the buying of votes, which notoriously flourished in mid-Victorian constituencies.

In his budgets, nothing gave him greater pleasure than sniping away constantly at every little expenditure. He worried about the spread of a "spending spirit" in society, and especially in government. "Economy," he once said, "is the first and great article . . . in my financial creed."[4] He was parsimonious because he "firmly believed, as the best men among whom he spent his youth had believed, that the misery of the poor was due chiefly to public extravagance, and the waste and misuse of the nation's resources."[5] But the result was often to make him a miserly politician at war with his own generous impulses. He developed a petty joy at minor victories in spending matters that tarnished his prestige and harmed his governments. As one contemporary said, "Gladstone divides me. Half of him I respect·deeply, and the other half seems not worthy of satire."[6]

---

ious in the 1840's and 1850's. In the 1870's and 1880's, the first serious talk of nationalization began, and the idea became reality in the 1940's and 1950's. The Labour Party is now engaged in a rethinking of the dogma that for so many years gave it its reason for existence. The argument going on now over nationalization as a concept is like that which began over *laissez faire* as a concept around the turn of the century. The great difference is that there is no Gladstone and his radiant memory associated with nationalization. It may be easier, therefore, for Labour to modify that dogma than it was for the Liberals to escape the rigidities that came to characterize the *laissez faire* concept in its later years.

4 Morley, *Gladstone*, II, 62.
5 Hammond, *Gladstone and the Irish Nation*, p. 126.

After Gladstone's budget triumphs in the 1850's, foreign affairs again intervened. The Crimean War broke out in 1853, and Gladstone before long was once more on the unpopular side. At first he supported the war as a means of enforcing "the public law of Europe against a wanton disturber."[7] But as the carnage proceeded—some 300,000 men died in this "minor" war—he came to realize it was being fueled more by a virulent Russophobia in the British mind than by a desire to restore international law. He began calling for settlement of the war on the basis of a collective European guarantee of the rights of the Sultan's Christian subjects in the Balkans. Speaking out of the somber Augustinianism that seemed always to be in his mind, he warned that warfare beyond this goal was simply pandering to a "base lust for conquest." He was called a pious fanatic, a conceited clown, and even a traitor, but he remained ironical and indifferent to the criticism, for he was convinced that he was right.[8]

Two years later—in 1857—he was attacking a new war with China, appealing to the British to take "the higher ground of natural justice . . . that justice which binds man to man; which is older than Christianity, because it was in the world before Christianity; which is broader than Christianity, because it extends to the world beyond Christianity; and which underlies Christianity, for Christianity itself appeals to it . . . "[9] In the same year he condemned Palmerston's efforts to halt the building of the Suez Canal. Such a project, Gladstone insisted, even if under French auspices, could only be a boon to all mankind.[1]

At the end of the decade the Italian war of liberation began, and Gladstone found himself irrevocably split off from his colleagues in the Conservative Party, for they supported

---

[6] Quoted in Hammond and Foot, Gladstone and Liberalism, 2nd edn., p. 9.
[7] Morley, Gladstone, I, 484.
[8] W. E. Gladstone, Speech of the Right Hon. W. E. Gladstone on the War and Negotiations, Commons, Aug. 3, 1855 (pamphlet; London, 1855); Morley, Gladstone, I, 550–6; Magnus, Gladstone, p. 121.
[9] Morley, Gladstone, I, 563; W. E. Gladstone, War in China, Speech, Commons, Mar. 3, 1857 (pamphlet; London, 1857).
[1] Hammond and Foot, Gladstone and Liberalism, 2nd edn., p. 59.

the established governments. He was warmly committed to
the idea of national self-rule, both from his Canningite inheritance and the devotion to vigorous self-governing communities that he had derived from his Greek studies. Homer's
attractive picture of the emergence of the Greek peoples from
inchoate formlessness into a lively and self-respecting national
group appealed to Gladstone's romantic nature. He believed
in self-government because of its moral effect on men's natures. Self-government in his view gave men freedom to
struggle with evil, eagerness to accomplish great civic goals,
manliness, a concern for others, dignity, and self-respect.[2]

Gladstone now took the step that made his break with
Conservatism final. As a major figure in the legendary meeting that in June 1859 was held in Willis's Rooms, he helped to
bring about the fusion of Whigs, Peelites, and Cobdenite
Radicals that finally led to the emergence of the Liberal Party
in Parliament as a continuing organization. At this meeting, it
was agreed to support a government under Lord Palmerston,
with Gladstone as Chancellor of the Exchequer. Though
Gladstone disliked Palmerston's nationalism, "the overwhelming weight and interest of the Italian question," he later
wrote, "and of our foreign policy in connection with it . . . led
me to decide without one moment's hesitation."[3] Under Palmerston the British government thereafter played what was
perhaps the critical role in helping a unified Italian nation to
come into being.[4]

[2] Hammond, *Gladstone and the Irish Nation,* pp. 719–20.
[3] Magnus, *Gladstone,* pp. 138–41.
[4] I should here take note of the controversy that has surrounded the
origin of the Liberal Party in Parliament. I have followed Donald
Southgate's treatment (*Passing of the Whigs,* pp. 290–3), which is
similar to that in Halévy's *Victorian Years,* p. 424. McCallum accepts
this view in "Liberal Outlook," in Ginsberg, ed., *Law and Opinion in
England in the 20th Century.* But Norman Gash has recently held that
this needlessly postdates the emergence of the party; that the name
"Liberal Party" was in current use in the mid-1830's and that it consisted largely of the Whigs (*Reaction and Reconstruction in English
Politics,* pp. 165–6). What it thereafter lacked, until, one gathers, the
emergence of Gladstone, was an effective leader and a program. Halévy
himself points out that in 1847 the Whigs officially adopted "Liberal"
as their designation in the election of that year (*Liberal Awakening,*
p. 180 n.). My own view is that if in the mid-1840's "the Liberals were
in need of a policy and a leader" (Gash, *Reaction and Reconstruction
in English Politics,* p. 189) and remained in this condition into the

Gladstone was now passing through one of the more profound experiences that life provides. He had had Conservative associates, and for many years he had represented Tory-Anglican Oxford in Commons. He now joined the world of the Liberals and the masses. When Oxford threw him out in 1865 he took Dissenting, industrial, and egalitarian Lancashire, "the cockpit of modern English politics,"[5] for his constituency. He was joining a social milieu whose frame of reference, whose whole perspective on the world, differed sharply from that held by the men among whom he had moved before. This necessarily affected his ideas. "The individual who finds himself in [a new social group]," Peter Berger writes, ". . . becomes more prone every day to share its basic assumptions. That is, we change our world views . . . as we move from one social world to another. Only the madman or the rare case of genius can inhabit a world of meaning all by himself."[6]

From another standpoint—one especially applicable to the orator Gladstone, who was always highly sensitive to his surroundings—the important aspect of his new situation was that he had acquired a new audience. "Deliberately, intuitively, or unconsciously," Tamotsu Shibutani has observed, "each person performs for some kind of audience; in the drama of life, as in the theater, conduct is oriented toward certain people whose judgment is deemed important."[7] Seeking his audience's approval, the person involved tends to adopt its perspective on the world and its values. In the

---

1850's, then it is difficult to regard them as a party. Perhaps the best resolution of the difficulty is to think of the term "liberal" as an adjective before 1859, and as a specific party name and affiliation after that date.
[5] *Times*, Aug. 21, 1879.
[6] Peter Berger, *Invitation to Sociology: A Humanistic Perspective* (Garden City, N.Y., 1963), p. 64.
[7] Tamotsu Shibutani, "Reference Groups and Social Control," in Arnold M. Rose, ed., *Human Behavior and Social Processes: An Interactionist Approach* (Boston, 1962), p. 129. I have drawn my general discussion of this phenomenon from this essay and from Tamotsu Shibutani, *Society and Personality: An Interactionist Approach to Social Psychology* (Englewood Cliffs, N.J., 1961), Ch. viii, "Social Status in Reference Groups."

language of social psychology, the audience becomes his reference group.

To complicate the situation, however, audiences need not be present in real life. They may consist of an idealized image of the Middle Ages, or of "posterity," or of an intensely admired past figure. Simple men, predictable men, act for the single audience that surrounds them in their life. Complex men like Gladstone act for many audiences—which suggests why men found him incomprehensible. Jesus Christ, Aristotle, St. Augustine, Dante, Edmund Burke, the Homeric Greeks, and the whole of European civilization—these were his audiences. The important new development now in his career was that he was adding to them the massed North Country and Scottish multitudes before whom he was to spend so much of the rest of his life.

One has the feeling that the audience to which Gladstone increasingly turned after 1859 was the one for which he had been searching all his life. He could now achieve a full release of the drives within him by taking on the causes and the enemies of the North Country, of the Nonconforming sects (Dissenters), of the ethnic minorities, and of the unfranchised masses. It was now, perhaps, that the man of small property, Vincent's archetypical Liberal voter, gave his whole heart to Gladstone. Whatever the reasons, whether Gladstone simply adopted the world view of the multitude, or could give fuller expression to the one growing within his own mind, the years after his shift of parties were to see an acceleration of his movement leftward. Certainly everything pulled him in this direction. Democracy seemed on the rise everywhere, the old Whig and Radical leaders were growing tired, and the rising Liberal forces in the country were looking for a vigorous and exciting leader.

Gladstone thereafter ruled Parliament through the electorate. He was imposed upon the oligarchies in Lords and Commons by social forces coming from every direction. "Gladstone exercises such a sway over the constituencies," observed the Duke of Argyll in 1881 in a private letter, "that the members are afraid to call their souls their own." His extraordinary transit across the spectrum of British political life, from right to left, meant that within the space of a few years he had captured the loyalties of men from many walks of life.

> He stood at once for the serious aristocracy, the High Churchmen, the industrialists, the cheap press and radical agitation, the provincial towns, Dissent, and the working class. So quickly did he evolve, that differing impressions of him, mutually exclusive in the long run, but all favourable, were co-existent in the minds of great classes, and Gladstone obtained that support of the general interest he looked for, from a party which was a confederation of all classes, each acting in their own interests. By the velocity of his evolution toward many-sidedness, he temporarily squared the political circle.[8]

He introduced his new directions in 1860 by repealing the paper duties, in a tumultuous struggle in which the Lords were humiliated, making cheap newspapers—and therefore political information—available to the masses. He also in this way won the lasting devotion of the new popular newspaper press that was revolutionizing British politics and becoming the voice of the rising Liberalism. Gladstone was afforded a clamorous reception in the North Country shortly after this victory, astonishing him and angering the aristocracy, who were now beginning to look upon him, as Lord Clarendon put it, as "an audacious innovator with an insatiable desire for popularity."[9]

He soon was launched upon the strange course of events that led to the Reform Bill of 1867. Few periods in his life have given rise to such conflicting explanations. Was he in favor of widespread enfranchisement, or opposed? It is clear that he felt powerfully attracted by what seemed to him to be happening to "the intelligent working man," as he would put it, and believed that such workingmen should be admitted not only to the suffrage but also to a new status in British life.

[8] Vincent, *Formation of the Liberal Party*, pp. 227–8.
[9] Southgate, *Passing of the Whigs*, p. 299.

"We are told," he said in a speech to a vast Lancashire audience in 1862, "that the people cannot be trusted—that they are fit for nothing except to earn daily bread—that you must not call them to the exercise of higher functions, or look to them for enlightened views." How then, he asked, explain what had made such an impression on his own mind, the stoic and high-principled endurance of unemployment by the working classes in the North Country during the cotton famine induced by the American Civil War? Taking unemployment as their share of the burdens imposed by the fight to end slavery, they had used their enforced leisure, he said, not in rioting, but in attendance at schools and the betterment of their minds.[1] Workingmen, when employed, were saving their money, living thriftily, eschewing the revolutionary violence of Chartism, and striving mightily to elevate themselves.

In May 1864, after having urged the trade unions to put pressure on Parliament if they wanted the vote, he ridiculed at length the fears of those who warned of social revolution if the franchise were widened. The laborers would only join together as a class, he said, if they were made to continue suffering exclusion. The time had come to recognize the great moral change that had come over the common people. They had acquired education, self-command, and a respect for order. Indeed, he said in Commons—in one of the boldest statements of his career, which he immediately and characteristically qualified—"I venture to say that every man who is not presumably incapacitated by some consideration of personal unfitness or of political danger is morally entitled to come within the pale of the Constitution."[2]

The sensation these words caused was extraordinary. He was a leading figure in a government that had theretofore largely shared with the Tories an implacable hostility to suffrage reform—Lord John Russell, as always, being the

[1] W. E. Gladstone, *Address and Speeches Delivered at Manchester on the 23rd and 24th of April, 1862* (pamphlet; London, 1862).
[2] Speech, Commons, May 11, 1864, *Hansard*, Third Series, CLXXV, 312–27.

honorable exception—and now he seemed to be calling for universal manhood suffrage. Loud "volleys of cheering and counter-cheering [broke out in the House]. Two whigs ran off to tell Phillimore that Gladstone had said something that would make his hair stand on end." Gladstone was reviled as a Tom Paine, a leveler, an inciter of mass uproar, and a wild preacher of the divine right of mobs. The *Quarterly* observed bitterly that he had become the first Radical candidate for the premiership.[3]

Gladstone lost his Oxford seat in 1865, went to Manchester to pronounce himself "unmuzzled," and introduced his suffrage-reform bill in 1866. He thereafter went about the country belittling Tory fears of the masses. A wide suffrage in America, he pointed out, had not weakened the government there, but had instead given to it the strength it had needed to fight through the terrible Civil War. The common people would bring disinterestedness and a better moral climate to the Parliament because—as he was to say often in later years —they had not been corrupted by the temptations of power and wealth.[4] He called upon the nation to accept the fact that all the currents of history showed this step to be in the predestined course of events.

> You cannot fight against the future. Time is on our side. The great social forces which move onwards in their might and majesty, and which the tumult of our debates does not for a moment impede or disturb—those great social forces are against you; they are marshalled on our side; and the banner which we now carry in this fight, though perhaps at some moment it may droop over our sinking heads, yet it soon again will float in the eye of heaven, and it will be borne by the firm hands of the united people of the three kingdoms, perhaps not to an easy, but to a certain and to a not distant victory.[5]

[3] Morley, *Gladstone*, II, 121–7; Southgate, *Passing of the Whigs*, p. 300; Briggs, *Making of Modern England*, pp. 495–6.
[4] W. E. Gladstone, *Speeches on Parliamentary Reform in 1866* (London, 1866), *passim*; Speech, Commons, April 27, 1866, *Hansard*, Third Series, CLXXXIII, 144.
[5] Speech, Commons, April 27, 1866, *Hansard*, Third Series, CLXXXIII, 144.

But the events of these two years, 1866 and 1867, were so confused as to place these words in a perplexing light. Gladstone's 1866 bill, which was defeated, was considerably more moderate than the reform bill enacted by Disraeli in the following year. Furthermore, Gladstone's own behavior raised questions. He would emerge for great declarations on the cause, and then be silent for months on end, even disappearing to the continent for recreation at times critical to the passage of the reform. His letters contain remarks that may be construed as issuing from a reluctant dragon, one who aimed at slowing down the wheels of history.

Maurice Cowling makes it clear that no one actually wanted to give real power, in any major way, to the working classes. Gladstone seems genuinely to have been concerned to bring the "intelligent and independent" laborer into the voting population, but felt the illiterate and impoverished masses below them would only be more fodder for corruption. Disraeli seems to have felt that there were groups naturally part of the Conservative interest in the countryside, men who looked to the landowners with respect and admiration, who would help the Conservative Party if enfranchised. Even more insistent in the minds of these two men was their determination to maintain and increase the coalitions in the general population that lay behind their two parties. Complicating the whole situation was the fact that the Premier in 1867, Disraeli, actually commanded only a minority in Commons. The Reform Bill of 1867 was in fact everybody's business, amendments and counteramendments arising from all sides of the House, so that it is impossible to be certain of its authorship. When Disraeli astonished everyone by switching to a limited form of household suffrage, thus increasing the numbers of people to be enfranchised, he was simply accepting an amendment offered by an obscure member of Commons. When Gladstone offered amendment after amendment that transformed this proposal into a genuine household suffrage arrangement, was he sincere in his efforts, or merely challenging the ever-mocking and elusive Disraeli, and finding to his alarm that Disraeli was indeed ready to go the whole way? The record is equivocal. As Cowling observes, the material available "can be read either way."[6]

Two events seem to have moved Gladstone firmly and finally leftward in this embroglio. When a group of Liberals —the so-called Cave of Adullam—violently opposed his first moderate movements in 1866 in the direction of reform, Gladstone moved toward broader reform to make certain that the Liberal Party in the country would not lose its emerging hold on the working classes. When Disraeli's own bill in 1867 went even further than he had in enfranchising the masses, thus endangering his left again, he was driven toward ever more generous reform proposals, almost, Cowling believes, in a fit of irritation and impatience. Both Gladstone and Disraeli were scrambling for a solid majority in the country at large, Disraeli in a desperate bid to make his party the majority party after thirty years in the wilderness, Gladstone in an equally determined effort to retain Liberal/ Whig control. He was successful. In the election of 1868, the voters, unbeguiled by Disraeli, gave the Liberals a large majority and thereby elevated Gladstone to the premiership for his first and greatest ministry, the famous reform ministry of 1868–74.[7]

There is little reason to doubt that Gladstone, for all his qualifications, was sincere in his great utterances in these years. He was coming to place a great deal of faith in the moral wholeness of the common English people, and increasingly less in that of the upper classes. As he said in 1866, "we cannot look, and we hope no man will look, upon [a wider franchise] as upon some Trojan horse, approaching the walls of the sacred city, and filled with armed men, bent upon ruin, plunder, and conflagration."[8] Is it really true, he asked in Liverpool,

---

[6] Maurice Cowling, *1867 Disraeli, Gladstone and Revolution: The Passing of the Second Reform Bill* (Cambridge, England, 1967), p. 333.
[7] For an example of a vigorously anti-Gladstone interpretation, cf. Gertrude Himmelfarb, "The Politics of Democracy: The English Reform Act of 1867," *The Journal of British Studies*, VI, 97–138. Unlike Cowling, Himmelfarb finds Disraeli holding a sincere faith in the soundness of the whole nation and therefore of the common people, and Gladstone desperately trying to fight off major enfranchisements.
[8] Speech, Commons, March 12, 1866, in Gladstone, *Speeches on Parliamentary Reform in 1866*, pp. 60–1.

that the best we can look for . . . is to see gathered together a small and privileged class within the fortified precincts of what we call the Constitution, and outside of it the huge toiling masses of the community, who are to be regarded . . . as an invading army?[9]

He had come to the view that the ordinary man had both the intellectual capacity to understand great issues and the moral character to act rightly upon them. When he spoke to his audiences, he assumed that they were serious and reflective. His speeches moved freely over all areas of statecraft, as if they were given on the floor of Commons itself. Faced with an unexpectedly large gathering at a railway station in Perth as he returned from giving a brief speech in the town in 1879, he mounted a small platform and launched into a detailed discussion of foreign affairs even though he had to compete with the clangor and bustle of a trainyard. As he said, "gentlemen, though you are a vast assembly, meeting here in circumstances of some inconvenience, and though the subject is one not free from difficulty, I have so much reliance on your intelligence as well as upon your patience, that I am confident you will clearly understand what I want to convey to you."[1] His whole career after 1860 is testimony to the assumption that he was sincere in such statements. In the most literal sense, he went to the people.

When he did so, he gave them the sense that they were being invited to join him in making moral judgments on public events of worldwide importance. He appealed confidently to a sense of compassion he was sure was in them—and which, perhaps, they therefore felt. The ordinary man standing in Gladstone's audiences was made to feel as though he had become a classless man, a disinterested man, a moral agent in the world. "To make a man in this sense a God is an object of all great art, and Gladstone never lost this power."[2]

Public adulation moved him deeply and gave him strength and self-esteem. Lonely among politicians, and con-

[9] Speech, Liverpool, April 6, 1866, ibid., pp. 79–80.
[1] London *Times*, Dec. 2, 1879.
[2] Hammond, *Gladstone and the Irish Nation*, p. 706.

vinced that the spirit of justice was in the common people, Gladstone found joy and peace in their cheers. "It is clear from his diaries that Gladstone sat back in his carriage with a confidence and a spirit immensely strengthened and encouraged by the friendship of a thousand unknown faces . . ."[3]

With Gladstone finally at the head of the Liberal Party, the full tide of Gladstonian Liberalism could begin. Confident that the doctrines of Adam Smith would solve the problem of poverty, Gladstonians thenceforth were fundamentally interested not in the economic reforms that absorbed later generations of Liberals, but in wiping away the institutional arrangements that embodied and symbolized the superior status and power of the Anglican, English, and aristocratic ascendancy. Donald Southgate, noting that Gladstonian Liberalism was most of all concerned with matters involving social status, described it as tending

> to loosen the control of superiors over inferiors, to threaten established churches, to erode landlord privileges, to imperil the political predominance of the aristocracy. It was far less sharply differentiated than Whiggism from the more robust and positively democratic and decidedly anti-aristocratic creed of Bright, whom Gladstone admitted into the cabinet. Not without reason did the *avant-garde* of the intelligentsia, and working class leaders impregnated with the seeds of middle class Radicalism, look with hope to Gladstone as the parliamentary champion of Progress.[4]

The Gladstone government of 1868–74 was the first of the modern governments in Britain. It came to office not just to administer, and perhaps to legislate a reform as strong public pressure for particular steps bore in upon Parliament, but to enact a sweeping program. Strong in talented ministers, led by a Premier at the peak of his powers, and moved by a conviction that there surged behind them all the "social forces" of which Gladstone had spoken, this government went far to transform British life. Mass common education at the elementary levels was for the first time created by the

[3] Ibid., pp. 708–9.
[4] Southgate, *Passing of the Whigs*, pp. 324–35.

Forster Education Act of 1870, so that literacy was no longer a monopoly of class; civil service was extended; Oxford and Cambridge were opened to men of all faiths; the army was virtually restructured, largely ending its existence as a preserve of the aristocracy; the court system was reorganized, bringing order out of chaotic, overlapping jurisdictions; and in a milestone event that reshaped British politics, voting was made secret by the Ballot Act of 1872.

To Gladstone's mind, the premiership that came to him in 1868, and again in 1880, in 1885, and in 1892, was given to him by God for two great purposes. One of these lay in foreign affairs, where he felt that his primary task was to awaken and keep alive an English conscience.[5] The United Kingdom, he wrote the Queen at the outset of his administration, must at long last retreat from the flamboyant contentiousness bred into her by her solitary twenty-year struggle against Napoleon. That struggle had led her to believe she had unlimited resources, responsibilities, and rights to glory. In this spirit, she had spent the succeeding half-century cherishing her lonely eminence and intervening almost at will in local problems throughout the world.

The time had now come to begin using England's credit and power more thriftily. The government must begin working for a *common* European public opinion that would achieve the objectives Britain had been seeking to win by unilateral action. Cooperation and mutual action, not irritating demonstrations of pride and power, must be the new order.[6] Thus Gladstone insisted on arbitrating the American *Alabama* claims, and he accepted the arbiter's judgment despite protests from those whose sense of national pride was offended.

His other great task, as he saw it, lay in taking up the crusade upon which Edmund Burke had labored so long: ending English misrule in Ireland. In these years, when the fight over Irish reform was at its most arduous, he came to read Burke almost daily, confiding to his diary, "what a

[5] Hammond, *Gladstone and the Irish Nation*, p. 164.
[6] Gladstone to General Grey (the Queen's Secretary), April 17, 1869, in Morley, *Gladstone*, II, 316–18.

magazine of wisdom on Ireland and America . . . *sometimes almost divine*." As he wrote to a friend in 1884, "I venerate and almost worship him . . . I would he were now alive . . ."[7]

Ireland had been on his mind for many years. After an 1845 visit in France with Guizot, during which he learned with dismay how the English treatment of Ireland looked to Europeans, he wrote to his wife, "Ireland! Ireland! that cloud in the west, that coming storm, the minister of God's retribution upon cruel and inveterate and but half-atoned injustice!"[8] It was his habit of mind, however, to ignore great problems until it became clear that public opinion was aroused to them, so that they had come within the range of what he liked to call "practical politics." He let the Irish problem stay at the back of his consciousness while in the 1840's and 1850's he carried through the long remaking of British economic policy, and then turned to securing a wider franchise in the 1860's. After the Reform of 1867, he felt that a new force—the mass vote and the compassion of the common man—had been brought into public life that would allow him finally to deal with the Irish question. At the same time, a violent outbreak of Irish protest against the Church of Ireland thoroughly awakened public opinion to the Irish problem.

The new direction his mind was taking was revealed in a speech he gave in Southport during the 1867 campaign, when there was great anger at a recent outrage of the Fenians. Gladstone warned his hearers not to confuse Fenianism with the whole of the Irish people. Ireland, he said, had real grievances, and it was the British duty to remove them.[9] When the message came to him in 1868 that the Queen planned to appoint him Premier, he was chopping down a tree—his favorite recreation—on the grounds of his estate at Hawarden. "After a few minutes the blows ceased, and Mr. Gladstone

---

[7] Morley, *Gladstone*, III, 280; Gladstone to G. W. E. Russell, Oct. 13, 1884, in Lathbury, *Correspondence on Church and Religion*, II, 326.
[8] Hammond, *Gladstone and the Irish Nation*, p. 68; Gladstone to his wife, Oct. 12, 1845, in Lathbury, *Correspondence on Church and Religion*, II, 265–6.
[9] Hammond, *Gladstone and the Irish Nation*, pp. 80–1.

resting on the handle of his axe, looked up and with deep earnestness in his voice and with great intensity in his face, exclaimed, 'My mission is to pacify Ireland.' "[1]

He began with no experience of Ireland, and with no real knowledge of its problems, only a sense of shame. His importance as a British leader in these years, in fact, was that he was capable of feeling disgraced about Ireland. To an extraordinary degree he had acquired the capacity to look at Ireland "not as England but as Europe saw her."[2]

The judgment of Western civilization weighed on his mind with painful force. "Go into the length and breadth of the world," he asked in 1886, "ransack the literature of all countries, find if you can a single voice, a single book, in which the conduct of England towards Ireland is anywhere treated except with profound and bitter condemnation."[3] What would future historians say of the British Empire, he wondered in 1884. They "will say that in that history there was one chapter of disgrace, and that chapter of disgrace was the treatment of Ireland."[4]

The principal barrier to his proposed reforms lay in the English mind—and here his faith in the compassion of the common man was first severely tested. Ireland's ills in a real sense were the product of English prejudices, English fears, English misconceptions. As Charles Stewart Parnell said to his brother after encountering harsh prejudice at Cambridge even though he was a Protestant, "These English despise us because we are Irish."[5]

The emotional barriers between Ireland and England grew worse as the years passed. After mid-century, Irish economic distress worsened, and the Irish reacted by violent attacks on landlords and their agents who were demanding increased rent payments or seeking evictions. Lawlessness became a way of life in Ireland. The Irish developed a callous life style in which cruel men were praised and admired. Like many Negroes in the United States in the 1960's, the

---

[1] Morley, *Gladstone*, II, 252.
[2] Hammond, *Gladstone and the Irish Nation*, p. 48.
[3] Morley, *Gladstone*, III, 340.
[4] Ibid., III, 40.
[5] Hammond, *Gladstone and the Irish Nation*, p. 149.

Irish felt imprisonment was no embarrassment. Those jailed for violations of law were looked upon not as felons but as prisoners of war.

While the Irish displayed all the traits of victimization, the English were growing more convinced of the righteousness of authority. The very lawlessness and violence of the Irish, resorted to in a desperate attempt to obtain social justice, made the English even less disposed to grant it. In Commons the Irish members thought of Ireland in terms of evictions; the English thought of the murders, burnings, sheep killing, and riots. "Each side thought the other callous, and every debate on coercion soon passed beyond the short reach of reason."[6] Gladstone found coercion in any form— from child rearing to religious belief—distasteful, and regarded even

> the briefest suspension of ordinary liberties [in Ireland] repugnant, [requiring] atonement . . . But to many a Whig the Crimes Act regime was more creditable to the British Government than preceding dispensations . . . when violence and intimidation reigned. The insubordination of the Irish, so far from calling for the grant of self-government, increased reluctance to consider it.[7]

Since everything authoritative in the English temperament reacted in anger to everything rebellious in the Irish character, Gladstone was indispensable to the Irish cause. When the Irish problem finally came fully before the English people, it was essential that the issues be brought before them by a man "so powerful and resolute that he could move and hold the imagination of the English people and force new and strange views upon them."[8]

The first step he took was to disestablish the Church of Ireland. It had never fulfilled, he said in Parliament, nor would it ever fulfill in the future, the objects of a religious establishment. It was not the national church, for only one Irishman out of nine belonged to it. It was not the church of

6 Hammond, *Gladstone and the Irish Nation*, p. 293.
7 Southgate, *Passing of the Whigs*, p. 405.
8 Hammond, *Gladstone and the Irish Nation*, p. 65.

the poor, for its members owned nine tenths of Ireland. It was certainly no longer serving any missionary function, for its share of the Irish population had steadily dwindled over more than a century. The only purpose it served, indeed, was to keep alive "the remembrance of bitter animosities, and . . . the principle of religious inequality and religious ascendancy."[9] It was the sign and badge of the Anglican Ascendancy in Ireland, an ascendancy Gladstone attacked with the same passion Burke had shown.

> I decline entirely [he said] . . . to draw a distinction between this and that religious persuasion; to cover one with privileges and to doom the other to exclusion, in order that the minority may be liable to the reproach of purchased loyalty, while the mass of the people may see themselves condemned to be held in less estimation.[1]

After a hard fight stretching over several months, Gladstone won this campaign. He then turned to consider that festering sore of Irish life, the land problem. Its origins lay in the eighteenth century, when the government eliminated peasant ownership by the penal laws and allowed enormous holdings to pass into the hands of a relatively small group of Protestants, the objective being to duplicate the English agricultural system. In the English system, landlords coordinated production over large areas and furnished the capital needed to prepare land for production and equip it with facilities. Tenant farmers provided only their labor. In Ireland, however, the landowners generally did not furnish capital, taking only the land and demanding rents. Drainage, the building of cottages, the provision of equipment—all had to come from the tenant. At the end of his agreement, he could be evicted with no compensation, and the land, now more valuable, turned over to a new tenant at a higher rent.[2]

In the nineteenth century, furthermore, most landowners decided to clear their land entirely of tenants in order to

---

[9] Speech, Commons, April 30, 1868, *Hansard,* Third Series, CXCI, 1651.
[1] Ibid., p. 1664.
[2] This and the following discussion is drawn from Hammond, *Gladstone and the Irish Nation, passim.*

allow for more profitable sheep culture. After the potato famine of the 1840's, the government aided the clearance process further by wiping out entirely such rights as tenants still possessed—except in Protestant Ulster—and stimulating hundreds of thousands of evictions. Lord Palmerston, himself an Irish landowner, coined the hated slogan: "Tenant's right is landlord's wrong." By the 1870's, in consequence, much of Ireland was torn by disorder.

In his Land Act of 1870, Gladstone gave all of Ireland the rights that Ulster tenants possessed, that of compensation for improvements and disturbance in the case of eviction. Furthermore, in a first step toward modifying the rigid law of contract and the rights of property, the ordinary courts were empowered to fix rents where they were "exorbitant." The act, however, was ineffective, for the courts usually ruled in the landlord's favor. The depression of the 1870's made it impossible for thousands of tenants to pay their rents, many evictions were made, and social disorder increased alarmingly.

In 1881, during his second ministry, Gladstone presented to Commons the revolutionary proposal—one that in effect ended the idea that property rights were absolute—that a Land Court be established to have complete control over rents, compensation, and all other differences between landlords and tenants. He frankly admitted that this was

> a great departure from the principles of free contract . . . It is, if I may say so, the one really Radical proposal in this Bill . . . I do not disguise it. But I ask you to observe this— . . . it is required by the circumstances of the country . . .[3]

It was impossible to legislate for Ireland any longer, he insisted, on theoretical grounds of *laissez faire* and free contract. One of the royal commissioners had proposed that this be done—"exactly," Gladstone acidly observed, "as if he had proposed to legislate for the inhabitants of Saturn or Jupiter" —but it was clearly out of the question. Steps had to be taken to establish "something like equal justice in Ireland," for there

[3] Speech, Commons, April 7, 1881, *Hansard*, Third Series, CCLX, 60.

were too many "harsh and grasping and even cruel landlords who, though few in proportion to the whole, have it fatally in their power to compromise the best interests of other men." It was certainly absurd to expect that rents could be fairly established in the market place when there was land scarcity and land hunger. Similarly, social disorder was inevitable when evictions without regard for improvements were made.[4]

After an arduous struggle, his Land Act of 1881 was enacted, and the peasant proprietary was inaugurated that eventually came to form the foundation of Irish agriculture, thereby making the Irish countryside much more similar to that of Denmark or France than to that of England.

By now Gladstone was thoroughly hated by the aristocracy. Their distaste for him had begun in the 1850's, with his inauguration of inheritance and land taxes and his talk of a "poor man's budget."[5] As reform followed reform, most of them striking at Anglican and aristocratic privileges, their resentment swelled into hatred. It was Gladstone who inaugurated civil service, thus ending the dispensing of patronage, a prized source of aristocratic power and prestige. His nationalizing of Oxford and Cambridge opened them to all Britons and at the same time thoroughly reorganized them. In 1860 his humiliation of the Lords over the paper duty and in 1868 his termination of mandatory tithing to the Church of England, combined with his dramatic swing to the masses and the events of his great reform ministry of 1868–74, made the estrangement permanent.

It was not until 1876, however, that Gladstone began to use as violent language on the upper classes as they used on him. In that year he suddenly seemed to find the enemy. Through almost forty-five years of public life, his speeches had been remarkably impersonal and high-minded. Like Burke's, they showed a concern with generalized problems of unspecified location, such as misinformation, harmful passions, and misconceptions. They were not those of a man who saw a great social enemy to be attacked and subdued. But

[4] Ibid., pp. 585–609, 890–926.
[5] Morley, *Gladstone*, I, 463; Southgate, *Passing of the Whigs*, pp. 298–9.

after the mid-1870's, he became a social critic of near-Jeffersonian harshness.

The cause of this transformation was the massacre of tens of thousands of Christian men, women, and children in Bulgaria by the Turkish government, and the apparent indifference of Disraeli and his Tory administration to this event. Disraeli seemed concerned only to prevent Russia from displacing Turkey as overlord of the Balkans, in the guise of protector of the Christians.

A large part of the nation was outraged, and Gladstone, reacting either to the public excitement or to his own inner feelings—the matter is in some dispute[6]—burst out against the Tories. He insisted that the time had come to recognize the distinct national groups in the Balkan Peninsula and to give them self-rule. Neither Turkey nor Russia should any longer scramble over these territories. The national groups should instead be allowed to join the family of nations, with a common European protection of their independence.

He was aroused most of all by the atrocities, however, and made almost frantic by a conviction that Britain should launch a great effort to get the Turk entirely out of the Balkans—the eastern outpost, in his mind, of Christian civilization. He dashed off a violent pamphlet, the sale of which mounted swiftly to the hundreds of thousands of copies, attacking the Turks as "the one great anti-human specimen of humanity." Then came the famous words:

> Let the Turks now carry away their abuses in the only possible manner, namely by carrying off themselves. Their Zaptiehs and their Mudirs, their Bimbashis and their Yuzbashis, their Kaimakams and their Pashas, one and all, bag and baggage, shall I hope clear out from the province they have desolated and profaned.[7]

It is clear from R. T. Shannon's account of this dramatic year that the Bulgarian crisis had long been in the making.

[6] R. T. Shannon takes the view that Gladstone was a tardy convert to the cause, joining it because it gave him a new opportunity to establish a vital relationship with the masses again. Cf. his *Gladstone and the Bulgarian Agitation 1876.*
[7] Morley, *Gladstone*, II, 553–4; Magnus, *Gladstone*, pp. 241–2.

For years Dissenters—the Methodists, the Congregationalists, the Baptists, and the other Protestant sects of Nonconformity —had been swept by evangelical revival campaigns. By the 1870's, the Nonconformist mentality had reached such a state of excitement that England had become "a religious society in a deeper and completer sense than any western country since the Reformation."[8] A "taut Victorian conscience" was created, ready to break out in quite the same way, one surmises, as did the intensely excited religious mind of the "Burned-Over District" in western New York in the 1830's and 1840's when it boiled over into the crusade to abolish slavery.[9] The Turks provided for Nonconformity the enemy that slavery and the South had provided for the American "ultras." Gladstone told a visiting deputation that the English sympathy for the Bulgarians was the same sympathy that had ended in the emancipation of the Negro.[1]

In the heat of this campaign, Gladstone and Dissent finally formed their lasting partnership. It was far more than a marriage of convenience. Gladstone's deepest religious convictions were mirrored in those of Nonconformity, and the entente had been in the making since Gladstone's swing to the masses in the 1860's. At that time he began removing the badges of the Dissenters' social inferiority. Now, in the 1870's, the enthusiastic response of Dissenting audiences to his appeals on the Bulgarian issue convinced him he was right in believing that the masses were morally superior to the aristocracy. From this time onward his social contacts with Dissenters became close and continuing, and their political support of him devoted and enduring.[2] The tone of this commitment is clear in the remarks of the *Congregationalist*, which even before the Bulgarian agitation got underway observed warmly of him:

> the nonconformists of this country have long cherished a
> loyalty more fervent [toward Gladstone], we are inclined

[8] Shannon, *Gladstone and the Bulgarian Agitation*, p. 28.
[9] Cf. Whitney R. Cross, *The Burned-Over District* (Cornell, 1950), *passim*.
[1] Shannon, *Gladstone and the Bulgarian Agitation*, p. 30.
[2] Ibid., pp. 162–4; Morley, *Gladstone*, II, 134.

to imagine, than that with which he has been regarded by any other section of the community. He, beyond all other modern statesmen, with perhaps here and there a doubtful exception, gave us the impression of a man who regarded politics as a part of Christian duty.[3]

The aristocracy in general opposed Gladstone on the "Eastern Question." Lord Hartington, now the official leader of the Liberals in Commons since Gladstone had "retired" after his 1874 defeat, tried to dissuade him, saying he would hate to see public opinion worked up to a point where that question overpowered everything else. Even many Radicals were still influenced by the Palmerston tradition, and so distrusted Russia that they were willing to go along with Disraeli. Intellectuals of the older John Stuart Mill, humanitarian tradition supported Gladstone, but many of the younger ones, Darwinists who scoffed at the Gospel and talked of superior races and the benign uses of power in the hands of great nations, turned away from him. What eventually became Liberal Imperialism would seem to have had its first baptism of fire in this agitation.[4]

Gladstone, in turn, began lashing out with invective that permanently embittered British political life. The "upper ten thousand," he said, constantly resisted everything that was right and good. "When did the Upper Ten Thousand ever lead the attack in the cause of humanity? Their heads are always full of class interest and the main chance."[5] In 1878, when the Russians attacked Turkey and Gladstone approved their action on the ground that the European powers in general had shirked their duty, he was hooted by members of Parliament, his windows were broken by a mob, the Court openly refused to shake hands, and the Duke of Sutherland publicly described him as a Russian agent.[6]

Gladstone, however, was not to be intimidated. He now began to attack the Tory mind in a way that expressed not

[3] *Congregationalist,* February 1875, quoted in Morley, *Gladstone,* II, 505–6.
[4] Southgate, *Passing of the Whigs,* pp. 357–8; Shannon, *Gladstone and the Bulgarian Agitation,* pp. 171–237.
[5] Magnus, *Gladstone,* p. 245; Morley, *Gladstone,* II, 557.
[6] Magnus, *Gladstone,* pp. 246–9.

only his fundamentally Augustinian outlook upon life but also the deepest and most persistent element in the Liberal image of the enemy. The Tory, Gladstone said, was in his heart a bully. He loved to dominate. He craved authoritative power, always identified with those at the top, and more than anything else wanted to experience the thrill of exerting his will over others. The "sympathies of British Toryism," Gladstone observed in an 1879 magazine article, "have regularly gravitated to the side of power . . ." Under Disraeli, he said, the Tories had gone all over the world forcing weaker peoples to give in to their will, most notably in South Africa and in Afghanistan. In the latter country, their machinations were being challenged by the equally autocratic Russians, and "We shall now see how the genuine bully can crouch before his equal . . ." "Such language as this," observed the shocked *Times,* "is happily new in our political controversies . . ."[7]

Preparations were now underway for Gladstone to launch his famous Midlothian campaign, which ever after captured the imagination of Liberals, figuring in their historical memories as the "coming of age" of Liberal politics. It was in these dramatic days that the young Scottish nobleman Lord Rosebery emerged as a national figure of high importance, for his role as Gladstone's intimate associate and patron in the campaign elevated him to pre-eminence among Scottish Liberals. "The passions aroused by the . . . Midlothian campaign," Robert Rhodes James remarks, "did not abate for a decade . . ." For the first time a leading British statesman of Premier rank went to the people in an extended oratorical campaign, and after months of speechmaking before tumultuous crowds turned out the sitting government. The nature of British political life was thereafter permanently changed.[8]

The Midlothian campaign took place in November and December of 1879 and in March and April of 1880. It involved scores of major and minor addresses and many skillfully staged mass rallies based on Rosebery's witnessing of a

[7] W. E. Gladstone, "The Friends and Foes of Russia," *The Nineteenth Century* (January 1879), pp. 168–92; London *Times,* Jan. 1, 1879.
[8] James, *Rosebery,* pp. 88–102; Robert Kelley, "Midlothian: A Study in Politics and Ideas," *Victorian Studies,* IV (1960), 119–40.

Democratic political campaign in New York. Tens of thousands of Englishmen and Scotsmen rushed to catch a glimpse of the great man as he stopped briefly to give speeches at railroad stations and hotels, or to cheer again and again during his long orations.

Gladstone's strategy was to present a connected series of addresses, each of them dealing with a separate topic, that would in sum present a comprehensive discussion of the whole range of public policy. As he wrote to Rosebery beforehand, it was his plan to make the whole series of speeches comprise his attack against the government. He would discuss domestic issues in detail, and then make an indictment of the government in its foreign affairs "everywhere!"[9]

In speech after speech he dwelt at great length on taxation, land, Ireland, and free trade. He attacked Disraeli's government for having established a whole system of government that was destructive to the nation and its best interests. This system, he said, was fundamentally authoritarian and illiberal, constituting in reality a covert subversion of parliamentary government. The ministry acted wilfully, on its own initiative, and misled the Commons by deceit or by silence. Its unsettling policies at home and abroad were so profligate and unpredictable that businessmen could not arrange their affairs. Taxation drained them of the funds needed to bring about recovery from the long depression into which the nation had plunged almost as soon as Disraeli took office in 1874.

Gladstone was harshest in his denunciation of the government's conduct of foreign affairs. The Tories, he said, centered their whole regime on base appeals to national pride and passion. These disfiguring emotions, once aroused, made the nation so irrational that it unthinkingly supported an autocratic and imperious policy abroad. The United Kingdom must above all, he insisted, reorient its foreign policy and restore the fundamental principles of peaceful international relations. Expressing ideas remarkably parallel to the values most prominent within minority-group politics, Gladstone called

[9] Letter, Gladstone to Lord Rosebery, Nov. 14, 1879, in Rosebery Papers, National Library of Scotland, Box #18.

upon the British people to return to what he described as the most fundamental and necessary of all assumptions in foreign affairs, the equality of nations. Throughout his assertions on foreign policy he constantly returned to this theme: the world was essentially a community of equal states, and its principles of interaction should be those that were applied between the citizens of an enlightened nation. Humankind constituted a family, he insisted, and Britain was just one of its more fortunate members. She was no more entitled to claim special privileges or special immunities than would be the members of a domestic family or the citizens in a nation. As he said at West Calder, "nations are knitted one to another in the bonds of right, a bond without distinction of great and small; . . . there is equality between them, the same sacredness defending the narrow limits of Belgium as attaches to the extended frontiers of Russia, of Germany, or of France." Without strict adherence to this principle, he warned, not only would British safety be endangered, so also would be "the best and most fundamental interests of Christian society." Without equality there could be "no such thing as public right, and without public international right there is no other instrument for settling the transactions of mankind except material force."[1]

A vital concern in the world community, he said in a classically Burkeian utterance, was the building of a system of public law, the most sacred duty of any government. The Tories, he said, had wantonly ignored this duty. The Treaty of Paris, for example, had ended the Crimean War in part by stipulating that no single power was thenceforth to deal with a Turkish problem, as the Russians had sought to do in 1853. Yet the Tories had violated this principle by their single-handed attempt in 1876 to hold back Russia in the Balkans.[2]

Even worse, they had made the Anglo-Turkish Convention, which was "one of the grossest breaches of the public law of Europe that ever has been put upon record."[3] While the powers had been gathered in Berlin in 1878 to settle the Turkish matter properly, Disraeli had unilaterally devised

[1] London *Times*, Nov. 28, 1879.
[2] London *Times*, Dec. 6, 1879.
[3] London *Times*, March 19, 1880.

this separate agreement with Turkey. Furthermore, he had done it secretly, "not in the light of day, but in the darkness of the night, not in the knowledge and cognizance of other powers." If international relations were to be peaceable, diplomacy must be carried on in the open, so that all powers had the opportunity of observing and preparing their own policy. As it was, the convention was an arrogant declaration, he said, that Britain was specially privileged.[4]

"In the principles of foreign policy, gentlemen, as I have professed them from my youth," he said, "it is a cardinal article that we are to set up no claim for ourselves which we do not allow to others, and that all who depart from that principle are committing treason against public law and the peace and order of the world." When the Tories took Cyprus and other territories with the justification that they were simply safeguarding the route to India, they were saying that a

> little island at one end of the world, having possessed itself of an enormous possession at the other end of the world, is entitled to say with respect to every land and every sea lying between its own shores and any part of that enormous possession, that it . . . has a preferential right to the possession or control of that intermediate territory in order, as it is called, to safe-guard the road to India . . . This, gentlemen, is a monstrous claim.[5]

No nation should take major international steps unilaterally. Multilateralism in all great matters was essential to everyone's security, for in this way you "neutralize and fetter and bind up the selfish aims of each." Common action was fatal to selfish aims; it would lead to common objects, and these common objects would lead to the common good of all.[6] The highest embodiment of this ideal, the true agency to which all nations should appeal, was what he repeatedly called the "Concert of Europe." The concert, or what he else-where called "the united authority of Europe," and then more sweepingly "the united authority of the civilized world," was

[4] London *Times*, Nov. 28, 1879.
[5] London *Times*, Dec. 6, 1879.
[6] London *Times*, Nov. 28, 1879.

the proper body to deal with great questions. "Modern times," he said, "have established a sisterhood of nations."[7]

In such a world community the true basis for all foreign policy should be a compassionate attitude of mind—an attitude, he said, that Disraeli's appeal to pride and dominance could never create. The British people should learn to view the actions of other nations not jealously but with understanding. The human family must be judged with the same indulgence men applied to their own country. Above all, Britons should look upon war in a new way. They should care about what happens to their human brethren on the other side of the lines. They should take to their hearts the real meaning of the universality of human experience. Britain's burden of guilt, he said to an audience largely of women gathered in Foresters' Hall in Dalkeith, was the result of having deluged many a hill and valley with blood. The Zulus had done no more than would patriotic Britons, for they were defending their own country. In Afghanistan, the wanton attack launched by Disraeli's government had spread wild destruction. In a famous utterance, he warned:

> Remember that the rights of those savages, as we may call them, and the sanctity of life among the hill tribes, and the happiness of their humble homes amid the winter snows . . . are as sacred in the eyes of Almighty God as are your own. Remember that He who has united you together as human beings of the same flesh and blood, has bound you in mutual love, and that mutual love is not limited by the shores of this country, nor limited by the boundaries of Christian civilization; that it passes over the wide surface of the earth, and embraces the meanest as well as the greatest in its wide scope.[8]

War was in some circumstances necessary, he said. One kind of war, the war for liberty, was not just acceptable, it was a duty. When he had been Prime Minister in 1870, he said, he had taken steps to fight France or Germany if either attacked Belgium, as for a time appeared possible. He justi-

[7] London *Times*, Nov. 28, 1879.
[8] London *Times*, Nov. 27, 1879.

fied his steps on the ground that "we should have gone to war for public right, we should have gone to war to save human happiness from being invaded by tyrannous and lawless power. That is what I call a good cause, gentlemen."[9]

Britain had a great mission, which was to spread freedom in the world. But what had the Tories done? "Gentlemen," he said in concluding an address in Glasgow, "amid the whole of this pestilent activity . . . this distress and bloodshed, which we have either produced or largely shared in producing, not in one instance . . . did we either do a deed or speak an effectual word on behalf of liberty."[1] The most glorious pages in the history of British diplomacy, he said, were those concerned with the creation of the kingdom of Belgium, and the unifying of the disjoined provinces of Italy.[2] Therefore the real friends of Britain were the small countries of Europe, where liberty was strongest and where, also, the danger of invasion by autocratic power was the greatest. These nations looked to the Liberals with approval, while the great empires frowned on them.[3] The advance of freedom, he insisted, was the most real kind of progress imaginable. By ending suffering and shame, by uprooting slavery, by giving security to life, property, and honor, "you accomplish a great, blessed work."[4]

There would be constant unrest until the Tories of the world recognized that nationalism was an unquenchable fire. National groups must be allowed to govern themselves. How absurd it was, he asserted, for Turkey and Russia and Austria to be haggling over control of the provinces in the Balkans, for in the long run the push of emerging nationalism would have its way. The succession in these nations must eventually pass "to the people of those countries, to those who have inhabited them for the many long centuries."[5] This was because, as he said elsewhere, the most powerful force that

[9] London *Times*, March 18, 1880.
[1] London *Times*, Dec. 6, 1879.
[2] London *Times*, Nov. 28, 1879.
[3] W. E. Gladstone, *Midlothian Campaign: Political Speeches Delivered in November and December 1879 and March and April 1880* (Edinburgh, 1880), pp. 75, 90.
[4] London *Times*, Dec. 1, 1879.
[5] London *Times*, Dec. 1, 1879.

acted upon the peoples of the world, aside from religion, was nationalism.[6]

What Gladstone was calling for was a pluralistic world, rather than a world divided up between three or four monolithic empires. Implicit in his appeals was the view that the world should enjoy its diversity of tongues and nationalities, each of them equal in status and in law, all treasured for their unique share of the human spirit. It had to be a world, however, in which there was a sense of community, a sense that would bind people together in friendliness. It was the highest responsibility of governments to foster these feelings. A Briton of what Gladstone would term the Tory mentality would look coolly on the fallen forms of Zulus and Afghans, for they were not, emotionally speaking, part of his world. But a Briton fully aroused to a sense of brotherhood would share the suffering of his fellows and would avoid violence.

Universalism and inclusiveness, as always, were the Gladstonian keynotes. He always explained by reference to the larger picture, by including all things within an interdependent whole. For this reason, the campaign was a powerful and concentrated attack against exclusiveness, against denial of the equality and the unity of mankind.

After the Midlothian campaign came to its climax, the Tories were swept from office, bringing in the troubled Gladstone government of 1880–5. The story of this unhappy government is well known. Gladstone made serious errors of judgment; Bismarck and others scoffed at his idealism; and his foreign policy proved more difficult to apply than to describe. After he made the shocking mistake of authorizing intervention in Egypt to "restore order," his administration was practically destroyed by the subsequent warfare and ever deepening involvement this decision entailed in just the same way that, almost a hundred years later, Lyndon Johnson's administration was destroyed by the war in Vietnam. So se-

[6] Gladstone, *Midlothian*, p. 61.

verely did Gladstone's Egyptian policy violate Gladstonian precepts in foreign policy that John Bright in despair resigned from the ministry, and many other Liberals turned away from their chief in anger.

Gladstone's two accomplishments in his second ministry were the Irish Land Act of 1881 and the enfranchisement of the rural laboring class in 1884, a step that added two million voters to the existing three million. While the rural worker, he said, was perhaps too ready to follow the lead of his social superiors, "we are [yet] firm in the faith that enfranchisement is a good, that the people may be trusted—that the voters under the Constitution are the strength of the Constitution."[7]

The Reform Act of 1884 opened the last chapter of his career, for it gave the rural Irish masses a voice for the first time. Recognizing this, Gladstone warned in the electoral campaign of 1885 that if the Irish expressed themselves unequivocally in favor of Home Rule, then for all their determined objections to the proposal, the English would have to let all other subjects stand aside and give Home Rule its full day in court.[8] As Burke had said, only at their peril can governments defy the general feeling of great communities.

The result in Ireland was as he had predicted. Home Rule—that is, the Nationalist Party—secured fantastic majorities. In Cork, for example, 300 voters supported the Tories, 10,000 the Nationalists. "As a supreme electoral demonstration," John Morley wrote in 1903,

the Irish elections of 1885 have never been surpassed in any country. They showed that neither remedial measures nor repressive measures had made even the fleeting shadow of an impression on the tenacious sentiment of Ireland, or on the powerful organization that embodied and directed it. The Land Act had made no impression. The two Coercion

[7] Speech, Commons, Feb. 28, 1884, *Hansard*, Third Series, CCLXXXV, 106–34.
[8] Speech, Edinburgh, Nov. 9, 1885, in William Ewart Gladstone, *Speeches of the Right Hon. W. E. Gladstone, M.P., with a Sketch of His Life*, ed., Henry W. Lucy (London and New York, 1885), pp. 167–8. Hereafter cited as Lucy, *Speeches of the Right Hon. W. E. Gladstone*.

Acts had made none. The imperial parliament had done its best for five years [but Ireland still wanted Home Rule].[9]

Gladstone therefore began his last struggle, the struggle that split his party, sent the Chamberlain Radicals and the Whigs completely over to the Tories, and left the Liberals weak and distracted until their victory in 1906. At this distance of time it is difficult to recapture an understanding of how huge and unavoidable the Irish problem really was, and how inevitable that Gladstone should try to solve it. It concerned everyone in the Anglo-American world—and to a good extent elsewhere. American politics were affected by the violent demands of the Irish-Americans for aid to the home country. Ireland itself was practically in a state of insurrection year in and year out. Terrorism, murder, burnings, and widespread suffering disfigured Irish life. The British Parliament was all but brought to a standstill by the obstructionism of the Nationalists. There was really no avoiding the issue. As Algeria obsessed the world in the 1950's and Vietnam in the 1960's, Ireland drew all eyes in the 1880's.

Gladstone had enormous odds to fight. He was asking the English to forsake their Protestant fellows and hand Ireland over to the detested Irish Catholic masses. He expected the Whigs, who owned so much of Ireland, to trust to the mercies of an Irish parliament certain to be dominated by Irish tenants. In an increasingly tense European world where nations felt their safety absolutely depended on centralization, he advocated the breaking up of a centralized power. To men like John Bright, who was consumed with bitterness toward the Irish Nationalists because for years they had almost immobilized the House of Commons, and to Joseph Chamberlain, whose pride had been inflamed by Irish attacks, Gladstone asked the impossible. They were to trust Charles Stewart Parnell, to forget their contempt for the Nationalist M.P.'s and place the government of Ireland in their hands. Men who had tried for decades to govern Ireland according to English standards were to admit that they had been wrong. Gladstone was asking, in short, for justice for

[9] Morley, *Gladstone*, III, 254.

the most despised minority group in British life. Given the circumstances of British life, it was too great a request to make.

He made his appeal to Parliament in early April 1886. The time had come, he said, to recognize that governing Ireland from London had proved to be impossible. Repressive legislation, presumed to be temporary, had become permanent. Crime had become a way of life. Juries could not be formed, individual liberty was wiped away by intimidation on both sides, respect for law and contract was far gone—and the situation was growing worse. In spite of all efforts to enforce the law, it was "discredited in Ireland . . . in . . . that it comes to the people of that country with a foreign aspect, and in a foreign garb." Why not move finally, then, to the "comparatively natural and simple, though not always easy, expedient of stripping law of its foreign garb, and investing it with a domestic character?"[1]

People wanted to pass their own laws, he observed, no matter how enlightened were the laws that others were willing to pass for them. This was what the American Revolution had demonstrated. This was what the British had slowly learned to grant to the English-speaking colonies they still possessed. "Do not let us disguise this from ourselves," he urged. "We stand face to face with what is termed Irish nationality."

Irish nationalism, he went on, was not an evil; it was simply an unavoidable fact. The sixty-mile channel would never go away; the people of Ireland were a separate nation. "These, Sir, are great facts. I hold that there is such a thing as local patriotism, which, in itself, is not bad, but good." The Welsh, the Scots, the English themselves all possessed it, and it did not destroy their imperial patriotism, nor would it in Ireland provided that the Irish could enact all legislation having to do with purely local affairs. The only reason they had been disloyal in the past was that they had been ruled by alien laws. The English must now build unity not upon the power of coercion, which is illusory, but upon "the affections,

[1] Speech, Commons, April 8, 1886, *Hansard*, Third Series, CCCIV, 1036–51.

the convictions, and the will of the nation . . ."²

The House of Commons rejected his appeal, and he turned to the people. In his Home Rule Manifesto, issued for the election of 1886, he called on Britons to forget their prejudices, recognize Irish nationalism, and give him the majority he needed. By now, he was attacking the upper classes openly and bitterly. Who were the enemies of Home Rule, he asked?

> [They are] to be found, as I sorrowfully admit, in profuse abundance [in the world of] station, title, wealth, social influence, the professions, or the large majority of them—in a word, the spirit and power of Class. These are the main body of the opposing host.

These were the self-same opponents, he went on, who had fought free trade, free navigation, public education, religious equality, and a wider vote. On these and many other great issues the classes had fought uniformly on the wrong side, and had uniformly been beaten by a "power more difficult to marshal, but resistless when marshalled—by the upright sense of the nation."³

Wales and Scotland and Ireland went heavily for him in 1886, but England went heavily against him, and he lost. The ensuing years of Conservative coercion in Ireland, however, were so sickening that Gladstone was returned to the premiership in 1892 for one last effort. He rose again in the Commons to propose Home Rule, appealing once more to duty, to honor, and to equity. He pointed to the unanimous state of foreign and colonial opinion, and above all to the will and conviction of the Irish themselves. "Can you hope in these days," he asked, "to govern Ireland against the fixed convictions of the great mass of the nation? . . . Ireland is against you, Scotland is against you, Wales is against you," and even a near majority of the English had finally supported the plan.⁴

² Ibid., pp. 1052–85.
³ W. E. Gladstone, *Home Rule Manifesto: Address to the Electors of Midlothian*, May 1, 1886 (pamphlet; London, 1886).
⁴ Speech, Commons, April 21, 1893, *Hansard*, Fourth Series, XI, 992–1006.

What really lay behind all the resistance to Home Rule, he asked? It was fundamentally a prejudice against Irishmen.

> It amounts to this: that the Irish people are to be deliberately, and by this Parliament, depressed below the standard level of civilised mankind. That is the real explanation. What is [the Liberal Party's] mission? We have made it our mission, and, I rejoice to think, our glorious mission, to carry freedom, so far as we are able to do so, throughout the world.

They had given it to Britons in the colonies, even when the majority were convicts or the children of convicts, and the results had been happy indeed. The same graces had been given to a mass of Frenchmen in Canada, and to Dutchmen in Africa.

> But the Irishman! [The Irish were to be the exception, for it was said they would use the power wrongly,] and you deny to them not the name of men, but the proper consequences of the acknowledgment of that name.[5]

The cause of Home Rule, however, was lost. Commons this time passed the bill, but the Lords rejected it. It was by now clear to Gladstone, though not to his colleagues, that decreasing the power of the House of Lords had to be the next great item on the Liberal agenda, for the Lords had brought practically all reform to a standstill. It had become an almost totally reactionary body, to a degree incredible to twentieth-century eyes.

Gladstone first began talking of the need for organic reform of the Lords in the 1884 controversy over the reform bill of that year, initially thrown out by the Lords. When they quickly dismissed his Home Rule bill in 1893 after literally months of labor in Commons, and mutilated or defeated many other important bills, he renewed his proposals. Parliament should be dissolved, he said, and the issue of Lords reform debated in the ensuing campaign. His colleagues in

[5] Ibid., pp. 1004–5.

the cabinet disagreed, and he was left to push the issue on his own. The last speech he made in the House of Commons, given in 1894, was a vigorous assault on the House of Lords, and even "in my last conversation with him in 1897," John Morley wrote, "he held to his text that we ought to have dissolved [on the issue] . . ."[6]

After the Lords defeated Home Rule, Gladstone's government stumbled on for a time. He found himself faced within his cabinet with an urgent demand for major increases in expenditures for the navy, in light of what was felt to be the rising threat to British security in the form of growing navies abroad. He could not agree. He had become known, he said, not simply as a British but as a European statesman. "My name stands in Europe as a symbol of the policy of peace, moderation, and non-aggression." He had "uniformly opposed militarism," and he was determined not to relent.[7] The parting of the ways between the first and the second generation of Liberals had finally come, and Gladstone resigned on March 3, 1894, Lord Rosebery succeeding him as premier.

He had three more years of life. He lived long enough to see Joseph Chamberlain become Colonial Secretary in a Tory government, and to learn of the ill-fated Jameson Raid in South Africa, though not, happily, long enough to see the Boer War begin. Enough had happened, however, to give him a dark view of the future. The armaments race, he said in 1897, was certain to end in war. It was clear to him, he observed grimly, that the old fears of democracy and science had become obsolete. "Materialism and militarism," he said, will "be the Devil's agents during the twentieth century."[8]

In William Gladstone, the British nation received its Thomas Jefferson, its first chief executive whose enemy was the aristocracy and who became an internationally famous

[6] Morley, *Gladstone*, III, 124–39, 504–5, 511.
[7] Ibid., 507–8.
[8] Magnus, *Gladstone*, p. 432.

figure symbolizing liberal values. From the midpoint in his career—and even earlier—the ever mounting theme in his evangel, the resonant note that in time polarized British political life, was his attack on what he saw as the Tory mentality and all its works. Its prejudice, its distaste for and distrust of the common people; its instinctive reaching for the tools of coercion to enforce its will; its lust to dominate at home and abroad; its contempt for weakness and toadying to strength; its appetite for blood and its callousness to suffering; above all, its arrogance—these were the targets of Gladstone's apostolate. He was concerned primarily with the emotional facts of nineteenth-century life. The will to dominate, and the fears and distrusts it produced, should be replaced by compassion and cooperation. Self-respect should be achieved by equality of status in religion, in political functions, in opportunities for a just share in the dynamic economy, in the right of living not under alien laws and institutions but under one's own.

In all of this, the enemy was clearly perceived. As Gladstone put it at the end of his last address in Midlothian:

> Unfortunately we cannot make our appeal to the aristocracy . . . [except to the Liberal fragment among them]. With that exception in all the classes of which I speak, I am sorry to say we cannot reckon upon the aristocracy—we cannot reckon upon what is called the landed interest, we cannot reckon upon the clergy of the Established Church in either England or in Scotland . . . We cannot reckon on the wealth of the country, nor upon the rank of the country, nor upon the influence which rank and wealth usually bring. In the main these powers are against us, and there are other powers against us, for wherever there is a close corporation, wherever there is a spirit of organized monopoly, wherever there is a narrow and sectional interest apart from that of the country, and desiring to be set up above the interest of the public, there, gentlemen, we, the Liberal party, have no friendship and no tolerance to expect.[9]

Jeffersonian in his social criticism, Gladstone was Jeffersonian too in the confusing nature of his political legacy.

[9] Gladstone, *Midlothian*, p. 82.

Which Gladstone did one see? Was it the miserly Premier who pared away at every tiny expense and came to symbolize the penny-pinching policy of traditional *laissez faire* that condemned all government expenditures for social services? Or was it the flaming orator who encouraged the masses to think of the government as responsive to their desires, attacked the aristocracy, and insisted that entrenched ideas must always give way when challenged by circumstances? Gladstonian parsimony inspired Treasury officials long after his departure, creating within the government a hard core of dogged and usually insurmountable resistance to the inauguration of increased spending for social services. His faith in the ability of Smithian free enterprise to solve the problem of poverty, when linked to the proper moral virtues, and his consequent distaste for socialism and what he called "construction," made his most devoted followers fatally resistant to the demands of the social masses whom Gladstone had aroused. Gladstone had criticized Evangelicalism as creating spiritual appetites that it could not satisfy, and he left it in good part for that reason. But in his relations with the masses, in a certain sense he did the same thing.

In good part, this situation grew out of the very qualities in Gladstone's mind that pulled him to Liberalism, and made him its prophet and its saint. His universalism drew him out of the exclusiveness and the rigidities of his early Toryism, but it also made him a man who instinctively thought of great and sweeping problems, rather than of issues that were immediate and local. It was Ireland that obsessed him, and beyond Ireland, Britain's role in the politics of the world community. Many Liberals in Parliament were restive and irritable while Gladstone expended whole sessions and entire administrations on the problems of Ireland. Like American workingmen during the campaign against slavery, they heartily wished that similar energies could be spent on issues closer to home. It is revealing that the issues that impelled Gladstone finally to leave the Conservatives and join in forming the Liberal Party lay in foreign policy. The nature of the world community, and how nations should properly act in their relations with one another, were the topics most fascinating to Gladstone. More than any other man in Anglo-American civilization, he fashioned the Liberal-Democratic philosophy of internationalism, bequeathing it, through Woodrow Wilson, to the twentieth century.

Again, however, the legacy was ambivalent. Gladstone's foreign policy placed nonintervention at the head of its list of cardinal virtues, but elsewhere it insisted upon a contradictory value: the transcendent importance of political liberty, and of law and order. This outlook upon the world proved to have built into it just as powerful incentives to intervention as the frank nationalism and the self-professed *Realpolitik* of the Tories. As Gladstone himself had warned in Midlothian, the war for liberty was a supreme duty. He was, he said, quite prepared to go to war with either France or Germany to save the independence of Belgium, and his political inheritors, in 1914, did just that. Gladstone's intervention in Egypt to restore law and order began a complex and painful involvement that was to last for sixty years, and his maladroitness turned the whole nation against him.

Nothing was to reveal more clearly the paradoxes inherent in Gladstonian foreign policy than the Boer War, when Liberals opposed to the war and Liberals in favor of it both called on Gladstonian values to justify their stands. Foreign policy should carry a moral charge, of this both factions were convinced. But was the moral value to be the protecting of the rights of small nations as against large, or the ensuring that Britons within the Boer states should have the right to vote and equality before the law? The dilemma was irresolvable.

However, for all the ambivalences built into Gladstone's domestic and foreign policies, there is little difficulty in discriminating the thrust of his argument and distinguishing it from that of his political enemies. Gladstone was a compassionate man, and he communicated to his age the idea that statesmen should rightfully be concerned with the disadvantaged, the degraded, the exploited. Those who hated him among the aristocracy had few doubts as to what he advocated. They saw in him a Premier infuriatingly ready to listen to every malcontent with a grievance, or so it seemed. The very activity of his enormously vigorous premierships was appalling to them. Every line of authority seemed to lead to Gladstone, and they were all active. His governments, for all their Gladstonian political economy, were continually engaged in enacting reforms, in the piecemeal, evolutionary, Burkeian fashion. Circumstances were in reality the dominating consideration. Could the Irish land situation, given its actual nature, be solved only by jettisoning the idea of free contract and private property? Then so be it. It was a radical thing to do, Gladstone said, "I do not disguise it. But . . . it is required by the circumstances of the country."

The Liberal message, as Gladstone expressed it, was to present the nation with the alternative of an open society, pluralistic and unprivileged, founded on what he saw as the solid moral health of the common people and devoted to the elimination of the great symbols of degradation and inferior status. Pragmatic, evolutionary, and compassionate, it would be a society receptive to change and possessed of a universalist vision of membership in the brotherhood of mankind. Its fundamental perspectives would lead to foreign policies that eschewed arms, dispensed with colonies, stressed international law, and cherished with special care the small nations of the world. Their mission, Gladstone said—in words with a curiously American ring—was to spread freedom. He was calling for a polycentric world, where self-respect—the vital center of Gladstonian Liberalism—would become the common property of mankind as self-government took the place of imperial dominion. Self-government for each national group, and complete free trade, would be the foundation stones for a stable and peaceful world.

So far as the Anglo-American nations are moved by the ideal of the world community, in which all nations are equal, so far has the influence of William Gladstone proved lasting and fertilizing. Similarly, too, so far as governments loyal to these values also find themselves involved in interventions, some of them begun in idealism and continued in grief, the paradoxes of William Gladstone, like those of Thomas Jefferson, continue to be with us.

Chapter 7

SAMUEL TILDEN:
THE DEMOCRAT AS SOCIAL SCIENTIST

William Gladstone emerged as the great popular leader of British Liberalism in the 1860's, and he pursued his spectacular course through the next thirty years. During this period, two men served as the principal figures in the Democratic Party in the United States, Samuel Tilden and Grover Cleveland. Both were New Yorkers. Tilden helped lead the Democratic Party back to unity after the shattering experiences of the Civil War, shaped much of its economic thought, and almost captured the White House in 1876. Eight years later his legatee, Grover Cleveland, won the presidency in the first Democratic victory since before the Civil War, and he held the office for two separated four-year terms, leaving the White House in 1897. The Tilden and Cleveland political careers in fact span the whole of Gladstone's sixty years in politics, for as Tilden entered politics in the 1830's, so Cleveland left it in the mid-1890's. The two men illustrate, therefore, what it meant to be a Democrat in the United States at the same time that Gladstone was illustrating what it meant to be a Liberal in the United Kingdom.

New York State, like Lancashire in English politics, was the cockpit of nineteenth-century American political life. The entrepôt of the immigrants and the first state to possess a city with more than a million inhabitants, it was the earliest to grapple with modern urban politics and its babble of tongues and religions. The focus of financial power and transportation, and the possessor of the largest bloc of electoral votes, New York developed a political life that was of central importance in the politics of the nation, especially in the politics of the Democratic Party. From the election of 1836—by which time two organized parties on modern lines had appeared—to that of 1900, seven of the thirteen men whom the Democrats nominated for the presidency came from New York. In the comparable period, none of the twelve men nominated by the Whig-Republicans came from that state. New York, the state of the ethnic minority groups, was peculiarly the state of the Democratic Party.

New York bore a special resemblance to Great Britain. It was the scene of the most extensive colonial effort to create an aristocracy similar to that in the home country, based on large landholdings, tenant farmers, and rule from above. The Dutch transplanted feudalism to the Hudson Valley with considerable success, and the English who came after them, dealing with a conquered people, followed the same plan. In New York, "their manors were more numerous, more persistent, more thoroughgoing, and more prosperous . . . than elsewhere in America."[1] The Hudson Valley was a great community of landlords and tenants quite dissimilar from that in any other colony, but much like that in England.

New York's early political attitudes were also shaped by the fact that it was uniquely the battleground of America. Containing the strategic routes to Canada and to the Great Lakes, New York saw heavy fighting in the French and Indian Wars, the Revolutionary War, and the War of 1812. Hostility to Britain, for many New Yorkers, was the result of bitter personal experiences, affecting generation after generation and renewed endlessly in the telling. "In no other state is there a local legend of the Revolution so rich in tragic drama. Nowhere else was civil strife so poignant; nowhere else were fought such numerous and such critical campaigns."[2]

After 1790, an influx of New Englanders began moving

[1] Dixon Ryan Fox, *Yankees and Yorkers* (New York and London, 1940), pp. 19–20.
[2] Ibid., pp. 16–17.

into New York as the Yankees undertook the "swarming" that spread hundreds of thousands of them westward for a thousand miles. They carried with them their own Revolutionary memories, their highly developed political skills, their aggressive puritanism, and their pride in themselves. Connecticut's impact on the state of New York alone is dramatically demonstrated in the fact that a majority of the delegates to the New York constitutional convention of 1821 were either born in Connecticut or were sons of fathers born there.[3]

In 1790, the Tildens moved westward from Connecticut as part of this migration, settling just across the New York border not far from Albany.[4] They were a family with bloody memories. Forebears had been in the French and Indian Wars, one had died on a British prison ship during the Revolution, and others had fought in the New York militia. In their eyes, anyone associated with the British side or who seemed to ape British ways—which included Alexander Hamilton and the Federalists—was an enemy. They were Jeffersonian to the core.

Samuel Tilden was born in 1814. He was a sickly child who became a withdrawn and precociously intellectual youth. Kept at home because of his many illnesses, he never acquired playmates. He was to move through life always a remote and lonely little man, erect and cold-mannered, largely friendless, admired for his power of mind but not liked by his contemporaries. The older members of the family doted on him when he was a youth, however; he was the bright recluse, the brainy young man who was sick most of the time, pampered, deferred to, and sought after for advice. The role of detached oracle was to be the one he played throughout life.

He was an outsider, with an outsider's view of life. Forced from his early days to be an observer and not a participant, he developed a manipulative, almost bloodless attitude

---

[3] Ibid., pp. 220–1.
[4] The general biographical information in this chapter is drawn from Alexander C. Flick, *Samuel J. Tilden* (New York, 1939); and John Bigelow, *Life of Samuel J. Tilden*, 2 vols. (New York, 1895).

of mind. He preferred dealing with those kinds of human problems that could be quantified, analyzed, and restructured. He enjoyed computing distances, populations, taxes, national income, and expenditures. He had a passion for order in his personal life and in the world around him. If he was confronted with a jumble of facts, he would fling himself on them until he could see the pattern linking them together. The man who was not a monomaniac, he once said, was not worth a damn. This character made him a brilliant political administrator, for he enjoyed working out the votes and factors in every precinct. His legal fortune came from this same talent for understanding complex situations, especially those created by the confused railroad boom of the mid-century period.

The Jacksonian world of the 1820's and 1830's, in which he was reared, was in constant economic turmoil. The Anglo-American boom that caused such an acceleration of life in the English North Country transformed the northeastern American states as well. Hundreds of thousands of eastern Americans and Europeans migrated out into the basin of the Great Lakes via New York's Erie Canal. Towns appeared or were transformed overnight, new inventions induced technological change, new trade patterns impoverished whole communities and enriched others, business conditions and private fortunes oscillated wildly up and down. A host of new opportunities crowding in on the businessman created the hustling, anxious, dollar-conscious American that Alexis de Tocqueville watched with such amazement when he visited Jacksonian America.

The boom and bust sequence "was the primal experience of Jacksonian life . . . [It] fixed the content, tone, and terms of politics for as long as Jacksonianism counted in America."[5] The Whig temperament found the new opportunities exciting, and held out Hamiltonian visions before the people, urging them to build more canals, open more resources, and erect tariffs to stimulate more industry. They urged that the

[5] Marvin Meyers, *The Jacksonian Persuasion: Politics and Belief* (New York, 1960), p. 103.

destinies of the country be placed in the hands of the financiers and businessmen who sat at the centers of trade.[6]

The attitude of most Jacksonian Democrats was fundamentally different. They often participated in the boom, sometimes acquiring great wealth in the process, but they were apprehensive. Heirs of Jefferson, and sharing in a kind of cousinship the basic attitudes of the Radicals and Peelites in Britain, they were afraid that much of what they saw was not progress, but destructive speculation based on special privileges. When the government supported internal improvements—canals, bridges, and roads—they suspected corruption, in the instinctive reaction that all Liberal-Democrats inherited from the eighteenth-century English, "True Whig" tradition. They grieved over the loss of the early Republic, in their idealized memories a land of simplicity and virtue. They wanted to dismantle the apparatus of government aids to business and restore the America-that-was. To them, "extraneous forces within society, powerless on their own to prosper and persuade, [had conspired] . . . to seize the government and convert it to an engine of despotism, theft and corruption."[7] They saw around them a conspiracy of clever men who lived by their wits, profiting from the toil of those who lived by the sweat of their brow.[8] In brief, while the Whigs spoke to the hopes of Americans, Jacksonians spoke to their fears.

The focus of Jacksonian anxieties was the Bank of the United States. With headquarters in Philadelphia and branches throughout the country, the Bank held the federal government's funds and was free to invest them in ways that would direct the growth of the economy as it saw fit. Possessed also of the power of discount over the currency of other banks, it was a financial institution of great power and apparent irresponsibility. To Jacksonians, it represented aristocratic control in a burgeoning democratic age, as well as all the conspiratorial specters that seemed to be at work behind

[6] Cf. Glyndon G. Van Deusen, "Some Aspects of Whig Thought and Theory in the Jacksonian Period," *American Historical Review*, LXIII (1958), 305–22.
[7] Meyers, *Jacksonian Persuasion*, p. 212.
[8] Ibid., p. 281.

the scenes, creating booms and busts—in both of which clever men at the center of power could profit—by manipulation of the paper currency.[9]

The anti-Bank, anti-paper-money point of view was not a new one in American politics. It began with Thomas Jefferson—indeed, it had its origins in hostility to the Bank of England—and had been kept alive by Jeffersonians ever since. In the 1820's, workingmen, intellectuals, and members of Congress constantly agitated the question. At the end of a tirade against the United States Bank in Congress, Thomas Hart Benton of Missouri cried out: "Gold and silver is the best currency for a republic . . . [It] suits the men of middle property and the working people best; and if I was going to establish a working man's party, it should be on the basis of hard money; a hard money party against a paper party."[1]

The culmination of years of agitation came in July 1832, when President Jackson vetoed the rechartering of the Bank in a spectacular message to Congress condemning "artificial distinctions" brought about by laws that "make the rich richer and the potent more powerful," and injure the "humble members of society—the farmers, mechanics, and laborers—who have neither the time nor the means of securing like favors to themselves . . ."[2]

Samuel Tilden shared in all these events and attitudes. The ethos of the Tilden family was intensely historical and political. Tilden was told over and over again of the Revolution and the War of 1812, and of the dramatic days of the early republic when Hamilton and Jefferson had founded the two parties. He absorbed an exciting sense of the immediacy of these controversies. Once fixed in the political polarities of this family obsession, he never questioned its assumptions, for he was to be a man of unusually fixed and rigid views. When he carried into the post-Civil War decades a sense that the struggles of the Old Republic still lived, breathed, and were pertinent, he was only bearing witness to the mental set he

[9] Both Meyers, *Jacksonian Persuasion,* and Schlesinger, *The Age of Jackson,* provide descriptions of anti-Bank attitudes.
[1] Schlesinger, *Age of Jackson,* pp. 80–2.
[2] Quoted in ibid., p. 90.

had acquired long before in the Tilden family home.

The Tilden family idolized Thomas Jefferson, and when the Jefferson *Memoirs* were published in 1829, a copy was immediately placed in young Samuel's hands. It became his textbook on politics, his imperishable and unchallengeable source of inspiration. When he was twenty, he was quoting Jefferson; in his sixties, the Civil War behind him, he was doing the same. "I read [the *Memoirs*] over and over again," Tilden remarked long after, "and thus became thoroughly imbued with Jeffersonian political ideas."[3]

What Tilden drew most of all from Jefferson was the view that there is an inevitable social conflict going on at all times between unscrupulous men of wealth—the aristocracy in American terms—and the people. Tilden constantly dichotomized politicians, in the Jeffersonian manner, into good people by nature unsullied, and bad ones by nature greedy and self-seeking. His writings were filled with such phrases as "the plundered ploughman and beggared yeomanry," the "clear-headed and stout-hearted yeomanry," the noble people with "their firmness and integrity of purpose," embodying the "moral sense and purpose of the community," and always in danger from "its selfish and fraudulent interests."[4]

He was to be personally caught up, during the course of his lifetime, in the dilemma that Marvin Meyers has seen facing all Jacksonians: the conflict between the lure of progress and profit-making in so buoyant an economy, and the nostalgic pull of the Old Republic, when life was felt to be innocent, calm, and virtuous. Tilden was always fascinated by the spectacle of the westward movement.[5] He was

---

[3] Quoted in Bigelow, *Tilden*, I, 15–16.
[4] See Speech, "Currency, Prices, and Wages," New Lebanon, October 3, 1840, in John Bigelow, ed., *The Writings and Speeches of Samuel J. Tilden* (New York, 1885), I, 158; Letter to Albany *Argus*, October 20, 1837, ibid., I, 75; Letter to *Columbia Sentinel*, April 11, 1833, ibid., I, 19; Address, Buffalo, August 10, 1875, ibid., II, 217.
[5] Cf. Bigelow, Tilden, I, 356; Speech, New York Constitutional Convention, in Bigelow, *Writings and Speeches*, I, 350; Speech, Union Square, New York City, September 17, 1866, ibid., I, 342; First Annual Message, Albany, January 5, 1875, ibid., II, 37–8; Speech, Buffalo, August 10, 1875, ibid, II, 214–15; Second Annual Message, Albany, January 4, 1876, ibid., II, 238; Speech, New York City, November 8, 1877, ibid., II, 494.

to be an early participant in the railroad boom, becoming a millionaire in the 1850's through his work as legal consultant to perhaps half the railroad lines in the Northern states.

But he always looked backward. He was never at home in the mobile and fluid new America. He was happiest walking in the hills of New Lebanon, or, late in life, enjoying the bucolic pleasures of his country estate, Greystone, which he turned into a model farm, lavishing on it the affection not to be found in the cold face he turned to the outside world. He suffered throughout life from the illnesses typical of inner tension. He talked frequently of the past, regarding "himself as a living ancestor . . . who gained courage by looking backward." His fundamental attitude was not forward, in joyous contemplation of a bright new world, but backward, grieved at the steady snapping of the ties with the past.[6]

It is not surprising, therefore, to see in the writings of his Jacksonian period the typical Jacksonian anxieties. He preached, as Meyers says of Jacksonians generally, "a decalogue of moral prohibitions," rather than "an articulate set of social ends and means."[7] A modest foray into content analysis shows how prominent in his mind was the classic Jeffersonian and indeed Gladstonian belief that the disorders of the time were caused by adventurous Whig political and economic policies.[8] He continually condemned such things as:[9]

1833:
  rashness and extravagance in action or opinion
  inconsiderate and extravagant generalizations
  the impulse of passion
  extravagant doctrines

[6] Flick, *Tilden*, p. 528.
[7] Meyers, *Jacksonian Persuasion*, p. 254.
[8] I have been guided in this approach by John A. Garraty's innovative article "The Interrelations of Psychology and Biography," *Psychological Bulletin*, LI (1954), 569–82, in which he describes methods of content analysis that can be helpful to historians.
[9] These have been drawn from: "Van Buren and the Nullifiers," *Columbia Sentinel*, September 12, 1833, in Bigelow, *Writings and Speeches,* I, 22–6; Open Letter to William Leggett, New York *Times*, March 25 and April 4, 1837, ibid., I, 45–54; Letter to Albany *Argus*, September 28, 1837, ibid., I, 57–64; and Speech, "Currency, Prices and Wages," New Lebanon, October 3, 1840, ibid., I, 103–61.

transient enthusiasms
speculative beliefs
1837:
new-fangled doctrines
exaggerated ideas
stimulating to constantly increasing excesses
excitement in banking and trade
1840:
rash adventures in a rising market
tempting the enterprising from the ordinary pursuits of
   industry
diverting from agriculture to trade and speculation
attracting swarms of settlers by visions of easy and sudden
   wealth
traversing the country to engage in traffic and speculation
streets filled with speculators
hazardous adventures
improvidence and unproductive expenditure
wild and ruinous projects

Tilden's father was a close friend of Andrew Jackson's protégé, Martin Van Buren, and the Tilden home was a frequent gathering place for members of Van Buren's following, the so-called Albany Regency. Soon Samuel Tilden was a permanent part of the Van Buren entourage. In a political movement that possessed vivid economic fears but little trained expertise, Tilden was valued for his understanding of economics, for he was deeply read in Adam Smith and remarkably *au courant* with the latest economic thinking from abroad.

Being part of the Van Buren world intensified Tilden's political perspectives, for Van Buren had struggled upward against the hostilities of the Hudson Valley aristocracy and was devoted to the egalitarian ideas of Thomas Jefferson. Almost more important to him, however, was the malevolent figure of Alexander Hamilton, who in his autobiography dominates the scene. In his youth he had watched Hamilton in New York politics with mingled fascination and alarm. To Van Buren, the Democratic mission was always to combat what he saw as Hamilton's hatred of democracy and his plan for destroying the republic by the mechanism of a central bank run by aristocrats.[1]

The New York Jacksonians were remarkably close to the world of British reform. It was in these years, in fact, that the monolithic Anglophobia of the heirs of Jefferson began to be replaced by a new feeling. They began to see that a Liberal Britain was rising beside the Tory Britain of their party imagery, a Liberal Britain that looked to America for much of its inspiration. "English radicals [of the Age of Reform] saw the America of the Age of Jackson as an incandescent example," Frank Thistlethwaite has written. The America that John Bright and Richard Cobden praised so highly, the America of free schools and free churches and free votes, was, to British out-groups, "the hope of the world, just as for the insiders of the establishment, it was a subversive influence deeply to be feared." In British politics, American achievements, actual or idealized, figured constantly in the Radical attack against the established order.[2] " 'The Americans,' wrote the *Westminster Review*, 'possess a greater amount of happiness than the same numbers have ever enjoyed before,' and Jeremy Bentham, himself, wrote to President Jackson that he was 'more of a United States man than an Englishman.' "[3]

Van Buren was in Britain during the debate over the Reform Bill of 1832, watching in excited approval from the galleries of Parliament. Like all Jacksonians he cheered on the Chartists of the 1840's and grieved at their failure. He later urged Democrats to cast off their prejudice against England. They should realize their cousinship, he said, with leaders like Robert Peel, who braved the hatred of the aris-

[1] Cf. Martin Van Buren, "The Autobiography of Martin Van Buren," ed., John C. Fitzpatrick, *Annual Report of the American Historical Association for the Year 1918*, II; and Martin Van Buren, *Inquiry into the Origin and Course of Political Parties in the United States* (New York, 1867), especially p. 166 for his concise statement of his theory of politics.

[2] Thistlethwaite, *America and the Atlantic Community*, p. 40.

[3] Ibid., pp. 42–3. Cf. also David Paul Crook, *American Democracy in English Politics 1815–1840* (Oxford, 1965), for a full description of this aspect of the Anglo-American connection.

tocracy to serve "the happiness and welfare of the masses."
Public opinion in Britain, Van Buren said, had gained as
much and in some ways more control over the British government than it possessed in the United States. It was now
clear that America no longer stood alone in the world as a
free country, but had been joined in this eminence by Britain.

> A line of separation, as yet not fully disclosed, has thus
> been drawn between England and America, on the one
> hand, and the antagonistic systems of the old world, on the
> other, which promises to endure as long as anything that
> depends upon the will or the action of man, and thus inter-
> ests of the greatest magnitude have become the subject of
> common and equal concern to the two former Nations.
> Every assault upon those interests, whether immediately di-
> rected against them in Great Britain or in the United States,
> must be regarded as an attack upon both and will, it is to be
> hoped, be met with equal spirit by both.[4]

Despite the great numbers of Irish Catholics in their
ranks, the Democrats, because of their allegiance to ideas
shared with the British Liberals, began to acquire the name
of the English party. In New York elections in the 1840's they
were stigmatized as "Free Trade men," who used "British
Money in our Elections," and were the "allies and hired instruments of British manufacturers."[5] Practically all the Jacksonian appeals for humanitarian reforms in the prisons, in the
legal system, in education, and in imprisonment for debt
showed the influence of Jeremy Bentham and the Utili-
tarians.[6] William Cobbett's attacks on labor exploitation encouraged those Jacksonians who were trying to create a
viable labor-union movement in the United States, and his
condemnation of paper money was similarly widely read and
utilized by Jacksonians engaged in the hard-money fight.[7]

Most important of all, however, were the ideas of Adam
Smith. His criticisms of soft money, monopolistic business,

[4] Van Buren, "Autobiography," pp. 460–1, 465, 481–4, 493.
[5] Benson, *Concept of Jacksonian Democracy*, p. 161.
[6] Merle Curti, *The Growth of American Thought* (New York, Evanston, and London, 1964), pp. 363–6.
[7] Schlesinger, *Age of Jackson*, pp. 317–18.

the greed of the wealthy, and government aids to business fertilized every stream of Jacksonian thought. Working men took up his labor theory of value, and anti-Bank men quoted his insistence that banks were too important not to be controlled by the government, as well as his view that many small banks were better and safer than one great institution. As Theodore Sedgwick said in 1838, Adam Smith's "voice has been ringing in the world's ears for sixty years, but it is only now in the United States that he is listened to, reverenced, and followed."[8]

Many British Radicals traveled to the United States, some to fight in American political campaigns, others to return to Britain with renewed zeal. An American tour for British Radicals became the early-nineteenth-century counterpart of the eighteenth-century Grand Tour in France for scions of noble houses. America was an "overpowering attraction" to them, a place of infinite promise for human betterment. They thought of the United States "not as a foreign country, but as a projection across the Atlantic of their own aspirations, an experimental ground for those reforms which in Europe were Utopian but which in America were possible." From Joseph Priestley to Robert Owen, they crossed the Atlantic to found utopian communities. In the 1840's came the *émigrés* from the failure of Chartism, who brought an industrial and agrarian radicalism—some of it Irish in origin—to American reform.[9]

Even more important were the extensive and lively contacts maintained between English Dissent and the United States. The American Revolution, Robert Southey observed, "made the Dissenters feel once more as a political party in the state. New England was more the country of their hearts than the England wherein they had been born and bred."[1] In 1838 the *Edinburgh Review* could observe of this connection that the very strongholds of Dissent in England—Liverpool and Manchester—

[8] Ibid., pp. 314–15.
[9] Thistlethwaite, *America and the Atlantic Community*, pp. 39–75.
[1] Quoted in Thistlethwaite, *America and the Atlantic Community*, p. 77.

are allied by close mercantile ties to Boston and New York; and the alliance of mind is closer still . . . Affinity of opinion has produced between members of these parties on each side of the Atlantic, a sort of cousinship and similarity of manner and tone of thought, not to be met with between any other classes in the several countries. The slight peculiarities, both of habit and mind which appear to characterise well educated Americans of the Eastern States are more nearly to be matched among the higher classes of dissenters in the great provincial towns of England than anywhere else; and an English Unitarian, especially if connected by family and acquaintance with the select people of that sect in his own country, is pretty sure of meeting in America not only with the kind and hospitable reception which all travellers with good recommendations can procure, but with a sort of family greeting.[2]

The same was true of Quakers, Presbyterians, Congregationalists, Methodists, Baptists, and Episcopalians, to greater or less degree. In both countries these sects resounded to the same controversies, exchanged delegates, experienced the same storms of evangelicalism or reaction, and worked together for spiritual regeneration and moral reform. Drink, war, and slavery were the trinity of evils they jointly attacked. Above all, they shared with the Radicals a dedication to the ideal of mass education, in the form of secular common schools for everyone, publicly supported.[3]

For reasons to be discussed further on, however, humanitarian reformers from Britain, especially if they were concerned with fundamentally moral issues, did not necessarily find their American partners in the Democratic Party. Its secularism, and its alliance with the South, complicated matters.

---

[2] Ibid., pp. 77–8.
[3] Ibid., pp. 76–150.

The Bank Veto in 1832 transformed the nature of American politics. In the 1820's, there had been great confusion in political alignments, especially in the state of New York,[4] arising from the fact that the Jeffersonians had been in power for so long and the Federalists had collapsed. The Bank issue struck so deeply, however, that it clarified all political factions and established a voting pattern that lasted for many years. The Whig Party came almost spontaneously into being, formed out of heterogeneous groups unified by their hostility to Andrew Jackson. They believed that President Jackson had overstepped his authority in vetoing a duly enacted law simply on the ground that it was bad policy, and in summarily dismissing two Secretaries of the Treasury until he got one who would agree to withdraw the government's deposits in the Bank before its charter expired. The issue that they cried up and down the country was "executive tyranny."

Hostility to the idea of a strong executive, a Whig principle in both the United States and in Britain, must not be confused—as observed in the previous chapter—with hostility to a strong government. The American Whigs, heirs of Hamilton, wanted a strong government, conceived of as a total institution, which would make major interventions in the economy in pursuance of specific legislation. Congress, however, should be supreme in matters of national policy and legislation, the President's veto being an instrument for disallowing legislation only on legal and constitutional grounds, not on grounds of policy. Furthermore, within the executive branch itself, they believed in the traditional aristocratic and oligarchical method of rule by a collection of notables, each cabinet minister being largely on his own. They did not like a strong executive on the model of an Andrew Jackson—or a William Gladstone—who might become a popular tribune. Except for the case of Theodore Roosevelt, this would appear to be a lasting distinction between the parties, as the administrative style of Hoover and Eisenhower, as compared with that of Franklin Roosevelt and Kennedy, reveals.

The Whigs also disliked other features of Jacksonianism,

[4] Cf. Alvin Kass, *Politics in New York State, 1800–1830* (Syracuse, N.Y., 1965).

such as "rotation in office"—stigmatized as the "spoils system." The Whig Party in the United States, like that in Britain, preferred deferential patterns of social organization and leadership in which positions in government service went to men not because of their expertise, or their readiness to serve as functionaries of a political party, but because of their social status in the community. Jacksonians, on the other hand, called for rotation in office not simply to repay political debts, but because they intended to depersonalize public office. Public posts were no longer to be shaped to their occupants, but were to have duties prescribed and explained by statute, so as to fit efficiently into a more coherently ordered structure of government. Where the Whigs thought of government service as "a function of private social status . . . in which a gentleman, once appointed to an office, private or public, expected to be continued therein, and the functions of his position fitted to his capabilities," the Jacksonians thought of public office as open equally to all, for its tasks would be standardized and easily mastered.

The Whigs were out of tune with the new patterns of American life not only in government and party organization, but in business organization as well. Efficiency and large structures with interchangeable parts were demanded by the new continental economy and government, and the Whigs had to reshape themselves in this image. That they maintained their fundamental hostility to vigorous executive leadership, however, is shown in the presidential performance of Abraham Lincoln in the 1860's. A devoted Whig, he let his cabinet members largely run their own departments and exerted almost no leadership at all over Congress, simply executing such laws as it passed.[5]

After the Bank Veto, the Jacksonians could finally take on the mantle of Jefferson, for which all factions had theretofore been scrambling, and proclaim a crusade against the moneyed aristocracy. Coincidentally, they began calling

[5] Cf. Lynn L. Marshall, "The Strange Stillbirth of the Whig Party," *American Historical Review*, LXXII (1967), 445–68; Donald, *Lincoln Reconsidered*, pp. 187–208.

themselves the Democratic Party, the party, in their rhetoric, of "the farmers, mechanics, and laborers" struggling against the tyranny of the Bank.

Until recent years, it has been traditional among historians to accept this self-description as accurate. Some historians—most notably Bray Hammond—have advanced the view, however, that the Jacksonians were misleading their era, as well as subsequent historians. In his view, the Jacksonians did not mean what they said about banks, hard money, and the struggle against the aristocracy. They were simply businessmen who wanted to destroy the Bank—seen in this context as a moderating influence—so they could make money more easily. They were hypocrites.[6]

As will be discussed at greater length later in this chapter, it would be unwise to ignore the fact that the Jacksonians, as devotees of Adam Smith, were interested in unleashing the economy, and that many of them were businessmen with bourgeois rather than reformist values. It also certainly seems likely that the Jacksonians were supported by the same men of small property, working alone and anxious in a speculative economy, who were behind the Liberal Party in Britain. But the conspiracy theory of history always has a fatal weakness in its evidence. It relies, fundamentally, on certain assumptions about the way men behave in politics, rather than on a body of evidence. One either shares the assumptions, or finds the Hammond case unconvincing—as, in fact, I do.

Recent studies have shown the same picture in America that J. R. Vincent has found in his study of the Victorian pollbooks. In reality, there were bankers, businessmen, farmers, and workingmen in both the Democratic and the Whig parties. Democrats and Whigs came from strikingly similar socio-economic backgrounds, despite the Democrats' claim that they were the party of the common people, and the Whigs' preference for elitism. Only a few percentage points separated the two parties in voting totals, which could not

6 Cf. Bray Hammond, *Banks and Politics in America from the Revolution to the Civil War* (Princeton, 1957).

have been the case if the Democrats had actually been the party of the common people.[7]

In actual fact, many influences operated within the politics of New York State in addition to the single one of economic class membership. Merchants in New York City who dealt in domestic goods tended to vote Whig, but those dealing in British imports were free traders and Democratic. Manufacturing towns voted Whig, probably because that party was identified with economic nationalism and protective tariffs, but a study of three hundred New York City bankers reveals them to have been divided almost equally between the parties.

Most important of all the factors that governed party membership were what Lee Benson has called ethnocultural differences. The Democrats were the party of the ethnic minorities. They were attacked after their victory in 1844 for having won through an "avalanche of Germans, Irish, Swiss, Prussians, French, Russians, and Poles."[8] Such groups as the French Canadian *Québecois* moving down into New York voted almost unanimously Democratic, as did French merchants in New York City. Dutch farming counties were comfortably prosperous, and by the traditional view should have voted Whig, but they instead voted strongly Democratic, apparently through a deeply rooted anti-British and therefore pro-Jeffersonian bias. They were also intensely localist in their outlook, in the classic manner of the European peasant, and they preferred the states' rights localism of the Democrats. The Irish Catholics, of course, went en masse to the Democrats, impelling English, Scottish, and Welsh immigrants into the Whig ranks. The Germans also gravitated largely to the Democrats and away from the nativist Whigs, who were the voice of anti-immigrant and anti-Catholic sentiment. Though the Germans were never to be so politically active as the Irish, who had been highly politicized in their struggle against the English, they were nevertheless to be a reliable Jacksonian voting group.[9]

[7] Cf. discussion of this topic in Chapter 1, and in Benson, *Concept of Jacksonian Democracy, passim.*
[8] Benson, *Concept of Jacksonian Democracy,* p. 175.
[9] Cf. Ernst, *Immigrant Life in New York,* p. 165.

There is impressionistic evidence to the effect that there were also "party differences in *moral attitudes and ways of life*." The Whigs, as befitted a party devoted consciously to elitist values—which does not mean a party exclusively *composed* of the elite—claimed to be the party of "decency" and "respectability." At all class levels and in most localities, this self-description would seem to have been true, for Democrats more than Whigs seemed to value the lusty, individualistic, hard-drinking qualities associated with the Mike Fink or the Davy Crockett stereotype, "or their *urban equivalents and manifestations*." Towns settled by New England immigrants that can be found to have been demonstrably puritan in ways of life tended to vote Whig; rough lumbering towns and others like them tended to vote strongly Democratic.[1] That these same attitudes existed among the Irish and Germans is suggested by the fact that, as their historians have noted, they disliked the Whigs' temperance activities.

The Whigs also claimed to be the party of religion, and the Democrats, working in the Jeffersonian tradition, were the party of secularism, the "godless" party. The New England immigrants who settled in such numbers in western New York were strongly puritanical and religious, and they were at the same time devotedly Whig. They demanded that the government enforce a moral code on drinking, Sunday activities, dancing, and other amusements of this type. In important ways, the aggressive puritanism of western New York—the "Burned-Over District"—which began with the anti-Masonic explosion of the 1820's and culminated in the abolition crusade, affected all of New York politics. Calling for a "Christian party in politics," the new puritans set off a long conflict with the Democrats over such issues as prayer meetings, temperance, and Sunday laws. Party differences on these matters were "distinct, passionate, and enduring."[2]

---

[1] Benson, *Concept of Jacksonian Democracy*, pp. 198–203.
[2] Ibid., pp. 3–46, 198–207.

When Martin Van Buren succeeded Andrew Jackson as President in 1837, he was immediately faced by a severe depression. His principal response was to carry the anti-Bank campaign even further. He proposed the Independent Treasury plan, by which the federal government would withdraw its funds entirely from the many private banks to which they had been distributed during the fight with the United States Bank and place them in its own depositories. At the same time, it would accept only gold at the treasuries, not bank notes. This would reduce the power of banks to speculate in risky investments with public funds, deny special privileges, and, he hoped, strike at the root cause of depressions.

Sound-money men were delighted. Frank Blair of Missouri, a prominent Jacksonian, called it "the boldest and highest stand ever taken by a Chief Magistrate in defence of the rights of the people. [It is] . . . a second declaration of independence." Radical Democrats everywhere wrote congratulatory letters to the White House. Many in the business community, on the other hand, reacted in horror. "The message is a heartless, cold-blooded attack upon our most valuable and most cherished classes of citizens," the New York *Gazette* bitterly observed.[3]

In this circumstance, Samuel Tilden received his first major public opportunity. A law student in New York City, he went to Tammany Hall to speak in favor of the Independent Treasury plan before a jammed audience of radical Democrats. The ultimate goal of the plan, he said, was to separate government and business and thereby to strike at the corrupt marriage that had as its only purpose the interests of wealth against the people. Each nation in the world, he said, had experienced the struggle of the few to dominate the many. The wealthy were always linked together by mutual interest, which arrays them

in an organized class which acts in phalanx and operates through all the ramifications in society; concentrating property in monopolies and perpetuities, and binding to it political power,—it has established an aristocracy more potent,

[3] Schlesinger, *Age of Jackson*, p. 236.

more permanent, and more oppressive than any other which has· ever existed. Such at this moment is practically the ruling power in nearly every civilized nation. The capitalists and landed proprietors [of England] wield the whole political power of the State for their own benefit . . . Monopolies overspread the land, paralyzing individual effort and exhausting the life-blood of the body politic. The burden of the gigantic machinery of State, the Church establishment, the pauper system, and the national debt, crushes the laboring classes, on whom exclusively it is made to fall.

Was not the same conspiracy at work in America? Had not that been the objective of the moneyed and powerful ever since the days of Alexander Hamilton? They had created a mammoth bank as the nucleus for their money power, they had tried to limit the suffrage, and they had built a lasting combination of political factions and moneyed interests that still aimed at the same objectives. The radical democracy, he said, wanted only that the banks should be on an equal standing with everyone else. "We excite no prejudice against wealth, we merely refuse to it exclusive privileges, either in business or in politics. We claim an equality, not of social conditions, but of political rights."[4]

In 1840, while still in his law studies, he put together his matured economic views in a long speech dealing with currency, prices, and wages. Based on the purest Adam Smith principles, with admixtures of David Ricardo, it expressed exactly the economic concepts that the Peel government was to implement in the 1840's. Tilden so skillfully applied these ideas to American conditions that his speech was published as a sixty-page pamphlet and widely praised, most notably by William Gouge and Condy Raguet, prominent Jacksonian economists, and sent to England.[5]

His main purpose was to demonstrate that sound money was absolutely vital to workingman, farmer, and businessman alike; that Whig policies created inflation, which bore cruelly

[4] Address to the Farmers, Mechanics and Workingmen of the State of New York, Tammany Hall, February 26, 1838, in Bigelow, *Writings and Speeches*, I, 79–87.
[5] Cf. Bigelow, *Writings and Speeches*, I, 101–2; Schlesinger, *Age of Jackson*, pp. 79–80, 117.

on those who, like the workingman, had little power to raise their income when prices rose. As Peel later wanted to make England a cheap country to live in, to help the working classes, so Tilden wanted to do the same for the United States.

The real source of wealth, he said, was the productivity of the workingman, not the supply of the currency. If, as in England, the taxes that supported an established church, a profligate government, and, through tariffs on wheat, the income of landowners were designed to be paid by the laboring man, why should he work hard? The weight of taxation, and its distribution, was therefore critically important to productivity, and thus to national wealth.

Freedom of industry was equally important in creating a productive economy. All artificial burdens must be removed from the entrepreneur and the laboring man. Long apprenticeships were a hindrance to productivity, as were all forms of monopoly, for such arrangements always resulted in a harmful misdirection of capital and labor and reduced productivity. "Unequal legislation, monopolies, and exclusive privileges of every description not only lessen production, but even alter the distribution of what is produced, invariably to the injury of the laboring classes."

This was why Jeffersonians had opposed from the beginning the Hamiltonian principle of a strong central government and manipulative legislation. Public debts, internal improvements, and all other such devices were a curse to the economy. These Whig measures

are a part of the same system of interference with the pursuits of industry and the private business of individuals,—in a word, of over-government, which curses the rest of the world; and their tendency is to consolidate power in a great central government, surrounded by magnificent establishments, and crushing by its weight the industrial masses.

The clearest and most immediate danger to the working classes, however, lay in fluctuations in the money supply, which endlessly produced rises and slumps in price levels and in business activity. It was no good to argue that a central bank was an essential regulator. Tilden sought to demonstrate, by discussing in detail and with extraordinary sophistication every bank panic since the 1820's, that the Bank of the United States had in fact operated in a wildly speculative way, exaggerating both the booms and the collapses. This arose from two causes: the greed that inevitably attached to the possession of so great and so uncontrolled a power; and fundamental misunderstandings of the currency system.

Men foolishly believed, he said, that printing unsupported paper money would create wealth. To understand the fallacies this view contained, it was necessary to look at the American economy as a part of the world economy, not simply by itself, as Whigs, with their selfish nationalism, were wont to do. Inflation of the money supply would indeed lead to rising prices in the short run, but it would also cause a flight of gold, for foreign creditors would demand payment in specie instead of in depreciated currency. Central banks in the United States would be forced to adopt the same policy to meet their foreign commitments, businessmen would learn that their local banks had no gold at all, confidence would collapse, and panic and depression would ensue.

In one of the biological images of which he was so fond, Tilden observed that currency "is to business what the blood is to the animal system." Just as too much created agonies of congestion, so too little created enervation and collapse. A proper balance, created only by natural forces, would be established by a sound-money policy—by which he meant paper money based on and freely convertible to gold, therefore limited in volume—that would allow the international gold-standard mechanism to keep prices fairly stable. When prices began to rise, gold would flow out of the country, banks would be forced quickly to reduce their currency issues, and prices would fall again. When they began to drop below the world level, gold would therefore be more valuable in the United States and would flow back into the economy, banks could issue more currency again, and the price level would rebound to the world level. The "necessary amount of currency in a country [would therefore be] . . . just so much as will keep the channels of circulation filled to a level with the currencies of the rest of the commercial world."

The essence of this system, however, was its automatic, "natural" operation. Artificial efforts to control it through the device of a central bank would only set it awry. Let the international gold standard operate freely, and businessmen and farmers could carry on their operations in confidence, and laborers would be spared the miseries of inflation.[6]

Tilden spent the 1840's in a whirl of political activity. He sat on party committees, helped to organize public meetings, drew up resolutions, scratched off campaign documents, went to caucuses and conventions, and rose rapidly within the party. As a young lawyer in New York City, he was strategically located to aid Martin Van Buren's political activities in the metropolis, and he became a member of Tammany Hall. In 1843, at the age of twenty-seven, he was appointed corporation counsel of New York City. In the following year, he attended the Democratic national convention, edited a partisan newspaper in New York City, and worked closely with Governor Silas Wright, a Jacksonian in the classic mold.

In 1845, he entered the New York Assembly and brought to an end the long Anti-Rent War in the patroon estates of the Hudson Valley. It was an issue tailor-made for a politician who, in the Adam Smith tradition, was hostile to land monopoly. Tenants were bound to leases extending for as long as three lifetimes, were subject to feudal duties, and had the prospect of endless rent payments ahead of them. A form of guerrilla warfare had broken out in the affected regions, and law and order had almost completely collapsed. It was an extremely complex legal and financial situation, and few

[6] "Currency, Prices, and Wages. —The Pretensions of the United States Bank to Regulate the Currency Exposed," in Bigelow, *Writings and Speeches*, I, 123–64.

Tilden's description of the international money flow was an excellent statement of David Ricardo's "Price-Specie Flow Mechanism," which dominated monetary thought until the 1930's. Tilden's economic writings show, in fact, a high degree of economic sophistication. He was obviously exceedingly well informed about what economists were saying and about the monetary and other economic problems of his day, I am informed by my colleague Walter Mead of the University of California, Santa Barbara, Economics Department.

could understand it. After intensive study, Tilden was able to make a long report that brought order out of the chaos in a way reminiscent of Gladstone's Irish land acts. At Tilden's recommendation, the great estates were broken up by special taxes, leases longer than ten years were prohibited, and tenants' leases were converted into reasonable mortgages. It was a masterful achievement, and he gained quite a new prominence and popularity in the state.[7]

In 1846, Tilden took a major role in the New York constitutional convention. Dominated by Democrats, the convention spent much of its time seeking to make certain that the heavy program of internal improvements being carried on by the government of the state of New York—particularly in canals—would be brought to a halt. The Democrats were also moved by the classic Smithian fear of corporations that Jacksonians had long expressed. For years they had been attacking the arrangement by which incorporation was a special privilege to be given out only by specific legislative charter. This system, they said, only perpetuated corruption and monopoly. In 1834, the prominent Jacksonian publicist William Leggett had stated that every grant of the right of incorporation "is directly in the teeth of the doctrine of equal rights." The answer, he believed, was to enact a general law by which any group could form a corporation so long as they met certain minimum requirements. This would throw open all such businesses, including banking, to universal competition.[8]

In his last major achievement as a Jacksonian reformer, Tilden led the movement within the convention to place a general-incorporation provision within the constitution. Duly enacted into statute form by the legislature, the general-incorporation policy threw open to everyone who could meet stated requirements the opportunity of incorporation. The results seem to have been exactly those predicted by Adam Smith. The general-incorporation law, which was quickly copied by other states, opened the way for such an explosive

[7] Cf. Henry Christman, *Tin Horns and Calico: An Episode in the Emergence of American Democracy* (New York, 1961), an excellent book on the Anti-Rent War.
[8] Schlesinger, *Age of Jackson*, pp. 188–9.

development of the economy that it helped to bring on the first specifically industrial boom in the United States, that of the 1850's. "Of all the business corporations of the country in the first half of the nineteenth century, nearly half were established during the fifties."[9]

By mid-century, therefore, the Jacksonians and their British counterparts had carried through most of Adam Smith's program. Smith had called for an end to the mercantilist state, in which the government intervened in the economy in major ways to aid businessmen. This kind of arrangement, he had said, featured a wide array of special privileges such as tariffs and chartered monopolies. Its principal effect was to enrich the privileged and to exploit everyone else. Most of all, it resulted in a limited and restricted economy bound in by illogical and regressive regulations. Wiping out special privileges and rigorously separating the government from the economy would have the great effect of unleashing the economy, setting off dynamic forces within it that would lift everyone upward in a steadily mounting rise to affluence. Speculation and collusive tendencies would have to be carefully watched, however, and special care taken to maintain a stable currency system.

In this spirit, the British Peelites and Radicals had practically eliminated the tariff system, and the American Democrats had made major reductions in what was already a relatively low American tariff (in the Walker Tariff of 1846, carried against severe Whig criticism). The Americans moved both to attack monopoly and to free the economy by enacting the general incorporation system, while the Peelites, catching the problem at a later stage, began to require that corporations conduct their business in certain ways, so that speculation and dishonesty would be checked. By divergent means, the Jacksonians and the Peelites and Radicals moved to establish sound money: the Britons by reforming the Bank of England, and the Americans by striking down the Bank of the United States—deemed by them to be inveterately speculative—and placing the government's funds in its own vaults, thereby removing a great pool of capital from the hands of

[9] Allan Nevins, *Ordeal of the Union* (New York, 1947), II, 244–5.

speculative bankers. Thereafter they relied on Adam Smith's idea that the money system would be best governed by competition among many small banks.

There are manifest paradoxes in this general system of policy. On the one hand it called for unleashing the economy, and on the other for curbing speculative and inflationary pressures. Its principal weapon against inflation and speculation was sound money; its principal devices for freeing the economy were to widen the market through elimination of tariffs and the striking down of monopolies. As it turned out, Smithian economics was better at freeing the economy than at controlling businessmen and their speculative and exploitive appetites. Its success, in fact, was in creating the dynamic economy; its failure was in so releasing the businessman from all control that he grew into a giant figure who dominated all of society. There is every reason to understand why Bray Hammond and Richard Hofstadter have taken the view that the Jacksonians were really businessmen jealous of the privileges of other businessmen. They were in fact engaged in removing restraints on the economy; many of them did thereafter lose themselves in busy schemes of personal enrichment, whether in banking or in railroads or in industry. The Manchester Radicals were without question triumphantly middle-class. It has long been a temptation to think of British Liberalism as in its heart of hearts bourgeois, striving in the Corn Law fight not so much for low food prices for the poor as for low wage levels for the employer, made possible by cheap food.

They also preached the classic middle-class virtues of hard work, self-denial, and the struggle for success. These were the virtues they held out before the working classes in the nineteenth century, and that the working classes, at least through much of the century, seemed to accept. In a dynamic Smithian economy, Liberal-Democrats believed the real road upward for the common man lay in the adoption of a certain kind of character. A growing economy would solve all social ills. Sloth alone prevented success. Gladstone was impressed by the workingman in the 1860's because he was saving his money and getting an education. It was in good part for these new moral qualities, Gladstone argued, that the workingman could rightfully claim the vote. Certainly the prospect of a militant and class-conscious labor movement received little sympathy among either Democrats or Liberals. Their stated reason was that this kind of unionism threatened a new kind of monopoly, but was their real reason simply a reluctance to pay higher wages? They demanded, too, a rigorous separation of government from business. Their stated reason was that this would keep the economy dynamic; that the old way had been productive simply of privilege and stagnation. But were they simply concerned to protect their own freedom to exploit workingmen?

The ambiguity is irresolvable. The best recourse seems to lie not in either castigating or praising the Liberal-Democrats, but in taking the view that every idea system has within it contradictory potentialities. It is the human condition that what is apparently good has within it the seeds of its own corruption; that each principle, as each person, possesses in the same instant both destructive and creative qualities, which are often at work at the same time. There is no reason to doubt the sincerity of the Adam Smiths and the William Gladstones; and there is no reason why the ideas in which they believed should have been uniquely free from the human paradox. Each reformist ideology presents features, when it becomes an orthodoxy, that later reformers find repellent.[1]

In any event, the Liberal-Democrats believed that in Adam Smith's ideas they had the answer for poverty, for aristocratic and capitalist exploitation, for war. And if they did not get peace, they certainly seemed to get prosperity. In

[1] There are those within the contemporary liberal comumnity, for example, who are nagged by doubts that nationalization and the bureaucratic state have wholly beneficient results. The liberal orthodoxies of the nineteenth century produced *laissez faire* monsters that have afforded generations of twentieth-century social scientists ample opportunities for the full employment of their talents of analysis and criticism. Yet they may be blind to strong-government monstrosities in their own time—huge military systems, ossified bureaucracies, unproductive state industries—that will lead later generations of social scientists to doubt the sincerity of those reformers from the Progressive era onward who began building the system, and of those scholars who, like the Adam Smiths and the Jeremy Benthams of an earlier day, inspired their creation.

one of the most extraordinary demonstrations of the way in which events can consolidate ideas, the Liberal-Democratic successes in enacting the Smithian program were followed by an amazing period of prosperity. Probably stimulated by the sudden influx of gold and silver bullion from the California and Nevada mines after 1849, both the United States and Great Britain experienced an expansion of their economies in all directions in the 1850's and into the 1870's. After the miseries of the worldwide depression in the 1840's—the "Hungry Forties" of famine and unemployment and sullen outbreaks of political and social violence—the prosperity of the 1850's produced the euphoria of the mid-Victorian years. For a generation, until the collapse of the mid-1870's, everything in economic life seemed to confirm what Adam Smith had predicted: that the dynamic economy would lift everyone upward. Gladstone could explain to the Commons in contented detail, year after year, how the average man's standard of living was bounding upward. The United States experienced in the 1850's its most explosive economic boom, and after the hiatus of the Civil War, the "Great Barbecue" continued with unabated zest.

During the Civil War, however, a tragic regression—as the Democrats saw it—took place in the United States. The Republicans finally gained both the presidency and large Congressional majorities on the strength of their anti-Southern policies. They took the opportunity to re-create the mercantilist state, enacting the first major protective tariff in American history, establishing a federal currency that eliminated the currency of state banks, and launching major programs of internal improvements in the form of land grants and subsidies to railroad companies and river and harbor projects. Under their leadership, the government and the entrepreneurs became friendly and cooperative partners once again.

These enactments crystallized the terms of politics in the United States for the next half-century. While Gladstone was free to turn to noneconomic problems, the American Democrats were still forced to carry on endless arguments with the Republicans over economic policy. The Democrats were battling a counter-reformation, while the British Liberals were moving on to the next problem, finding a new Liberalism to deal with the consequences of the old.

As the country began its long boom in the 1850's, Samuel Tilden found his law practice growing more exciting and remunerative. The railroad scramble produced intricately complex problems between competing roads that he was well suited to analyze and reorder, and fees poured in. Before the Civil War began he was a rich man, and during and after that conflict he became a millionaire.

In consequence he found much less time for politics. It had become, in any case, an arena that attracted him less and less. The Smithian revolution had been largely completed, and the country was growing excited over just the kind of moral issue, in the abolition crusade, that had little appeal to such a man as Tilden. The Democratic Party split on the issue—as the Liberals were later to divide over Home Rule. In the late 1840's he helped Martin Van Buren in his campaign for the presidency on the Free Soil ticket, writing much of what Van Buren said against the spread of slavery into the new territories. But in the 1850's, when the slavery controversy became more openly anti-Southern and more directly concerned with the cry for abolition, he lost interest in the Free Soil movement and took an increasingly less active role within the Democratic Party, turning instead to his legal activities and his life in New York City.

He was revolted by the abolitionist crusade. Abolitionism was a movement that emanated from the world of evangelical Christianity. The Burned-Over District in western New York, where the devotedly religious puritanism of New England had its flowering in the 1830's and 1840's, was in many ways the wellspring of abolitionism. Tilden, however, was never a particularly religious man, maintaining only a nominal membership in the Presbyterian Church throughout his life. He opposed the new puritans' moralism in politics, taking forthright stands against them on such issues as the temperance campaign. They were generally Whigs in their partisan affiliations, furthermore, and this heightened his hostility. It is not surprising that he found their abolitionism distasteful.

He was not alone in this hostility. Jacksonians were generally opposed to abolitionism on the ground that it distracted attention from social issues within the Northern states. Jacksonian workingmen's organizations distrusted the abolitionists, for they seemed to be indifferent to the "wage slavery" that existed in Northern factories. Although opposed to slavery as an abstract proposition, workingmen concentrated instead on their own objectives.[2]

Martin Van Buren and the Dutch farmers from whom he sprang were moved by additional considerations. They seem clearly to have been prejudiced against free Negroes. The Dutch farmers had owned slaves, did not like having them taken away, and opposed social and political equality for them.[3] The Catholic Irish of New York City were also enemies of the free Negroes in that community, because of competition for unskilled jobs. The very idea of abolition was anathema to them, for they feared a flooding of Northern labor markets by released slaves. The Civil War draft riots in New York City in 1863 were "the bloodiest race riots of American history." Laborers hunted down Negroes, killed them, and drove thousands from the city permanently.[4]

The Irish were not a reformist influence within the Democratic Party in the middle decades of the nineteenth century. Like the French Canadian *Québecois*, the Irish Catholic in America was strongly influenced by the fact that

[2] Cf. Joseph G. Rayback, "The American Workingman and the Antislavery Crusade," *Journal of Economic History*, III (1943), 152–64; Schlesinger, *Age of Jackson*, pp. 232, 424–7; Leon Litwak, *North of Slavery: The Negro in the Free States* (Chicago, 1961), particularly pp. 84–90 for the attitudes of Northern Democrats.

[3] Benson, *Concept of Jacksonian Democracy*, pp. 8, 208–13, 295–7. For Van Buren's view, see "Autobiography," pp. 132–8, and *Inquiry*, pp. 354–8.

[4] Albon P. Man, Jr., "Labor Competition and the New York Draft Riots of 1863," *Journal of Negro History*, XXXVI (1951), 375–405; Williston H. Lofton, "Northern Labor and the Negro During the Civil War," ibid., XXXIV (1949), 251–73; Williston H. Lofton, "Abolition and Labor," ibid., XXXIII (1948), 249–83.

his church was in a determinedly conservative phase. The revolutions of 1848 and the Italian wars of national unification—which took the Papal States from the Pope—made Pius IX (1846–78) a violent enemy of liberalism and social reform. The Vatican Council of 1870 proclaimed papal infallibility, which caused sharp reactions throughout the religious world. In 1876 Pius's famous *Syllabus of Errors* condemned socialism, communism, "Clerico-Liberal Societies," the public schools, religious toleration, rationalism, and naturalism. He summed up his message in these words: "It is an error to believe that the Roman Pontiff can and ought to reconcile himself to, and agree with, progress, liberalism, and contemporary civilization."

To a social group as devoted to Rome as the Irish—both the Catholic Irish and the *Québecois* considered Rome their capital, their faith being coterminous with their ethnic identity—these words were accepted without question. They reinforced, indeed, what was apparently a social conservatism brought with them from Ireland. "Irish journalists denounced penal reform as violating the basic law of punishing him who needed punishment, ridiculed abolitionism as 'niggerology,' opposed the public school movement, sneered at reform third parties, and condemned utopian socialism." The answer for suffering was charity; the answer for the bitterness they carried with them from Ireland, and had reinforced in the slums and prejudice and grinding exploitation of America, was hatred of England. Fenianism drained off the passions built up in Irishmen by their wretched lives.[5]

---

[5] Arthur Mann, *Yankee Reformers in the Urban Age: Social Reform in Boston, 1880–1900* (New York, 1966), pp. 24–7. Daniel P. Moynihan, in his brilliant essay on the New York Irish in *Beyond the Melting Pot*, pursues these matters in depth. Irish conservatism, he writes, has meant that though they knew how to use organization to gain office, they "just didn't know what to do with their opportunity. They never thought of politics as an instrument of social change—their kind of politics involved the processes of a society that was not changing" (p. 229). In the modern period their illiberalism led great numbers to follow Joseph McCarthy enthusiastically, thus beginning to break down their monolithic loyalty to the Democrats. Revealingly, however, McCarthy's campaign seemed to appeal to the Irish most of all when it became an assault against the key institutions of Anglo-Saxon Protestant supremacy: Harvard, university professors, the State Department, and the alliance with Great Britain. Profound changes within the Roman

In addition to the prejudices of the ethnic minorities they represented, there were also venerable and authoritative intellectual roots to Democratic race ideas. Jefferson's "Query XIV" in his *Notes on Virginia* held that Negroes were naturally inferior in both body and mind to whites. Furthermore, abolitionism was an idea emanating from religious groups, and if there was any legacy that Jefferson handed down, it was an active suspicion of clericalism in politics.[6]

As a last consideration, the whole idea of abolitionism violated *laissez faire* in its crudest form. An activist government was exactly what Jacksonians did not want. The new puritans in politics, calling for abolitionism and temperance and blue laws, gave the impression that there were many things to be done. The voice of the people must be felt. The government must be used.[7]

All this represents a principal difference between the Liberals and the Democrats. This was why there was a tendency in mid-century Britain to think of the Republicans as the Liberal Party of the United States. Its fundamentally Hamiltonian character was obscured by its having become the vehicle for moralism and abolitionism. For this reason, when the zealous young Liberal intellectual E. L. Godkin arrived in America in the 1850's, he joined the Republicans.

It is clear, in any event, that Samuel Tilden's ideas on the Negro were derivative from the intellectual and political tradition within which he worked.[8] He fought abolitionists and the vote for free Negroes, and like Van Buren soon forgot the anti-Southern enthusiasms of the Free Soil movement—which was primarily aimed at saving the new territories for white men by keeping out the Negro slave.

Catholic Church and the Irish community itself presage equally great changes soon to come in Irish politics in the future.
[6] Peterson, *Jefferson Image*, is essential on this whole subject: pp. 92–3, 167, 172–3, 175–6.
[7] Cf. Benson, *Concept of Jacksonian Democracy*, pp. 35, 186–200.
[8] While his views were clearly derivative, he perhaps gave them added intensity on his own count as well. It is interesting to note that Tilden's personality was of the type that has been observed to be predisposed to racial prejudice. An important discovery, Gordon Allport observes, "is . . . that people who are rigid in their perceptions and style of thinking tend to be prejudiced against Negroes, Jews, and other groups." *Pattern and Growth in Personality* (New York, 1961), p. 269.

Tilden and Van Buren shared with most Northern Democrats a feeling that the Union was more important than ending slavery. Tilden was not a "Hunker"—the name for New York Democrats who were openly pro-Southern in the 1840's—but as the slavery issue grew more bitter in the late 1850's, he began to argue that the race question should be left in the hands of the white Southerners. At the height of the crisis, in 1860, he was so alarmed by what he seems to have seen coming more clearly than most, that he came out of his political semiretirement to publish, during the last days of the presidential campaign, what has been called the "most influential of all his public writings," the Kent Letter.

His primary argument in the Kent Letter was that slavery should be left alone. The tragic fact in American politics, he said, was that a large part of the Northern population had got the idea that something had to be done about slavery, even though—in his view—slavery in a Southern state was no more the federal government's concern than slavery in Brazil. Northerners at the very least wanted slavery to be kept where it was, and not allowed to spread. This would be disastrous, Tilden said. If the Southern whites and Negroes were forced to remain where they were, their growing numbers would soon exhaust their resources, resulting in poverty and despair. The discouraged whites would free their slaves as no longer profitable and emigrate alone, leaving behind them the unambitious Negro, thus turning the Southern states into black republics. Was this what Northerners wanted?

If the reply was that consequences should not deter from doing what moral right and duty commanded, Tilden had a ready response. "No man," he said, "has the right or duty to impose his own convictions upon others." Certainly this was true, he said, when what was involved was a mere theory which held that "slavery is a wrong, without reference to any condition of time, place, or circumstances."

Consider what the facts showed, he said. The westward movement was naturally following paths imposed upon it by geography and culture. The "current of Northern emigration does not deviate largely from certain parallels of latitude.

The current of Southern emigration, tending in the same general direction, spreads out, perhaps deflects, to the southwest." The Northern current was several times as large in volume as that in the South, and it "tends to press southwardly the line where the two touch each other."

Thus Southern migration moved to the southwest, carrying slavery with it, "withdrawing and moving toward the tropics," following the curve of the Gulf shore southward. Since cotton culture in the Deep South was especially profitable, slaves were being sent southward from the states of the upper South. Thus the border states were being steadily drained of their slaves and by natural forces being transformed into white states.

The time had come, therefore, to turn once again to the master philosophy that in every other matter had proved so useful: Leave it alone. "Would it not, on the whole, be better to let the black man go toward the tropics as best he may, bond or free," Tilden asked, leaving "white men for the governing power" in the regions left behind? What wise man in possession of these facts could feel that he should "deal with them on any artificial system of human devising?" But:

> It is too late! It is too late! We are upon the breakers. Whose eye quails now? Whose cheek blanches? It is not mine, who felt "a provident fear" and have done all I could . . . My mind is filled, my heart swells with the thought, that yon wave which towers before us will engulf more of human happiness and human hopes than have perished in any one catastrophe since the world began.[9]

Tilden returned to active political life in the years of the Civil War. He was a "War Democrat" who supported the leadership and policies of Abraham Lincoln. He continued to disagree, however, with the idea of abolition. Helping Horatio Seymour with his inaugural address as governor of New York in 1862, he put in a passage predicting that abolition of slavery to restore the Union would create a military despotism. He founded in New York City the Society for the Diffu-

[9] Letter to William Kent, October 26, 1860, in Bigelow, *Writings*, I, 289–330.

sion of Political Knowledge, which among other things was actively anti-abolition. In one of its pamphlets, Samuel F. B. Morse sought to prove by copious Biblical quotations and ethical argumentation that slavery was a good thing, "one of the indispensable regulators of the Social system, divinely ordained."[1] In 1864, Tilden stood before a gathering of Wall Street bankers and merchants and lashed out at abolition as a "crude scheme of philanthropy," an attempt to reconstruct human society that could only fail. How could the laws of New York and Vermont be imposed on the South? Somebody must run the South after the war, he said, and since Northerners could not do it, and the Negro was obviously unfit for self-government, the nation must ultimately rely on the white race.[2]

In 1868, as chairman of the Democratic Party in New York, he took up the topic again for his last major effort on the theme. The Republicans, in their Radical Reconstruction policies, had only one reason, he said, for making the Negroes the governing power in the South. They wished to use the votes of the gullible ex-slaves to get twenty United States senators and fifty representatives out of the occupied Southern states and their carpetbag governments. Three million barbarian Negroes had thereby been placed in a position where, with their fanatical Northern leaders, they could rule the whole nation.

> The grim Puritan of New England—whose only child, whose solitary daughter is already listening to the soft music of a Celtic wooer—stretches his hand down along the Atlantic coast to the receding and decaying African and says: "Come, let us rule this continent together!"

They were faced, he said, with the monstrous situation in which three million Negroes had ten times as many senators as the four million whites of New York State. Joining with their Northern allies, the Republicans—who were traditionally hostile to immigrants, but unaccountably friendly to

[1] Cf. the Papers of the Society for August 1863, No. 12.
[2] Speech to Wall Street Bankers and Merchants, November 1, 1864, Tilden Papers, Manuscript Division, New York Public Library.

Negroes—they would doubtless vote to admit Negroes to the suffrage in Nothern states and take it away from Irishmen and Germans. "Do you think they would not assert the superior rights of negroes born in this country," he asked, "over foreigners?"

The whole policy was madness. America was a great experiment that could succeed only if its people had intelligence and virtue. The nation was a biologically limited partnership between citizens that was intimate and complex. Who had been admitted to this partnership in the past? Only those who could be taken naturally into the family. Those whose entrance into the family was repugnant to Americans must always be "separate and incapable of amalgamation with the mass." For this reason, America had always refused to admit into its self-governing partnership "inferior or . . . mixed races." He had opposed on this ground, he said, the annexation of Mexico. Certainly the swarming millions of Chinese could never be admitted, nor the American Indians.

On the other hand, immigrants from Europe had provided superb stock for the nation. "Races have a growth and culture," Tilden observed, "as well as individuals." Immigrants from Europe came here simply to rejoin their kindred. They were admitted to the family openly. Indeed, such liaisons would doubtless lead to a higher kind of mankind. But as to the Negro? Reverting to his most powerful imagery, he put it categorically:

> In our body politic, as in the human system, what can be digested and assimilated is nutrition; it is the source of health and life. What remains incapable of being digested and assimilated can be only an element of disease and death. The question in respect to it is always this,—whether the vital forces are strong enough to prevail over it and excrete it from the system.[3]

All the elements of Tilden's world view were revealed in these utterances: the mechanistic and biological images, the

[3] Speech, Democratic State Convention, Albany, March 11, 1868, in Bigelow, *Writings and Speeches*, I, 395–420.

atmosphere of remoteness and scientific observation, the hostility to coercive moralism, the complete unconcern for the Negro, and the triumphant application of *laissez faire*, the "master philosophy."

Tilden was in every way a product of the self-consciously "scientific" naturalism that came into European and American thought in the middle of the nineteenth century. He liked to fill his writings with naturalistic images. He would speak of the way men were "interlaced with each other by the numberless ties which spring up and grow around and grow over individuals living in one community"; about the way in which political parties provide "the nerves of sensation which convey intelligence to the intellect of the body politic . . . [and] the ligaments and muscles which hold its parts together, and move them in harmony"; or about "the organism of Government." He preferred to think of social processes as naturally orderly and harmonious, using such terms as "the great machinery of trade," and "the influence of the several parts of the social mechanism."[4]

Tilden was the sole representative among the Liberal-Democratic leaders of the cast of mind typical of Benthamite Utilitarianism in Britain. Jeremy Bentham and his Philosophic Radicals also approached Britain's problems in Tilden's forbiddingly mechanistic and quantifying way. Their whole intention was to create a science of society as Newton had of the physical world. While Gladstone, Burke, and Jefferson had been humanists and moralists in search of an encompassing social ethic that would make their countrymen more compassionate, Tilden was a social scientist concerned with quantifiable facts and rationalized institutional arrangements. The sense of outrage against economic privilege was prominent in his mind, but it was set in a forbiddingly cold outlook on the world.[5]

---

[4] For these and other images, see Bigelow, *Writings and Speeches*, I, 68–70, 86, 129, 130, 158, 294, 295, 306, 318, 325–6, 335, 485; II, 11, 191, 197, 489, 496.

[5] It is revealing that the first books he had read to him when he grew too old for an active life were the biographies of Jeremy Bentham, James Mill, and John Stuart Mill. One wonders what he made of J. S. Mill's turn toward socialism, after having spent much of his career

Tilden's scientism was typical of attitudes widespread among academicians and reformers in the northeastern United States. They were expressed in 1865 in the founding of what became the American Social Science Association, a body consciously modeled after a similar group in Britain. Its goal was the "scientific" study of all social problems in a search for underlying principles and structures. As in the British group, the American society organized discussions, disseminated information, and supported research in numerous areas, with the overall goal of improving society. Morally neutral, yet creating in its members all the enthusiasm of a religious sect, the association insisted that it was not philanthropic, but rather a body concerned with social science, which would go "behind the effect to the cause," preventing, rather than relieving, "the error existing among men." The "men who made up the Association envisioned the neutral, detached state— honest, efficient, above politics, opposed to all special interests, and dedicated to strict *laissez faire* in economic matters."[6]

Recognizing a kindred spirit in Samuel Tilden, they invited him to speak to them in 1876, while he was governor of New York. In response he delightedly enthused at length on their common passion, the analysis of society through the use of statistics and scientific analogies.

You assume that the complex phenomena of society, its grand tides of movement, its successions of changes, growth and decay of populations, mortality, pauperism, crime, are capable of being analyzed, studied, and reduced to formulas. Now, gentlemen, it seems to me that no more important object of investigation could be presented to the human mind. I am quite sure that the application of the same philosophy which has achieved such grand results elsewhere will astonish you . . . Even those uncertain things that depend on the human will are capable of being studied, of being analyzed, of being classified, and their results stated.

as a typical Utilitarian. When Tilden visited Britain in the late 1870's, he was immediately elected to membership in the Cobden Club.
[6] Irwin Unger, *The Greenback Era: A Social and Political History of American Finance, 1865–1879* (Princeton, N. J., 1964), pp. 136–7.

Such analytical methods, as Tilden saw them, pierced through the confused, chaotic, and scrambled screen of immediate experience to reveal the greatest insight of all.

> Gentlemen, how is it that this great multitude of individual wills and individual tastes, acting separately and independently, find themselves averaged and compensated until everything tends to and everything results in an equilibrium of forces? It is that the Divine Being has impressed upon everything order, method and law.[7]

In the 1870's, Samuel Tilden became nationally prominent as a fighter against political corruption. It is on this ground that he is best known in textbooks of American history. As the most prominent leader of the Democrats in New York State, he was inevitably drawn into the controversy when sensational revelations made it clear that William Marcy Tweed had built a bipartisan ring in New York City, operating out of Tammany Hall, that was taking millions from the taxpayers.[8]

Historians have generally forgotten—if they have ever properly recognized—what a problem political corruption actually was to the men who faced it throughout the Anglo-American world in the eighteenth and nineteenth centuries. One of the principal results of the comparative research undertaken for this book, in fact, has been to reveal how pervasive and severe a problem it was in all three countries. Nothing obsessed the American colonials so much as the fear that the eighteenth-century system of British government, which seemed to be *built* on corruption, was going to be forcibly introduced into American life by such means as the Stamp Act and other laws. Swarms of dishonest officials, they believed, would soon be sent over from Britain to collect the revenue. Corruption was more than a morally reprehensible system of government to them; it was the principal means by which free government throughout the empire was in the

[7] Address, Saratoga, September 5, 1876, in Bigelow, *Writings and Speeches*, II, 375–9.
[8] Cf. Alexander B. Callow, Jr., *The Tweed Ring* (New York, 1966), for a skillful description of this whole controversy.

process of being destroyed. Edmund Burke regarded political corruption as perhaps the key problem in the British government, and built much of his career around his attacks on the system. Thomas Jefferson aroused the Democratic mind to the threat of corruption, and the Jacksonians talked constantly of the way in which it was being used by their enemies to destroy both the republican experiment and democracy.

The issue became similarly important in Canadian politics, shaping the whole nature of post-Confederation Liberalism in that country. Corruption at the constituency level was also a principal reason for the demand for the Reform Act of 1832, and all subsequent suffrage legislation. Gladstone fought corruption almost all of his career. This was what he meant by "economy in government." He encountered corruption directly in Midlothian and created the civil service, secret balloting, and corrupt-practices acts to deal with the problem. He sprang from a political generation that regarded governmental profligacy in the form of sinecures, special grants, and lavish facilities for those in power as a principal cause of the misery of the poor.

In short, no theme was more central to Liberal-Democratic ideology than the constant attack against corruption. It was seen not simply as a moral blot, but as the means by which aristocracies rooted themselves in power and exploited the people. Indeed, undermining the government and the people with dreams of ill-gotten gains was, to Liberal-Democratic eyes, the very device by which Tories and Whig-Republicans got into office. No problem, therefore, more seriously threatened the success of the emerging democratic experiment.

Corruption had of course become, by the post-Civil War decades, perhaps the most destructive single illness in U.S. and Canadian political life. At every level and in every state, corruption made it almost impossible to move toward the solution of any other social problem. Government had practically broken down; the whole democratic experiment seemed to be failing miserably. The term "American-style politics" had a clear meaning throughout the Anglo-American world and elsewhere. Mass parties seemed to lead inevitably to corruption in government. Nothing was more frequently referred to in the arguments going on contemporaneously in Britain over the widening of the suffrage. Corruption in America, it was said, was not "retail," as it was in England, but "wholesale," existing not simply in constituency elections, but in the very proceedings of legislative bodies. The result of American-style politics, said Robert Lowe, was that members of Congress were "traffickers in office, bankrupts, men who have lost their character and been driven from every respectable way of life, and who take up politics as a last resort."[9]

Men in America who were deeply devoted to the democratic experiment felt it all as a wound upon the spirit. "It is not necessary for me to attempt to paint the state of political corruption to which we have been reduced," Henry George said in California as he called for the election of Samuel Tilden to the presidency in 1876.

> It is the dark background to our national rejoicing, the skeleton which has stood by us at the feast. Our Fourth of July orators do not proclaim it; our newspapers do not announce it; we hardly whisper it to one another, but we all know, for we all feel, that beneath all our centennial rejoicing there exists in the public mind to-day a greater doubt of the success of Republican institutions than has existed before within the memory of our oldest man.[1]

It is clear that the fight against corruption was hardly the precious plaything of the moralistic middle classes it is often described to be. Men like Samuel Tilden and Grover Cleveland in the United States and Alexander Mackenzie in Canada were almost spontaneously plucked out—in Cleveland's case, from total obscurity—and forced to the top to meet an urgent need. Their particular blend of qualities was desperately needed, indeed demanded, by the age—and by al-

[9] Henry Pelling, America and the British Left: From Bright to Bevan (New York, 1957), pp. 14–15.
[1] Henry George, The Question before the People. What Is the Real Issue in the Presidential Campaign? (pamphlet; San Francisco, 1876), p. 5.

most no other, which explains in part why they have less than heroic stature in subsequent histories of the period. The fighter against corruption is not a congenial figure to the twentieth-century mind, either in personality or in function. His principal task was to say "no." Subsequent generations have needed and praised affirmation, not negativism.

Tilden clearly understood what was at issue in the struggle over corruption in New York. As he said in 1875, "it is not to ourselves alone that we are to look when we consider what is involved in this controversy. The whole United States, and indeed other countries, are interested in it. The cause of free government has been dishonored and imperilled by the abuse, maladministration, and peculations that have recently prevailed in the country."[2]

He had a theory of government ready at hand to explain corruption. It simply grew out of a perverted local application, he said, of the centralist doctrine that the Republicans had always preached. The Albany legislature of New York State had taken the power of self-government away from the people of the city of New York and had placed it in the hands of a small, self-appointed commission, which then proceeded, unchecked by the local people, to divide up the municipal treasury. "The cancer which reached a head in the municipal government of the metropolis," he said in a characteristic utterance, "gathered its virus from the corrupted blood which pervades our whole country."[3]

The Tweed Ring presented Tilden with an unavoidable conflict between his political values and his intense loyalty to his party. Tweed was a Democrat, and a harsh internecine fight was in the offing. Tilden moved reluctantly and hesitantly at first, but at length he gave himself to the problem of pursuing Tweed, and he stuck with it year after year until the ring was crushed completely. In the course of the fight he became governor, in 1874, and in that post he went on to

[2] Speech, Utica, August 12, 1875, in Bigelow, *Writings and Speeches*, II, 227.
[3] Pamphlet, "The New York City Ring: Its Origin, Maturity, and Fall" (New York, 1873), in Bigelow, *Writings and Speeches*, I, 600; Municipal Reform Message to the Legislature, Albany, May 11, 1875, in ibid., II, 119–35.

wage a similarly spectacular battle with the Canal Ring.[4]

Samuel Tilden had become the symbol of reform. Men began talking of him for the presidency. Possessed, now, of a national audience, he began to speak once more out of his Jacksonian inheritance, fulfilling in this way his larger role in the history of the Democratic Party, which was to deliver the Jacksonian point of view, largely unchanged, to the postwar generation. His success in this task grew not simply out of his new eminence, but from his extraordinary intellectual prestige among Democrats in the 1870's and 1880's. He carried not only the aura of the great period of Jackson and Van Buren, he was known to have been one of its leading intellectuals. Democrats were in awe of his power of mind, and of the ideas he expressed with such fluency and confidence. Few ordinary politicians understood economics, and in the complex postwar economic situation, the money question "was an intellectual labyrinth that easily confused the untrained and the ill-informed. The man who attempted to thread its twists and turns without special knowledge risked finding himself hopelessly befuddled." In these circumstances, common people and politicians alike "turned to the 'experts' for guidance."[5] In Tilden, they found not only an expert, but also an expert who was at the same time leader of the Democrats in

[4] This is the most controversial period in Tilden's life. Was he not only a reluctant dragon but an insincere one as well who took action only after the *Times* had exposed the corruption, and then limited what he did to what could not be avoided? For this view, see Alexander Callow, *The Tweed Ring;* Mark D. Hirsch, "Samuel J. Tilden: The Story of a Lost Opportunity," *American Historical Review*, LVI (1951), 788–802; and Mark D. Hirsch, *William C. Whitney, Modern Warwick* (New York, 1948).

My own conclusion is that Hirsch and Callow would have made a different judgment if they had understood more fully Tilden's character and career. They find him cynically opportunist; I think he was simply a strange and uncongenial little man with a talent for exciting dislike among historians. He was always slow to act until the facts were all in; he had a quite understandable reluctance to start an explosive fight within the party, which was practically like a religious order to him; he was annoyingly elusive and given to manipulative maneuvers that went unexplained. When the facts were clear, however, he skillfully and implacably led the campaign to smash Tweed. As Callow states, the last words on the Boss's lips before he died were "I hope Tilden and Fairchild are satisfied now." Tilden was indeed a reluctant dragon, but I find it impossible to doubt he was a sincere one.

[5] Unger, *Greenback Era*, p. 35.

the most populous state in the Union, victorious over the greatest corruptionist in the land, and—perhaps most important in the America of Horatio Alger—a self-made millionaire.

In considering the relatively sterile performance of the Democrats in these decades one must bear in mind that the Jacksonian thought Samuel Tilden delivered to the 1870's had passed through the selective perceptions of an intense but narrow personality. Jacksonianism as he transmitted it was restricted in scope and bereft of the warmth, the humanity, the multiformity and creativity that had characterized so much of Jacksonian thinking. Tilden's views were logical, abstract, and even-tempered, not lusty, growing, and humane.

His mind and career constitute a clear demonstration, if one were needed, that the Liberal-Democratic political and social message possessed potentialities that were not particularly attractive. The rational mode of social analysis exemplified by the Benthamites could produce monsters as easily as the anti-intellectual traditionalism of the Tories. The skeptical reductionism of a Bolingbroke could function well as an integral part of a robust and many-sided personality such as Jefferson's, but in the mind of a self-confessed monomaniac like Tilden, it could create a peculiarly limited social vision.[6]

When he began speaking out on larger national problems in the 1870's he first called for a return to the ideas of Thomas Jefferson—whose responsibility for the concept of states' rights had made him anathema to many in the Civil

[6] Tilden also represents that stage in the evolution of a political movement that Harold Lasswell has written about. There is a cycle, he observes, which seems to characterize the life history of political movements. In the first stage, idea creators—men like Adam Smith, Thomas Jefferson, and perhaps even the Jacksonians—are prominent. In the next, the movement passes into the hands of men who are not innovators, but specialists in administration. At that point the new leaders change the emphasis in ideas from innovation and inquiry to repetition and rationalization. Codification and vindication become the obsession, not a search for new symbols and new categories. Tilden, in this sense, was the careful trustee of an inherited estate. He did not conceive it his role to bring in new intellectual capital. See Lasswell's chapter, "The Elite Concept," in Harold D. Lasswell, Daniel Lerner, and C. Easton Rothwell, *The Comparative Study of Elites* (Stanford, 1952), pp. 6–21.

War years. What the nation needed most of all, he said, was a revival of Jeffersonian democracy, a new victory for the people like Jefferson's in 1800.

> As the means of the reaction of 1800, Thomas Jefferson founded and organized the Democratic party. He stayed the advancing centralism. He restored the rights of the States and the localities. He repressed the meddling of government in the concerns of private business, remitting the management of the industries of the country to the domain of the individual judgment and conscience.[7]

With Tilden as one of its earliest exemplars, Jeffersonianism experienced a major renaissance in the latter years of the century. It swelled steadily in volume among Democrats, reaching its climax about 1900, "leaving the record of its progress in campaign buttons and banners and medallions, in party magazines, in pilgrimages to Monticello, even in verse and song." Many Democrats were firmly convinced that "touching the bones" of Jefferson would revive the shattered fortunes of their party. The men whom Merrill Peterson calls "code-Jeffersonians" believed that

> Jefferson, like the Messiah, would rise again. Jefferson was the Christ of the American government; they were his latter-day apostles. The mildest jest at Jefferson they regarded as blasphemous; the gentlest criticism they took as a personal insult. There were only two ways in American politics: Jeffersonian and Hamiltonian . . . They shared a fundamentalist habit of mind, though differing somewhat among themselves on the application of the fundamentals.[8]

The revival of Jeffersonianism was not a wholly beneficial influence on Democratic thought. The cluster of enemies and problems that Jefferson saw, and the agenda that he developed, was hardly appropriate to the ills of a more complex age, yet men like Tilden and the "code-Jeffersonians"

[7] Letter, Tilden to New York State Democratic Committee, August 1873, in John Bigelow, ed., *Letters and Literary Memorials of Samuel J. Tilden* (New York, 1908), I, 321.
[8] Peterson, *Jefferson Image*, pp. 250–65.

took on the Master's viewpoint almost without change, except to narrow it further. Their Jeffersonian fundamentalism gave them a "false consciousness"; that is, an outlook oriented to past rather than to present problems, and therefore blind to such new challenges as labor exploitation and urban squalor.[9]

Jeffersonianism nonetheless had rich resources for Democratic thought. Jefferson was concerned with much more than simply states' rights and limited government. He also bequeathed an almost Jacobinical commentary on politics. His pungent social analysis was what gave life and power to the things that Tilden and his successors said to their generation. Tilden spoke a great deal more of the conspiratorial activities of the wealthy and the power-hungry than he did of states' rights. He condemned the Republicans as a party still dominated by their master spirit, Alexander Hamilton, whose philosophy, Tilden said, was that "our American people must be governed, if not by force, at least by appeals to the selfish interests of classes, in all the forms of corrupt influence." These classes now possessed the Republican Party completely, and through it the government of the United States.

> The myriads of officeholders, with enhanced salaries, and often with illicit gains; the contractors and jobbers; the beneficiaries of Congressional grants of the public property or of special franchises; the favored interests whose business is rendered lucrative by legislative bounties or legislative monopolies; the corporations whose hopes and fears are appealed to by the measures of the government; the rapacious hordes of carpet-baggers who have plundered the impoverished people of the South at least ten times as much as Tweed's Ring did the rich metropolis, and whose fungus growth is intertwined with the roots of the Republican party; all these classes are not only interested in perpetuating existing wrongs, but they are the main agencies and instruments by which that work is done.[1]

[9] Ibid., p. 70. The term "false consciousness" is drawn from the sociologist Karl Mannheim, referring to "an orientation to traditional norms with which action in the existing situation cannot comply." See Karl Mannheim, *Ideology and Utopia*, tr. Louis Wirth and Edward Shils (New York, 1936), pp. 94–7.
[1] Ibid., pp. 321–3.

Republicans had long sought and gained revolutionary power, he said, by fostering illusions and wild ideas—such as abolitionism, great schemes of public enrichment, and hatred of the Southerner. They discarded all "the maxims and the habits of constitutional government for the expedience of the moment." They thrived in an atmosphere of hypocritical moralism, false finance, grasping centralism, and largesse to favored groups.[2]

As the White House came into view to Tilden in the mid-1870's, he began to speak out on economic matters for the first time since the 1840's. Great interest was taken in his utterances, for the nation was suffering severely in the long depression that began in 1873. Like everyone else, he was concerned about money issues as an explanation of the depression, and some of his principal contributions were on this theme.

The post-Civil War period in the United States was in fact spent in a continuous and incredibly complicated political argument over the money system. From 1862, when the Northern government had begun the issuance of "greenbacks"—fiat paper money with no backing in gold—the argument over what to do with this supposedly temporary addition to the money supply had gone on endlessly. As has recently been shown, the standard historical accounts of this long national obsession have been fatally simplistic. The business class was neither monolithically for sound money, nor monolithically Republican. As is now quite evident, class membership affords a poor index in these matters. One thing is clear: very large segments of the business community were Democratic because Democratic economic policies would help them. The key point, when it came to their voting behavior, was not their class membership, but their specific location within the economy. Merchants, bankers, manufacturers, and almost every other kind of economic grouping was divided against itself on the issue, for soft money or

2 Cf. Speech, Syracuse, September 17, 1874, in Bigelow, Writings and Speeches, II, 13; Letter to Evening Post, New York City, February 7, 1863, ibid., I, 333; Letter to State Democratic Committee, August 1873, in Bigelow, Letters and Literary Memorials, I, 323-4.

sound money would affect each specific element of the economy differently. If generalizations may be made, it would seem that established industries—like the textiles in New England—favored sound money, while new and growing ones in need of ready supplies of capital—like the iron industries in Pennsylvania—favored soft money. Similarly, those linked to foreign trade, like many of the railroads, certain kinds of raw-materials producers, many banking establishments, shipping lines, and mercantile houses with British connections, voted for sound money, while those oriented primarily to the domestic market and fearful of foreign competition wanted soft money and protective tariffs (soft money operating, in effect, to make foreign goods more expensive). Perhaps the only group generally unified in its stand were the entrepreneurs and promoters, who insisted that soft money would develop the economy and open its resources, since it would make capital more easily available.[3]

In this sense Liberal-Democracy was as much a businessman's creed as was its opposite. The Democrats did not attack all businessmen, but rather certain kinds of businessmen. Like Adam Smith, they celebrated an economic world that was dynamic, one in which everyone not only had a chance to get ahead, but had a social duty to do so. The men they condemned were those who sought special advantages in this race; who schemed behind the scenes to get government favors, to manipulate the money supply, to get ahead by the use of their wits instead of by honest labor and competition. This meant, however, that their rhetoric had an antibusiness cast quite unlike that of the Republicans. In Democratic hands the government characteristically thought of itself as performing its role best when it acted as a watchful critic of the business community, while the most congenial Republican role was that of friend and helpmeet to businessmen.

On the currency issue, Tilden continued to speak out of

[3] It is impossible here to describe this complex picture any more completely. The reader is referred to Robert Sharkey, *Money, Class, and Party: An Economic Study of Civil War and Reconstruction* (Baltimore, Md., 1959); and Unger, *Greenback Era.*

the Jacksonian sound-money tradition. This tradition by the 1870's had not only the combined prestige of Adam Smith, David Ricardo, and the Jacksonians behind it, but had acquired the luminous name of John Stuart Mill as well, for his *Principles of Political Economy* (1848) had become the dominant work on the subject, either directly or in the writings of numerous American economists.

There was a determined opposition to these ideas from American economists like Henry C. Carey, whose "American School" of political economy revived Hamiltonian mercantilism. He insisted that the idea of free trade and sound money was a British plot for preventing the development of American industry. The United States, he said, could develop its economy only behind the barrier of protective tariffs, which would keep out the destructive competition of British goods while new industries took root. An essential part of Carey's doctrine was a soft-money policy. Carey regarded "British monopolists" and "British agents" as the national enemy, working subversively through such American groups as the Free Trade League. As one writer of the American School put it, "The whole system of [British] political economy, from beginning to end, is an apology for tyranny, and the whole tribe of political economists are humbugs . . . and at their head stands the prince of humbugs, John Stuart Mill."[4]

Tilden, in his public utterances, took the view that the post-1873 depression was caused by the soft-money policy the Republicans had begun in 1862. A delusive boom based on government spending and inflated currency had taken place after the war, he said, but the uncertainty all this created had led to the inevitable collapse.[5] As he put it succinctly in 1874, "The fruits of a false and delusive system of government finances are everywhere around us. All business is in a dry-rot . . . Inflation no longer inflates . . . The truth is that our body

[4] Sharkey, *Money, Class, and Party*, p. 208.
[5] Address, Syracuse, September 17, 1874, in Bigelow, *Writings and Speeches*, II, 9–14; First Annual Message, Albany, January 5, 1875, ibid., II, 23–74; Second Annual Message, Albany, January 4, 1876, ibid., 237–95.

politic has been overdrugged with stimulants."6

More important to Tilden now as a cause of depression, however, was the weight of taxation. The mounting theme in his annual messages and occasional speeches as governor of New York was what he felt to be the mountainous load of taxation that the country was carrying. He called frequently —using the Gladstonian slogan—for "retrenchment and reform." The immense costs of the army of occupation in the Southern states, he said, together with the heavy expenditures for railroads, port facilities, and other internal improvements that the Republicans had set in motion, had absorbed so much capital that not enough was left in the hands of private citizens to get the economy going again.

As governor of New York he rigorously practiced what he preached. He not only crushed the Canal Ring, he slashed the heavy expenditures that former regimes had annually made on the Erie Canal, to the point where taxes in New York were soon at less than a third of their former level.

When he was nominated by the Democrats for the presidency in 1876, he called for a number of new policies. He argued that there be an end to the long experiment that had been made in race relations in the South, and a readmission of the Southern white to the constitution on equal terms with Americans elsewhere. The Southern states, he said, should be returned to the rule of white governments. Corruption in the national government, furthermore, must be eliminated, ending the "inefficiency, peculation, fraud, and malversation of the public funds [which had] . . . overspread the whole service like a leprosy."7

Most of all, however, he was concerned with economic policy. The first thing to be done, he said, was for the government to end its excessive consumption—as he saw it—of the country's capital. So much taxation had now to be raised to pay off the debt, he said, that the whole economy was

[6] Address of Acceptance of Gubernatorial Nomination, September 17, 1874, ibid., II, 10–11.
[7] This and the following are drawn from his only major statement during the campaign, his letter accepting the nomination: Albany, July 31, 1876, in Bigelow, *Writings and Speeches*, II, 359–73.

depressed. Spending must be sharply reduced. "This reform will be resisted at every step; but it must be pressed persistently."

Furthermore, a sound currency must be established by the resumption of Treasury specie payments—as, indeed, the Republicans promised to do, but by methods he condemned as delusive. When urged by followers to swing over to the soft-money position—the "greenback" position—on the ground that it had considerable popularity among many Democrats in the Western farming states, he refused, holding to his long-expressed belief that sound money was vital to the poor and to the consuming classes in general, since it would keep prices low. He said he would rather lose a million votes than permit that "the mechanics, the servant girls and laboring men should be robbed of their earnings."[8]

The fact that Tilden had had no difficulty making millions during inflationary times—he had made his fortune during the 1850's and the Civil War—and that he had held to this essentially Jacksonian view throughout a long political career make it seem likely that his statement, despite its pompousness, was sincere. At the time, however, he was bitterly attacked by inflationists as a tool of the moneyed interests, whose investments would presumably be rendered more valuable by the high interest rates created by a restricted money supply. Tilden's own wealth made him an ideal whipping boy on the issue, both then and since. He was the first genuinely wealthy man to run for the presidency, and there were endless references to "Sammy's barrel" during the campaign.

What was happening to the Democratic Party was the first opening out of a division within its ranks on money issues that was to have the most fateful consequences for the party in the future. American wheat farmers by the 1870's had fallen on terrible difficulties. Far more subject to world fluctuations in price than in the simpler Jacksonian days, they were beginning to suffer the effects of the long-term decline in wheat prices that affected the world market through most

8 Flick, *Tilden,* pp. 317–18.

of the second half of the nineteenth century. Because they were producers whose income came from the market, some of them began to call for an inflationist money policy that they hoped would raise prices. The number making this appeal grew swiftly after the free-silver idea began to take hold, silver coin being much more attractive to the farmer than the paper currency (greenbacks) he traditionally distrusted.

Democrats in the consuming groups—that is to say, in the cities—had a different relation to currency matters. Their economic interest (to the extent that these matters may be so baldly stated) was in low food prices. Put in the simplest terms, sound money had the same relation to the American worker and consumer that free trade in grains (the Repeal of the Corn Laws) had to their British counterparts. So helpful to workingmen was the long-term decline in food prices in the late nineteenth century that the laboring classes in Britain and in the United States generally experienced a significant increase in real income.

Historians have generally not taken full account of these matters. In American historiography, an agrarian bias has led historians to take on face value the pleas and diagnoses of the Western farmer, and to accept as valid their attacks on Samuel Tilden and Grover Cleveland as conservative "gold bugs" who cynically resisted the path to social justice. My purpose in this discussion is not to propose that the standard position on the money problem be summarily dismissed, but only that it may be taken as an open question again that Tilden meant sincerely what he said when he took the view that his policies were designed to help the working man and the consumer, and that in fact they would have.[9]

The truth of the matter is that the post-Civil War period

[9] It is very difficult to dispense with historical stereotypes. This is shown in the fact that even Irwin Unger, who devotes his *Greenback Era* to disproving the simplicities of Charles Beard's historical views, seems still to be thinking within Beard's fundamental framework, which was to regard all sound-money men as "conservative," apparently using the term in its modern sense. This term is used throughout *Greenback Era* in Beard's way, though the information within the book clearly demonstrates how poorly it describes the actual facts. Even bankers were divided on the issue, let alone industrialists, farmers, and laboring men. In that maelstrom, who was the liberal and who the conservative?

yet awaits the kinds of multidimensional studies that we now have of the age of Jackson. Voting behavior has been almost uniformly described on economic class grounds, with the result that at crucial points the explanation cannot explain.[1]

In the most corrupt and famous electoral count in the nation's history, Tilden lost the election of 1876, though he clearly had a popular-vote majority. The major reason for his defeat, ironically, was that he was too good a Jeffersonian who obviously practiced what he preached. Southerners in Congress, when the critical votes were taken, decided—after intensive behind-the-scenes maneuvering—to swing the victory to the Republican, Rutherford B. Hayes. The record of Tilden's governorship made it chillingly clear that he meant what he said about slashing expenditures on internal improvements. The South desperately needed its ports and rivers and bridges and railroad system rebuilt after the destruction of the Civil War and the neglect of the Reconstruction years. The Republicans were clearly more friendly to such measures, for they had constructed internal improvements all over the Northern states.

Montgomery Blair, an old Jacksonian, explained Tilden's defeat as having been caused by precisely the same political and economic forces he and Tilden had fought in the Age of Jackson. "The jobbers and monopolists of the North made common cause with the Southern oligarchy," he said. They

[1] After a brilliant analysis of the economic factors in American life in the 1870's, based throughout on an implied assumption that these matters bore directly upon politics, Irwin Unger is forced to explain the puzzling fact that the greenbackers' appeals had no discernible effect on the election of 1876 by the formula that "traditional party loyalties" were stronger than considerations of class interest. Democratic voters, led by some unexplained allegiance to their party, "held their noses and swallowed Tilden." Unger, *Greenback Era*, p. 317. Such "explanations" simply tell us how much we do not yet know. It is possible that the sound-money position was in fact appealing to the urban masses. This supposition is borne out by what is now known of voting patterns in the 1890's, discussed in the next chapter. It is probable too, going on the British and the Jacksonian example, that a variety of ethno-cultural factors were at work.

had promised internal improvements and return of white governments to power in Southern states in exchange for a Hayes vote. A great scheme to launch a Southern transcontinental railroad, the Texas and Pacific, played a central role in the whole proceeding. "Tom Scott's railroad played the role in the seventies that Nick Biddle's bank played in the thirties."[2]

For the next four years, Tilden thought of himself, and was referred to by Democrats, as "President" Tilden. He maintained that on this ground he was prevented from taking any other public post. In 1880, the party turned to a Civil War hero, Winfield S. Hancock, in a vain attempt to capture the "bloody shirt" emotion the Republicans had exploited for so many years. After this failed completely, in 1884 the Democrats returned again to New York for their nominee. Grover Cleveland had suddenly appeared as a fighting governor, and behind his banner the party finally recaptured the White House, after a quarter of a century in the wilderness. The next twelve years were to be pre-eminently Cleveland's.

There were many in 1884, however, who had thought to make Tilden the nominee again, for he had become a sentimental favorite. A number of delegations went to the Democratic national convention of that year pledged to him. He was much too ill, however, to take on the responsibility, and he swung his support behind Cleveland, who admired Tilden's ideas. During the campaign, Tilden's contribution was to issue an attack on the Republicans that showed how strongly the original vision still figured in his larger view of politics:

> All history shows that reforms in government must not be expected from those who sit serenely on the social mountain-tops enjoying the benefits of the existing order of things. Even the divine Author of our religion found his followers not among the self-complacent Pharisees, but among lowly-minded fishermen. The Republican Party is largely made up of those who live by their wits, and who

[2] For all of the above, see the analysis of this crisis in C. Vann Woodward, *Reunion and Reaction* (New York, 1956), especially p. 228.

aspire in politics to advantages over the rest of mankind, similar to those which their daily lives are devoted to securing in private business.[3]

Cleveland appointed a close Tilden associate as his Secretary of the Treasury, and for the better part of two years Samuel Tilden finally had an almost daily supervision over the financial policies of the United States government. The end, however, was not far away. In August 1886, Samuel Tilden died, and Grover Cleveland, who had already been clearly moving out on his own independent path, was now wholly in possession of the leadership of the party.

[3] Letter to Committee from National Democratic Convention, October 6, 1884, in Bigelow, *Letters and Literary Memorials*, II, 654–5.

Chapter 8

GROVER CLEVELAND:
THE DEMOCRAT AS SOCIAL MORALIST

Sometime in the mid-1880's, the mood cracked. The optimism of the high Victorian era in Britain that had begun in the prosperity of the 1850's, and the "age of confidence"[1] that ensued in the United States in the booming years that followed the Civil War, gave way to a mood of despair. The depression of the 1870's, which had struck both countries, seemed only subconsciously to have shaken confidence, but real anxiety became the dominant mood when, after some years of upturn, the mid-1880's witnessed another serious depression. Labor violence, farm protests, the rage of the Irish peasant, and the upsurge of socialist doctrines and anarchist movements created widespread convictions that the whole social order was sick. Instead of a classless and contented equalitarian America subsisting on sturdy individualism and open opportunity, instead of a dynamic Britain in which anyone could get ahead if he adopted the proper virtues, it now seemed clear that the Anglo-American community represented slums, exploited farmers, hopeless poverty, and shameless wealth. The laboring classes in both countries had formerly been content to accept the middle-class virtues as their road to prosperity, but now began to turn away in distaste and to listen to those who talked of strikes and of class war.

[1] The term used in Higham, *Strangers in the Land.*

For many decades the Radicals—the Cobdens and the Brights—in Britain had looked to America as the shining example, the proof of all their ideas about the secular, equalitarian, and *laissez faire* state. Now the sobering news came from across the water that class conflict had become just as fixed in America as at home. The younger generation of British radicals therefore began to look away from America to Europe. In a real sense, collectivism took hold of the radical British mind precisely because of its disenchantment with conditions in the United States, where Cobden's and Bright's favorite formula of free schools and free churches and free votes did not seem to have worked and the basic economic and social questions remained still unsolved.[2]

In the turmoil that shook the United States in the 1880's, one great fact seemed prominent in the nation's consciousness: the country had become corrupt in deep and disturbing ways. Tilden had almost been carried to the White House on the strength of this feeling in the 1870's. The prosperity that followed may have temporarily dulled the emotion, reinforcing the Republican view that some deviltry was a small price to pay for the vast developments that were being carried through. But the obsession with corruption continued to grow, most notably in New York, which was in so many ways the example of what was happening in the nation at large. Both political and economic corruption were flagrant in the state, and it was to produce in Grover Cleveland the principal spokesman for the idea that the ills of the nation resulted chiefly from a moral corruption that had taken hold of its people.

Cleveland's leadership had therefore a significantly different quality from Tilden's. In a real sense, Cleveland was to be a Liberal-Democratic leader more in the Gladstonian and Jeffersonian tradition, for he was fundamentally a moralist.[3] Cleveland accepted completely the Jacksonian

[2] Cf. Pelling, *America and the British Left,* Ch. iv, "The Rise of Economic Radicalism and Socialism."

[3] It is important to note the difference between the nature of their moralism and that, say, of the aggressively religious who were in the Republican camp. With the exception of abolitionism, Liberal-Democratic moralism was fundamentally concerned with society, not with

economic analysis and held the same image of the economic enemy, but "selfishness" and "sordidness" were the key words in his vocabulary, not mechanistic metaphors like Tilden's "machinery of trade" or "flow of currency." He felt and expressed a massive sense of outrage, the same emotion that was driving Gladstone forward in his Home Rule battles in these years. It was in good part because Cleveland expressed so well the prevailing mood of the nation that he, alone among Democrats until Franklin Roosevelt, received more popular votes than his Republican antagonist in three successive presidential elections. This extraordinary ascendancy made the dozen years from 1883 to 1895—until the rise of William Jennings Bryan—the years of the Cleveland democracy.[4]

Grover Cleveland was known in 1881 only to the community of Buffalo, New York, and then simply as a stolid bachelor lawyer of forty-four who weighed 250 pounds, wore a walrus mustache, and had labored long within the local Democratic Party. He was popular among the Germans, and had once been a courageous sheriff of the county. Three years later, he was elected to the presidency of the United States.

There was no precedent for such a meteoric rise, nor was there ever to be its equal thereafter. "In him we got a president," Woodrow Wilson wrote in 1897, "as it were . . . by immediate choice from out of the body of the people, as the Constitution has all along appeared to expect . . . ." The Progressive editor William Allen White wrote in 1902 that Cleveland had been

> swept onward by the tidal power that was moving in the protesting hearts of the people . . . He did not make the

personal conduct—temperance, dancing, Sunday laws, and the like. (The Canadians show some variation in this matter.)
[4] The peculiarities of the Electoral College gave the victory to the Republican candidate in the election of 1888, the second of Cleveland's three campaigns.

wave, he rose with it. The revolt against Republican rule
was brutal, unplanned—a barbaric yawp of disgust . . .
[The] soul of the people was sick of politics, and was
nauseated at all politicians.[5]

His upward course began when an awakening of the
civic conscience in Buffalo against a local system of malo-
dorous corruption led to his being elected mayor in 1881. He
began immediately, in his implacable and uncompromising
way, to clean up the city, vetoing proposal after proposal as
they emanated from the corrupt city council. He displayed in
this a knack for the strong phrase, saying in one widely
quoted veto message that the granting of a contract to a man
whose bid was $100,000 above all others constituted nothing
less than "a most barefaced, impudent, and shameless scheme
to betray the interests of the people."[6]

When words like these were read by Tilden men in Albany, who were looking despairingly for a strong young man
to reunite the shattered party behind the cause of civic reform, they were delighted. They gave him their vigorous
support, ran him for governor over bitter Tammany protests,
and had him in the governor's mansion in Albany by the beginning of 1883. During the next two years he battled Tammany bosses on patronage matters and slashed away at spe-
cial-interest legislation. He vetoed a long series of proposals
that would have granted funds, special privileges, and immunities to banks, railroads, subway companies, electric
power corporations, and even ice houses. Carried along by an
inexhaustible physical strength, he worked steadily, day and
night, winnowing out everything questionable from the mass
of paper before him and carefully writing out his pungent
veto messages. He attacked the taxation system for ignoring
large fortunes in stocks and bonds, allowing "the rich, by
shirking taxation . . . [to add] to the burdens of the poor." He
criticized the liberality of the laws governing corporations,

[5] Woodrow Wilson, "Mr. Cleveland as President," *Atlantic Monthly*,
LXXIX (1897), 289; William Allen White, "Cleveland," *McClure's
Magazine*, XVIII (1902), 324–5.
[6] Veto of Street Cleaning Contract, June 26, 1882, in George F. Parker,
ed., *The Writings and Speeches of Grover Cleveland* (New York, 1892),
pp. 435–7.

which he condemned as speculative influences, and demanded that the state begin to exercise its "paternity" and "provide a simple, easy way for its people whose money is invested . . . to discover how the funds of these institutions are spent, and how their affairs are conducted."[7]

This nonstop performance made Cleveland a national figure. "For two years, as governor of New York, Grover Cleveland stood the one strong, looming figure in the nation."[8] Independent Republicans, revolted by the corruption in their party and particularly by the long ascendancy of James G. Blaine, the symbol of unprincipled subserviency to vested interests, began defecting to Cleveland's side. Many supported him as early as the gubernatorial election of 1882. As the presidential election of 1884 approached, the defection of Independent Republicans swelled to a stampede.

The adhesion of the Independent Republicans—the Mugwumps, as they came to be called for obscure reasons—to the Cleveland Democrats was an event of major importance, not only in United States affairs, but also within the larger framework of Anglo-American politics. In effect, it made the Cleveland Democrats even more the American counterpart of the Liberal Party in Britain. Almost the sole difference between the Liberals and the Democrats had been the absence of such a group within Democratic ranks. Men possessed of a strong sense of moral purpose—men to whom abolitionism was an appealing cause—had long been deflected from the Democrats to the Whig-Republicans by the hostility to such reforms that the Jacksonians had displayed, and by the attitudes and nature of their constituency: the Irish, the Germans, and the Davy Crockett type in rural and urban life. The Democrats had a disreputable air, and educated men in mid-century who came from respectable families found the Republican Party not simply the place for men of moral sensitivity but the only party that seemed a congenial milieu for gentlemen. A principal inheritance that the

[7] State of New York, *Public Papers of Grover Cleveland, Governor* (Albany, 1883), pp. 36–7, 59, 62–3, 68–9, 91, 93–101, 122–32; State of New York, *Public Papers of Grover Cleveland, Governor* (Albany, 1884), pp. 4–5.
[8] White, "Cleveland," pp. 324–35.

Republicans received from their predecessors, the Whigs, was the reputation of being the party of the established, the party of gentility.

There were great hopes among young educated Republicans at the end of the Civil War that the nation was about to begin a new day of reform and national vitalization. They were convinced that the renaissance would be undertaken by the Republican Party, fresh from its victories and dedicated to the ideal of a strong national government directing a unified nation. More to the point, they thought of themselves, the young men of education and good family and moral sensitivity, as the leaders of such a dynamic Republican Party. Henry Adams wrote from England, where his father had been ambassador to Britain during the war, "We want a national set of young men like ourselves or better, to start new influences not only in politics, but in literature, in law, in society, and throughout the whole social organism of the country—a national school of our own generation."[9] When he came home from London, he arrived looking forward eagerly to an eminent career in American politics like that enjoyed by comparable young men in England.

It had been natural for E. L. Godkin to gravitate to the Republicans when in the 1850's he arrived in America steeped in British Liberalism. He had "been conditioned to look on politics as a moralistic, purposive, ideological social process," and the Republicans, he said, were "the party of good government, of virtue, of knowledge, and understanding." The Democrats, on the other hand, with their Tammany Hall and Irish Catholic image—particularly repellent to a Protestant Irishman like Godkin—and their alliance with slave owning Southerners, were the party of "the most ignorant and vicious elements in the community."[1] He shared the great hopes that were in the air after the war, and the exciting sense that cerebral Republicans like himself would be leading and directing the work. His intellectual godfather,

[9] Ernest Samuels, *The Young Henry Adams* (Cambridge, Mass., 1948), pp. 145–6.
[1] Morton Keller, Introduction, to the John Harvard Library edition of *Problems of Modern Democracy: Political and Economic Essays* by E. L. Godkin (Cambridge, Mass., 1966), pp. xviii, xxxix.

John Stuart Mill, wrote him in encouragement, saying that "the great concussion which has taken place in the American mind must have loosened the foundations of all prejudices, and secured a fair hearing for impartial reason on all subjects such as it might not otherwise have had for many generations."[2]

Godkin founded the *Nation* in 1865, joining to it in the 1880's the New York *Evening Post,* which he directed until 1900. Through these publications he became the voice of the Mugwumps, exerting an extraordinary influence on the opinions of the educated, professional, and reforming classes. "To my generation," wrote William James, "Godkin's was certainly the towering influence in all thought concerning public affairs, and indirectly his influence has certainly been more pervasive than that of any other writer of the generation . . ."[3] Through the latter decades of the century he urged classic Gladstonian Liberalism upon the Independent Republican mind—as befitted a man whose father was one of Gladstone's advisers—calling at first for Negro equality, and then, as that issue faded, for low tariffs, honest and abstemious government, no aids to business enterprise, sound money, and hostility to imperialism. He helped to create the characteristic Mugwump attitude, which was that all issues, as he insisted in true Gladstonian fashion, must be judged by moral rather than by crudely practical standards.[4]

The hopes of Godkin and his audience were to be sadly disappointed. They were successful in creating an integrated and remarkably vigorous structure of intellectual life in the postwar decades, expressing itself in social-science associations, journals of literature and public affairs, and the "new" universities founded upon research and the advancement of knowledge. But men of education, of lineage, of respectability, and of moral concern were not wanted in the new political and economic order, as Henry Adams soon found to his lasting dismay. The Republican Party had unsuspected resources of corruption of its own. It became primarily de-

[2] Quoted in ibid., pp. xiv–xv.
[3] Quoted in ibid., p. viii.
[4] Ibid., pp. xiv–xxxi.

voted to the wishes of the entrepreneurial classes at all levels, and it identified almost completely with the material values that the Independent Republican mind deplored.

In Richard Hofstadter's view, the subsequent behavior of the Mugwumps arose from a feeling that they were being rudely displaced by a new class. A status revolution had taken place in American life; the older elite, with their local wealth and high social position, were submerged by the oceanic rising of the new industrial order. Coarse new men with great fortunes made the Mugwump feel shrunken and ineffectual. The Republican Party had become a strange world of corrupt bargains, millionaire senators, and endless chicane.[5] Expertise and a disinterested social conscience had no place in that world. As the Peelites had chosen the wrong partners in the Tory squirearchy a generation before, so the Mugwumps had chosen the wrong partners in the entrepreneurial Republicans.[6]

They therefore began agitating for civil-service reform. The function of such a reform was clearly, in their minds, to be that of the earlier civil-service reform in Britain: it would ensure places in public service for men of education and breeding, since in these years the two went together. Civil service would not only establish an efficient and honest government that could resist the importunities of businessmen, it would minister to the Mugwumps' wounded sense of being left out.

For, ironically, the Mugwumps had come to share the minority-group status of such elements as the Irish Catholics. All the things that the civil-service reformer believed in had been cast aside.

---

[5] Richard Hofstadter, *The Age of Reform, from Bryan to F.D.R.* (New York, 1955), pp. 134–43.
[6] I take it from the writings of Irwin Unger and Robert Sharkey, previously cited, that of all the interest groups in the economy, the entrepreneurial class (if it may be spoken of as a class) was the most uniformly Republican, when economic groupings alone are considered. My own studies in California politics and economics in this same period lead me to believe that this generalization is sound. Cf. Robert Kelley, "Taming the Sacramento: Hamiltonianism in Action," *Pacific Historical Review*, XXXIV (1965), 21–49.

John Stuart Mill was his philosopher and William E. Gladstone his ideal statesman. . . . He favored free trade in an age of growing protectionism. He demanded hard money when cries for currency expansion grew louder. He hated monopoly and rapacious capitalism when big business swept all before it. He disliked unions, strikes, and radicals, but these all became more common. He was engulfed in the city of his fathers by an increasing flood of immigrants from eastern and southern Europe. He opposed imperialism, but in the twilight of his career witnessed America's most hypernationalistic war. The reformer stood for little government in a period when the civil service proportionately grew faster than the population, and he called for civil service reform while the blatant spoilsman reached his zenith. The reformer was an outsider, philosophically as well as politically.[7]

In these circumstances, Godkin's feeling of identity with the Republicans grew progressively more tenuous. As James G. Blaine, with his seamy past and his outspoken Anglophobia, grew more dominant within the Republican Party in the 1880's, Godkin and the Mugwumps became more restive. When Blaine was nominated for the presidency in 1884, Godkin led a wholesale defection of Mugwumps to the Cleveland ticket. In June 1884, three columns of letters from Independent Republicans appeared in *The New York Times* in support of Cleveland, signed by such luminaries as Carl Schurz, Henry Ward Beecher, Charles F. Adams, Jr., President Charles Eliot of Harvard, and most of the Harvard faculty.[8]

Thereafter, for as long as Cleveland led the Democratic Party, the Mugwumps were his warmest supporters, and among his closest associates. As Woodrow Wilson described it, if Cleveland "spoke and acted for the views of any body of men . . . he was the leader of those independent Republicans who had broken with their own party, and were looking for

[7] Ari A. Hoogenboom, *Outlawing The Spoils: A History of the Civil Service Reform Movement 1865–1883* (Urbana, Illinois, 1961), pp. 21, 196–7.
[8] Allan Nevins, *Grover Cleveland: A Study in Courage* (New York, 1932), p. 157; Rollo Ogden, "Edwin Lawrence Godkin," in *Dictionary of American Biography*, Allen Johnson and Dumas Malone, eds. (New York, 1931), VII, 347–50; Unger, *Greenback Era*, pp. 131–44.

some one who should open a new era in party politics and give them efficient and public-spirited principles to believe in and vote for again."[9]

One of the best examples of these men was Richard Watson Gilder, poet, patron of the arts, and vigorous advocate of civil-service and slum-housing reform in New York City. For many years he edited the *Century* magazine, a journal of literature and public affairs in the English Liberal style that played a significant role in the nation's intellectual life. He became one of Cleveland's most intimate friends— though he remarked that Cleveland never quite seemed able to forget he had been a Republican—and after Cleveland's death wrote one of the best descriptions of him.[1]

The Mugwumps taught Cleveland a great deal. He was already a Jacksonian—especially in currency matters, where the Tildenites had instructed him—but the social vision that in time he displayed as President proceeded from a much broader perspective on the world than that provided by Tildenism alone. In his long battle on the tariff and in his foreign policy, it is clear that Grover Cleveland had become a Gladstonian Liberal, American-style.[2] The whole world view of British Liberalism—which was fundamentally harmonious with his Jacksonian inheritance—came to him with the Mugwumps. The result was a different kind of presidency than observers of him would have predicted when he was in the governor's mansion in Albany.

The similarity between the Gladstonian Liberals and the Cleveland Democrats is heightened by another consideration. Just as the advent to power of Gladstone's governments from 1880 onward signalized a new day for the Irish, so the advent of Cleveland's government meant a new day for the

[9] Wilson, "Cleveland," p. 292.
[1] William B. Cairns, "Richard Watson Gilder," *Dictionary of American Biography*, VII, 275–8; Richard Watson Gilder, "Grover Cleveland: A Record of Friendship," *Century*, LXXVIII (1909), 483–501, 687–705, 846–60; LXXIX (1910), 24–31.
[2] When Richard Watson Gilder, in a typical Mugwump gesture, sent a copy of John Morley's *Life of Gladstone* to Cleveland as soon as it was published, Cleveland's reply was revealing: "I desire to thank you for it from the bottom of my heart. Somehow I don't get much chance to read now-a-days; but this book I shall read." Letter, Cleveland to Gilder, March 21, 1904, in Nevins, *Letters*, p. 575.

South. Cleveland's election in 1884 was widely regarded as the signal that the South was once more to be "brought . . . back into the Union," with a renewed opportunity of "impressing itself upon the national policy." The loyalty issue that Democrats had had to struggle with for a quarter of a century, especially in the form of "bloody shirt" oratory on the Republican side, slowly subsided in the Cleveland years.[3]

It was not that Cleveland actually pushed forward a program of legislation for the Southern white. The key element was rather—as in so much of minority-group politics— the stimulus to self-respect that came with symbolic recognition by the highest authority in the land. When Cleveland appointed Southerners to his cabinet, visited Gettysburg but refused to make a speech, praised the unveiling of a statue of a much-loved Confederate general, fished in Illinois but declined to visit Lincoln's tomb, and took steps to return Confederate battle flags to their states, Southerners were grateful, and professional rebel haters in the Northern states—especially the Grand Army of the Republic, the veterans' organization—were enraged. At a later time Cleveland was to lose the South's loyalty completely, but in his three presidential campaigns it was with him solidly.[4]

One of the principal features of the troubled 1880's was the reappearance of virulent anti-alien nativism, and this had the effect of solidifying the Democratic loyalties of another traditional Democratic voting bloc, the ethnic minorities. The Republicans led in diatribes against all immigrants and against Catholics in particular as sources of the nation's terrible difficulties in these years. Patriotic societies of all sorts came into being to preach the nativist dogma, and the Grand Army of the Republic—an inveterately Republican body— and such organizations as the British-American Association

[3] Paul H. Buck, *The Road to Reunion*, 1865–1900 (New York, 1959), pp. 280–1.

The Democrats' concern for the South did not mean, of course, concern for the Negro, but for the Southern white. By Cleveland's day, even the Republicans had long since forgotten their zeal for Negro equality—those of them who had possessed it. E. L. Godkin was uncomfortable at the idea of social equality for the Negro, and he dropped it from the columns of the *Nation* as soon as he could.

[4] Nevins, *Cleveland*, pp. 322–4, 332–4.

and the Loyal Orange Institution made anti-Catholicism and nativism practically their *raison d'être*. Primarily an urban phenomenon concentrated in the Northeastern states and in the older Middle West, the nativist agitation of the 1880's swelled into a national crusade in the anxieties of the depression-ridden 1890's.

> The period resounded with organized campaigns to arouse a vigorous "Americanism." Flag exercises, replete with special salutes and pledges, spread throughout the public schools along with agitation for inculcating patriotism. Among well-to-do, status-conscious circles, over a dozen hereditary patriotic societies sprang up in the early nineties to cultivate a keener, more exclusive sense of nationality. Beginning with the Sons of the American Revolution in 1889, these prestige organizations embarked on a round of banquets, receptions, and celebrations. Their principal theme was always the dire importance of perpetuating the pure American spirit of one's ancestors.[5]

Anti-Catholicism reached heights of bigotry, depicting the Catholics as leading America to disaster through the fomenting of labor strikes and even through such diabolical plots as runs on the banks to precipitate depressions. The American Protective Association, a secret society that swelled to more than a million members, demanded oaths that members would never vote for a Catholic. It attracted great numbers of the predominantly Protestant immigrants from the Scandinavian countries, stimulated ugly vigilante outbreaks against Catholics, and described the Republican Party as the only bulwark the nation possessed against the threat of a papal *coup d'état*. By the mid-1890's, the APA began dying away as the nativist hysteria passed its peak, but in the Cleveland years it was a power in the land.[6]

The Irish Catholics and other such threatened ethnic minorities were therefore fervent supporters of Cleveland and the Democrats, who continued to oppose all proposals for immigration restriction and to provide a political home

[5] Higham, *Strangers in the Land*, p. 75.
[6] Ibid., pp. 35–95.

for the minority groups. Even when radical Irish Catholic reformers like John Boyle O'Reilly began to emerge in the 1880's from the generally conservative Irish Catholic world, they clung loyally to the Democrats and refused their support to more radical parties. O'Reilly's devotion to the Democrats

derived from his belief that it was the party of the masses, whereas the Republican Party was that of the classes, and, even worse, the inheritor of the anti-Irish and anti-Catholic prejudice of Know-Nothingism. In city, state, and national elections, he urged the readers of the *Pilot* [his Boston newspaper, widely popular among the Irish] to vote *en masse* for Democratic nominees, although he had the very awkward task of explaining away Cleveland's anti-parochial school bias. When Benjamin F. Butler, the idol of the Irish in Massachusetts, bolted the Democratic Party and ran for President in 1884 on the Greenback and Anti-Monopoly ticket, the Irish editor warned his people that a vote for the General would be a vote lost to Cleveland and hence one for Blaine, the leader of the anti-Irish party. Yet O'Reilly admired Butler to the point of idolatry and approved his platform . . .[7]

In the decade when Gladstone was fighting for the Irish in the British Parliament, therefore, Cleveland and the Democrats played the same role in the United States. The result was the full re-emergence behind Grover Cleveland of the minority-group coalition—composed of the Southern white and the largely Catholic ethnic minorities in the North—that had been the underpinning of the Democratic Party in the years before the Civil War.

The recruitment of the Mugwumps, furthermore, re-established the Democratic link with the large segment of the intellectual classes that had been a principal feature of the Jacksonian Democratic coalition. The journals of opinion and the faculties of the great universities to an extraordinary degree were behind the Cleveland presidencies.

[7] Mann, *Yankee Reformers in the Urban Age,* p. 39.

What kind of a man was Grover Cleveland? The adjectives spring easily to mind, for they are well known: stolid, courageous, unreflective, determined, high-minded. They were applied to him in his own time, and they have been the stuff of history ever since. A prominent Mugwump, Carl Schurz, wrote that Cleveland had been elected precisely because his talents were so nonpolitical. He was not fascinating; he had no eloquence and no personal magnetism; he displayed nothing romantic in his history; and he had not the ability to be all things to all men.

> People saw in him a man conscientiously devoted to his duties, honest in his zeal to understand and to perform them without regard to personal advantage, and maintaining with dauntless courage what he thought right against friend and foe alike—a personality of exceptional strength and trustworthiness, commanding confidence.[8]

This, the standard picture of Cleveland in history, for all its evident truth, is an incomplete portrait. It depicts Cleveland as a man with no larger view of politics whatever. Even Allan Nevins's classic biography is largely unconcerned with Cleveland's ideas, and deals rather with his courageous character.[9] His most recent biographer describes him simply as the mindless leader of "the Bourbon Democrats, who were the conservative spokesmen of business in the party. Their function was to prevent control of the government by farmers, wage earners and inefficient, irresponsible, corrupt officeholders."[1] That this fundamentally Beardian view leaves much to be desired seems clear when Cleveland's background and his ideas, heretofore largely neglected, are examined.

Grover Cleveland was a minister's son, and a Democrat whose political lineage went back to the Jacksonians. Curiously, his biographies have left these matters largely unex-

[8] Carl Schurz, "Grover Cleveland's Second Administration," *McClure's Magazine*, IX (1897), 634.
[9] Cf. Nevins, *Grover Cleveland: A Study in Courage*.
[1] Horace Samuel Merrill, *Bourbon Leader: Grover Cleveland and the Democratic Party* (Boston, 1957).

plored. Such questions still remain as, What was the nature of the Presbyterianism within which he was reared? Set beside his larger view of politics, does the profile of the one resemble that of the other? Similarly, what was there in the Jacksonian outlook that may be found in Cleveland's as well? Once these questions are explored, a new rationale for understanding Cleveland's presidencies appears. Cleveland himself looks rather different from the picture of him given to us by the standard accounts.

Cleveland's own testimony points to the religious line of analysis. "I was reared and taught in the strictest school of Presbyterianism," he once said of his childhood years, which were spent near Syracuse, in the heart of western New York. To the "precious precepts and examples of my early days," he went on, "I owe every faculty of usefulness I possess, and every just apprehension of the duties and obligations of life." During noontimes, in Sabbath school, in three church sessions every Sunday, and in a family circle "Hallowed and sanctified by the spirit of Presbyterianism," he was rigorously taught the faith. Though the Shorter Catechism, he said, was difficult for a boy to understand, "those are not apt to be the worst citizens who were early taught, 'what is the chief end of man?' "[2]

He was not a churchgoing man in mature life. He was rather the kind of minister's son who veers away from the childhood pattern of life, enjoying the saloons and the songs. Buffalo, to which he moved to spend twenty-five years in law practice, was a rough-and-tumble port city on Lake Erie. Here Cleveland "observed that the Germans of Buffalo were, on the whole, about the best citizens; and he was happy sitting on a sanded floor with an old German landlady to refill his glass."[3] Yet there was another side to his nature that

---

[2] Address, Ninth Annual Meeting, Actors' Fund of America, New York City, Jan. 3, 1890, Albert Ellery Bergh, ed., *Grover Cleveland: Addresses, State Papers and Letters* (New York, 1909), pp. 196–200; Address, Northern and Southern Presbyterian Assemblies, Philadelphia, May 23, 1888, Cleveland Papers, Series Five.

[3] Louis Filler, ed., *Democrats and Republicans: Ten Years of the Republic—From Harry Thurston Peck's Twenty Years of the Republic* (New York, 1964), quoting from the Cincinnati *Enquirer*, March 25, 1885.

showed the strong persistence of his early training. All his life his friends saw two Clevelands, one jovial and fun-loving, the other stern and unbending in his work and responsibilities, beclouded, as it were, by a pall of duty.[4] Cleveland's case is another reminder that it is what is learned early in life that must be examined, despite later appearances.

What did it mean to be a Presbyterian in western New York in the years of Cleveland's youth? It meant being reared in the Burned-Over District, one of the great battlegrounds of American religion. Here took place in the Jacksonian years the explosion of revivalistic fervor that spawned, among other faiths, the Adventist churches, the Mormon churches, and John Humphrey Noyes's Perfectionism. Methodists, Baptists, Disciples of Christ, Universalists, Presbyterians, and many others crossed and recrossed western New York, setting off whirlwinds of evangelistic religion. As Whitney R. Cross describes it, a "veritable host of evangelists . . . swarmed over Yankeedom, old and new, preaching every shade of gospel, heresy, and reform to a people who for a generation had been saturated with spiritual and moral intensity. The impulse to eccentricity and radicalism was thus broadly and deeply planted."[5]

The social psychology that for a number of years came to dominate western New York was expressed in the "ultra" cast of mind. True believers charged with the fire that a conviction of direct contact with God can give were confident they were the agents of the operation of the Holy Spirit in the here and now. Moved by an urgent belief that Christ was soon coming to usher in the millennium, and called upon by their faith to purify the world in preparation for that Coming, ultras set off clamorous reform crusades. The concept of sin was expanded far beyond its normal human boundaries. The slightest transgression now became a stench in the nostrils of God. Men of solid reputation for probity and good will found themselves accused of radical sinfulness for petty acts. At the same time, the ultra was typically convinced that

---

[4] Nevins, *Cleveland*, pp. 58–9. See also letter to C. D. Wilson, April 5, 1907, in Allan Nevins, ed., *Letters of Grover Cleveland, 1850–1908* (Boston, 1933), p. 614.
[5] Cross, *Burned-Over District*, pp. 187–8.

all the world's ills could be solved by one or another great and simple reform to be achieved now, immediately, by one bold cleansing stroke.[6]

They were determined to use governments—as in the days of the Puritan past—as divine instruments to reshape American life in accordance with the imperatives of the newly recharged faith. It has been observed that the churches of New England were only partially out of the frame of mind induced by generations of existence as state churches. "Again and again, confronted by special problems or opportunities, they reverted to the old custom of using government or tax monies to support church work."[7] Anti-Masonry, temperance campaigns, agitation for Sunday laws, and similar ultra crusades increased the turbulence of the Jacksonian years. So vigorous did this new Yankee clericalism become that some suspected a new linkup of church and state. The temperance campaign in particular led many to cry "Priestcraft! Church and State!" A labor paper charged that "political anti-Masonry is neither more nor less than a Church and State intrigue."[8] In time, this political activism, frustrated in the temperance crusade, moved on into the long campaign for abolition of slavery.

All of this, which was so like contemporary Evangelicalism in England and the Free Kirk movement in Scotland, had been largely set in motion in western New York by the Presbyterians—a fact that caused their fellow churchmen elsewhere painful concern. Presbyterians in the Burned-Over District, in fact, were a special type quite unlike the ruggedly orthodox Presbyterians in New Jersey, Pennsylvania, and the Southern states. New Jersey by the end of the colonial period had acquired the heaviest concentration of Scots in the colonies. In 1746, Princeton University was founded (as the College of New Jersey) specifically to train Presbyterian min-

[6] Ibid., pp. 198–208. Usually a reform such as temperance. The ultra was typically not a critic of the economy.
[7] Franklin Hamlin Littell, *From State Church to Pluralism: A Protestant Interpretation of Religion in American History* (Garden City, N.Y., 1962), p. 47.
[8] Cross, *Burned-Over District*, pp. 131–2; Benson, *Concept of Jacksonian Democracy*, p. 195.

isters, and it maintained close ties with Scotland thereafter. Purified of any free-will tendencies by its reaction against the Great Awakening of the 1730's and 1740's, the Presbyterianism that flourished among the Scots and the Scotch-Irish of Pennsylvania and the Southern states was sternly Calvinist.[9]

Presbyterians in the Burned-Over District, however, were originally New England Congregationalists of the more enthusiastic and religiously liberal sort who, by the Plan of Union, became Presbyterians when they entered New York.[1] They led the early revivals in western New York, and continued thereafter to bring on a new outburst of self-conscious, inspired, and triumphant evangelicalism. Leading Presbyterian revivalists like Charles Finney were not trained ministers, carefully schooled in the creedal beliefs, the scholastic distinctions, and the fundamental theology of Presbyterianism. Finney did not even know the Westminster Confession of Faith, working instead directly from the Scriptures. Since the revival situation seemed to demand an assumption of personal choice, Finney and other evangelists unconsciously moved toward free will. The rigorous determinism of traditional Calvinism disappeared, and the emphasis thereafter in this branch of the Presbyterian Church was toward Perfectionism, with all the radical changes in theological world view that this implied.[2]

Presbyterians outside the "infected" area reacted with distaste. They detested religious enthusiasm. "Dignified clergymen, whatever their theology, objected to being called antichristian merely because they hesitated to act like common ranters."[3] More than this, they were outraged by unorthodox theology. The Princeton divines, the theologians for American Presbyterianism, were deeply aroused by the free-will heresy. They and the Scotch-Irish Presbyterians had long believed they had opened the gates to heretical beliefs when they had agreed in 1801 to the Plan of Union, and now their

---

[9] Cf. Leyburn, Scotch-Irish: A Social History, pp. 242–6, 278–95; Graham, Colonists from Scotland, pp. 142–6; Pryde, Scotland, p. 21.
[1] Cross, Burned-Over District, pp. 14–22.
[2] Ibid., pp. 159–60.
[3] Ibid., p. 163.

fears were confirmed. They began a counterattack. By heresy trials and annual battles in the Presbyterian General Assembly the conflict was carried on for years within the Church. By 1837 the Old School had a clear majority at the Philadelphia meeting, and four synods in western New York containing almost half the membership of the Church were bodily excluded—at almost the same that a similar disruption was taking place among Presbyterians in Scotland.[4] The American Home Missionary Society, which had long been the Church's principal arm in western New York, shifted wholly to the conservative side, and many congregations split off from the infected synods to join orthodoxy. Eventually, many Presbyterian ultras moved out of the Church and erected Congregational bodies, making that sect as large in the Burned-Over District as the Presbyterian.[5]

Ultraism, meanwhile, was in process of collapse. In reaction, disillusioned ultras were finding their way back to orthodoxy, where strict fundamentalism and an exclusive concern for simply saving souls and not transforming the world was the mode.[6] The "radicalism of the reform movements and the heresy of perfectionism turned moderates into conservatives and prepared a substantial portion of each major denomination for a contest to determine which could best prove its utter orthodoxy."[7]

This was the context for the Cleveland family's entrance into western New York in 1841. It explains two things left largely untouched by the Cleveland biographies—one apparently unimportant, the other of central concern: the move of the Cleveland family from New Jersey to western New York; and why the Clevelands, father and son, were Democrats.[8]

Richard Falley Cleveland was a firmly orthodox Presbyterian minister who had been trained for the ministry at Princeton. He was clearly part of the counterattack against heresy. He was doubtless sent to the Syracuse region in western New York as an emissary of sanity, of the true faith, to

[4] Discussed below, in Chapter 9.
[5] Cross, *Burned-Over District*, pp. 259–61.
[6] Ibid., pp. 252, 277.
[7] Ibid., p. 257.
[8] Cf. Nevins, *Cleveland*, pp. 15, 44.

train his congregation in the stern doctrines of the Shorter Catechism. He became a principal figure in the American Home Missionary Society, which was orthodoxy's leading agency in the battle against the heresiarchs.

Furthermore, the ultras against whom the long campaign for the true faith was mounted were Whigs, attracted to that party by its activist ideas about government, its concern for "morality" and "decency," and its friendliness to religion in politics. The Whigs, in effect, were the state-church party in American politics. Many in New York State seem to have become Democrats precisely because they disliked the ultras. As Lee Benson has shown, much of New York politics can be explained by the instinctive reaction of the Dutch, the Irish Catholics, and the workingmen's movements against the puritans of the Burned-Over District. The latter wanted to attack the Masons and the Catholic infidels, free the slaves, end drinking, and create a collectivist atmosphere of active government intervention in private morals. Their whole style of life—righteous, sin-hating, abstemious, austere—revolted those of more robust life styles, who seem in consequence to have largely voted Democratic.[9] One suspects the same could be said of Cleveland's Germans, with their boisterous conviviality.

These considerations may explain why the Clevelands were staunch Democrats. The "enemy" in their lives was Whig, enthusiastic and activist in politics and religion, and abolitionist. Nothing illustrates this difference more graphically than the fact that Benjamin Harrison, Cleveland's Republican antagonist in the presidential elections of 1888 and 1892, was a Presbyterian of the "ultra" type. While Cleveland was an orthodox young Presbyterian in New York, Harrison was an "ultra" Presbyterian in Ohio. He attended Miami University in Ohio, a Presbyterian hotbed of revivalism and abolitionism, and almost became a minister. Unlike Cleveland, he remained active in the Church, spending forty years as a deacon and Bible-class leader.[1]

[9] Benson, *Concept of Jacksonian Democracy*, pp. 165–207, 288–328.
[1] Cf. Harry J. Sievers, *Benjamin Harrison: Hoosier Warrior* (New York, 1960), pp. 55, 59–65, 111–28.
When it is considered that George Brown and John A. Macdonald

When the Clevelands found distasteful the abolitionism and flamboyance of the Frémont presidential campaign of 1856—the first Republican presidential effort—they were therefore reacting not against single issues, but against a whole complex of negative associations and cherished dislikes. It was ironic that the ultras drove orthodox Presbyterians, Irish Roman Catholics, and agnostic New York City intellectuals and workingmen into the same party.[2] It was never a comfortable working partnership, which points up again the classic observation that in politics as in war, "The enemy of my enemy is my friend."

The Presbyterianism of Cleveland's youth, as befits a counterrevolution, was therefore in a state of victorious, energetic orthodoxism. Creed, doctrine, and dogma were emphasized, not vitalism. In Cleveland's time the teacher was the key figure in the Church, not the preacher. Parishioners were drilled in the specifics of doctrine, not led to apply them to the ills of the larger world. "Instruction in the Catechism," Charles A. Briggs of Union Theological Seminary in New York City later observed, "was almost universal. Lectures upon the Confession of Faith, and in exposition of the Scriptures, on Sabbath morning and at the weekly lecture, were heard gladly by the people." The reigning mode of Biblical interpretation was sternly fundamentalist. When many years later the dramatic discoveries of higher criticism excited the religious world, Cleveland's reaction was revealing: the "Bible is good enough for me, just the old book under which I was brought up. I do not want notes, or criticism, or explanations about authorship or origin, or even cross-references. I do not need or understand them, and they confuse me."[3]

in Canada were also different kinds of Presbyterians who led opposing parties, one gets the feeling that Anglo-American politics in the nineteenth century constitute in a curious way a family argument among Presbyterians. Other Democratic Presbyterians were Andrew Jackson, Samuel Tilden, William Jennings Bryan, and Woodrow Wilson. On the Republican side in the post-Civil War period, James G. Blaine also came from the Presbyterians, though of necessity he joined a Congregational church when he finally settled down in Maine.
[2] Cross, *Burned-Over District*, pp. 168, 207; Benson, *Concept of Jacksonian Democracy*, pp. 195–6.
[3] Charles A. Briggs, *Whither? A Theological Question for the Times*

It says much about American Presbyterianism that the key document utilized in its teaching was the Shorter Catechism. The other fundamental statements prepared by the Westminster Assembly of Divines in the 1640's—the Confession of Faith and the Larger Catechism—have a different temper. They are relatively flexible, subtle, and qualified. It is possible in them to see not only the sterner attributes of God, but also to see in Him a deity concerned about the fate of mankind, lively in His appreciation of the complexities of the human condition, and ready to enter into a many-sided relationship with man in which love would be a major element. The Shorter Catechism, however, through its brevity, contains a much more austere, simplistic, and demanding Calvinism. American Presbyterianism from time to time modified the Confession and the Larger Catechism, but the Shorter Catechism, upon which the Church concentrated, was retained without change. The result was to make American Presbyterianism perhaps the most theologically conservative of all branches of the Calvinist world.[4]

The consuming center of attention in the Shorter Catechism is the awesome transcendent sovereignty of God, not His saving concern for mankind nor His vitality. He is seen as stern, demanding, unbending. Twin to His sovereignty is man's duty, which is inexorable, imperative, inescapable. One must worship God not through gratitude or love or adoration, but because of duty. "The scriptures principally teach," says the Third Answer, "what man is to believe concerning God, and what duty God requires of man."[5] The most important section in the Catechism is that concerned with morals, for the first rule revealed to man by God, the Catechism states, "was the moral law." No mere man "is able in this life," the Catechism warns after scores of forbidding questions and answers developing all the nuances of sin and the moral law, "perfectly to keep the commandments . . ." Furthermore,

(New York, 1889), pp. 40–1; Gamaliel Bradford, "Grover Cleveland," *Atlantic*, CXXVI (1920), 656.
[4] Briggs, *Whither?*, p. 17–18, 27–8, 31.
[5] The edition here relied upon is that in the Rev. H. Humphrey, ed., *The New England Primer, Containing The Assembly's Catechism* . . . (Worchester, Mass., ca. 1852).

"Every sin deserveth God's wrath and curse, both in this life and that which is to come." So imperative was this punishment, indeed, that two of the major Presbyterian theologians of Princeton orthodoxy, Charles and A. A. Hodge, held that God is bound to practice justice by punishing sin, thus denying him the freedom to love and to forgive. "Christian love," wrote Briggs despairingly, "has been overwhelmed by law."[6]

Briggs's despair, however, was the grief of a liberal professor of theology at Union, not at Princeton, who was trying more or less from the outside to change the temper of the Church. The measure of his failure may be seen in the publication in 1901, by the Presbyterian Committee of Publication, of E. W. Smith's orthodox *The Creed of Presbyterians*, which by the 1920's had become much the most widely read book ever written in America on Presbyterianism.[7]

Smith proclaimed the Presbyterian as "pronouncedly and preeminently" a doctrinal church. What, he asked, was the most prominent and pervading quality of its basic documents? Ethical concern, expressed as "the practical 'duty which God requires of man.'" God's holy laws, Smith warned, covered every aspect of life; we were forever accountable to them. No other creed, he observed, was so devoted to divine law. Nowhere else but in the Westminster Standards could be found "such an unfolding of the heart-searching claims of that law," especially in the stern Shorter Catechism, the "consummate flower" of the Westminster Assembly. Why was the Shorter Catechism so demanding, so filled with hard sayings? Because "there are hard sayings in the Bible." The Standards, therefore, had never been popular with "the rationalistic and unregenerate world."[8]

The dominant theme of Presbyterian faith, Smith observed, was its "exaltation of God." He was "the Absolute and Ever-Blessed Sovereign, infinitely worthy of love, worship,

---

[6] Briggs, *Whither?*, pp. 57–60, 93–6. Charles Hodge's orthodoxy is presented in *What Is Presbyterianism?* (Philadelphia, 1855), and the views of the father of Princeton orthodoxy, Archibald Alexander, may be seen in his *Thoughts on Religious Experience* (Philadelphia, 1844).
[7] E. W. Smith, *The Creed of Presbyterians* (Richmond, Va., 1901), "Preface to the Study Class Edition," dated 1924, pp. ix–x.
[8] Ibid., pp. 22, 26, 34.

and obedience . . ." At the peril of the soul, God's will and order must be obeyed. "Not," Smith warned, "is it pleasant, or popular, or profitable; but, is it right? Is it what God would have me do? This is Calvinism's first question."[9]

God being great and glorious, man's sins were "heinous and fatal." The enormity of them and the punishment they deserved were "beyond man's calculation and conception." Sin was utterly loathsome and deadly. Left to himself, man was hopelessly condemned, hopelessly miserable. Only God's inscrutable decision—made, as the Shorter Catechism puts it, "out of his mere good pleasure"—would save degraded man. But the feeling of salvation, when it came, placed a man's feet upon rock. He was sure; he was confident; he had in him a divine energy springing from the confidence that "through him is working out eternal purposes of good . . ." Thus he had invincible strength, the strength of a man who knew himself to be a man of destiny. "Alone among men he may be, but only more consciously allied with God." Steeled with the conviction that he was working out God's commands, the Presbyterian would go to his work and troubles "shielded by a panoply more invulnerable, and nerved by a courage more unconquerable, than any other faith could bestow."[1]

Predestination and Providence were the core doctrines to this faith. They meant that God had a plan for the world (predestination) and moved to carry it out (providence). Rooted in Calvinism, in short, was the belief that God rules, and actively so. He had authority; he had "a right to exercise dominion; [and] for the good of the universe that right should be exercised . . ." He was "no absentee Deity, sitting outside the universe . . . He is 'everywhere present, upholding, directing, disposing, and governing' all creatures, actions, and things from the greatest even to the last."[2]

Official creeds and their explanations have imbedded in them an ideal character type. Presbyterianism, as Smith's explanation of it clearly shows, aimed at the creation of a particular kind of man. He should have a preternaturally strong

9 Ibid., pp. 44, 46.
1 Ibid., pp. 48–54.
2 Ibid., pp. 157–8, 160–1.

and imperious sense of duty, joined to a conviction that law (creed, doctrine, principle) was pre-eminent, was fundamental to the order of the universe, and must be both obeyed and preserved. Strength, stability, and a readiness to act vigorously in this world in carrying out God's wishes should go together with personal humility, probity, and a stiff-necked insistence upon just dealing. Precisely because it was centered on the moral law, Presbyterianism, Smith wrote, was "admirably fitted to be . . . the spiritual food of stalwart souls, the nurse of a supremely massive and masculine type of piety."[3] Presbyterians should make good businessmen, through their trustworthiness and diligent hard work. They should also make energetic public officials, for they would see the universe as held together by the active will of a vigorous God who acts through them. They would certainly be monolithic in character. "Calvinism," wrote Smith with grim pride, "plies men with hammer and with chisel . . . and the result is monumental marble. Other systems leave men soft and dirty; Calvinism makes them of white marble, to endure forever."[4]

It would be absurd to say that all Presbyterians were of this character. But whatever its failure or success in producing its ideal type in the mass of its members, Presbyterianism would seem to have had much success with Cleveland. Placing Cleveland against the background of his Presbyterianism suggests a rationale for explaining his actions and ideas too persuasive to ignore. It seems only reasonable to conclude that Cleveland's faith helped shape his character, for he fits the archetype so well. Carl Schurz's words again come to mind: "a man conscientiously devoted to his duties, honest in his zeal to understand and to perform them without regard to personal advantage, and maintaining with dauntless courage what he thought right against friend and foe alike—a personality of exceptional strength and trustworthiness, commanding confidence."[5]

The word "duty" is one of the most prominent words in all his letters and speeches. "I have often thought," he wrote

[3] Ibid., p. 24.
[4] Ibid., pp. 62–3.
[5] Schurz, "Grover Cleveland's Second Administration," p. 634.

an intimate friend in 1885, "how solemn a thing it is to live and feel the pressure of the duties which life—the mere existence in a social state—imposes . . ."[6] Upon leaving office after his first term in 1889, he said, "We know that we have espoused the cause of right and justice. We know that we have not permitted duty to country to wait upon expediency."[7] In 1892, aroused by the turmoil within his party and convinced that he must run again for the presidency, he wrote that "it is an exceedingly high duty to do all that is within legitimate human reach to win success in November."[8] Embattled and downcast in 1894, during his second administration, he wrote a close companion, "I am sure I never was more completely in the right path of duty than I am now . . ."[9] What rewards wait for the self-made man who considers the welfare of society? he asked in an 1897 Princeton address. Not wealth or fame, though they may come, but a much more valuable reward: "consciousness of duty well and faithfully performed. Popular applause is, of course, gratifying; but there are times when a man's own satisfaction with his conduct is a better criterion of real merit." The last words that came from him were "I have tried so hard to do right."[1]

Furthermore, he *knew* he was right. In Smith's words, his feet were on the rock. "Do you know," he wrote a friend in 1895, "that I have never been so sure that there is a high and unseen Power that guides and sustains the weak efforts of man? I feel it all the time . . ." In the work of "public life and effort," he wrote Gilder in 1906, "God has never failed to clearly make known to me the path of duty."[2] In seeming obedience to Smith's injunction to ask not whether something was pleasant, or popular, or profitable, but rather whether it was right, Cleveland was remarkable not only for taking steps he was warned were unpopular, but also for being delighted when he could take them. Gilder said he had never

[6] Letter to Wilson S. Bissell, June 25, 1885, Nevins, *Letters*, p. 65.
[7] Address, New York, April 27, 1889, Bergh, *Addresses*, pp. 169–70.
[8] Letter to William F. Vilas, June 30, 1892, Nevins, *Letters*, pp. 289–90.
[9] Letter to Richard Watson Gilder, Dec. 26, 1894, Nevins, *Letters*, p. 374.
[1] Grover Cleveland, *The Self-Made Man in American Life* (New York, 1897), pp. 22–3; Gilder, "Grover Cleveland," *Century*, LXXIX, 31.
[2] Letter to E. C. Benedict, Feb. 25, 1895, Nevins, *Letters*, pp. 380–1; Letter, Mar. 18, 1906, ibid., p. 605.

seen Cleveland more pleased than he was after writing his anti-free-silver letter in 1892, thereby supposedly throwing the presidency out the window. It showed that "he cared more for principle than for the Presidency." He always insisted that obstinacy was his principle virtue, once saying that "if every man in the country abandons this issue, I shall stick to it."[3] Speaking of how he and John G. Carlisle, his Secretary of the Treasury, had struggled together to save the currency, he observed, "We were just right for each other; he knows all I ought to know, *and I can bear all we have to bear.*"[4]

Cleveland's Presbyterianism was congruent not only with his character but with his presidency as well. It was in the nature of Presbyterianism to assume the rightful existence of power and the necessity for its use. The active sovereignty of God, one of Calvinism's key concepts, implied that what was needed in the world was energy, direction, authority, decisiveness, used primarily by reference to a divine plan or to divine values rather than to human purposes or considerations. Cleveland respected authority. He held its symbols in awe. He often spoke of the feelings called up in him when he thought of the sovereignty embodied in the office of the presidency. It was a thing, he said, "full of solemnity; for this sovereignty I conceive to be the working out or enforcement of the divine right of man to govern himself and a manifestation of God's plan concerning the human race."[5]

From the beginning of his meteoric career, therefore, and throughout it—as mayor, governor, and president—he showed a vigorous executive temper. He characteristic mode of leadership was that of interposing an uncompromising negative in the spirit of the "thou shalt nots" of the Decalogue and the Shorter Catechism image of God. Like Andrew Jackson, he built his presidency, just as he had built his governorship and mayoralty, primarily upon a long series of vetoes.[6]

[3] Gilder, "Cleveland," *Century,* LXXVIII, 491; Bradford, "Cleveland," 663.
[4] Gilder, "Cleveland," *Century,* LXXVIII, 848.
[5] Address, Clinton, N.Y., July 13, 1887, Cleveland Papers, Series 5.
[6] The veto as an essential tool of democratic leadership was much

There was more to it, however, than just a string of vetoes. He took pains in one of his longest messages as governor of New York to praise a bill giving major executive powers to the mayor of New York City. Almost as soon as he became President he fought a successful struggle with the Senate over the power of the President to withhold certain papers from the Congress on the grounds of executive privilege.[7] He was delighted with Albert Bushnell Hart's book, *The Coercive Powers of the Government of the United States of America,* taking the unusual step of writing Hart to praise the work.[8] It is revealing that the four *Presidential Problems* upon which he chose to write after his final exit from office were essentially crises in which he could display executive power. His whole discussion of the Chicago strikes and riots in this book displayed a bone-and-marrow instinct for the rightfulness and the transcendent necessity of authority and of obedience to that authority. He was absolutely undivided in his mind as to the imperative need for the national executive to move in swiftly and powerfully to assure obedience to duly constituted authority, in this case the injunctions of the courts.[9]

Most of all, however, Cleveland showed his appetite for the use of power in his struggles for a lowered tariff and sound money, the two great passions of his presidential years. In these and other controversies, Cleveland emerged as a strong executive in the Gladstone-Peel-Jackson tradition. He clearly thought of himself as a tribune of the people, and he was quite impatient with Congressmen. Rule by a collection of notables, by oligarchy, was not the mode in the Cleveland presidencies. Senators overshadowed the White House in Re-

---

praised by Jacksonians. Cf. Meyers, *Jacksonian Persuasion,* pp. 249–51, 260–1. In his first term, Cleveland would appear to have issued more than twice the total vetoes of all his predecessors—most of them, of course, concerning pension bills.

[7] Message, Mar. 17, 1884, *Public Papers of Grover Cleveland,* Governor (1884), pp. 80–7; Special Message to the Senate, Mar. 1, 1886, *A Compilation of the Messages and Papers of the Presidents,* comp. James D. Richardson (Washington, D.C., 1913), VII, 4960–8.

[8] Letters, Cleveland to William C. Endicott, May 4, 1891, Nevins, *Letters,* p. 253.

[9] Cf. Grover Cleveland, "The Government in the Chicago Strike of 1894," *Presidential Problems* (New York, 1904), pp. 79–117.

publican regimes, but not when Cleveland was there.

No President since Lincoln dominated the stage of national politics as Cleveland did in his two terms, and not since Andrew Jackson had there been an executive so vigorous in his relations with Congress, or within his own government over his cabinet chiefs. He was much more man than partisan, Woodrow Wilson observed in his 1897 assessment, "with an independent executive will of his own; hardly a colleague of the Houses so much as an individual servant of the country; exercising his powers like a chief magistrate rather than like a party leader."[1] He staffed his second cabinet entirely out of the circle of his close friends and associates, as if he intended openly to show both his independence of party and his predominance in his administration. "It was singular," Wilson observed, "how politics began at once to centre in the President, waiting for his initiative, and how the air at Washington filled with murmurs against the domineering and usurping temper and practice of the Executive. Power had somehow gone the length of the avenue, and seemed lodged in one man."[2]

Thus, duty, certainty, and vigorous authority were prominent in Cleveland's mind and character. There was also veneration of law. To the Shorter Catechism mind, God was seen as organizing and ordering the world through law. Divine injunctions, expressed in creeds, principles, and rules, held the world together. They disciplined man, aided him in the dark scramble of life, and saved him from his natural selfishness and cupidity. It was vital to preserve such principles in their original purity as they were passed across the generations. To ignore, to replace, to attack the creed was heresy, a damnable crime.

When placed against this background, Cleveland's behavior in the long currency crisis of the 1880's and 1890's takes on a new aspect. In his party there was a deeply rooted traditional creed, developed by the Jacksonians and sanctified by the Gladstonian Liberals, that held that sound money was fundamental to the health of the economy and to social jus-

[1] Wilson, "Mr. Cleveland as President," p. 289.
[2] Ibid., pp. 295–6.

tice. What behavior could be more natural to the Shorter Catechism mind than to hold to these principles with firmness and confidence? Creeds were to be upheld, not to be cast aside by the nation simply because men claimed that they were uncomfortable or outmoded.

Against this background, too, Cleveland's revealing alternation between optimism and pessimism throughout his public career may be seen as a phenomenon integral to his most fundamental outlook. He constantly protested his faith in the goodness of the common people, in words and circumstances that attested to his sincerity—the term perhaps best descriptive of his character. He was reared in the Jeffersonian and Jacksonian view that the people were good, and only their exploiters were bad.

As President, he had a feeling about his relationship with the people that was almost monarchical. It was certainly, on his part, an intimately personal emotion. Perhaps it came from the circumstances of his meteoric rise. The most important fact about Cleveland may have been the way in which he was so summarily plucked from obscurity and hurried to the White House, for he seems to have derived from this— quite understandably—an unshakable conviction that the mass of the people were on his side; that he owed his election not to party or to politicians, but to an almost mystical bond between himself and the nation at large. He always felt that he could intuitively know public opinion; that politicians could tell him nothing. Had he not built his whole career out of refusing to do what politicians did? When he did something party workers warned him against as unpopular, did not the public applaud? Did he not win a plurality of the popular votes in three successive presidential elections?[3] Was he not justified in being—like Gladstone, it must be observed —personally aloof from politicians? For both men, their power base lay not in the Parliament or in the Congress, both of which found them puzzling and irritating, but in the people.

Cleveland developed out of all this a curious paternal

[3] Cf., on this point, Gilder, "Cleveland," *Century*, LXXVIII, 491–2.

feeling toward the American people. As he wrote to a friend after his first presidential victory in 1884, he wanted only to "be of service to my people." A year later he was writing, "God is good to me, and after all the American people are pretty nearly right. At any rate, while I scold a good deal I love them and am grateful to them." When he was elected for his second term in 1892, he spoke in New York City of "the obligation I have entered into with the best and most confiding people of the world." And his faith in their goodness seemed to survive every vicissitude. In the darkest days of his second administration, he wrote a friend, "You know my supreme faith in the American people. While I believe them just now deluded, mistaken, and wickedly duped, they will certainly return to sound principles and patriotic aspirations, and what I may suffer in the period of aberration is not important."[4]

Fundamental to Cleveland's mind, however, was a deeply rooted pessimism. He was a Calvinist who considered the world dominated by sensual greed, grasping egoism, and a callous disregard for one's fellows. It was this conviction, strongly reinforced by his Jacksonian inheritance but rooted in his religious world view, that gave such bite and authority to his presidential performance and led to his major accomplishments.

The Cleveland presidencies, then, like the Gladstone premierships, derived their motivating force from an essentially religious inspiration. Both men were moralists, not rationalists. They relied for their basic views of man and society on the Scriptures, not on the dry provender of Locke and Bentham and Mill that it is usually assumed sustained the left center—the Liberal-Democratic mind—in Anglo-American politics. To what extent they were representative is, of course, a difficult question. But it seems at the least significant that the Gladstones and the Clevelands provided the kind of man most frequently found in leadership positions in Liberal-Democratic politics.

[4] Cleveland to Wilson S. Bissell, Nov. 13, 1884, and September 24, 1885, Nevins, *Letters*, pp. 48, 78–9; Address, New York City, Nov. 17, 1892, Bergh, *Addresses*, p. 343; Cleveland to Don M. Dickinson, Feb. 18, 1896, Nevins, *Letters*, pp. 429–30.

As President, Cleveland's principal accomplishment perhaps lay in making civil service a reality. This task involved him in arduous and seemingly endless labors. In Cleveland's day, Presidents spent literally months deciding on thousands of appointments. The White House halls were clogged with applicants and their friends; constant pressure from all directions was applied upon the President, and party harmony rode or fell on whether this miserable applicant or that one filled a petty postmastership in some remote corner of the country. An important function of the presidency, in fact, was to serve as the nation's personnel office. Cleveland struggled his way doggedly through all of this, trying as best he could to fight off the almost hysterical demands of Democratic politicians denied access to the public trough for a quarter of a century, and working steadily toward the classic Gladstonian Liberal goal, urged on him by the Mugwumps, of an educated civil service holding appointment by passage of examinations. It is enough to say that while at the beginning of his term it was a specific exception to the norm for a government post to be under civil service, at the end of his second term, in 1897, it required a specific exception for such a post not to be.[5] The great reforms of the Progressive period after 1900, based as they were on the existence of a nonpolitical and professional civil service possessed of expertise and efficiency, were thereby rendered possible. Perhaps even more important to the Mugwump mind, the glaring contrast in this regard between Britain and the United States that so many educated observers pointed to, and that caused such remark among British ruling circles, was largely ended.

While he labored on the civil service in his first administration, he worked as well on the extraordinary problem created by the pension system. What had begun as a means of caring for *bona fide* veterans disabled by their war service had mushroomed into a carnival in which Congress poured out pensions with a lavish hand to all manner of persons

[5] Schurz, "Cleveland's Second Administration," p. 643.

whose relationship to the Civil War had been at best tenuous. Excused by some on the ground that it helped dissipate the embarrassingly large surplus that was beginning to pile up in the government's vaults—in preference to lowering the tariff —pension expenditures were at such a fantastic level that even in 1888, after Cleveland had been hacking away at the system for years, they amounted to 31 per cent of the government's total expenditures. It was in putting a stop to this system that Cleveland won his record in the issuance of vetoes. The whole system, he said again and again, was a perversion of proper use of the public funds and a demoralization to the people. There "can be no doubt," as he said in one of his veto messages, "that the race after the pensions offered by this bill would not only stimulate weakness and pretended incapacity to labor, but put a further premium on dishonesty and mendacity."[6]

While he was in the midst of this struggle, which involved hundreds of veto messages, he wrote the veto of the Texas seed bill that has ritually been selected out for single treatment by historians as a demonstration of his heartless and incomprehensible conservatism. "I do not believe," he said in this veto, with scores of pension vetoes still to write and a hard-won position to maintain, "that the power and duty of the General Government ought to be extended to the relief of individual suffering which is in no manner properly related to the public service or benefit."[7]

Cleveland's main concern was to cleanse the nation's economic system. As the first Democrat to hold the power of the presidency since the Republicans had reintroduced the mercantilist state during the Civil War, he was therefore the first to begin the disassembling of what was to Democrats a vast system of corruption. The elaborate mechanism of government aids to business, the rape of the western territories by land grabbers and railroads; all these and more, to Cleveland, grew out of the "selfishness" and "sordidness" he saw blighting American life. He was more worried about the

[6] Veto Message, Feb. 11, 1887, *Messages and Papers of the Presidents*, VII, 5134–42; Fourth Annual Message, Dec. 3, 1888, ibid., VII, 5382.
[7] Veto Message, Feb. 16, 1887, ibid., VII, 5142–3.

spoliation of the West by railroads, land grabbers, lumbermen, and many other such groups than by any other early problem in his first administration. He stopped all land-office activity for a major investigation of fraudulent claims, and in his Second Annual Message, in late 1886, he castigated the great frauds that had taken place. A beneficient system designed to create family farms, he said, had been corrupted into a monstrous system of land monopoly. Cattle kings, land syndicates, railroads, and lumber barons had wrongfully appropriated incredible expanses of the national domain. He condemned the "colossal greed" of the culprits, and forced them to return more than eighty million acres. He went on in his second administration to attack the speculative elements and local interests that had twisted all land laws to their advantage, beginning the process of setting aside great regions as national forests.[8]

Of major importance, too, were controls established over railroads during his administration. He had always regarded business corporations, in the classic Smithian tradition, with distrust. As early as 1882, when he accepted the nomination to run for governor of the state of New York, he warned that "when by combination, or by the exercise of unwarranted power, [corporations] oppress the people, the same authority which created them should restrain them and protect the rights of the citizen." As governor he demanded they be required to make public declarations of all their financial operations.[9]

When in 1886 the decisions of the U.S. Supreme Court took away the power of the states to regulate the rates of railroads, he told Congress that since this "important field of control and regulation [has] thus been left entirely unoccu-

[8] Nevins, *Cleveland*, pp. 225–7, 359–60; Second Annual Message, Dec. 6, 1886, *Messages and Papers of the Presidents*, VII, 5106–8; Fourth Annual Message, Dec. 3, 1888, ibid., VII, 5379–80; First Annual Message, Dec. 4, 1893, ibid., VIII, 5886; Second Annual Message, Dec. 3, 1894, ibid., VIII, 5975. Many executive decrees establishing national forests are included in ibid.
[9] Letter of Acceptance, Oct. 7, 1882, in George F. Parker, ed., *The Writings and Speeches of Grover Cleveland* (New York, 1892), p. 5; Annual Message, Jan. 1, 1884, in *Public Papers of Grover Cleveland* (1884), pp. 38–9.

pied," the Congress should consider taking action. Many in
his party clung to *laissez faire* views that condemned all attempts at regulation, but Cleveland agreed with those in the
Congress who urged that they follow British practice and
establish a strong and independent commission to control
rates, discriminations, and other such matters. When the In-
terstate Commerce Commission law came before him in February 1887, he ignored discussion of its constitutionality and
signed it. Though unprecedented in American practice, it was
quite in keeping with his belief that the sovereign power
should not simply be recognized, but actively used. He gave
painstaking care to selecting the ICC commissioners and
made strong appointments. For a short time—until the courts
in 1890 hampered its powers—the ICC had great effects on
rates.[1]

It was the tariff question, however, that became the dominating issue in Cleveland's mind. When this happened, the
course of American politics was changed. In the long years
since the Republicans first established the protective-tariff
system during the Civil War, the tariff had become one of the
accepted facts of American life. Added to again and again, it
had become so impregnably rooted in the American system
that for a long time Democrats had paid it little attention.
Samuel Tilden hardly uttered a word on the tariff.

But to the Mugwumps, it was perhaps the greatest question of all. What was more inspiring or more central to British Liberalism than the fight over the Corn Laws? Or the
triumphant series of later victories by which Gladstone had
wiped away all barriers to free trade with the world? What
was more confidently assumed in the Liberal mind than the
link between free trade and world peace? Nothing could be
more alluring to the Mugwumps than to play the same role in
America that William Gladstone had played in Britain, and
to win the very kind of victory he had sanctified.

From the moment of Cleveland's election, "the tariff reformers . . . exerted every possible ounce of pressure upon
Cleveland, talking with him, writing him letters, and sending

[1] Nevins, *Cleveland*, pp. 355–6; Second Annual Message, Dec. 6, 1886,
Messages and Papers of the Presidents, VII, 5111.

him books." Cleveland found that the same men who urged civil service reform on him, the men who represented the intellect of the reforming world and who seemed in a special sense uniquely his following, were also the ones most fervently advocating lower tariffs. Economists, professors, political liberals like Carl Schurz, and the older generation of New England reformers like Charles Francis Adams, Jr., led the movement. In November 1885, they formed the National Tariff Reform League to give momentum to their cause.[2]

In June 1886, Cleveland dramatically responded to these importunities. Opening what was in effect a new era in American politics, he began to summon Congressmen to the White House for the purpose of arguing with them for a lower tariff. For a time he even threatened the calling of an extra session. He forced and narrowly lost a tariff vote in the House after the elections of 1886 had given some encouragement to the low-tariff side, and followed up this defeat by the sensational Tariff message of 1887, in which he called again for action by the Congress. Meanwhile, the tariff-reform movement, startled and energized by the fact that the White House was suddenly on its side, gained new impetus all over the country.[3]

The Cleveland presidency now seemed to come fully alive. "The breath of affairs was at last in his lungs," Woodrow Wilson later wrote, "and he gave his party a leader, of a sudden, in the plain-spoken, earnest, mandatory tariff message of December, 1887." Without consulting the party leaders, at one stroke in this message he settled the main issue of the next campaign. "Some resented his action as a sudden usurpation; others doubted what they should think; a few took the changed aspect of politics with zest and relish. It was bravely done."[4]

The Tariff Message of 1887 was in fact an extraordinary document. Never before had any President ever devoted his entire annual message—usually a portmanteau collection of utterances on all the concerns before the government—to one

[2] Nevins, Cleveland, pp. 280–2.
[3] Ibid., pp. 289–98.
[4] Wilson, "Cleveland," p. 294.

topic alone, and it caused a national sensation. Its tone heightened the response, for Cleveland was unequivocal. The fundamental cause of the nation's difficulties, he said—the immense surplus in the treasury in the midst of widespread suffering through low wages and unemployment—lay directly in the "vicious, inequitable, and illogical" system of protective tariffs. It must at once be revised and amended, for its "primary and plain effect [is to] raise the price to consumers of all articles imported . . ." It also raised the prices of all other articles like them produced within the country. This whole system of taxation, which bore directly on the necessaries of life, must be drastically changed. The common people, he said, were in effect being forced to pay an extra tax directly into the hands of domestic producers. It was impossible simply to wipe the tariffs away, and he had no intention of calling for complete free trade, he said, but something had to be done to change a system designed to ensure "immense profits instead of moderately profitable returns." A hundred years after the nation's founding, he asked caustically, must the country still listen to the argument that "infant industries still [need] the highest and greatest degree of favor and fostering care that can be wrung from Federal legislation"?

Did the protective tariff help the workingmen, as Republicans had always alleged? Not so, for only a minority actually worked in protected industries, and even they were consumers, paying much more in high prices than they received in wages. What was needed was a greater degree of internal competition to keep prices down. It was notorious, he said in a bitter aside, "that this competition is too often strangled by combinations . . . The people can hardly hope for any consideration in the operation of these selfish schemes."[5]

He lost the battle for a new tariff in 1888, but he was thoroughly aroused to his cause. It had become a part of a much larger and more compelling vision, a vision of the nation as sick to its core with special economic privilege and materialism. When he lost the election of 1888—getting a

[5] Third Annual Message, Dec. 6, 1887, *Messages and Papers of the Presidents*, VII, 5165–75.

popular-vote plurality, but not an electoral-college majority—
before he turned the White House over to Benjamin Harrison
he issued in December 1888 one of the most radically leftist
annual messages ever to come from the White House. Nothing less than a violent attack on the power elite of the nation
for their corrupting of a once innocent society, his Fourth
Annual Message was a restatement of the Jacksonian social
analysis. Heavy with the rhetoric of Cleveland's day, it was
at once ponderous and eloquent. It sounded like nothing
so much as the evangelist Jeremiah crying woe, the land is
defiled, its inheritance is made an abomination.

America, Cleveland said, had originally been a place in
which the government looked only to see that each man left
the other alone and had a clear field ahead for individual
achievement. It had been a frugal government because the
people were frugal. Combinations, monopolies, and great ag-
gregations of capital were sternly prevented or controlled.
The people were not attracted by the pomp and glitter of
undemocratic nations. Their lives were plain and simple; they
enjoyed sturdy competition; and they worked hard to enno-
ble mankind and to solve the problem of free government.
They strove, in short, to achieve the God-given destiny that
awaited them.

After a century, how fared the country? Great and
wealthy cities, filled with luxury, immense factories, a mad
race for riches, and massive concentrations of capital in few
hands: these were what met the eye. There was glitter, but
there was disease as well. The cities were crowded and constantly growing, for the countryside was swept by a distaste
for farming. Country boys left the "simple and laborious life"
of their fathers and joined the chase for easily acquired
wealth. Meanwhile, luxury and degradation lived side by
side. The common lot of poor men was heavy toil for tiny
wages.

Fortunes were no longer made by hard work, by enlightened foresight, and by sturdy enterprise, but by arrangements in which the government discriminated in favor of
manufacturers. Unreasonable profits came largely from exploiting the masses. Workers, meanwhile, found themselves

steadily more remote from their employers as corporations grew large and impersonal. Classes were rapidly forming, "one comprising the very rich and powerful while in another are found the toiling poor." Trusts, combinations, and monopolies ruled the land, "while the citizen is struggling far in the rear or is trampled to death beneath an iron heel." The corporations that laws should carefully control so that they served society were swiftly becoming the masters of the people who had allowed their appearance.

Throughout the unhappy land, therefore, the kind of patriotism that expressed the simple affection and trust the people earlier had felt for their government was being replaced by "selfish greed and grasping avarice." In unconcealed arrogance, men disregarded anything but their own personal interest. They jealously kept every inch of advantage they had, and by combining together perpetuated their advantages by controlling legislation or intimidating and corrupting the people into misuse of the ballot.

"Communism," he said, "is a hateful thing and a menace to peace and organized government; but the communism of combined wealth and capital, the outgrowth of overweening cupidity and selfishness . . . is not less dangerous than the communism of oppressed poverty and toil, which, exasperated by injustice and discontent, attacks with wild disorder the citadel of rule." Those who said that the government should care for the rich, and the rich would care for the poor, mocked the people. The boast of free institutions was that they served the humblest. Giving into wealthy hands the control of society would make free institutions "a glittering delusion and the pretended boon of American citizenship a shameless imposition."[6]

In the years between 1888 and 1892, Cleveland went back and forth across the country condemning these evidences of what he saw as a new life style in American society. He called out for·a new model of citizenship in a society that had become egoistically personalist in an extreme degree. It is not too much to say that the theme of national decay

[6] Fourth Annual Message, Dec. 3, 1888, ibid., VII, 5358–85.

became his obsession—though he protested his faith in the people. Look to the past, he urged merchants in Boston, and see how far they and their kind had fallen from original innocence. The businessmen of the early Republic were self-reliant, wanting no favors for themselves or for others. But now businessmen were invited to become the dependents of the government's favor, and beneficiaries of its taxing power. The "spirit of selfishness is abroad in the land," he said, and it filled the air with demands for special privilege from the government. "Vile, unsavory forms rise to the surface of our agitated political waters, and gleefully anticipate, in the anxiety of selfish interest, their opportunity to fatten upon corruption and debauched suffrage."[7]

The past had been forgotten, he said in New York City, and the great labors and sacrifices that had made the country. Why? Because of the "impetuous race after wealth which has become a characteristic of our people." The growing "selfishness and sordidness," the cynical attitude toward patriotism and morality in government, the attitude that politics was a career for personal gain like any other, had all combined to create a departure from the principles on which the very system of government rested. "Point to your immense fortunes," he said, "to your national growth and prosperity; boast of the day of practical politics, and discard as obsolete all sentiment and all conception of morality and patriotism in public life," but do not entertain the delusion that these things mean that the nation was on a safe course.[8]

The American government was only suited to a frugal and economical people, he said in Ohio. It could only survive if it was in the hands of men who had acquired strength and self-reliance by self-denial and by living in circumstances in which they had been forced to acquire economic habits. Such a thrifty and careful people would make the government in their image. Tragically, however, the Republicans derided cheapness and economy within the home in their drive for

[7] Address, Merchants Association of Boston, Dec. 12, 1889, Cleveland Papers, Series 5.
[8] Address, Washington's Birthday, New York City, Feb. 22, 1890, Cleveland Papers, Series 5.

higher tariffs and higher prices, and were reckless and wasteful with the public money, showering it upon businessmen. This showed, he warned, that "something is wrong with us . . ." "We, who are proud to call ourselves Jacksonian Democrats," he said in New York City, were also, like Jackson, "boldly and aggressively [attacking] a political heresy opposed to the best interests of the people and defended by an arrogant and unscrupulous party."[9]

When he was elected in 1892 for a second term, it was in this spirit that he gave his Second Inaugural Address. The nation, he warned, was like a strong man who could be confident in his strength, yet find hidden within him a terrible disease that could lead to collapse. The very strength of the nation had given rise to a heedlessness about the laws that governed its national existence. Americans could no longer enjoy the corrupt luxury of a belief that they could expect from the government "especial and direct individual advantages." This spirit degraded to a mechanism of craft the great system established by the Founding Fathers. Honest patriotism had been perverted into self-interest. Men no longer admired and supported their sacred government out of a sense of duty, but instead because of a "pitiful calculation of the sordid gain to be derived from their Government's maintenance." The love of a sovereign, he might have said as a good Calvinist, is a duty, not something given in the expectation of a return.

What, then, was his prescription for America in the month of March 1893, as his second administration began? All bounties and subsidies must be refused, he said. There could be no more reckless scrambles for unearned pensions from the government. Frugality and economy must again reign, for the opposite simply encouraged personal lives of prodigality and extravagance in the populace. The tariff would now without further question be lowered, for the six-year campaign he had launched in 1887 had finally been won, and the people had given their clear mandate not only by

9 Address, Thurman Birthday Banquet, Columbus, Ohio, Nov. 13, 1890, Cleveland Papers, Series 5; Address, Business Men's Democratic Association, New York City, Jan. 8, 1892, Cleveland Papers, Series 5.

placing him in the White House, but by giving the Democrats their first control over both houses of Congress since the 1850's. The people demanded the lifting from their lives of the "inordinate and unequal advantages too long enjoyed by the few." Furthermore, the enormous trusts and combinations that were formed for the purpose of limiting production and fixing prices must be attacked "to the extent that they can be reached and restrained by Federal power . . ."[1]

Cleveland's second administration was begun in triumph and spent in tragedy. Within weeks after his inauguration a disastrous worldwide depression began, one comparable in severity—and in its political effects—to that of the 1930's. It was, as it has recently been called, "an earth-shaker."[2] Cleveland was fated to be a depression president, and he was not prepared for the challenge. He knew how to use a mandate, not how to build a new one. He was pitifully adrift when his task was to create a favorable public opinion, rather than calmly to act as its chosen instrument. He was accustomed to ignoring politicians, and now he needed above all to attract their support and sympathy. He clung to his belief that he intuitively knew what the people wanted, despite the uproar. He was in consequence a blind and rigid political leader who shattered his party, refused to listen to advice from those counseling compromise, and faced with inflexibility a massive revolt in the Southern and Western wings of his party over the question of currency inflation.

The currency question had returned to haunt him. The inflationist campaign that had earlier taken the form of Greenbackism had taken new life and new form by the 1890's in the Free Silver movement. First the Populists, and then growing numbers of Democrats—with William Jennings Bryan at their head—began calling for the free and unlimited coinage of silver at a ratio with gold that would result

[1] Second Inaugural Address, March 4, 1893, in *Messages and Papers of the Presidents*, VIII, 5822–4.

Cleveland clearly expected that the best way to attack the trusts was through lowering the tariff. Cf. Letter to Patrick Collins and others, Cleveland Papers, Series II, Vol. 215.

[2] Carl N. Degler, "American Political Parties and the Rise of the City: An Interpretation," *Journal of American History*, LI (1964), 47.

in an apparently massive inflation of the currency. American wheat farmers were in such desperate straits that they made the Free Silver campaign a powerful and clamorous movement that would soon reorient the whole structure of American politics.

Cleveland's own position in the controversy was clear and unshaken. All the voices he trusted, whether Jacksonian or Gladstonian, instructed him in the classic Liberal-Democratic principles. Fundamentally internationalist in their character, these principles aimed at the maintenance of low prices on food and other necessaries and a stable, nonspeculative economy. Sound money was to be the principal disciplining mechanism, along with competition, for keeping the potentially fruitful appetites and activities of the businessman from verging into disastrous speculation and exploitation. In depression times, sound money was essential to restore confidence.[3]

From his first message on the problem in the 1880's to his last in the 1890's, Cleveland never questioned these orthodox principles of Jacksonian finance, received from such venerable hands. He persistently held that the United States could not maintain a bimetallic currency alone in the world, and that the two metals would part company entirely as gold was drained from the Treasury either by panic or by the profit that could be made by exchanging cheap silver coin for the more valuable gold. This would be disastrous, he said in 1885, for gold was "still the standard of value and necessary in our dealings with other countries . . ." Furthermore, bankers and speculators would inevitably get richer if the free-silver experiment were tried, for clever men at the seats of power can always profit from price rises and declines, while "the laboring men and women of the land, most defenseless of all, will find that the dollar received for the wage of their toil has sadly shrunk in its purchasing power."[4]

---

[3] For the way in which these concepts came to Cleveland through the influence of Tilden, see Nevins, *Cleveland*, pp. 113–14, 132, 201–4.
[4] First Annual Message, Dec. 8, 1885, *Messages and Papers of the Presidents*, VII, 4926–31. Cleveland, like Tilden before him, was accused then and has been since of making such statements out of the merest hypocrisy. Historians have largely accepted the views of the Populists,

Eight years later, locked in the silver struggle of 1893, he quoted Tilden, whom he described as "one of the greatest statesmen our country has known," to the effect that "the very man of all others who has the deepest interest in a sound currency and who suffers most by mischievous legislation in money matters is the man who earns his daily bread by his daily toil."[5]

In his hands, the faith was secure, for he had the sureness of discipleship. He *knew* that he was right. As he said in 1891 before the Young Men's Democratic Association in Philadelphia, he was saving the "ark of the covenant," the true principles of the Democratic Party.[6] "Is it ordained," he asked a Southern friend when the free-silver campaign began building up, "that I am to be the instrument through which Democratic principles can be saved . . . ? I shall be obedient to the call of my country and my party. Whatever happens no one shall say that I refused to serve in a time of evil . . . [when the nation was faced by] the free-coinage heresy."[7]

In one sense, perhaps no other issue engaged deeper levels of Cleveland's personality than this one. It must be remembered that Cleveland's beloved father had been a heresy fighter. It is hard to escape the feeling, when reading Cleveland's attacks on the "heresy" of free silver, that he was

---

expressed typically by Mary Lease of Kansas (save for her anti-Semitism), who said, "The capitalistic press rejoiced in the power of Grover Cleveland, the American agent of Jewish bankers and British gold." Walter T. K. Nugent, *The Tolerant Populists* (Chicago and London, 1963), p. 108. Charles A. Beard, the patriarch of this school, wrote simply that Cleveland was "as clay in the hands of New York bankers directed by J. P. Morgan . . . " *The Rise of American Civilization* (New York, 1934), pp. 329–34. The "gold-bug" thesis, which describes the Cleveland Democrats as concerned only for the interest rates of financiers, has been echoed in Merrill, *Bourbon Leader*. As in my remarks on Tilden, I shall only suggest here that these views are founded on a misunderstanding of the real nature and function of currency, of currency history in the United States, and of the Liberal-Democratic tradition within which Cleveland was operating.

[5] Special Session Message, Aug. 8, 1893, ibid., VIII, 5836–7.
[6] Address, "Principles of True Democracy," Jan. 8, 1891, Cleveland Papers, Series 5.

The word "principles" figures constantly in his utterances and writings. See: Gilder, "Cleveland," *Century*, LXXVIII, 489–90; many letters in Nevins, *Letters*, pp. 46–7, 80, 162–3, 246, 258, 262, 272–3; Bergh, *Addresses*, pp. 329–30.
[7] Cleveland to L. Q. C. Lamar, May 1, 1892, Nevins, *Letters*, pp. 279–80.

given greater strength and inflexibility in this struggle by a sense, whether or not it was consciously realized, that he was fulfilling the role sanctified by his father. To fight the destroyers of venerated creeds and principles was in Cleveland's mind, one suspects, an ennobling opportunity.

Not only traditional British Liberalism, but also contemporary British opinion solidly supported Cleveland's stand. The silverites may have been suffering from paranoid delusions in their elaborate theories about an international gold conspiracy, an "Anglo-American Gold Trust," centering in the Bank of England,[8] but they were quite right in believing that the British were determinedly devoted to the gold standard. Gladstone thought the free-silver idea arrant nonsense. Arthur Balfour, soon to be a Conservative Prime Minister, seems for a time to have become enamored of a special form of silverism—international bimetallism—and even persuaded one of Cleveland's closest advisers, William C. Whitney, of its efficacy, but this was a distinctly minority voice and Cleveland would have none of it.[9]

Being attacked as a British agent, as he was in this controversy, was nothing new to Cleveland. As early as 1887, a Congressional body called Cleveland's tariff-reduction proposals "a direct attempt to fasten upon this country the British policy of free foreign trade." Cleveland's association with the ideas of British Liberalism, in fact, was one of his chief burdens in the tariff controversy, for the Republicans knew as well as everyone else that British influences were anathema to Irish Catholic voters. Whatever Cleveland did was twisted so as to make him appear a British agent. Republicans trumpeted their hostility to Britain in the same way they had their hostility to the South. Cleveland therefore faced the loyalty issue coming and going. Nothing cost him more agonized efforts in the 1888 presidential campaign than his attempts to short-circuit the pro-British accusation.[1]

[8] Cf. The analysis of this strain in Populist thought in Hofstadter, *Age of Reform*, Ch. ii, "The Folklore of Populism."
[9] Mark D. Hirsch, *William C. Whitney: Modern Warwick* (New York, 1948), pp. 475–510.
[1] Nevins, *Cleveland*, pp. 391, 428–31.

> The Republican plan of campaign was simple. It was . . .
> [to] be what was known as "working the free trade
> racket." The Country would be put in an uproar . . . about
> "free trade," the breaking down of industry and the end of
> good wages . . . [They] were to be impoverished and beg-
> gared by the lowering of customs barriers and a deluge of
> foreign goods, especially out of England . . . Every utter-
> ance in an English newspaper, every remark, however cas-
> ual, by an Englishman at home or in this country . . . was
> gleaned, quoted and brought forward . . . as proof that it
> was American to be for the Republican ticket and un-Amer-
> ican to be for Mr. Cleveland.[2]

The principal reason Cleveland did not suffer more among
the Irish from this charge in the elections of 1888 and 1892
derived from the ironic fact that at the same time the Republicans were playing the anti-British theme, they could not
forbear from joining in nativist anti-Catholic campaigns.

Cleveland was drawn inescapably to the currency controversy at the outset of his second term because the gold reserve
in the Treasury was dropping catastrophically. The depression
which began as soon as he took up the office in 1893, widespread panic induced by the Free Silver campaign, and the
effects of the Sherman Silver Purchase Act of 1890—which
allowed the free exchange of silver coin for gold—combined
to produce a crisis situation. Cleveland resolved, therefore,
that his first and most imperative duty, even before moving on
the tariff question, was to secure the repeal of the Sherman
Silver Purchase Act. What followed was a long and bitter
struggle, stretching out over many months, in which he exerted over Congress every ounce of his executive power. "It
was the President's victory," Woodrow Wilson observed, "and
every one knew it . . . Such a stroke settled what the course of
congressional politics should be throughout the four years
of Mr. Cleveland's term, and made it certain that at the end
of that term he should either have won his party to himself or
lost it altogether."[3]

[2] Ellis Paxson Oberholzer, A History of the United States Since the
Civil War (New York, 1937), V, 39–40.
[3] Wilson, "Cleveland," p. 297.

As it turned out, Cleveland lost it. The South and the West completely revolted. In effect, two Democratic parties came into being. Prosperity did not return with repeal, as Cleveland had said it would, and he grew increasingly alienated from his party. Practically no senator would even talk with him. Lonely, abused on all sides, Cleveland grew bitter and depressed while remaining convinced that he was right. He found it impossible to credit Silver Democrats with any sincerity at all. In his eyes they were charlatans, chameleons, opportunists playing on the ignorant credulity of a sorely distracted people. "I am near the point," he wrote in 1897, "of believing them to be conspirators and traitors and, in their relations with the honest masses, as confidence sharks and swindlers." He considered William Jennings Bryan and Bryanism as a "sort of disease in the body politic." The silverites had "burglarized and befouled the Democratic home."[4]

By the time he had finished the silver-repeal fight and could turn to tariff reform, he had made far too many enemies and had lost the momentum of his early administration.[5] Using ruthless patronage pressure, he was able to force a tariff-reduction bill through the House, but the Senate eviscerated it, causing him to lash out publicly at "party perfidy and party dishonor." How could the Democratic Party face the people, he said, "after indulging in such outrageous discriminations and violations of principles"? If thorough tariff reduction were only achieved, he pleaded, there would be a "quick and certain return of prosperity."[6]

But he had failed utterly, and his administration entered the endless dog days that made the rest of his term a hell for him. He knew that he had powerful interests in the business world principally to thank for his tariff failure. "The trusts and combinations—the communism of pelf—whose machina-

---

[4] Letter to Charles Fairchild, April 2, 1897, Nevins, *Letters*, p. 473; Gilder, "Cleveland," *Century*, LXXVIII, 856; Letter to Judson B. Harmon, July 17, 1900, Nevins, *Letters*, pp. 532–3.
[5] Cf. J. Rogers Hollingsworth, *The Whirligig of Politics: The Democracy of Cleveland and Bryan* (Chicago and London, 1963), pp. 26–7. On the South, see C. Vann Woodward, *Origins of the New South, 1877–1913* (Baton Rouge, 1951), pp. 271–80.
[6] Letter to Congressman William L. Wilson (made public), July 2, 1894, in Nevins, *Letters*, pp. 354–6.

tions have prevented us from reaching the success we deserved," he wrote a friend, "should not be forgotten nor forgiven." The courts had frustrated practically all trust prosecutions, however, and his anger could only be expressed in a blistering attack on the trusts in his last message to Congress.[7]

In the midterm election of 1894 the Democrats suffered one of the more stunning defeats in American political history. Having taken over the majority of both houses behind Cleveland in 1892, they not only lost their majority in 1894, they lost it catastrophically. The watershed in American politics that has traditionally been the 1896 election of the Republican William McKinley to the White House should more accurately be placed at 1894. The oscillation that for decades had taken place in Congress, first one party and then the other winning majorities, was suddenly terminated. For a generation thereafter the Republicans were to dominate American political life completely. Even the election of Woodrow Wilson on the Democratic ticket in 1912 occurred because the Republicans split among themselves and ran two candidates.

The reasons for this turn of events have only begun to be explored. What seems clear is that the suffering created by the massive collapse of the economy in the depression of the 1890's made economic questions absolutely paramount. Urban voters reacted in alarm against the rural inflationist uprising in the Democratic Party set off by the silverites. For the first time, ethnic minorities began shifting to the Republican side. The consumer-producer split within the Democratic Party had begun to work its disastrous results. As Bryan and the Westerners and Southerners took over the party, the Eastern and Midwestern urban working and consumer groups that the Jacksonians and Cleveland had always represented went over to the Republicans.

In short, the cities voted for sound money. "Free silver . . .

[7] Cleveland to Congressman Thomas C. Catchings, Aug. 27, 1894, ibid., pp. 354–5; Nevins, *Cleveland*, pp. 723–4; Cleveland to E. C. Benedict, Jan. 1, 1897, Nevins, *Letters*, pp. 466–7; Fourth Annual Message, Dec. 7, 1896, *Messages and Papers of the Presidents*, VIII, 6176–7.

would be inflationary and therefore contrary to the interests of all urban consumers, whether bankers, petty clerks, or factory workers," Carl N. Degler writes. When William Jennings Bryan ran in the election of 1896, he was rejected in urban areas all over the country that had long been Democratic.[8]

The Republican victories in the cities revealed to party leaders the fact that in half a dozen Midwestern states, the foreign-born workers tipped the victory to the Republicans by their votes. McKinley would have been defeated without their support. In consequence, the Republicans began to turn away from nativism, at least for a number of years. The literacy test for immigrants that they had passed in 1896 as a first step toward immigration restriction—Cleveland vetoed it, to Theodore Roosevelt's infinite disgust—was the last major step in this direction that the Republicans were to take for many years.[9]

They had thereafter the extraordinary good fortune of being the party in power when prosperity returned in the late 1890's, stimulated by the influx of enormous new supplies of gold bullion from discoveries in South Africa, Colorado, and the Yukon. Free silver disappeared as an issue, for farmers found market prices rising buoyantly. At the same time, the Republicans' vigorous ideas about using national power to develop the economy, and, after the rise of the Progressive Republicans, to enact major reforms, seemed to have finally gained for them a strong hold on the loyalties of the voters. After 1894, they became the majority party in the country, holding that ascendancy—with the exception of the Wilson years, themselves accidental—until the depression of the 1930's.[1]

[8] Degler, "Political Parties and the City," *Journal of American History*, pp. 48–9. Cf. also Hollingsworth, *Whirligig of Politics*, pp. 17, 28–9, 55–7; and Samuel P. Hays, *The Response to Industrialism: 1885–1914* (Chicago, 1957), p. 47.
[9] Higham, *Strangers in the Land*, pp. 104–5.
[1] Degler, "Political Parties and the City," *passim*.

Cleveland's foreign policy as President had been, in its fundamental Gladstonianism, radically different from that of the Republicans. He had begun the rebuilding of a strong navy, but he also withdrew the Republicans' proposed canal treaty with Nicaragua in 1885 on the ground that it was coercive and expansionist. He insisted that the basic concept of an internationalized canal be retained as American policy. Any isthmian canal that might be constructed, he said, should "be removed from the chance of domination by any single power," thereby immediately stirring up accusations that he was pro-British.[2]

His response when the Hawaiian annexation episode blew up after 1893—the episode that Ernest R. May sees as the beginning of America's imperialist years—was typically Liberal-Democratic. He thought the whole tawdry business of the "rebellion" against Queen Liliuokalani and the interposition of the American force quite disgraceful. As soon as he became President for his second term he withdrew the treaty of annexation that the previous Republican administration had laid before the Senate, stating that "right and justice" and "national honesty" should be the only touchstones in American foreign policy. Every nation, he warned the Congress, whether weak or strong, has the same rights. There is an international morality that governs and condemns such arrogant spoliations.

> The law of nations is founded upon reason and justice, and the rules of conduct governing individual relations between citizens or subjects of a civilized state are equally applicable as between enlightened nations. The considerations that international law is without a court for its enforcement and that obedience to its commands practically depends upon good faith instead of upon the mandate of a superior tribunal only give additional sanction to the law itself and brand any deliberate infraction of it not merely as a wrong, but as a disgrace.

He tried to restore in Hawaii the *status quo ante bellum,* but the Queen was determined to make heads roll, leaving him

[2] First Annual Message, Dec. 8, 1885, *Messages and Papers of the Presidents,* VII, 4912–13.

embarrassed and everything indeterminate until the Republicans took over the White House in 1897 and secured annexation.[3]

Like Gladstone, he had found it difficult to apply Liberal-Democratic moralism in international affairs, but he had tried hard. Charles Francis Adams, Jr., paid him the ultimate accolade. In a revealing Mugwump observation, he told Cleveland that, with regard to his Hawaiian policy, "I remember no stand taken by a government so morally sound and dignified . . . since the similar stand taken some years ago by Mr. Gladstone towards the victorious African Boers [after the battle of Majuba Hill in 1881]."[4]

In the same vein, Cleveland decided that the British— under the Conservative Premier, Lord Salisbury—were riding roughshod over the rights of a small and defenseless nation in the Venezuela boundary dispute, and he determined to make them desist. Ironically, his actions in this crisis gave a stimulus to the bumptious and chauvinistic jingoism that was growing in the United States in these years, but he saw his steps simply as a rightful intervention in the interests of a weak neighbor. He told the British government through diplomatic channels that they should arbitrate the issues at stake. When Salisbury's government—still used to thinking of the United States as a minor power in world affairs—treated his request with insouciance, he exploded in anger. His message in 1895, publicly announced, was nothing less than an ultimatum in which war was threatened. "Many still living," Joseph Chamberlain's biographer observed in 1934, "remember like yesterday with what stupefaction the Venezuelan ultimatum was received."[5] A great furor arose in both countries, reveal-

[3] Ernest R. May, *Imperial Democracy: The Emergence of America as a Great Power* (New York, 1961), pp. 3–38; Special Message, March 9, 1893, *Messages and Papers of the Presidents,* VIII, 5825; Special Message, Dec. 18, 1893, ibid., VIII, 5892–904.
[4] Charles Francis Adams, Jr., to Cleveland, Nov. 18, 1893, Nevins, *Letters,* p. 339.
[5] May, *Imperial Democracy,* p. 48.

Chamberlain, the former Radical who in 1881 had described the Republicans as the Liberal Party in America, was by 1895 Colonial Secretary in Salisbury's Conservative government, thus making clear what the true parallels were between the American and British parties. As the campaign for protective tariffs that he soon launched demoning how much America and Britain had grown together, and how fundamentally obsolete was the Anglophobism that had been so long a stock in trade in American political life—and that was not to disappear completely for another generation. From all sides in both countries a clamor arose to find a settlement of the difficulty, war being "unthinkable." Measures were found to save face, the Venezuela dispute was settled, and when the dust had subsided a startled European world suddenly realized that the United States had emerged as a great power.[6]

The result was to inaugurate the shift in Anglo-American relations that thereafter saw the two nations put a final end to stiffness and hostility, at least officially, and begin the "special relationship" that has existed ever since, despite periodic difficulties. The British delivered their interests in the Western Hemisphere into American protection, relinquished their claim on joint operation of an isthmian canal, and grounded their foreign policy thereafter on an assumption that the American relationship had always to be kept a friendly and co-operative one. The immediate result was what Carl Schurz called an achievement that by itself would have been enough "to make an administration memorable for all time," a formal treaty of arbitration between Britain and the United States. That it foundered in the Senate, Richard Watson Gilder later observed, was in Cleveland's mind "the greatest failure and grief" of his second administration.[7]

It was typical of Cleveland, therefore, that in his post-presidential years he should become one of the most determined leaders of the anti-imperialist movement.[8] The popu-

strated, the real British counterpart to the Republicans was the Conservative Party.
[6] Ibid., pp. 33–65.
[7] Schurz, "Cleveland's Second Administration," p. 642; Gilder, "Cleveland," *Century*, LXXVIII, 858. There is an abundant literature on Anglo-American diplomatic relations in this period, the *rapprochement*, and its ensuing effects.
[8] Cf. E. Berkeley Tompkins, *The Great Debate: Anti-Imperialism in the United States* (in press); and E. Berkeley Tompkins, "Scylla and Charybdis: The Anti-Imperialist Dilemma in the Election of 1900," *Pacific Historical Review*, XXXVI (1967), 143–61.

lar enthusiasm over imperialism left him aghast; he could never understand it. "It seems to me," he said in 1898, "that the ears of our people are closed to reason." "My pride and self-conceit have had a terrible fall," he said in the following year. "I thought I understood the American people." The pith of the anti-expansion argument, he wrote in 1899, was that "The use of power in the extension of American institutions presents an inconsistency whose evil and dangerous tendency ought to be apparent to all who love these institutions and understand their motives and purposes."[9]

He was horrified at Theodore Roosevelt's foreign policy, saying in a public address at Carnegie Hall in New York City that the way Roosevelt had acquired the Panama Canal route had shamed America, violating "our national honor . . . good name . . . and, above all, our national morality." Roosevelt's election in 1904 staggered him. He was so surprised that "for a moment, the idea has entered my mind that a change in the character of our countrymen has taken place." When Richard Watson Gilder suggested the preparation of a biography in 1905, he replied, "I am by no means sure that it would be in tune with the vaudeville that attracts our people and wins their applause."[1] He was, of course, right. The day when his character type had been popular had largely passed. The twentieth century has at no time found the Clevelands of this world to be interesting people.[2]

Despite his disappointments, Cleveland clung to his paradoxical faith in the Whole People. They might be afflicted by selfishness, sordidness, and a delight in carnival attractions, yet they were in his mind still sound. In his last year—1908—he wrote:

[9] Cleveland to John G. Carlisle, Oct. 21, 1898, Nevins, *Letters*, p. 506; Cleveland to Edward M. Shepard, Jan. 12, 1899, ibid., p. 508; Cleveland to Bolton Hall, Oct. 8, 1899, ibid., p. 518.
[1] Address, Carnegie Hall, New York City, Oct. 21, 1904, Cleveland Papers, Series 5; Letter to A. B. Farquhar, Dec. 12, 1904, Nevins, *Letters*, pp. 590–1; Gilder, "Cleveland," *Century*, LXXVIII, 491–2.
[2] It may be held that Hoover and Eisenhower were of Cleveland's type, but Hoover was seen primarily as a brilliant engineer with an international standing as a philanthropist, and Eisenhower as a great and (apparently) universally admired general. Cleveland was elected and admired for his character alone, with no other luster to his name.

I have always been such an optimistic American and have always had such complete faith in the saving power of American good sense, that I cannot make myself believe but that we shall weather all storms and find the bright daylight in due time. Though occasionally a feeling of discouragement comes over me, I am glad to say it is only temporary.[3]

To the end, therefore, the essential contradictions in Cleveland—the ambivalences inherent in his faith and in his political world view—persisted. He was torn between an optimism induced by the conviction that America was carrying out God's plan, and a pessimism characteristic of the Calvinist view that mankind is degraded. Devoted to a determinist faith, he derived from it the stimulus to be an energetic and strongly willed executive. His appetite for active power led him to reinvigorate the American presidency, yet he was content to spend his vast energies on only a few campaigns. It is true that it was not yet in the tradition of the presidency for the man in the White House to be a prolific creator of proposed legislation, and that in contrast to most of his predecessors he was genuinely in the tradition of Jackson, Peel, and Gladstone. Yet the fact is that his immensely vigorous presidency produced little of major consequence, save the establishment of the civil service and the beginnings of conservation.

Cleveland's career embodied the paradoxes of Jacksonianism as well. Jackson and Cleveland spent much of their presidencies attacking unearned wealth, monopolies, and social exploitation, yet both were satisfied with surprisingly little in the way of program. Out of all the sound and fury of Jacksonianism, what emerged as the Jacksonian agenda? Destroy the U.S. Bank and establish sound money. Cleveland's Fourth Annual Message in 1888 depicted a nation sick to its core, defiled, shallow, led astray by false gods, ground under the iron heel of wealth and power. What was the answer? Lower the tariff. This would supposedly end the monopolies, terminate special privilege, and clarify American life, bringing prosperity and honest toil in its wake.

[2] Cleveland to A. B. Farquhar, Feb. 11, 1908, Nevins, *Letters*, p. 623.

It was doubtless this disparity between diagnosis and prescription that led so many then and since to see Cleveland as the front man for the moneyed interests. Such an interpretation, however, misses the essential point. Cleveland operated within a political tradition devoted to only a few large and essentially negative goals. Cleveland, the British Liberals, and the Jacksonians were moved by a political world view that concentrated most of its force in one central conviction: that the root cause of social oppression and economic disorder was a corrupt relationship between business and aristocracy and the government. Prevent the distribution of special privileges to businessmen, and moral and social health would flourish, founded on the sturdy vigor of honest men who ask no favors. More than this, stable prosperity, based on free interchange between nations, would ensue. Since in their long reign after 1860 the Republicans had indeed distributed favors, Cleveland and the Democrats conceived it to be their principal task to take them away.

Cleveland was superbly equipped for this task. His religious outlook made him a powerful social critic who turned the White House into a pulpit from which to castigate the major sources of corruption in American life. All that was sordid and selfish, as defined by the political creed he inherited and venerated, was singled out for the burning word and the slashing veto, handed down with the confidence of authority. He was convinced he spoke alike for the people, whose inner convictions he felt he uniquely divined, and for the principles of the true and righteous political faith.

As a depression President he was disabled by the very virtues that made him strong and confident. The Presbyterianism in which he was reared made him a powerful opponent of heresies, but not an innovator. It was too creedal, too concentrated on preserving the "ark of the covenant." To the Shorter Catechism mind, what was not contained in the original vision handed down from the sainted past was not simply irrelevant, it was a threatened falling away from "principle." It was this attitude that could lead him to say, of Jefferson, that his principles were issued in a "spirit of prophecy," and were applicable "in all times to come and in all stages of our country's growth and development."[4] When conditions changed, and new principles were called for, he was faced with a social function for which he was not equipped, the recognition and acceptance of new ideas—of which there were many in the air. His Presbyterianism could lead to social criticism, but it enjoined denial, not creation; faithfulness to the received vision, not inspired heterodoxy.

He refreshed the nation's idea of the presidency by dramatically assuming the role of tribune of the people, a role largely forgotten since Jackson's day. He thought of himself as deriving his power from the nation at large and not from limited and oligarchical circles in society and in the Congress. But Cleveland was misled by this conception into thinking he could neglect the arts of Congressional diplomacy. He failed to invest his apparently strong presidency with the strength that comes from political skill. When he could operate within the negative powers of the presidency—those that are relatively free from Congressional interference—he was successful in his blunt and forceful way. But when major enactments were called for, he faltered seriously. He assumed from his real popularity in the nation at large that he could rely primarily upon exhortation. It is probable, indeed, that his very notion of sovereignty, derived from his Presbyterian understanding of God, led him to rely on the righteousness of his requests.

The example of William Gladstone may have helped to lead him astray. The Liberal-Democratic tradition by Cleveland's time had come to embody not only the ideas that Gladstone so luminously expressed, but his personal political style as well. Gladstone symbolized the exhorter in politics, and the exhorter in a special mode: the exhorter as preacher. Since the Liberal-Democratic tradition as he had fashioned it assumed that the key battles in public life were those that went on within each man's character—between selfishness and the lust to dominate on the one hand, and self-denial and

[4] Address, Democratic Club, New York City, April 13, 1891, Cleveland Papers, Series 5; Address, New York City, April 27, 1889, Bergh, *Addresses*, pp. 165–70.

compassion on the other—it naturally flowed from this tradition that exhortation was the most critical function in political life. Gladstone at Midlothian was not simply the first British political leader of prime-ministerial rank to go about the country exhorting masses of citizenry, he was the first such politician to do so in the Anglo-American world. American Presidents or presidential candidates limited themselves to rare utterances, and in the White House to statements that were bland and official. Jackson's Bank Veto was a startling departure in his time, so much was it a diatribe on social opression. When Andrew Johnson made his tragic stumping tour in 1866 against the Radical Republicans, he was savagely criticized and defeated in the ensuing Congressional elections.

Cleveland was introducing quite a new style to the American presidency, therefore, when he made it a pulpit. His Tariff Message of 1887 was sensational, and it was followed thereafter by his bitter Fourth Annual Message in 1888, his attacks against corruption during his interregnum, and his somber Second Inaugural in 1893. Perhaps as a minister's son he unconsciously concluded, from having watched the abject faces in his father's church, that burning words alone would lead to action. Perhaps he assumed from Gladstone's successes that exhortation by itself would lead to legislation, forgetting the much greater hold of the British premiership over the Commons, and Gladstone's assiduous work with party whips.

Whatever the reasons, his Congressional relations were seriously defective, and his most cherished objectives were lost. There were several critically important occasions during his second term when he might have salvaged major victories by the arts of compromise and conciliation, but these arts were not simply beyond him, they were beneath him. He could not compromise "principle," for that would convict him along with his enemies. When exhortation failed, he bludgeoned his opponents with the patronage weapon. After that weapon had been used to win his one major legislative victory, the repeal of silver purchase, it was thereafter blunted and ineffective.

On the other hand, he was assaulting an extraordinarily

solid and resistant fortress in his campaign against the tariff. Jackson had invested his presidency with luster by his attack on the United States Bank, and there is some evidence that Cleveland had this example in mind as he battled for tariff reduction. The logic of the situation and of history, indeed, made the tariff his inevitable target. Just as the United States Bank had been the large and visible symbol of the corruption that the Jacksonians assailed in their day, the tariff was the embodiment of corruption in Cleveland's presidencies. Unfortunately for Cleveland, however, the tariff as an institution was much more rooted than the United States Bank. He led, too, a Democratic Party severely divided against itself on the issue that had unified them before, the money system. A determined president who was fixed on having his way, he found the politicians he led to be a distracted force engaged in internecine struggles, and he could not bring himself to mollify them. The result was a shattered crusade, an ineffective presidency, and a flat historical image.

Chapter 9

GEORGE BROWN AND
ALEXANDER MACKENZIE:
SCOTTISH LIBERALISM IN CANADA

At the time of the American Revolution, the Province of Quebec extended far westward beyond its present boundaries, running out beyond the Great Lakes. In 1791, since English-speaking settlements had begun to appear in the region west of Montreal, Quebec was reduced to its present size and given the name of Lower Canada, and Upper Canada (now the Province of Ontario—the name "Ontario" being established at Confederation in 1867) was created for the English-speaking and placed under English laws. For almost half a century, the two provinces carried on their separate lives. In 1840, in a determined attempt to swamp the French Canadians and turn them into Britons, the two were merged into a unified Province of Canada, under one government. Twenty-seven years later, after interminable wrangling, the two original provinces were given back their local governments and autonomy, and the Maritime Provinces joined them in the Confederation of 1867, establishing the Dominion of Canada with its common government in Ottawa.

George Brown and Alexander Mackenzie both emigrated to Canada from Scotland in the 1840's, during the period when Quebec and Ontario constituted the unified but sorely distracted Province of Canada. Brown settled in Toronto, where he founded the *Globe*, and rose to eminence in short order. In the 1850s, he entered the provincial parliament, fashioned the Liberal Party largely in his image, and led the way to the creation of the Dominion of Canada in 1867. Alexander Mackenzie took up his residence in the far-western tip of the peninsula of Ontario, then an almost untouched frontier, and made his way laboriously upward to modest wealth and status as a building contractor. He became one of Brown's close supporters and friends in the 1850's, took over the leadership of the Liberals after Brown had largely retired from active politics in 1867, and served five difficult, depression-ridden years as the first Liberal Premier of Canada from 1873 to 1878. When he resigned the party leadership in 1880, the pronouncedly Scottish period of Canadian Liberalism came to an end, but the Scottish characteristics of Liberalism in Canada had become firmly established.[1]

The antagonism between French-speaking and English-speaking Canadians, which led to the Confederation of the Dominion of Canada, is one of the better-known examples in modern history of ethnic conflict. What must be understood about Canada, however, is that the English-speaking are also divided among themselves by ethnic and religious hostilities. Within the province of Upper Canada (the terms "Upper Canada" and "Ontario" will be used interchangeably) there has been an almost constant political melee from its earliest days, a melee that is in many ways a reproduction in miniature of the controversies within the British Isles.

[1] In Great Britain, the practice is to refer to those living north of the Border as "Scots" and not "Scotch," the latter term, one is informed, being the name of a liquor and not of a people. In Canada, for unexplained reasons, the distinction seems to be without importance, and the latter term is the more common, at least in the twentieth century. "We referred to ourselves as Scotch and not Scots," John Kenneth Galbraith has recently written. "When, years later, I learned that the usage in Scotland was different it seemed to me rather an affectation." (John Kenneth Galbraith, *The Scotch* [Boston, 1964], p. 12.) For consistency's sake, and since Scotland in this case is so directly the referent, the British practice will be that used in this chapter.

The first settlements in Upper Canada consisted of thousands of Loyalists driven out of the thirteen colonies after the Revolution. Confiscations, mistreatment, sufferings—these were what Upper Canadians thought of when they regarded the United States, or republicanism, democracy, and social equality. Such memories are still alive in the twentieth century. "[Write a book] about our ancestor who was a judge in Massachusetts before they burned his house down and nearly murdered him," Jane Cameron urges her sister just before the Second World War in MacLennan's novel *The Precipice*. "The Americans admire themselves so much, it would be a good thing if somebody reminded them about the other side of their picture. They've become intolerably conceited and it would do them good if someone took them down a peg or two."[2]

If being driven out were not enough, in 1812 the Americans launched a war of conquest against Upper Canada, thereby making certain that Canada would never become a part of the American Union. Not only was the British Loyalism of the original settlers made far more intense, so also was a sense of Canadian nationalism created. "The place of this contest in Canadian history goes far beyond the military events involved: it goes to the roots of Canadian life. As a factor in the building of the Canadian nation, it is hard to see how it can be outranked . . . ."[3]

Because of the circumstances of Upper Canada's founding, British Canada and French Canada were to be in a curious way fundamentally alike. Both developed a loyalty that was non-Canadian in its object, in order to maintain their separate identities. Quebec, conquered by the British and discarded by France, developed a fervent loyalty to Rome as it fought to retain its own identity, becoming, its critics insisted, more Catholic than the Pope himself. British Canada similarly developed a fealty to Great Britain, to the Crown and to British institutions, in its determination not to

[2] Hugh MacLennan, *The Precipice* (New York, 1948), pp. 148–9.
[3] Arthur R. M. Lower, *Canadians in the Making: A Social History of Canada* (Toronto, 1958), p. 173. For general information on the history of Upper Canada, I have placed primary reliance on Gerald M. Craig, *Upper Canada: The Formative Years, 1784–1841* (Toronto, 1963).

become American. The Conservative Party in Ontario has been pre-eminently the party of an outspoken British loyalty, but the Liberals in that province shared the attitude too, in their own different way. When Alexander Mackenzie visited Britain in 1875 as Liberal Premier, he found to his disappointment that few there shared his devotion to the empire. "I have listened a lot," he wrote home, "and I conclude that Canada is more British than Britain."[4]

Those who looked south of the border to the United States for their inspiration, therefore, had small leverage indeed upon Canadian life. What patriotism and subversion have meant to Americans, loyalty and disloyalty to Britain have meant to British-Canadians. From the earliest days of Upper Canada, anything that smacked of American governmental practices—usually under the term "elective principles" —was to be shunned or condemned for that reason. Britain had always to be the referent—and not Liberal Britain, but Conservative, imperial, traditional Britain. "Throughout [Canadian history] it has been the conservative trends in English life that we have usually copied."[5] Almost by principle, therefore, Canada in the nineteenth century consistently delayed its movements toward the democratization of politics and society.

The American influence, however, could not be escaped. In population, Canada is a small nation next to a very large and powerful one. The American way of life and economy constitute the most prominent objects on the Canadian horizon. Furthermore, quite aside from the influence of the American example, Canada is a North American nation. Upper Canada in the 1830's looked American to British visitors not because it slavishly copied the United States, but because, as Gerald M. Craig observes, it shared similar frontier conditions, a similar freedom from feudal inheritances, and the same high premiums given to individual initiative and hard work.[6] Despite its determination to remain British, Canada could not avoid becoming an American country as much as it was a British one.

When Upper Canada was first established in the 1790's, the British government resolved not to make again the same mistakes—as it saw them—that it had made in the thirteen colonies. It determined that any tendency toward democracy would be counterbalanced by strongly aristocratic institutions. The governor was given sources of funds largely outside the control of the assembly; the land system was made distinctly aristocratic, with larger grants going to those of higher social status; a great deal of land, one seventh, was reserved to the Crown; and another seventh was set aside for the support of a "Protestant Clergy." This last arrangement was immediately interpreted by the governing authorities to mean the exclusive establishment and support of the Church of England in Canada. An Anglican bishop was soon appointed, and for a time marriages could be made only by Anglican priests. Education in the province was assumed to be primarily under the control of the Anglican hierarchy. In every possible way, Upper Canada was to be a mirror of Anglican, aristocratic England.[7]

Upper Canada was unlike the United States also in that its population was almost entirely British in origin. Most notably, Upper Canada was Scottish in tone and in leadership, retaining this characteristic for many years despite the fact that the Scots were equaled in numbers by the English by the 1850's, and numbered less than half of the Irish population (both Protestant and Catholic) in that decade.[8] When a reporter asked Sir Richard Cartwright at the end of his long career what groups were dominant in Ontario politics in the 1860's, he replied in some amusement:

> Oh, there you had tumbled into an almost perfect Scotch settlement. You had Sir J. A. Macdonald, Sandfield Macdonald, George Brown, Alexander Mackenzie, Oliver Mowat, Alexander Campbell, J. H. Cameron, W. Macdougall, and representatives of nearly every clan you could name . . .

[7] Craig, *Upper Canada*, pp. 5, 14–15, 21, 56, 183–6.
[8] In 1851, Upper Canada contained 176,000 Irish, 82,000 English, and 75,000 Scots. Lower, *Canadians in the Making*, p. 210.

I think Mr. Foley [an Irish Catholic] was almost the only prominent man in Ontario at the time who was not of Scotch origin.[9]

Most of the Scots were Liberals—or, as they were generally referred to before the 1860's, Reformers. Sir Wilfrid Laurier remarked that Scots Presbyterianism was the heart of Ontario Liberalism. "Locally there was no real competition," John Kenneth Galbraith writes of his heavily Scottish district in Ontario, "there were too many Liberals . . . Quite a few of the clansmen backed the Liberals . . . because they wanted the competitive reward of winning and even more because they wanted the unadulterated joy of seeing the Tories lose. They imagined or at least hoped that the Tories suffered terribly in defeat."[1] The career of John A. Macdonald in the nineteenth century demonstrates, however, that it was quite possible for a Scot to be not only a Conservative, but the greatest Conservative of them all. The explanation for this may in part be found in an examination of early settlement patterns.

The first Scottish settlements of any size in Upper Canada consisted of Highlanders fleeing from New York after the Revolution. Scottish Highlanders in the American colonies were notoriously Loyalist, and they suffered for it. Forced out of the United States, they settled in eastern Ontario, in the general vicinity of Kingston. In the ensuing years they were able to attract many emigrants directly from the Scottish Highlands, where economic conditions were depressed, so that before the War of 1812 eastern Ontario became Highlander in population—and Tory and Loyalist in politics.[2]

Some of the Highlanders were Catholic, and they would seemed to have leaned toward the Liberals. John Sandfield Macdonald—not to be confused with John A. Macdonald—who was premier of the united Province of Canada from 1862

[9] Sir Richard Cartwright, *Reminiscences* (Toronto, 1912), p. 9.
[1] O. D. Skelton, *Life and Letters of Sir Wilfrid Laurier* (Toronto, 1912), I, 22; Galbraith, *The Scotch*, p. 69.
[2] Stanley C. Johnson, *A History of Emigration from the United Kingdom to North America, 1763–1912* (New York, 1966), pp. 5–8; Helen I. Cowan, *British Emigration to British North America: The First Hundred Years* (Toronto, 1961), pp. 18–27.

to 1864, and first premier of the Province of Ontario (1867–71), sprang from this group. But eastern Ontario Liberals were always an equivocal element in Ontario Liberalism, reluctant to follow the lead of the Liberals around Toronto and to the west.

Eastern Ontario remained the heartland of Conservatism for many decades after the arrival of the original Loyalist settlements. In the 1840's the "strength of the Conservative party lay, where it had always lain before, in the long narrow strip of farming country, homeland of the first Loyalist settlements, which stretched from Toronto eastward to the old interprovincial boundary."[3]

It was to this world that the family of John A. Macdonald emigrated from Scotland in 1820. They had come from the far-northern Scottish highlands, by way of Glasgow, and they took up residence in Kingston, the principal town of eastern Ontario, settling among a strongly knit group of Highland families. The patriarch of the connection was Lieutenant Colonel Donald Macpherson, who had been fighting Yankees, off and on, for forty years. Loyalty to the Crown was the breath of life; disdain for Americans, and for everything American, was beyond question.[4]

The ex-British officer class that in substantial numbers settled in Canada—on bounteous land grants—was in fact one of the pillars of Canadian Toryism. They joined with governors, royal officials, and local magistracy and officialdom to form a Canadian version of the British ruling class. "Their presence in a district introduced a class consciousness which cut across the natural democracy of North America and . . . further divided a province already weakened by heterogeneity of origin."[5] Kingston joined to its Highland Scot character the influence of its naval base and military tradition, making Conservatism so monolithic in that district that Reformers hardly even came forward as candidates.[6]

It is not surprising, therefore, that from the beginning of

[3] Donald Creighton, *John A. Macdonald: The Young Politician* (Boston, 1953), p. 102.
[4] Ibid., pp. 1–7.
[5] Lower, *Canadians in the Making*, p. 197.
[6] Creighton, *Macdonald: The Young Politician*, p. 41.

his political career John A. Macdonald spoke for the Canadian political tradition that strongly disliked the United States, glorified the British connection, and adopted the views of traditional Tory England. In his first important political utterances in 1843, Macdonald supported the Governor General, Sir Charles Metcalfe, in his struggle with the Reformers, who were trying to secure more control by the Assembly over the government. In a classic Conservative statement, he praised the Crown's prerogative as against the legislature, which in his view expressed primarily the low ambitions of party politicians. Those agitating against Metcalfe, he warned, were actually republicans in disguise.[7] Two years later, in the provincial parliament, he praised the law of primogeniture as essential to the maintenance of a sound and stable constitution.[8] In the same year he supported differential duties against American imports, insisting that Canadians needed to fear American, not British, manufactures.[9]

As eastern Ontario was the seat of Conservatism, western Ontario—Toronto being the dividing point—was the center of Reform. It was this region that tended to receive the heavily American immigration that moved into Upper Canada from the 1790's to the War of 1812. Perhaps half of Upper Canada's population, in 1820, was American.[1] The Americans constituted the first minority group in Ontario's history, in the sense that they were the object of attempts at repressive treatment by the socially dominant. They were much feared even before the War of 1812, and after the peace of 1815 the ruling groups in Upper Canada—known to history as the Family Compact—took many steps to halt further American immigration and to limit the political and property rights of those already resident in the province. The fight over the "alien issue" in the 1820's was the beginning of partisan politics in Upper Canada. It was in this struggle that the Reformers, representing western Ontario, first appeared as a distinct political grouping opposed to the Tories.[2]

[7] Ibid., p. 94.
[8] Ibid., p. 107.
[9] Ibid., p. 115.
[1] Craig, *Upper Canada*, pp. 115–16.
[2] Ibid., pp. 85–123.

The 1820's and 1830's were to be the period in which American influence on Upper Canadian politics was strongest. Many Reformers looked to Jacksonian America in admiration and worked hard to introduce elective institutions and republican simplicity and austerity in government. They attacked the aristocratic governing system in Upper Canada, pushed for separation of church and state, and called for a land system like that in the United States.

The most violent among these men was William Lyon Mackenzie, who was spiritually a transplanted Jacksonian.[3] A splenetic and tempestuous man whose newspaper screamed abuse at the authorities—for which he was repeatedly expelled from the Legislative Assembly—Mackenzie finally launched a direct, if tiny, assault against the government. Gathering about him a small band of American settlers, he set in motion the Rebellion of 1837. Involving hardly more than a brief brush between his men and a small group of militia on a back road leading out of Toronto, the Rebellion was nevertheless a major turning point in Canadian history. It led to the famous Durham Report, in which Lord Durham laid the basis for the later Commonwealth by holding that local self-rule had to be the basis of the empire. It led also to the Union of 1840, the effective breaking up of the Family Compact, and the beginnings of self-government. Psychologically, the Rebellion ended any possibility that Upper Canada would become Americanized. The influx of American settlers had in any event ceased, and Reformers had been scrambling to disassociate themselves from Mackenzie even before the Rebellion. He was too radical and pro-American. His cause was dead before the Rebellion began.[4]

Most of all, it was dead because a great inflow of British population had finally begun. In a conscious attempt to confirm the British loyalty of the province, Conservative authorities began actively encouraging British immigration in the 1830's. In the brief period from 1830 to 1833, Upper Canada's population increased 50 per cent. The new immigration was

[3] For a clear presentation of his Jacksonianism, see Lillian F. Gates, *"Mackenzie's Gazette:* An Aspect of W. L. Mackenzie's American Years," *Canadian Historical Review,* XLVI (1965), 323–45.
[4] Craig, *Upper Canada,* pp. 188–252.

loyalist in its sympathies. It was in these years that the Orange Order, the Irish Protestant association that was to be so staunchly Tory, began to grow greatly. Furthermore, many people of substance and standing were induced to emigrate to Canada, giving a major boost to the strength of the Conservative Party.[5] The influx, then begun, continued to swell. In the years from 1820 to 1850, Upper Canada evolved from a straggling line of settlements along the north shore of Lake Ontario to a populous province. Where there had been 95,000 in the province in 1814, there were 952,000 in 1851.[6]

The political trends in Upper Canada were therefore no longer toward Americanization, but rather once again in the British direction. This orientation was shared by both Conservatives and Liberals. The system of government that both desired was not that of the United States, where the people directly elected the executive, but rather that of Britain, where the executive is chosen at second hand, as it were, by the legislature. Fundamentally a more elitist system, the British arrangement carried with it not only the responsibility of the government to the legislature, but a royally appointed Governor General to represent the monarch, and the whole traditional panoply of ceremony, allusion, and titles of nobility. Nothing more dramatically illustrates the difference between Canada and the United States than the fact that the constitution for the Dominion of Canada, the British North America Act of 1867, was never submitted to a vote of the people—a fact pointed to by Frank Underhill, among others, as a possible source of its relative weakness.[7] Even George Brown rejected the idea of a referendum. The British government and the Canadian government approved the constitution; what else, he asked, was needed?[8]

That both parties were profoundly British, however, no more made them a band of brothers than were Liberals and Conservatives in Britain. Intense rancor was a major characteristic of Canadian politics in the nineteenth century. At one

[5] Craig, *Upper Canada*, pp. 227–32.
[6] Lower, *Canadians in the Making*, p. 190.
[7] Underhill, *In Search of Canadian Liberalism*, p. 16.
[8] J. M. S. Careless, *Brown of the Globe* (Toronto, 1963), II, 185.

point, in 1849, partisans actually resorted to burning down the legislative buildings in their anger at the passage of a law, the Rebellion Losses Bill. Violence was always just below the surface; legislative gatherings saw many personal encounters. Goon-squad tactics on both sides disrupted meetings and made campaigning dangerous to life and limb.

The root of the matter would seem to be that Canadian politics have their origin not in economic differences, but in ethnic and religious passions and hatreds. Of the three Anglo-American countries, Canada is the nation in which the power of group prejudice may be seen to be most clearly at work.[9] Even in contemporary Canadian politics, religion, ethnic identity, and regionalism are far more important in shaping Canadian voting patterns than class identity[1]—with the concomitant result, one might add, that Canada remains today a relatively weakly integrated nation doubtful of its identity and its nationhood.[2]

───────

Nothing better illustrates the many divisions among Canadians than the fact that even the Scots, as earlier observed, were divided against one another. In this division may be found the explanation for much of mid-century Canadian politics. It was a division that sprang fundamentally—

[9] This is a common observation. S. R. Mealing, "The Concept of Social Class and the Interpretation of Canadian History," *Canadian Historical Review*, XLVI (1965), pp. 201–18, has protested against the non-economic interpretation, but it seems to me that interpretations based upon economic class will not be particularly successful.
[1] See Robert T. Alford, *Party and Society: The Anglo-American Democracies* (Chicago, 1963), Ch. ix, "Canada: Pure Non-Class Politics?" pp. 259–86.
[2] One is reminded of James Madison's principle, enunciated in *The Federalist Papers*, that the politics of small countries are inherently embittered. In large societies, with their heterogeneity and complexity, the enemy is diffuse and indistinct, there are always many interests to balance others, coalitions tend to shift about, and majorities behind strong governments are difficult to form. In small countries, the search for an enemy—the most inveterate characteristic in political society—is easily satisfied, for the cast of characters is small. Lines of hostility, once established, are difficult to change. Group identities remain alive, and prejudices can more easily infuse every aspect of political and social life.

as did so much in Victorian politics—from religious differences. As Grover Cleveland and Benjamin Harrison were both Presbyterians, but rose through different parties in large part because they differed in their Presbyterianism, so John A. Macdonald and George Brown were different kinds of Presbyterians who ended up leading the Conservative and Liberal parties.

The division sprang from events in Scotland. The Church of Scotland—the mother church of Presbyterianism in England and North America—experienced the same wave of evangelical Protestantism that created the Burned-Over District in New York State and the Evangelical explosion in Gladstone's England. Within the Church of Scotland the Calvinism of John Knox had largely died away by the eighteenth century. What was called Moderatism suffused its preaching. Rooted in the calm and rational inquiry of the Enlightenment, cultivated in its tastes and repelled by enthusiasm, Moderatism was divided as by an abyss from the Evangelical movement.[3] Many Moderates in the eighteenth century were on good terms with David Hume, whose free-thinking rationalism and apparent atheism made him almost Satan himself to Evangelicals. Reminiscent of the dry Anglicanism against which Wilberforce and Gladstone railed, Moderate Church of Scotland ministers preached a quiet, intellectual, and legalistic moralism drawn largely from the literature of the day.

In the 1790's, Evangelicalism began to catch fire in Scotland. James Haldane, a wealthy Scot inspired by the example and the religious point of view of Charles Simeon, the great English Evangelical, undertook revival efforts through all of Scotland, preaching to vast audiences the fervent message of Christ and the Gospels that the English Evangelicals had placed at the center of Anglican preaching. Scottish Evangelicalism was also like that in England in being a vigorous revival of Calvinism, with its convictions concerning the depravity of the human soul and mankind's total reliance on God's grace for salvation. Haldane and his brother built

[3] The following discussion is drawn primarily from J. H. S. Burleigh, *A Church History of Scotland* (Oxford, 1960), especially pp. 286–308.

preaching tabernacles, established a college for the training of Evangelists, and organized a missionary society for work within Scotland. Violently disliked by the Church of Scotland —the Church's General Assembly anathematized him as a seditious radical in 1799—Haldane broke away entirely from orthodoxy and founded the Baptist Church movement in Scotland.[4]

Evangelicalism within the Church of Scotland, however, continued to grow in the following decades. By 1834, the Evangelicals were able to gain a majority in the General Assembly, and they launched an assault against the rigidities of the Church. They built hundreds of new churches, especially in the working-class districts that the orthodox Church authorities had ignored, and staffed them with earnest young Evangelical preachers. The Evangelical majority in 1834 took its boldest step, however, when it declared that no pastor could be intruded upon a congregation by a lay patron against its will. Since patrons had the power to appoint ministers and were generally wealthy aristocrats who detested Evangelicalism, and since many congregations were newly aroused by "vital" religion, the non-intrusionist declaration set off a major controversy.

Everything authoritative and aristocratic in the British upper-class temperament was challenged by the demand that a prospective new minister had to be approved by his congregation. It seemed dangerously democratic at a time when the ruling classes were horrified at democracy's advances; it threatened to stimulate the same demand within Anglican congregations; and it struck at one of the taproots of aristocratic status and prestige, the power of patronage, since pulpits carried with them a guaranteed income derived from tithes.

The Evangelicals were quickly taken to court. In a harsh and to many a brutally frank declaration that the state was supreme over the Church, the Scottish Court of Session ruled the non-intrusionist declaration illegal. The Church was declared to be wholly a product of secular legislation. The truly

[4] Ibid., pp. 309–13.

Calvinist and High Church position—that the Church was an independent spiritual community working in cooperation with the state—was thereby quashed. When an appeal was taken to the House of Lords in London, the Church of Scotland found itself in "words even more contemptuous and galling" informed that the right of patrons to appoint ministers was absolute, and that neither parishioners nor presbyteries had any role in the matter at all.

From 1839 a growing party began to emerge in the Church of Scotland, a party Evangelical and non-intrusionist that was to many Englishmen and to Moderate Church Scotsmen both lawless and fanatical. As Lord Cockburn put it, those in power in Parliament and in the government began to take pleasure at "winging Wild-Churchmen."[5] The many new Evangelical church buildings were declared illegal, and the internal system of Church administration came under secular attack. Certain, now, that the cause of true and vital religion was endangered, Evangelicals decided that the tie between Church and state must be completely broken. Having lost their majority in General Session, some 450 Evangelicals, out of the roughly 1,200 ministers of the Church of Scotland, withdrew from the Church in 1843, renouncing the income they had received as ministers of the established Church—the "Auld Kirk"—and forming the "Free Kirk," the Church of Scotland Free.[6]

These events, which together constitute the Great Disruption in nineteenth-century Scottish history, were incomparably dramatic to Scots both at home and overseas. The Church of Scotland was the only organized national body left to Scotland after the Union of 1707 had terminated the Scottish Parliament. Around the Kirk gathered the devotion that Scotsmen felt for their homeland. The openings and closings of its General Assembly were surrounded with all the pomp and circumstance appropriate to a national parliamentary body—as is still the case. The Church carried on much of the local government of Scotland and directed the schools. Though there were small bodies of Roman Catholics, Episco-

5 Ibid., p. 346.
6 Ibid., pp. 314–53.

palians, and other Dissenters in Scotland, by and large the Auld Kirk and Scotland had been one.

The Great Disruption, then, was a sensational event. To see a third of the Kirk's ministry withdraw, taking with them perhaps a third of the parishioners; to see Evangelical teachers give up their posts in the common schools, withdrawing to create separate establishments; to see whole new colleges created for the training of Free Kirk ministers; to see practically the whole of the missionary ministers of the Church leave to join the Free Kirk; to participate in, or to follow from abroad, the splitting up of congregations and the laborious construction of hundreds of new church buildings; to feel, most of all, the great sense of exhilaration and redeemed courage that swept over Evangelicals as they gave up the worldly privilege and wealth of the established Church for the glory of the Lord—to see all this was to witness a drama, a confrontation of holiness and wickedness, that could claim every resource of loyalty that a man had to give.

And so it was among the Scots of Upper Canada. Men's political loyalties either grew directly out of, or were profoundly affected by, the side that they took in the controversy. John A. Macdonald, if anything, had his Conservatism strengthened by the fact that he was never a Free Kirk Presbyterian. The "pious fervour and puritanical eccentricities of early nineteenth-century evangelism" did not appeal to him. He could never understand the intense moralism of the Free Kirkers, and at no time was he uncomfortable with the idea that church and state should be closely linked. He was "quite prepared to accept the old Conservative view that the state should recognize and assist the religious and cultural activities of the churches," provided only that this assistance go to all Christian churches, not simply to the Anglican.[7]

To George Brown, however, the absorbing cause of the Free Kirk was central to much of his life, and it led directly to his becoming a Reformer. The Free Kirkism that did so much to set the tone of Canadian Liberalism was hostile to state and church ties, fought against the idea of ecclesiastical

[7] Creighton, *Macdonald: The Young Politician*, pp. 29, 182.

tyranny and for the secular state—which meant, among other things, secular schools. Free Kirkism was also intensely concerned with personal and social morals, which led to an extraordinary sensitivity—as it seemed to Macdonald's Conservatives—to anything that smacked of corruption in public life.

Therefore, the most important influence upon George Brown as a public man was

> that which stamped him from the start: the deep-rooted religious convictions of his family. The Browns . . . looked with much disfavour on the temporal connections and lay patronage that had grown up in the Kirk over the previous century or so . . . [The] spirit of their religion was . . . the . . . emotional, outgoing faith of the nineteenth-century evangelical movement. [As with Gladstone] Family prayers, Sunday-school teaching for George, charitable work among the poor for his mother and elder sisters, all were an essential part of their lives.
>
> [The Liberalism of George's father, Peter,] was thoroughly related to his religious tenets. He warmly believed, and taught his son, that political liberty was grounded on religious freedom; that victory over authority in the church had led to the conquest of despotism in the state; and that the right—nay duty—of each man, to worship and serve God as his conscience dictated made necessary the freedom of religion from state interference, the citizen's freedom from clerical domination, and all those other freedoms that combined to produce free speech, civil liberties and self-government.[8]

George and Peter Brown emigrated to New York City from Edinburgh in 1837, where they watched in worried and prayerful concern the crisis within the Church of Scotland, as well as all the other controversies, political and economic, that agitated the Anglo-American world in the age of Jackson and Peel. Peter Brown had been an active Whig-Liberal in Edinburgh, supporting the economic doctrines of Adam Smith and both political reform and the destruction of all

[8] Careless, *Brown of the Globe*, I, 7–8.

aristocratic privileges. George's earliest political memories were of the torchlight processions and the heady excitement leading up to the Reform Bill of 1832.

The Browns, however, were unhappy in Jacksonian America. They disliked what they saw of Jacksonian democracy and "locofocoism."[9] Far from being egalitarian democrats, they shared with Alexis de Tocqueville the belief that democracy meant simply the tyranny of majorities. Peter Brown condemned "rule by the passions and ignorance of the multitude—an attitude he passed on to his son." When a quarter of a century later George Brown and John A. Macdonald began working together on a new constitution for Canada, though they were political enemies they agreed emphatically that they had no intention of creating universal suffrage.[1] American democracy was also burdened, in the eyes of the Browns, with the guilt of slavery. In his later years George Brown was to be one of the most active Canadian abolitionists, organizing help for escaped slaves and maintaining close relations with American abolitionists.[2]

Furthermore, they were intensely loyal to Great Britain and revolted by the Anglophobia they found in New York City. "It's as much a man's life is worth," George Brown observed, "to give expression to any British predilections whatsoever."[3] They were ready to listen, therefore, when fellow Free Kirkers began urging them to come to Toronto, bringing with them a newspaper they had founded in New York and taking up the Free Kirk battle in Upper Canada. In 1843, they assented to the call, and shortly were launched in the founding of the Toronto *Globe*, which became both the newspaper giant of Ontario and the voice of Scottish Liberalism in Canada.[4]

[9] A term referring to radical Democrats.
[1] Careless, *Brown of the Globe*, I, 16–18; II, 141–2.
[2] Ibid., I, 100–2; II, 212.
[3] Ibid., I, 22.
[4] Galbraith, *The Scotch*, p. 79. The leaders of public opinion in his community did not read much, John Kenneth Galbraith remarks, but they did "keep a close watch on the one unfailing guide to the sound position on all issues which was the Toronto *Globe*. Not even the Boston *Transcript*, which in its generally austere aspect it somewhat resembled, ever had such a committed clientele. The Scotch did not cite the views of *The Globe* with approval; they merely cited them."

George Brown shared most of Toronto's qualities: ambition for business success and political eminence; deep religious sensibilities; a dislike for American democracy; and preternaturally strong British loyalties. Toronto was the bastion of warm attachment to the British Empire. Its principal early population consisted of Protestant Northern Irish, whose garrison mentality—with its anti-Catholicism and loyalty to the Crown—made Toronto "Derry Walls" itself in the 1840's. The city's "wild and rabid" Toryism, as Charles Dickens called it, was to be legend.[5]

The Browns were not Tories, however. They might dislike universal suffrage and American institutions, but once back within a British community again they were vigorously Liberal—an eloquently comparative fact in itself. They supported the fight for responsible government in Canada,[6] which Canadian Tories assailed. When the Tories called responsible government nothing but republicanism in disguise, Peter Brown replied that it was instead a "happy medium between absolute monarchy on the one hand and the tyranny of a democratic majority on the other." As George Brown said in 1849, "What has republicanism ever done for freedom?" Stung by the constant Tory refrain that Reformers were disloyal, he put on the masthead of the *Globe* its permanent motto, "The subject who is truly loyal to the Chief Magistrate will neither advise nor submit to arbitrary measures."[7]

It was the battles within the Kirk, however, that claimed George Brown's closest attention. As soon as the Great Disruption took place in Scotland, emissaries left for Canada to explain to Upper Canada—which was in a real sense New Scotland—what had happened, and to solicit support. The Synod of the "Presbyterian Church in connection with the Church of Scotland," as the Auld Kirk in Canada was called, met in Kingston in July 1844. Presbyterians from eastern Ontario were Auld Kirk and Conservative; those from western

[5] Careless, *Brown of the Globe*, I, 26–30; Lower, *Canadians in the Making*, p. 265.
[6] "Responsible government" is another term for parliamentary or cabinet government. It provides for a cabinet, drawn from the majority party in the elected assembly, that governs the province in place of the royally appointed governor (excluding foreign affairs).
[7] Careless, *Brown of the Globe*, I, 30–4, 43, 94–7.

Ontario were Free Kirk and Reform. Perhaps these differences were more than simply religious, for the west of Ontario, settled largely by the later immigration that came in such extraordinary volume after 1820, consisted largely of Lowland Scots, while those in and around Kingston, as earlier observed, were Highlanders. The Browns were Lowlanders from Edinburgh; the John A. Macdonald connection were Highlanders. In Canada, apparently, there was recreated the split that in so many ways explains much of Scotland's internal history.[8]

A Great Disruption among Scots in Canada, in any event, was inevitable. Something less than half of those at the Kingston Synod withdrew to create the Presbyterian Church of Canada, the Browns being very busy in its organization.[9] They then went on, in the succeeding years, to lead the fight for what became a major goal of Canadian Reform, a complete separation of church and state.

George Brown was seeking a reform that would go far to Americanize Upper Canada, and the Conservatives, recognizing this fact, made the most of it. The more zealous Reformers of the older, Americanist variety frankly looked to a complete secularization of the state as a step toward what they admired south of the border. In the early 1840's, this variety of Reformer took on the name "Clear Grit," a term of uncertain origin that was quickly regarded as synonymous with "radical."

In essence, however, Clear Grits were not Jacksonian Democrats, but rather British Radicals along the lines of Cobden and Bright—to whom Brown liked to compare himself.[1] When the Clear Grit leaders were not Scots, they were from the English North Country. There was a lot of Chartism in their background. Some of them wanted to establish American elective institutions in Canada, and they displayed all the admiration of things American that John Bright himself expressed. Primarily, however, they wanted to use responsi-

---

[8] Ibid., I, 59–60, 71; cf. also Lower, *Canadians in the Making*, Ch. xiv, "The Great Days of Settlement, 1820–1850."
[9] Careless, *Brown of the Globe*, I, 59–60.
[1] Ibid., I, 69.

ble government to sweep away all aristocratic privileges in Canada, establish universal suffrage (in this, differing with George Brown), secularize the state, create free public education, and above all, wipe out corruption. Their basic complaint against the Family Compact and its successors in Upper Canada was not simply against its Anglicanism, or its refusal to let the executive power be swayed by public opinion, but against its corrupt use of the patronage power to buy off opposition. In the 1850's, the Grand Trunk railway, in place of the patronage, became for them the symbol and the source of the pervasive corruption that disfigured all of Canadian politics.[2]

For a number of years Brown waged a campaign to convert the more radical Clear Grits to the idea that British-style responsible government was more efficient than American elective institutions, more expressive of the people's will, less corrupt, and a better vehicle for maintaining liberty. Universal suffrage, he insisted, meant simply extravagance, and the dominance of ignorant mobs.[3] The practical achievement of responsible government in 1849, when Lord Elgin signed the Rebellion Losses Bill, and the passage of each year thereafter made fully elective institutions increasingly remote and less appealing. Much more pressing, furthermore, were church-and-state questions, and on this issue, in the 1850's, Brown and the Clear Grits became a working team.

The battle for secularization focused first on King's College, the Anglican institution in Toronto that was supported by public funds. Reformers wanted to replace King's with a secular, publicly supported institution open to men of all creeds. After years of agitation, they won their battle in 1849, when in one of the first pieces of legislation to be enacted by a fully responsible government in Canada, King's was replaced by the University of Toronto.[4]

[2] Craig, *Upper Canada*, pp. 189–90; Underhill, *In Search of Canadian Liberalism*, pp. 21–42, 48–52; Careless, *Brown of the Globe*, I, 109–14.
[3] Careless, *Brown of the Globe*, I, 113–14.
[4] Careless, *Brown of the Globe*, I, 56, 87.
The University of Toronto is an interesting expression in Canada of the same influences that in this general period founded the University of London and New York University. All three were specifically founded as "new wave" institutions: secular, freethinking, advanced

This led to a direct assault on the greatest problem of all, the Clergy Reserves. From the Act of 1791, when one seventh of the land in Upper Canada was set aside for the support of a "Protestant Clergy," the Reserves had been an almost constantly festering issue in Upper Canadian life. Poulett Thomson, Governor General in 1839, called it "the one great overwhelming grievance—the root of all the troubles of the Province—the cause of the Rebellion—the never failing watchword at the hustings—the perpetual source of discord, strife, and hatred."[5]

To the royal authorities in the early days, "Anglicanism," Arthur R. M. Lower writes, "was the focus of the lost cause which had to retreat from the new American nation to the Canadian bush . . . [The] new colonies must be of pure religion and undefiled, that is, they must be Anglican." Dissent, that hated apparent source of rebellion and disorder, must be left behind in the United States. This "is the fundamental point in British North American history after the American Revolution."[6]

By George Brown's day, however, the dream of an Anglican Canada had clearly grown to be impossible. Of those claimed by the various denominations in Upper Canada in 1840, approximately 96,000 were Anglicans, 88,000 were Presbyterians, 74,000 were Methodists, 50,000 were Roman Catholics, and 19,000 were Baptists.[7] In consequence, the majority continuously agitated the question of the Clergy Reserves.[8]

There were many who did not want Clergy Reserves abolished; they simply wanted them divided. This was John A. Macdonald's view, and that of Auld Kirk Conservatives like him. In 1840, an act along these lines was passed allowing Roman Catholics, Presbyterians, and Methodists to have a

in curricula, and radical in political orientation. All were protests against the church-dominated and conservative institutions then available. Samuel Tilden, in his student years, left Yale for New York University for exactly these reasons.
[5] Craig, *Upper Canada*, p. 273.
[6] Lower, *Canadians in the Making*, pp. 137–40.
[7] J. Bartlet Brebner, *Canada: A Modern History* (Ann Arbor, Mich., 1960), p. 232.
[8] Craig, *Upper Canada*, p. 18.

share in the proceeds from sale of Clergy Reserves land.[9] This line of policy, however, was criticized by Free Kirkers and all Clear Grits, who were opposed to any links at all between church and state.

In 1850, Clear Grits had their deepest convictions flouted in another way. In that year, the government of the united Province of Canada—listening to the combined voices of High Anglican Tories, French Canadians, and Irish Roman Catholics—made it mandatory in Upper Canada that municipal authorities provide public funds to support church-directed "separate schools" when twelve heads of families so requested. The act was protested by Upper Canadian Clear Grits as a direct assault on the secular public school system that, in contrast to Quebec, Upper Canada had been recently building.[1]

Brown, now thoroughly aroused, secured election to the provincial parliament in 1851 and began leading a campaign calling for complete separation between church and state and an end to what he saw as a growing French Canadian domination over Upper Canada. The government's recent actions, as he saw them, together with what the Roman Catholic Church was apparently doing elsewhere in Britain and throughout Europe, were evidence of a malign Catholic conspiracy to overturn free institutions everywhere.[2] "In our own country—in Upper Canada—do not popery and churchism," Brown asked in 1851, "combine to destroy our national common school system? . . . There can be no permanent peace in Canada till every vestige of church dominancy is swept away."[3] When supporters of the ministry pleaded that the only hope for a unified Canada lay in meeting the legiti-

---

[9] Brebner, *Canada*, p. 231; Craig, *Upper Canada*, p. 274.
[1] Careless, *Brown of the Globe*, I, 119–20.
[2] In both Britain and the United States violent anti-Catholic outbursts were underway in the 1850's. The "Papal Aggression" crisis in Britain in 1851, growing out of the re-establishment by the Pope of Catholic dioceses in Britain—using regrettably aggressive and truculent language—had a great influence in stimulating anti-Catholicism in Upper Canada. America's Know-Nothing movement doubtless had its effect as well. North America in these years received an enormous influx, for the first time, of Irish Roman Catholics, and they were received with hostility.
[3] Ibid., I, 127.

mate demands of French Canadians, whose whole way of life was built upon church schools, Brown harshly replied:

> If unity with the French is to come first and the voluntary principle after it—then we say we are quite satisfied that the reserves three years from now will be divided among the sects, and we will have sectarian education, sectarian grants and sectarian corporations to the heart's content of the veriest priest in the country.[4]

Brown quickly became the symbol of anti-Catholicism in Canada—even the Orange Order supported him for a while —and he remained so thereafter. His principal goal, however, was not to destroy Catholicism so much as it was to protect in Upper Canada the secular school system and society that his Free Kirkism and his Liberalism called for—a society in which there would be no privileges whatsoever for any religious group, in which all would have equal status. "Voluntaryism," in such a society, would be the ruling principle.

Voluntaryism, for the next several years the key term in Canadian politics, demanded that all churches be supported by the donations of their members, and not by Clergy Reserves income. Voluntaryism carried with it the vision of all children, of whatever sect, going to the same common public schools together, these schools being supported by secularized Clergy Reserves. Brown detested the thought that every child, in a separate school arrangement, would go to a Methodist school, or a Catholic school, or a Presbyterian school, thus shattering social unity. He shared with the British Radicals and Dissenters, in short, a dedication to the free and nonsectarian school system that existed in the United States. No other issue, perhaps, bound together American Democrats, British Radicals, and Canadian Reformers so much as the issue of public education. The victory for nonsectarian public schools had in fact been won only recently in the United States; the British Radicals hoped eagerly for it in England, and Brown was determined to achieve and protect it in Upper Canada.

[4] Ibid., I, 139.

In 1854, voluntaryism won its major victory, though a qualified one: the Clergy Reserves were reluctantly abolished by a Conservative ministry, but the funds they produced went to the municipalities rather than directly to the support of public education.[5] Almost immediately, however, the Conservatives outraged the Clear Grits again. At the end of the session of 1855, John A. Macdonald introduced and passed over Upper Canadian protests a bill that made it even easier for separate schools to be established in Ontario. The affair had all the hallmarks of conspiracy, and it created anger in Ontario, for the laws were enacted hastily at the end of the session at a time when most Upper Canadian legislators had already left the parliament for the long journey home, Quebec City still being the seat of government.[6]

Brown now shifted the point of his attack. He realized that as long as Upper and Lower Canada were equally represented in the parliament, as provided for in the Union of 1840, French Canada would always have predominant power. On religious issues most of its members voted as a bloc, and by finding allies among Conservatives or Irish coreligionists in Upper Canada, they could build lasting majorities. Voluntaryism in Upper Canada, in Brown's view, would be steadily undermined as the years went by. He therefore began in the latter 1850's to call for representation by population on the ground that Ontario's population had grown far larger than Quebec's, and that the existing arrangement was monstrous. French Canada, on its side, grew more determined to hold rigidly to the formula of equal representation.[7]

By this time, George Brown had become the unquestioned leader of Ontario Liberalism. His commanding figure, his self-confidence and driving impatience, his explosive and exciting oratory, his incredible energy, and, of course, his great newspaper, which daily spread his words throughout the province—all of these made Brown tower over those around him in the party. Clear Grittism was no longer a

[5] Ibid., I, 113–23, 197–8.
[6] Ibid., I, 203–8.
[7] Ibid., I, 114, 116, 203–8, 235–7.

movement that looked yearningly southward to the American model. Brown had won his long struggle with the Americanists, so that "when the Brownite Reform party finally took shape, it would express the outlook of middle-of-the-road Victorian Liberalism far more than radical, agrarian democracy."[8]

Brownite Liberalism was extremely middle-class. The Browns had been comfortably middle-class in Edinburgh, and after overcoming the misfortunes that sent them to America, George Brown had become a very wealthy man in Canada. The *Globe* was a great success, and Brown could enjoy the pleasures of being a kind of "laird" over large landholdings in Ontario. He was intimately connected not only with Canadian business interests, but also with the world of large business enterprise in the United States. When the Reform Party met in convention in 1867, Brown exulted that the delegates all came from the cream of society: "Wardens, reeves, J.R.'s, coroners, merchants, manufacturers—the pick of the local politicians, business men and professionals." Toronto, the heart of the Orange Order, remained in Tory hands, but most of western Ontario, in its common farmers and its substantial men, was Brown's.[9]

No event displayed more dramatically Brown's position and point of view in the economic order than the struggle he carried on with his workingmen at his newspaper plant in the early 1870's. An impatient and often autocratic man, he refused to negotiate a reduction of hours with the union, had some of its leaders thrown in jail on conspiracy grounds, and led an unrelenting battle against the resulting strike, calling it "a very transparent attempt to introduce amongst us the Communistic system of levelling."[1] He could never understand the demands of the labor-union movement. The Liberals, he said, had provided free schools, the vote for the common man, and social and religious equality. What more could be asked? It had been Liberal policy, he said,

---

[8] Ibid., I, 208.
[9] Ibid., II, 247.
[1] Bernard Ostry, "Conservatives, Liberals, and Labour in the 1870's," *Canadian Historical Review*, XLI (1960), 98.

that the honest son of toil needs no favours, requires no patronage,—that all he wants is a fair field and no favour; and the whole struggles of reform have been in order to break up the iniquities of class legislation, which have ever pressed most heavily on the lowest, and to secure that there be none insulted by exemption from burdens and consequent deprivations of rights, but that all shall bear their full share of national obligations, and hold in the same way their rightful part in national deliberations and in the performance of national work.[2]

In short, what Brown had created was not only a deeply religious party, but one that was a business party as well. The two were not, after all, at war with each other. Brown was an Evangelical, as were most of those whom he led, and as William Gladstone had said, Evangelicalism harmonized well with the money-getting pursuits. Its individualism, its emphasis on hard work and self-denial, and its rather narrow sense of social concern made it well suited to the businessman. Brown went about Ontario in the 1850's campaigning for temperance and against Sabbath desecration just like the puritanical "ultras" in New York State, but he also called for railroads and the full development of the canal system.[3] Through the columns of the *Globe* he was the first to begin advocating the addition to Canada of the great West beyond the Lakes. He urged Ontario to find its destiny in the limitless resources of that vast territory—and a counterbalance, as well, to the power of French Canada.[4]

Canadian Liberalism was perhaps even more keyed to economic development than British Liberalism. The great problem in Canada has always been the building of a nation. This has been more difficult in Canada than in the United States—if one ignores the Civil War—and certainly than in Britain. It is in major ways not yet accomplished. Practically all political persuasions have therefore had this problem as their first item of business. This has meant that economic development has been at practically all times the

[2] Quoted in ibid., p. 116.
[3] Ibid., I, 150–60, 237.
[4] Ibid., I, 231–2.

most pressing consideration for both Liberals and Conservatives, since it has generally appeared that such development was the most promising means of nation-building. The emphasis grew more urgent from the 1880's onward, for Canada had by that time entered its long slump, and emigration to the United States seemed to be draining away the life of the nation. Brown foreshadowed, therefore, what was to grow extraordinarily prominent in the Liberalism of Sir Wilfrid Laurier, an obsession with policies that led to national development of resources.

The differences in economic policy between the Brownite Liberals and Macdonald's Conservatives were therefore the differences that arise between two competing theories on how best to develop the nation. This was, of course, not unusual, for such was the case between Liberals and Conservatives in Britain and Democrats and Republicans in the United States. The Conservative Party that John A. Macdonald built in Canada, as Frank Underhill has observed, was "a Hamiltonian federalist party." Macdonald believed in a strong central government that used its power to develop the economy by direct aids to businessmen.

> A strong central government was needed to carry through the drive for westward economic expansion, to win the confidence and attract the capital of the investing classes whose support was necessary for this expansionist policy. The great interests of finance and industry and transportation must be tied to the national government by putting the national government solidly behind their ambitions for power and profit. So the "National Policy" lays the basis for the development of a many-sided economic life [through protective tariffs and railroad building].[5]

Out of this interlocking complex of Canadian financiers, railwaymen, and manufacturers, there would emerge a unified Canada that could stand up against the United States. It would have its own self-contained economy, one "based predominantly upon the St. Lawrence and its tributary routes . . ."

[5] Underhill, *In Search of Canadian Liberalism*, pp. 33–4.

Such a system could be consolidated "against American penetration . . . making [of] it a closed preserve to be triumphantly exploited by Canadian business enterprise."[6]

Brown attacked this whole line of policy. He was first of all devoted to the economic world view of Adam Smith. Furthermore, the St. Lawrence system, as Macdonald apparently conceived it, would make Ontario an economic vassal to Montreal. Brown called for free navigation on the St. Lawrence, insisted that there should be no discrimination against the use of the Erie Canal, and criticized all Conservative machinations that appeared to make banks in Upper Canada subservient to the Bank of Montreal.[7] He always worked for freer trade with the United States, supported the reciprocity treaty while it lasted, and led the vain negotiations in the 1870's to get it revived.[8]

Most of all, however, Brownite Liberals, like the Democrats in the United States and the Liberals in Britain, consisted of those men who suspected the worst whenever the government took a leading role in economic matters by direct aids to business enterprise. The Grand Trunk railway project, an expensive enterprise designed to link Quebec and Ontario, symbolized all of their fears. Undertaken by a private company with lavish Conservative assistance, it seemed endlessly to be running out of money and appearing before the parliament for more subsidies. By the late 1850's Brown was attacking the whole arrangement as a venal system for keeping the Conservatives in power. They bought political support in French Canada with money grants, he said, parceled out railway-construction contracts to their friends, and carelessly burdened Canada with an ever growing load of public debt. He found much to criticize in the fact that George Etienne Cartier, the leader of the Conservative ministry in 1859 and of the French Canadian *Bleus*, was at one and the same time Premier of Canada and solicitor for the Grand Trunk railway. When Cartier also opposed the acquisition of the Hudson's

[6] Ibid., p. 34. Cf. also Donald Creighton, *John A. Macdonald: The Old Chieftain* (Boston, 1956), *passim*, esp. pp. 118–22, 208–12.
[7] Ibid., p. 66, and Careless, *Brown of the Globe*, I, 160.
[8] These views are displayed throughout Careless's biography of Brown, but see particularly I, 150, 160; II, 106, 324.

Bay Company lands in the west as a threat to Quebec, since it would add weight to the English-speaking side, Brown's bill of particulars was complete. He could condemn the ministry as a corrupt coalition of French Canadians and Ontario Tories that would use French Canada's overweighted vote in the parliament to prevent Canada's western expansion and enact high tariffs, ruinous Grand Trunk railway bills, separate school measures, and a regime of venality and extravagance.[9]

To complete the circle, George Brown, like Samuel Tilden, Grover Cleveland, and William Gladstone, supported sound money. When the Macdonald government in 1866, perhaps copying the inflationist proposals of many Radical Republicans in the United States, decided to make a large issue of paper money, Brown opposed the idea. Meddling with the money supply, he said, was against the laws of political economy. It could have no other effect than to lead to more extravagance and more economic disarray.[1]

Brown's primary interest, however, lay not in economic matters, but in devising some means to protect Ontario from what he saw as domination by French Canada. As the late 1850's went by, it became more clear to him that simply building an increasingly monolithic Clear Grit party in Ontario on the issue of representation by population would not achieve that reform. The existing constitution of the united

[9] Ibid., I, 293–4; II, 8–9. See also Creighton, *John A. Macdonald: The Young Politician*, pp. 250–3.
[1] Ibid., II, 228–9.
The persistence of inflation as a Conservative-Republican policy must be emphasized. Disraeli wanted inflation in the 1840's and 1850's, as indeed the anti-Peelites had proposed since the immediate post-Napoleonic period. The Radical Republicans favored it, and such silver-purchase legislation as was passed in the later decades was enacted by Republican regimes. Even Balfour in the 1890's was an international bimetallist in British politics. The big change came in the 1890's for two reasons: Bryan made the Democrats an inflationist party behind the free-silver cry, and the Republicans saw how disastrous this proposal was in the growing new cities in a time of depression; and the influx of precious metals from South Africa, Colorado, and the Yukon ended the argument. The fact that Macdonald's Conservatives wanted inflation provides the appropriate explanation: inflation was a policy not simply favored by farmers, but by the entrepreneurial elements in the economy. Economic nationalism (protective tariffs) and soft money went hand in hand.

Province of Canada, with its equality of representation for Quebec, could never be changed in a head-on encounter between the two halves of the province. Many Clear Grits, recognizing this, began to call for a simple dissolution of the union, but Brown's reply was that Ontario could never live by itself; it would inevitably be absorbed by the United States. The true policy, he urged in the party's Toronto convention in 1859, was Confederation. By this means, Quebec and Ontario would take care of their local affairs—which emphatically included the schools—in local legislatures, leaving to a general government the oversight of all else. In a brilliant victory, he swung his party behind him, and the journey to Confederation was underway.[2]

The next eight years of Brown's political career were primarily concerned with the achievement of Confederation. Macdonald at first resisted the idea, for he believed in having all power unified in one central government—the British example was doubtless persuasive to him—but in time he agreed to the project, provided that it be a confederation not simply of Quebec and Ontario, but one that would include the Maritimes as well. Implicit in this proposal was the need for another railroad, this time one connecting the Maritimes with Quebec and Ontario. The Clear Grits, and their sometime allies in Quebec, the *Rouges,* suspected corruption again and turned against Confederation as another scheme to enrich Tory contractors and buy votes to keep John A. Macdonald in power. So determined was Brown to achieve the larger objective, however, that in time he gave up his resistance to the Intercolonial railway, saying it was a cheap price to pay for Confederation. Besides, he got Macdonald to agree that the great region beyond the Great Lakes would be speedily added to the new federation, thus providing Ontario with her outlet westward and promising a new counterbalancing force in Canadian politics. Thereafter, Brown alternately led and assisted in the climatic events that after 1864 moved on to the British North America Act of 1867.[3] When

[2] Ibid., I, 320–2.
[3] Ibid., II, 120–1, 157–8, 162–4. The essential account to read is Donald Creighton, *The Road to Confederation: The Emergence of Canada:*

he succeeded in getting the first agreement as to the nature of the constitution hammered out, he wrote a revealing letter to his wife. Everything they had long complained of was now settled: "Is it not wonderful? French Canadianism entirely extinguished! . . . You will say our constitution is dreadfully Tory—and so it is—*but we have the power in our hands* (if it passes) *to change it as we like.* Hurrah!"[4]

Brown's career as an active politician was now coming to an end. He had got what he had wanted for Canada: local rule within the provinces and a dominion committed to acquiring the great west. After 1867, he withdrew from direct leadership of his party, preferring to concentrate on his private affairs and to play the role of *éminence grise* behind the Liberal leadership. He remained a major force in Canadian political life until 1880, when he died a lingering death from gunshot wounds inflicted by a disgruntled employee, but the leadership of the Liberal Party had to pass on to other hands.

Brown had laid the basis, however, for a reorientation of Canadian political life that inevitably worked itself out in the ensuing decades. His efforts to protect Ontario from the Catholic threat had made the Liberals in Ontario a wholly Protestant body fighting to protect its public schools and to prevent what it saw as economic vassalage. Both apparently emanated from the same Conservative–French Canadian coalition that was centered in Montreal and its environs. But with the achievement of local autonomy over schools within the provinces—the existing rights of Catholics to have parochial schools being protected—the influences driving apart the Liberals and the Catholics, both French and Irish, began to lose their force.

Thereafter, all the other influences that throughout the world of Anglo-American politics made the Liberal-Demo-

---

1863–1867 (Boston, 1965); as well as W. L. Morton, *The Critical Years: The Union of British North America, 1857–73* (London and New York, 1964).
[4] Ibid., II, 171. In calling it "dreadfully Tory," Brown was probably referring to the power it gave the central government to disallow provincial legislation that Macdonald had insisted upon, and to its remarkably aristocratic features (senators appointed for life and the like).

crats the Catholic party began to have their way in Canada
as well. Brown's anti-Catholicism had been primarily defensive. It carried little of the anti-Catholic bigotry, the hatred of
Catholicism and the desire to see it destroyed, that the
Orange Order—so prominent in the Tory Party—expressed.
The Tories were the party of the British, who flaunted the
Union Jack at every opportunity and spoke darkly of the
"disloyalty" of the *Québecois*. They identified completely
with Conservative England on the issue of Irish Home Rule,
and quickly drove the Irish Catholics into the Liberal voting
ranks in Canada. Macdonald, furthermore, disliked the idea
of provincial autonomy. A centralist constitution was his policy, just as it was for the Republicans in the United States
and the Tories in Britain. But the venerable Liberal policy of
provincial autonomy in Canada, so like the equally Liberal-
Democratic policies of "states' rights" in the United States
and Home Rule in Britain, grew increasingly vital to be-
leaguered Quebec. The Conservatives tried determinedly to
use the power of the federal government to disallow provincial legislation; the Liberals argued vigorously against it, and
allowed it to fall into disuse.

The Liberals, too, began to develop the idea of a
uniquely Canadian nationality, one separate from Great Britain and inclusive of Quebec in a multi-ethnic community.
This was the concept that provided the bridge between
French Canada and the rest of the Dominion. The Liberals,
furthermore, were the party that stood out for the ideal of
social equality, of no invidious distinctions based on faith or
ethnic origin. Their fundamental world view led them to the
image of a pluralistic and equalitarian Canada, at least in
their official ideology, founded upon provincial—and therefore cultural—autonomy. Since cultural questions were of all
questions the most vital to the *Québecois*, it was only logical
that in time they should take up their residence within the
Liberal Party.

Two influences barred the way for some time. One lay in
Montreal, among those French Canadians who agreed with
Macdonald in his great vision of a business-oriented Cana-
dian economy led by entrepreneurs with the eager backing of

the government. Macdonald's dream for Canada envisioned an economy centered on the St. Lawrence, and necessarily upon Montreal; one sealed off, as it were, from the United States. This was an appealing dream to many in the French Canadian banking and entrepreneurial community.

The other influence was the Catholic Church. Mid-century Roman Catholicism was engaged in a great offensive against liberalism wherever it could be found, and the Liberal Party in Canada was anathema to it. The Quebec hierarchy was firmly devoted to the Conservatives—who, after all, inherited the state-church tradition of the Conservatives in Britain—and hostile to the Liberals. Everything waited, therefore, for a French Canadian leader who could persuade the *Québecois* that Liberalism was not really against their faith, no matter what the bishops said. When that leader appeared in the form of the intelligent and appealing Sir Wilfrid Laurier, the events were set in motion that by the 1890's were to make Quebec a Liberal fief, the Solid South of Canadian politics.

——————

All of this lay in the future as George Brown withdrew from the leadership of the Liberal Party upon the achievement of Confederation in 1867. The man who came forward now to lead the Liberals was his close friend Alexander Mackenzie, who, six years after the Dominion was formed, became the first Liberal Premier of the Dominion of Canada (1873–8). To a notable degree, he was cut from the same cloth as Samuel Tilden in the United States. Not only were they the leading figures in their parties in the same years, they also came to power primarily as fighters against corruption, symbolizing in their persons the values of determined civic purity. Both were convinced that corruption was the greatest evil of the age, that it sprang fundamentally from unnatural ties between business and government, and that the first and almost the only task of the statesman was to stand at the doors of the treasury and scrutinize every expenditure with painful care so as to deny public funds to the greedy. Similar in their personalities, in their intense partisanship, and in their political point of view, Mackenzie and Tilden have shared as well a relatively dim historical image.

Mackenzie was the archetypical dour Scot. Born and reared on the edge of the Highlands in Perthshire, he carried such a Scottishness in his accent, appearance, and manner that "Sandy" was his inevitable political nickname. His family was poor, and Alexander became a stonemason to make his way. The only laboring man in either Great Britain or Canada to rise to the premiership, he was often to be reminded of, and was sensitive to, his origins. In the western Lowlands of Scotland as a young man in the early 1840's—the years in which the Evangelical excitement was reaching its peak—he became a Baptist of the Haldane school. The Church of Scotland was too cold for a man who had built his whole life on a close sense of harmony with God, who prayed regularly and read the Bible daily.[5]

Evangelicalism in whatever form was pre-eminently a revived form of zealous Calvinism. Though Mackenzie was a Baptist, he was clearly a Scottish, that is a Calvinist, Baptist. He was reared in the belief that, as he put it, "the heart of man is by nature totally depraved."[6] He was to give witness to this belief all his days. His whole pattern of life was that of the puritan, making him in every way typical of small-town Ontario, where the way of life, it has been said, was "chocolate-brown with Calvinism."[7] He was a convinced sabbatarian, rising in Parliament on one occasion to support the closing of public canals on Sunday. He was reported as saying that the observance of the Sabbath day

> was a duty incumbent on them as a Christian people, and that they as legislators ought to do their duty in promoting the observance of the Sabbath. No good ever came of Sabbath breaking . . . He believed that the observance of the

[5] Thomson, *Alexander Mackenzie*, p. 9.
[6] A. Mackenzie et al., *Reform Government in the Dominion: The Pic-Nic Speeches Delivered in the Province of Ontario During the Summer of 1877* (Toronto, 1878), p. 70.
[7] MacLennan, *The Precipice*, p. 11.

Sabbath was in the interests of all legitimate labor, and that public servants were entitled to rest on that day.[8]

He totally abstained from all drink, and in his first campaign for public office ran for mayor of Sarnia, Ontario, on the prohibitionist ticket—though in later years he relented to the point of serving liquor in his home, and refused to propose prohibition until all the people were for the reform. In a curious but revealing act, he refused entirely, when being married, to say the words "with this body I thee worship."[9] It was altogether typical of him to write home shortly after his arrival in Canada in 1842 that "The Sabbath appears to be pretty well kept here, but there is very little true religion among the great mass of the population."[1]

His whole political career was that of a censorious critic, the function perhaps most natural to his character. He was a rigid, harsh, and highly concentrated man blessed—or cursed —with enormous self-control. He had such a sharp tongue that legend had it that he said "yes" more woundingly than John A. Macdonald said "no." In debate his most effective weapon was a sense of humor that cut and embittered.

Interested intensely in everything that surrounded him, he was fixed in his views once his mind was made up. Throughout life his rigidity drove away potential friends and allies, but he comforted himself with the belief—as did his fellow Calvinist, Grover Cleveland—that he was only paying the price of standing inflexibly upon principles. "I have always had a horror," he wrote after his fall from office in 1878, "of the policy of carrying on a Government by compromises of views on great questions."[2]

He was not the kind of man who could easily forget or forgive. Far more partisan than almost anyone else among his associates, he bitterly distrusted the political enemy. He stood out alone against coalition with John A. Macdonald in 1864

[8] William Buckingham and G. W. Ross, *The Hon. Alexander Mackenzie: His Life and Times* (Toronto, 1892), p. 241.
[9] Thomson, *Alexander Mackenzie*, pp. 18, 22, 26; Mackenzie et al., *Reform Government in the Dominion*, pp. 117–18.
[1] Buckingham and Ross, *Mackenzie*, p. 93.
[2] Ibid., pp. 535–6.

when the object was the writing of the new constitution. Whenever he was forced to refer to fellow party members who had deviated from what to him were clear party obligations, he used such words as "treachery" and "conspiracy"— and he meant them. One of his most revealing documents, the biography he wrote of George Brown, which he prepared after Brown's death, is filled with these attitudes.[3]

From the beginning of his career, Mackenzie suspected the enemy of having evil in his soul. As Sir Wilfrid Laurier later said, Mackenzie "was certain that the Tories had inherited most of Adam's original sin, and he usually had the facts at his fingers' ends to prove it." He hammered at them constantly on the floor of the House, looking for the corruption he knew was there. "We never had a better debater in the House . . . [He] knew his facts, he knew his men, he had a firm grip on principle and an inexhaustible fund of indignation . . ."[4] His letters in the 1850's were filled with observations like "wickedness in high places . . . traitors . . . hypocrites . . . corruptionists."[5] Reformers could never relax their vigilance, he said in 1877, "so long as this world is peopled by sinners, and controlled as it is sometimes by sordid motives."[6]

Like Cleveland, he was convinced that in fighting corruption in government he was battling to save the soul of all of society. He lived in a speculative and swiftly changing world, a world in which a scramble after money without regard for principle seemed to threaten the fundamental wholeness and moral health of the people, and he clung with greater determination to moral principles as their one salvation.

> You may depend upon it that if you once relax the laws of
> public morality in high places, the contagion will spread
> like a plague all over the community, you will induce social
> and financial disorder, and an utter want of principle will be

[3] Alexander Mackenzie, *The Life and Speeches of Hon. George Brown* (Toronto, 1882). See also Thomson, *Alexander Mackenzie,* pp. 53, 55, 59, 65, 66, 80, 334, 357.
[4] Skelton, *Life and Letters of Sir Wilfrid Laurier,* I, 221.
[5] Thomson, *Alexander Mackenzie,* p. 42.
[6] Mackenzie *et al., Reform Government in the Dominion,* p. 118.

infused not only into our Federal and Provincial Governments, but into the very centre of our municipal and school systems, which will bear its fruit for many years to come, and prove disastrous to our boasted system of self-government. (Loud cheers.)[7]

The focus of his attacks on corruption in the years before his premiership was the succession of railroad projects that from the 1850's John A. Macdonald's governments began launching: the Grand Trunk, to connect Ontario and Quebec in the original Province of Canada; the Intercolonial, to tie together the new Dominion by linking Quebec and Ontario with the Maritimes; and finally the grandest and most fantastic project of all, for a little country consisting of perhaps four million people, the Canadian Pacific, stretching thousands of miles across an empty continent to make the final connection, with British Columbia on the Pacific coast. Each of these projects involved not only the laying of rails, but also the construction of thousands of bridges, gradings, signals, warehouses, and many other such costly items. At the same time, there were also the locks, canals, wharves, and warehouses that Canada was simultaneously building in order to develop its water-transportation routes. The possibilities for corruption were practically endless. To put the country together and to develop it at the same time was an enormous task. The real challenge was to do it honestly.

Railroads, in point of fact, were the politics of the Dominion, and above all of the Conservative Party. "The day the Canadian Pacific busts," said a Conservative railroad minister in a particularly critical time, "the Conservative party busts the day after."[8] But whether Liberals or Conservatives were in office, they were constantly wrangling and worrying and laboring over railroads. "Consult the annals of Canada for [the half century after 1860] . . . at random," it has been remarked, "and whatever party may be in power, what do you find? The government is building a railway, buying a railway, selling a railway, or blocking a railway."[9]

---

[7] Ibid., p. 106.
[8] Quoted in Underhill, *In Search of Canadian Liberalism*, p. 35.
[9] Skelton, *Life and Letters of Sir Wilfrid Laurier*, I, 244.

Mackenzie always believed that the Grand Trunk and other railway schemes were largely designed to put lucrative contracts in Tory pockets. For this reason, he expected to find all sorts of putrid machinations in Tory accounts, and year after year "examined every detail to bare the misdeeds and unworthy motives he was certain lay at the bottom of every move."[1] When the Canadian Pacific project was launched, he attacked it as simply the Grand Trunk and the Intercolonial grown continental. It was wild, he said, it was extravagant— as indeed it seems to have been—and it would deliver later settlers into the hands of unscrupulous speculators because of the huge land grants given to the railroad's builders.[2]

Then there took place one of the most spectacular events in Canadian history: stolen letters, publicly revealed, proved beyond a doubt that all that Mackenzie had suspected was true. Macdonald and the Conservatives had in effect sold the Canadian Pacific railroad contract to a largely American syndicate in return for several hundred thousand dollars in campaign funds. Macdonald had ignominiously to resign in 1873, apparently—but only apparently—forever disgraced, and Alexander Mackenzie, the stonemason who had become the symbol of civic virtue, was Premier.

His five years in office (1873–8) were difficult and unhappy. He was not, for one thing, an exciting man. His political style was decidedly small beer after George Brown and Sir John A. Macdonald. He was also afflicted with the internal consequences of a repressive life style. Mackenzie's taciturn, stolid, and immobile countenance covered up a great deal of inner turmoil. He had constant stomach difficulties. He was a sensitive man, and the premiership was a burden for him. The calm assurance he displayed when he put together his government in 1873 was tragically given away in a letter he later wrote: "I was sick, sick, before it was done; really ill in fact."[3]

Like George Brown, Mackenzie sprang directly from Scottish Liberalism, and in his premiership he drew on this

---

[1] Thomson, *Alexander Mackenzie,* pp. 69–70, 76–7, 116.
[2] Thomson, *Alexander Mackenzie,* pp. 124–5.
[3] Thomson, *Alexander Mackenzie,* p. 172.

tradition. As a young man in western Scotland he had actively participated in Chartist gatherings, though he thought of himself as a Christian Chartist and was repelled by the more radical elements in the movement.[4] He was a thoroughly convinced free-trader. "I am old enough to remember the time," he said in 1877, "when the great anti-corn-law agitation was carried on in England. I have heard George Thompson and his compeers, Cobden and his friends, at meetings, denouncing these corn laws . . . and I remember that the farmers were almost rioting in some districts, believing it would be ruinous to them if the duty were abolished. The fact is that they became very much more prosperous since than they had been before."[5] "I believe myself," he said in Scotland in 1875, "that the principles of Richard Cobden, and the principles of free trade over the world, are the real principles of civilization . . ."[6]

He never wavered from these beliefs. He was convinced, as he said in 1867, that protectionism was not only "absurd" but also "necessarily evil."[7] Again and again, throughout his career, he returned to the attack. Tariffs produced monopolies, he insisted, which exploited the people. The only men who really benefited from tariffs—and they only apparently —were greedy manufacturers who fattened off the labors of everyone else. Tariffs only "make the rich man richer and the poor man poorer . . ."[8] He was fond of pointing to the United States under the Republicans as a repellent example of the exploitation and falseness of protection. Would the depression of the 1870's lift if Canada adopted higher tariffs, as the Conservatives insisted? Look at the United States. Examine the wages of labor, he said, how workingmen in America were reduced to beggary under protection. When farmers appealed for tariffs to raise their grain prices, he scoffed that all such prices were set in the English markets, and that they

[4] Ibid., p. 7.
[5] Mackenzie et al., *Reform Government in the Dominion*, p. 75.
[6] Alexander Mackenzie, *Speeches of the Hon. Alexander Mackenzie During His Visit to Scotland with His Principal Speeches in Canada since the Session of 1875* (Toronto, 1876), pp. 33–4.
[7] Thomson, *Alexander Mackenzie*, p. 94.
[8] Mackenzie et al., *Reform Government in the Dominion*, pp. 42–3.

were unavoidably depressed by the worldwide glut of grain.

Governments, he claimed, could never create wealth; they could only ensure it was equitably distributed. The only sound national policy, he said—echoing Peel—was to make Canada as cheap a country to live in as possible. An enlightened government must find markets abroad for Canada, for Canada was primarily a producer of commodities. Tariffs would only build up the fortunes "of a few manufacturers, and in the course of a few years, [ruin] . . . even those manufacturers, after they have accomplished the ruin of the working classes." At bottom, he insisted, protectionism was simply a return to class legislation and class distinctions.[9]

This last note—Mackenzie's concern with class distinctions—touches one of the fundamental concerns in his mind and career. Everything in his life and surroundings made this issue keenly sensitive to him. He was a poor Highlander, and a man with little formal education. If this were not enough, he was an Evangelical, and more than that, a Baptist, a sect even more detested than Evangelicalism by the orthodox. It was the fate of this sensitive man to be reared in a class-conscious world dominated by established aristocracies. In consequence, he was always both proud and on the defensive.

The first thing he had reacted against in Canada after his arrival in the 1840's was the privileged position of the Anglican Church and of the Church of Scotland. His earliest enemies were the social groups represented in the Tory-Anglican Family Compact. He was a passionate "voluntaryist" in the campaign against Clergy Reserves and for secular schools. The first things he began speaking of when he undertook to save his government in the "Pic-Nic" speeches of 1877 were the battles the Liberals had always fought for religious equality. The *Life* that he wrote of George Brown in 1882 is filled with a burning sense of grievance at the religious privileges that Reformers had struggled against in the 1840's and 1850's.

---

[9] Cf. Buckingham and Ross, *Mackenzie*, pp. 52–5; Mackenzie *et al.*, *Reform Government in the Dominion*, pp. 35, 42–3; Thomson, *Alexander Mackenzie*, pp. 249, 251, 260, 287, 340, 342, 358.

What have Tories always done in Ontario, he cried out in an 1867 debate, but work for inequality?

> The policy of the Tories or the Conservatives had been what their name indicated,—to conserve and preserve all old abuses,—a policy of restriction and ecclesiastical despotism, which they would have fastened on us, if they had had the power. The policy of Reformers, on the other hand, had been to secure that every man should stand upon perfectly equal terms in the eye of the law; that no church or other institution should receive special privileges from the State.
>
> The Conservative policy was here what it was in England, a restrictive one—one that cramped the energies of the people. It was the same policy as that which resisted the repeal of the penal laws against Roman Catholicism in Great Britain; which enacted corn laws to tax the bread of the people; the policy which would build up and perpetuate a State Establishment. This policy had been imported here and we had had the most deliberate, persistent, and systematic attempts made to engraft on our system the abuses against which the Liberals of Great Britain had fought for centuries.[1]

When he triumphantly returned to Scotland in 1875 as the Premier of Canada, he talked constantly in his many speeches of Canada's great achievements in establishing social and religious equality. "We have, as you are aware," he said in Dundee, "no difficulties to contend with such as divide many interests in this country. We have no Established Church. (Applause.) . . . We have . . . no kind of class legislation—no sundering differences." Ontario had not only a system of free public schools, open to every child, they also had the University of Toronto, "a great national establishment, amply endowed and free to every person of every creed or class or circumstance in life."[2] Canada was a place, he went on, where every man stood equal in the sight of the law, and where everyone had the same opportunity to rise by

[1] Buckingham and Ross, *Mackenzie*, pp. 222–3.
[2] Mackenzie, *Speeches in Scotland*, p. 23.

his talents as anyone else. Everything had to be got by hard labor, he said, and that was a good thing. It was the "fault of the individual and not of the political system" if a man failed to gain reasonable success and comfort. Self-cultivation and hard labor would win the prize for anyone who struggled for it in Canada. "The days of monopolies are ended; the days of class legislation, when one class was set over another, are ended . . ."[3]

He was not, however, an apostle of American equality pure and simple. Like Brown, he was loyal to Britain. It was characteristic of him that in the same speech quoted above he went on to deride the supposed equality boasted of in the United States. There was in America, "I venture to say, more class distinctions created by wealth than you will find in this country by titular distinctions connected with the landed property of the country. (Applause.)"[4] The British system of responsible government, he said elsewhere, "is more democratical, more like true liberty, than the boasted Republicanism of the United States."[5] Canadians therefore shared with Great Britain, he believed, the grand mission of vindicating the British system of government and spreading its blessings to all the world.

Sometimes this was a mission which he saw the British and the Canadians carrying forward jointly with the Americans, all being branches of the Anglo-Saxon race. They were a chosen people, he said in 1859 in a carefully prepared address on Anglo-Saxonism, sharing the great mission of spreading Christian civilization through their unique powers of self-governance, and their industrial prowess. The steam engine and the Bible, he said in a truly Victorian utterance, went hand in hand.[6] In Scotland many years later he returned to the same theme. What they had before them, he insisted, was a great work of "evangelization—speaking both in a Christian and commercial sense—for, sir, it is the mission of the Anglo-

[3] Ibid., pp. 35, 44.
[4] Ibid., p. 44.
[5] Mackenzie *et al.*, *Reform Government in the Dominion*, pp. 118–19.
[6] Thomson, *Alexander Mackenzie*, p. 54.

Saxon race to carry the power of Anglo-Saxon civilization over every country in the world."[7]

It was clear, however, that he thought of this mission as primarily a British one. Britain, he said in 1869, had the three great requisites of national greatness—unity, intelligence, and virtue—and this was why Britain was one of God's vehicles for carrying on civilization.[8]

> I am anxious as it is possible for any British subject to be [he said in Scotland] that [the glory of the British Empire] should be unsullied, that that power should never be abridged, and that English supremacy shall last till the end of time, because it means universal freedom, universal liberty, emancipation from everything degrading.[9]

In a curious way, Mackenzie seemed to have a particular relish for the physical symbols of power. Perhaps this came from his truculent and combative personality. In any event, for a Liberal he was remarkably military. He seemed to enjoy the feeling of being part of a great empire armed and militant. "I do not think there is anything so satisfactory," he once said, "as to have powerful possessions in all the important quarters of the globe . . ."[1] He was always interested in Canadian defense policy. As a young parliamentarian he made a particular point of criticizing the government's military arrangements, and he quickly turned out to serve as an officer during the excitement over the Fenian raids. He was proud of having founded Canada's military college; he hired a British officer to reorganize the forces; and in the 1878 Fenian crisis he supervised the mobilization with infinite care. Though Premier, he was actually also the Minister of Militia.[2]

When the rebellion led by Louis Riel broke out in Manitoba in 1870, Mackenzie's instinctive militantism erupted

---

[7] Ibid., p. 241.
[8] Thomson, *Alexander Mackenzie*, p. 113.
[9] Mackenzie, *Speeches in Scotland*, p. 60.
[1] Ibid., pp. 72–3.
[2] Thomson, *Alexander Mackenzie*, pp. 109, 331.

startlingly. The spectacle of rebellion against "law and order" seemed to enrage him. He attacked the Macdonald government for hesitancy, called upon the manliness of the House to rise up in wrath, and in a heated outburst insisted that the fundamental task for any society, the very first thing before it, was "to enforce its authority." After that, if necessary, grievances could be duly cared for. "He had but one view of the matter," he was reported as saying, "either restore order there peremptorily, or, cease to be a nation . . . They should send five, ten, twenty thousand men if necessary, but order should be restored."[3]

It was the height of irony, therefore, that Mackenzie had to suffer, like all Canadian Liberals, the continued Conservative accusation of disloyalty. On almost every issue—especially in economic matters, where Liberals called for reciprocity with the United States—Mackenzie had to refute what he once called the "very, very stale" charge that he was disloyal to the British connection and to British institutions.[4]

Like George Brown, however, his trips to Britain tended to make him more Canadian and less British. Both were typically Liberal in this reaction. Brown found the life of the British aristocracy boring when he was wined and dined in London in 1865. They "are a different race from us," he wrote home, "different ideas, different aspirations, and however well it may be to see what the thing is like—it takes no hold of your feelings, or even of your respect."[5] Alexander Mackenzie felt during his visit in Britain in 1875 that "class differences in Britain were so great that a conflict of classes was inevitably coming."[6] Like Brown before him, he reacted in bitterness at the sublime ignorance of the English concerning Canada. And like many provincials before him, from Thomas

[3] Buckingham and Ross, *Mackenzie*, pp. 262–3. It is impossible not to think of Cleveland in this connection, and his reaction to the labor strikes in Chicago. His dispensing of troops was apparently based on the same determination to restore not only order but also obedience to "proper" authority. Mackenzie and Cleveland, Calvinists both, would seem to have been similarly sensitive to questions of authority and law and order.
[4] Mackenzie *et al.*, *Reform Government in the Dominion*, p. 37. See also Thomson, *Alexander Mackenzie*, pp. 101, 116, 138.
[5] Careless, *Brown of the Globe*, II, 197.
[6] Thomson, *Alexander Mackenzie*, p. 240.

Jefferson and Adam Smith onward, he was offended by their condescending ways. In a classic Liberal-Democratic utterance, he later observed that it "has been the policy of English statesmen . . . from the first to consider colonists as inferior to themselves."[7] Wherever he went in Scotland in 1875, the dignitaries introducing him seemed to find it necessary to refer to his working-class origins, which made George Brown—an equally sensitive Scotsman and Canadian—fume at these "patronising references" as "the height of rudeness."[8]

Mackenzie returned to Canada in 1875, therefore, vowing to develop further what he called Canada's character of "manly independence."[9] He was thereafter more determined than ever to curb the flamboyant behavior of Lord Dufferin, the last Governor General who tried in any significant way to manipulate Canadian governments and affairs. He delighted in ruffling the feathers of London by sending emissaries directly to Washington without asking Colonial Office permission. Never again, he told his neighbors in Sarnia, would any British statesman think of interfering in treaty negotiations where the interests of Canada alone were concerned. Canada was no longer a colony, he said; it had "assumed the proportions of a nation."[1]

———

In their five years in office under Alexander Mackenzie (1873–8), the Liberals passed a number of enactments on the subject that was traditionally their special concern: making the political system purer and more democratic. They put all voting on the same day, ending the former arrangement that allowed the ministry to stretch out the balloting and to shift their forces strategically from place to place. The trial of controverted elections was taken away from politically appointed commissions and placed in the hands of the courts.

[7] Buckingham and Ross, *Mackenzie*, pp. 373–4.
[8] Ibid., pp. 416–17.
[9] Thomson, *Alexander Mackenzie*, p. 244.
[1] Ibid., p. 249.

Public balloting was replaced by the secret ballot, the franchise was extended, property qualifications for members of parliament were abolished, and strong measures against bribery and corruption were enacted.

Any hopes Alexander Mackenzie may have had for reducing the tariff were blasted, however, by the fact that a severe depression in Britain and America began almost as soon as he took office, and did not lift until after he had left the Premier's seat. Mackenzie shares with Martin Van Buren, Grover Cleveland, and Herbert Hoover the melancholy distinction of having been a chief executive during a disastrous depression. Execration in their time and a bad historical press thereafter have been their common lot, since they were not suited to the challenge.

Mackenzie did make an effort to break out of the economic dilemma. He could not lower tariffs because he needed them for revenue, but he could and did send George Brown off on another mission—a fruitless one in the Washington of Ulysses Grant—to get a reciprocity treaty with the United States. He could console himself, however, with the view that the Conservatives had caused the depression. He and Samuel Tilden had the same explanation of the prosperity that had existed before the collapse of 1873: it was caused by spending policies on the part of the government. As Tilden attacked the Republicans for their heavy spending on internal improvements, Mackenzie criticized the Conservatives under John A. Macdonald for having sent enormous sums circulating through the country in their railroad projects. This had created, he said, a "temporary and fictitious prosperity" that led inevitably to collapse.[2] The answer, as he saw it, lay in a course of rigorous government economy. As he told a supporter when the election of 1878 approached, "Remember,

---

[2] Mackenzie et al., Reform Government in the Dominion, p. 73. This has been a uniform Liberal-Democratic economic assessment. Speculative spending influences within the economy have been condemned by men of this persuasion since Jefferson pointed to them in the late 1790's as the cause for hard times, and Gladstone and the Jacksonians blamed them in the 1830's and 1840's. Gladstone in Midlothian, in 1879–80, played a variation on this theme: the hard times of the 1870's came from the speculative foreign policy of Disraeli, which had unsettled confidence.

economy is our role for the general election." They must discharge as many civil servants as possible![3]

He spent his premiership, however, not battling depression so much as corruption. At great cost to his popularity among Liberal Party regulars, he worked for the establishment of a nonpartisan civil service. He refused to fire those already holding non-policymaking posts in the government. This involved him in an almost constant struggle with importunate Liberals, who cared little for his reiterated cry, "honesty and efficiency," when they had a specific patronage matter in hand.[4]

He also took the Ministry of Public Works as well as the premiership, spending most of his five years in office grinding away hour by hour on the enormous volume of estimates, surveys, bids, and construction projects created by the government's simultaneous programs of railroad, canal, wagon-road, and telegraph-line construction. Public Works was by far the busiest office in the entire government. It carried out what was the major function actively placed in the hands of the Canadian government. It spent most of the national budget, for it was involved in the task most critical to the existence of the Canadian nation, the building of the transportation system. In this office more than any other—as historians and his contemporaries do not seem to have understood—Mackenzie could meet what was to him the severest challenge that Canada faced, the cleansing of its befouled reputation. Here he could do what he wanted more than anything else to do in government, to "resist the terrible pressure of friends and enemies alike for favours . . ."[5] Self-denial and moral cleanliness were the heart of his Calvinist faith. How else could he respond to the Canada of the 1870's, a Canada to his eyes, darkened by the sins of the Conservatives?

Both he and George Brown, like the Henry Georges of the United States in the same years, saw corruption—as embodied most dramatically in the Canadian Pacific scandal—as

[3] Thomson, *Alexander Mackenzie,* p. 304.
[4] Ibid., pp. 174, 232–3.
[5] Ibid., p. 171.

nothing less than a testing of their nation before the eyes of
the world. They regarded the Canadian Pacific bribery as a
personal shame that degraded the whole nation. When Macdonald resigned in disgrace in 1873, the *Globe* rejoiced that
"the hand of the defiler is removed from the Ark of the Covenant."[6] Mackenzie put it in the following words in 1877:

> When we assumed office we did so when a black cloud was
> hanging over the country, one which obscured the fair fame
> of Canada in sight of every civilized nation, and was
> watched alike by the people of England and the United
> States as belonging peculiarly to the people of Canada. It
> rested with the new Administration to dispel that cloud, and
> induce the people of the United States and Europe to be-
> lieve that all the public men of Canada were not tainted
> with the same sordid and corrupt motives which led to the
> commission of *that great crime.*[7]

The Public Works Ministry was not taken on by Mackenzie, therefore—as tradition would have it—simply because he was a narrow stonemason who knew only how to
deal with construction projects. It was assumed because here,
to Mackenzie, was where the government's real destiny had
to be faced. His was an admittedly narrow vision of public
service, and one that made younger and some older Liberals
impatient, but it was an austere and powerful vision all the
same, which may have had a great deal more relevance to the
real needs of democratic governments, at a time when they
were still a new and precarious experiment in the world, than
has been generally recognized.

That nothing else meant so much to him is eloquently
revealed in the "Pic-Nic speeches" that he gave in 1877. They
were undertaken in a desperate effort at rebuilding public
confidence in preparation for the election of 1878. The man
could not bring himself to spend his time, as he should have,
on the whole range of issues before the nation. By 1877 the
Conservatives had filled the air with charges that he, too, was
corrupt, and he could not get these charges off his mind. To

[6] Careless, *Brown of the Globe*, II, 310.
[7] Mackenzie *et al.*, *Reform Government in the Dominion*, p. 5.

an evangelical Baptist, and a sensitive man into the bargain, they must have been a torment. Obsessively, agonizingly, he answered in infinite detail every charge. Over and over again his audiences heard how he had established a system where contracts went to the lowest bidder, how he had worked out a special arrangement with his civil servants so that he never even saw the names of the bidders whose documents came before him. He would desperately say that there were all sorts of positive policy matters he could speak about, such as how best to people the new lands west of the Great Lakes, but he had to spend his time answering charges—and he would trail off on yet another long explanation of how it came about that the government had purchased a vast quantity of steel rails, just before the market price had slumped further.[8]

His ministry, so victoriously begun, was spent in drudgery, and it ended in a defeat so thorough that two years later he gave up the leadership of the party. He passed it on to Edward Blake, the leader of those Liberals who had found Mackenzie's leadership plodding and bereft of large vision— as indeed it was. In the losing campaign of 1878, however, he had written a not wholly discreditable epitaph for his leadership when he said that he was proudest of all that he had established a mode of government that no successor could completely destroy. He had created a style of government that was characterized by honesty, efficiency, and integrity. These, he said, were the watchwords.[9] What else, he doubtless asked himself, could Canada ask?

[8] Mackenzie *et al.*, *Reform Government in the Dominion*, *passim*.
[9] Thomson, *Alexander Mackenzie*, p. 332.

PART III

PART III

Chapter 10

IN RETROSPECT

This book has been concerned with two things: rediscovering the Liberal-Democratic argument, in the sense of its characteristic outlook on the nation and the world; and searching out the social and cultural forces that formed the Liberal-Democratic ranks, providing not only voting strength but also many of Liberal-Democracy's basic assumptions and ways of thinking. It remains now to undertake a summary view.

The Liberals and the Democrats had their origins in controversies that began in eighteenth-century Britain and spread outward to the larger Anglo-American world, carried across the Atlantic in the form of religious attitudes, ethnic identities, and an economic revolution that transformed in common the Anglo-American community. The politics produced by this situation contained one arresting feature: the existence of a constellation of outgroups of various kinds banding together in common self-defense behind the Liberal and Democratic banners. The Liberal-Democratic mind, produced in good part by these influences, was the expression in politics of those who conceived of themselves as being outside the real centers of power and prestige in society. Their grievances being not only economic and political but also emotional, they looked to politics perhaps more for emotional gratification than for concrete enactments to improve their situation. When their friends won an electoral victory, they shared in the triumph. If they had to suffer indignities in their private lives, in their public capacity they had experienced the sweet delights of being on top. Politics, for them, was a drama in which each man played a part, in which the gestures and utterances of great men carried heavy symbolic freight, in which years of degradation might be, if only for a few hours or days, assuaged in the leaping sense of victory that came when the chosen leader came out on top.

The argument between the Liberal-Democrats and their adversary had its eighteenth-century beginnings in the predominating power of England within the British Isles and the empire—and within that England, in the position of a landed aristocracy that was predominantly Southern English, Anglican, and aligned with a business community that received special privileges in return for the building of a great empire. The Scotsman Adam Smith, the Irishman Edmund Burke, and the colonial Thomas Jefferson all expressed in their separate careers the protests of the outsiders against English pretensions of superiority, Anglican pretensions of supremacy, and the business and landed community's credo that the nation would benefit if they were given special privileges by the government.

In varying forms, this was the argument that went on in nineteenth-century Anglo-American politics. Especially striking in the argument was the intimate intermixture of politics and religion. The political ideas of Gladstone and Cleveland —to speak of no others—clearly derived as much from their religious outlooks as from Adam Smith or any other of the intellectual sources commonly regarded as the wellsprings of Liberal and Democratic thought. Religious grievances were often the principal considerations that moved men into the Liberal-Democratic camp. Freethinkers, men of the secular outlook characterized by Jefferson and Samuel Tilden, found Liberal-Democracy their political refuge from the attacks of the aggressively religious. There were also many thousands of devout men, Protestants but not members of the Church of England, who resented Anglican privileges and superiority, and the links between the Church and the state. In different shapes, this situation in England repeated itself in Scotland, in Canada, and in the United States, where other men were angry at the Auld Kirk, or at activist puritans who wanted to use the state in the old way to achieve temperance or Sunday laws or control of education. What Liberal-Democrats wanted was the secular state, where no one had religious privilege and no sect need feel shame; where in politics and in the schools, everyone would stand on an equal basis, paying no penalty for their faith—or their lack of it.

The economic drives behind Liberal-Democracy may be found in the grievances of the man of small property in both Britain and the United States—the shopkeeper, the craftsman, the petty manufacturer—who was alone and anxious in a wildly fluctuating economy over which he had no control; who was conscious that others possessed special privileges that protected and enriched them. He feared speculative booms and busts, and he resented protective tariffs, banking systems controlled by wealthy insiders, and complex arrays of legal devices in aid of the landed. He alternately grumbled and loudly berated the comfortable and privileged aristocracy, whether it was the landed in Britain, or the rich businessman in America. A small man in a world where men like himself were demeaned by the hauteur and the condescending ways of big men, he found in his political party the one means open to him of smiting the established, the privileged, the complacent, and the powerful.

Other voters were also attracted to Liberal-Democracy for economic reasons. There were the urban consumers, who wanted the lower prices and the stability that seemed promised by sound money and low tariffs. There were also those businessmen whose enterprises were built on international trade or on established industries with solid markets. Railroads, shipping lines, various kinds of raw-material producers, banks engaged in foreign trading, business houses linked to transatlantic commerce, textile producers—these and many other elements in the business world found low tariffs and sound money to their advantage. Businessmen split widely, oftentimes in equal portions, in their loyalties. Contrary to some timeworn orthodoxies about the American past, the Democratic businessman was no more an anomaly than his counterpart, the Republican businessman. The key factor, when economic considerations affected a man's vote, was not the businessman's class membership, but the specific position of his enterprise in the economy.

The workers were similarly divided. Men who labored in industries that concentrated on the domestic market and feared foreign competition—in steel production, for example —tended to vote for the party that promised tariffs. Those in England whose ways of life were connected with the land voted predominantly Tory, through similar fears of foreign competition in foodstuffs. In industries that used steel, however, and wanted to be able to get it from the cheapest supplier, whether domestic or foreign—in railroad construction, for example—the economic interest of the worker could lead him to Liberal-Democracy. In the shipyards, in transport, in the ranks of the merchant marine, in textiles, there was a whole world that wanted no barriers to international trade.

Political divisions in the age of Gladstone emanated not only from religious and economic differences, but also from the animosities and the almost visceral distastes induced by social prejudice. Liberal-Democracy drew much of its strength from those who faced contempt because of their ethnic identity. The Scots and the Welsh voted Liberal in British politics in good part for this reason, since the Tories were so intimately identified with England. Similar tendencies displayed themselves among the North Countrymen in England itself, for they traditionally felt looked down upon as crude provincials by Southern England. In the United States, white Southerners—in so many ways a separate ethnic group in American life—the Irish Catholics and many other non-British groups such as the Dutch farmers in the Hudson Valley, the Catholic Germans, the French, and the eastern and southern European immigrants were similarly driven to the Democrats. In Canada, when religious differences were not the chief influence, the bitterness between ethnic groups ranged men on one side or another of the political fence. In Ontario, at least in the early period, even the Scots were split among themselves, Highlanders going one way and Lowlanders another—to the Liberals.

The Catholic Irish played the same role in the British

mind as the Negro in the American, polarizing attitudes and political alignments in both the United Kingdom and in the United States. Not only did anti-Irish prejudice produce almost interminable crises in British politics, it powerfully influenced American politics as well, for British immigrants flocked to the Republicans when they found the Irish Catholics ranged solidly within the Democratic Party. On both sides of the Atlantic, such friends as the Irish Catholics had were to be found among the Liberals and the Democrats.

Liberal-Democracy was not simply an aggregation of voting blocs. Looked at in another dimension, it was also a set of ideas about the nation and the world, fashioned not by the rank and file but by intellectuals, and carried out by that small body of men, the leaders of the parties. In other words, Liberal-Democracy was an alliance between the intellectuals and their relatively sophisticated ideologies and values, on the one hand, and the outgroups and their large and relatively uncomplicated grievances on the other. This is not necessarily a congenial alliance. Outgroups are not normally devoted to broad reforms beyond their own limited goals. Intellectuals have always found the minority-group character of the Democratic Party to be an advantage in ensuring loyal votes and a disadvantage in limiting commitment to libertarian values. The minority groups were Liberals or Democrats because they smarted from prejudice, but they were often prejudiced against one another. Scots detested the Irish and began turning away from Gladstone when he championed Irish Home Rule. The Irish Catholics voted *en masse* for the Democrats, but they battled Cleveland doggedly on civil-service reform, and when Gladstone the libertarian argued for the admission of atheists to Parliament, the Irish Catholics deserted him. The minority groups in the Northern states seemed markedly hostile to the Negro, which intensified the anti-abolition sentiments of the Democratic Party and made many Englishmen regard the Republicans as the Liberals of the United States. The Solid South, in its tacit alliance with Republicans in matters of social reform, has long been a trial to Northern ideologues within the Democratic Party.

Minority groups, furthermore, vote so solidly for one

party that their representatives, unchallenged by opposition, tend to grow old—and conservative—in office. When the Democrats are in power in Congress, the seniority rule usually places most committee chairmanships in Southern hands, for Southerners tend to have the longest uninterrupted Congressional careers. The consequences have rarely been happy for social and libertarian legislation.

Liberal-Democracy, therefore, may be perceived in two aspects. It was a voting bloc, and it was an ideology, the one not necessarily compatible with the other. How to bridge the gap? How to find an ideological tent large enough to encompass all of Liberal-Democracy, its followers as well as its leaders?

It is a central thesis of this book that the most inclusive as well as the most revealing aspect of a political tradition is to be found in its image of the enemy. Here leaders and followers seem to find the widest agreement. From this standpoint, political movements widely separated in time may be found actually to possess a kind of cousinship. It is a shared vision of the enemy that reveals the common nature of the Jacksonian Democrats and Franklin Roosevelt's Second New Deal; that makes it clear that the British and Canadian Liberals and the American Democrats were segments of a common political stratum. It is this consideration, in sum, that allows us to see with the fullest clarity the whole of the Liberal-Democratic persuasion.

How did the Liberals and the Democrats see their enemy? If we look in their speeches and writings, we will find abundant materials for the portrait. Tories and Republicans, as Liberal-Democrats described them, were men whom power and wealth had made corrupt and arrogant. Stuffed with pride, they attempted to impose their allegedly superior ways on others. The Irish must be Anglicized; native peoples must be subjected to their control; the economy must be directed, through the United States Bank or through monopolies, as they saw fit; power and place, as of right, should always go to them. Possessed of the habit of authority, they reached instinctively for the tools of coercion to enforce their will, whether in considerations of private morality or in rule over the American colonies. Special privilege—whether economic, religious, or social—was their distinguishing mark and their pride, for they regarded themselves as superior in virtue and capacity and therefore entitled to these marks of preference. It was right that they should be allowed to monopolize, to take up vast tracts of land, to keep Oxford an institution only for Anglicans. If not themselves actually wealthy or powerful, they toadied to those who were, in the fashion of the Anglicized Scot or the Anglophile Canadian who waved the Union Jack, attended the local equivalent of the Anglican Church, adopted an English accent, sent his children to private schools on the English pattern, and admired titles and badges of social rank.

Tories and Republicans—as Liberal-Democrats pictured them—regarded the nation as identified with and limited to themselves. They were convinced that only they were truly loyal, for how could a Scot be loyal to an English Britain, a French Catholic to a British Canada, an Irish Catholic to an Anglo-Saxon Protestant United States? How could a critic of the business and landed world be loyal to the most vital element in patriotism, the inviolability of property and prescriptive right? Distrust of everything "alien" was their hallmark, nationalism in economics and in foreign policy was their creed. They clung to the idea of the homogeneous nation, for they detested the idea of a pluralistic Britain, a multiethnic Canada, a polyglot United States. The Liberal-Democrat, in their eyes, was always essentially unpatriotic and disloyal. The Gladstones and the Clevelands favored wiping out tariffs and opening domestic markets to the foreigner, condemned imperialism, denied that power should be freely used to protect the nation's "interests," and vetoed immigration-restriction bills that would have kept out unsavory aliens. Similarly, the Mackenzies and the Browns criticized the Established Church, required the Crown's own representative to bow to the will of the local inhabitants, and grew more Canadian and less British as the years went by. What more was needed to establish the disloyalty of Liberal-Democracy?

In religious matters, Tories and Republicans actively cultivated the idea of the superiority of some religions over others, tried as long as possible to retain laws that discriminated against dissenters, and harassed others within their religious communions in attempts to enforce conformity. In Britain, they tried to keep non-Anglicans out of the circles of power; in the United States, the same exclusions were exercised against non-Protestants. When faced with the choice, Tories in the Church—as Gladstone saw them—were men who preferred to hold to the privileges and profits of the state connection and let the faith go. In the United States, where there was no established church, Whig-Republicans still showed the state-church mentality in their desire for government regulation of personal morals.

In politics, Tories and Republicans were men who were contemptuous of the common folk and sought constantly to hold back the direct impact of the people on the government. In contrast, Gladstone insisted that great public issues were matters to place before the public at large for their verdict, not secret mysteries confided only to the hands of a governing aristocracy. The roaring crowds of Midlothian symbolized the near-Jeffersonian faith that Gladstone came to have in the masses. They also confirmed the aristocracy in their belief that Gladstone had become a demagogue.

It is interesting to note that Liberal-Democracy did in fact appear to embody a distinctly separate governing style, that of the strong executive. The tendency among the Whigs and Republicans in the United States, and the Whigs and Tories in Britain, was to prefer rule by oligarchy, by a collection of notables, rather than by a popular tribune in the executive chair. They were never comfortable with a Peel or a Gladstone, with a Jackson or a Cleveland. When Republicans were in power, Congressional cabals ran the nation, and cabinet members directed the affairs of their departments with little presidential interference. When the Democrats came in with Cleveland, power seemed to travel the length of Pennsylvania Avenue, as Woodrow Wilson observed, and take up its domicile in the White House.

Tories and Republicans, as Liberal-Democrats saw the matter, ruled not simply through aristocratic elites, but through a skillful use of corruption. From Jefferson's day to Cleveland's, few issues so obsessed the Liberal-Democratic mind as this one. In the eighteenth century, Jefferson's generation regarded corruption as the major weapon being wielded by the Tories in an attempt to destroy the relatively recent liberal constitution that had come down to Britons and colonists alike from the Revolution of 1688. Burke made a campaign for "economical reform"—by which he meant eliminating sinecures and corrupt patronage—one of the central themes of his career. In nineteenth-century Canadian and American politics, Liberal-Democrats were convinced that corruption was the principal danger that faced democracy and responsible government. Mackenzie and Cleveland both believed that it was the enemy's chief means for deforming the government and debasing the morals of the people at large. Relying on discreet uses of corruption behind the scenes, they bent the government to their wishes, extracting privileges they could not win in the open market place of politics. Using similar devices in the economy, as Tilden said, they spread a speculative, grasping, and selfish spirit throughout the land. It was for this reason that Liberal-Democratic leaders like Mackenzie and Gladstone and Cleveland worked hard for a civil service. This was why the words that sprang most readily to Cleveland's mind in connection with the enemy were "selfish" and "sordid."

The economic ideas of the Liberal-Democrats were closely related to these concerns. They were convinced that there was an inevitable and eternal conflict going on in society between the community at large and those who wanted to use their superior social situation to gain special economic privileges. They regarded the whole Tory-Republican economic system—tariffs, bounties, land laws, absentee ownership, private banking systems, concessions, and public works in support of private enterprise—as a vast structure of corruption. Tory-Republicans might claim that it was the best means for developing and protecting the nation's economy, and for ensuring that its great spirits—its men of talent and family and position—were given the opportunities they deserved. But Liberal-Democrats from Adam Smith to Grover Cleveland regarded it as nothing more than the "mean, rapacious, monopolizing" spirit of the businessman and the landowner having its way.

Distrust the businessman, said Adam Smith, for he will always seek monopolies. His personal interests inevitably run counter to those of society at large. He wants high prices and low wages, which means that the mass of society— composed of consumers, always the special concern of Liberal-Democracy—will be exploited coming and going. Sidling up to the aristocrats who run the government, businessmen get special privileges in return for the illusion of a powerful nation or in return for cash. The result is a stultified economy clamped within all manner of restrictions and burdened with an excessive tax rate.

Perhaps the most dramatic expression of Tory-Republicanism—to Liberal-Democratic eyes—was in foreign policy. When Tories and Republicans were in power, they went about building, or trying to build, great empires, for they enjoyed being domineering over others. They bristled at their monolithic neighbors, the other great empires of the world, and used military and naval power at every opportunity, giving expression to their native appetite for combat. Something in the Tory, Gladstone said, made him crave power. Just as he liked the trappings of rank, so he enjoyed the symbols of domination.

The Tory-Republican's foreign policy seemed always to be a business of appealing to pride, passion, and contempt for other peoples. Inveterate hierarchs themselves, they seemed happiest when they could stir up the appetite for domination in the people at large. Teddy Roosevelt, Cleveland said, had made a vulgar carnival of foreign relations, arousing the people to frenzies of disfiguring nationalist passion. Coercing others to consent to their will seemed to be not simply the characteristic means of the Tory-Republicans, but an end in itself. The Tory mentality, in the last analysis, was what concerned Liberal-Democracy most of all.

What was the Liberal-Democratic alternative to all of this? It consisted of a complex program for action that ranged through every aspect of national life. It was not, of course, one that we can or should accept simply at face value. The positive Liberal-Democratic program was violated, either in deed or in statement, by many Liberals and Democrats. No political movement, as Reinhold Niebuhr has taught us, is free of its own corruptions. Disfiguring characteristics are not only present in every human being, springing, as they do, from inescapable self-regard, they are even more swollen and uncontrolled in social groups. Liberal-Democracy was not uniquely freed from the human condition.

It is difficult, furthermore, for a generalized picture of the Liberal-Democratic point of view not to be in conflict with many particulars, especially when so much of it must be based on what is implied by the deeds and words of Liberal-Democracy rather than on explicit utterances. But these things are in the very nature of intellectual history. And the record seems so persuasively clear: that Liberal-Democracy conceived of itself as engaged in a large social mission is abundantly evident.

The economic program began and practically ended with Adam Smith, with admixtures of David Ricardo on currency matters. The goal was the dynamic economy, an economy alike innocent of special privilege and beneficent to all. Liberal-Democracy condemned any attempt to shape the economy, through the use of tariffs and other devices, so as to direct the flow of investment capital to favored industries and economic interests. Governments must not delude themselves with the comforting illusion that their central position and superior knowledge equipped them to see what would benefit the nation most and to regulate accordingly. This not only created large and tempting opportunities for corruption, it also was an activity doomed from the outset. It was in fact impossible to direct so large and complex a system as a national economy from the center. Men's capacities, Smith said —expressing the skeptical rationalism of David Hume—were largely limited to an understanding of their own affairs. No one had a wide enough intelligence to comprehend the infinite subtleties of the whole nation's economy. That which was distant from us was inescapably vague and imprecise. Only the close at hand presented itself with reasonable clarity.

Control of the economy would be better achieved by relying on the natural competitive appetites of businessmen. When freed to operate under the discipline of the market place, and not under that of a distant and inefficient government, businessmen would be under a system of control that would constantly readjust itself to fit the ebb and flow of local conditions. Local initiative, moreover, would energize the whole economy, for every man knew best how to profit from his particular situation.

Contrary to the standard view, however, Smith did not call for a completely passive state. It had two great tasks before it. The first was to clear away all legal monopolies and all forms of artificial "aid" to specially favored businessmen. Tariffs had to be wiped away or reduced to such low levels that they produced only revenue and not protection. The right of incorporation had to be thrown open to all, on an equal basis, instead of being limited to a chosen few. Foreign trade had similarly to be made an open arena, ending the rule of chartered monopolies. Bounties for the production of specific goods, laws that prevented the free passage of land from hand to hand, specially chartered private banks with monopoly controls over the national currency, public works in aid of particular business enterprises—all of this inherited mercantilistic system of inefficient and corrupt controls had to be rooted out. By the 1850's, this aspect of the Smithian revolution was largely completed on both sides of the Atlantic. The Republicans were able to achieve a counterreformation thereafter, which set the terms of American politics for the latter decades of the nineteenth century—the Democrats expending their energies in attempts to re-establish Smithian economics—but the Liberals in Britain were saved this experience.

The second task for the government, as conceived of in the Smithian framework, was for it to establish controls and conditions that would indirectly supervise and support the economy. Schools must be provided to equip the working class—whose labor was the source of all wealth—with skills, and to rescue them from the degradation of ignorance. The banking system, so vital to all of the economy, required close watching and, if necessary, regulation. Businessmen and their proposals should be regarded skeptically, for the things they wanted were almost always in conflict with the public interest. Government must ensure that the ways were open for a "natural aristocracy" to rise from the middle and lower classes to lead the nation.

Perhaps most important of all, the government was to damp down speculation and keep the economy stable. The principal means for disciplining the rapacious appetites of businessmen, aside from an open market place directed by competition, was the maintenance of a sound-money system. Sound money would retard inflation and thereby dampen speculation; it would keep the price of food and other necessaries for the masses to a minimum; and it would benefit the consumer in many ways. Sound-money systems worked best when linked to an international gold standard. When selfish businessmen got an inflationary spiral started, gold flowed out of the country to meet the demands of foreign creditors, who would not accept the paper currency that inflation was depreciating. The loss of gold, in a sound-money system— that is, a system in which paper currency is backed by gold— resulted in a contraction of the currency, and the initiation of a downward spiral back to stable prices. When local depression occurred, gold would flow inward because of its higher value, currency would expand, and economic activity would again be brought up to a level with similar activity worldwide. In sum, in currency matters as in the tariff issue, Liberal-Democracy was consumer-oriented and firmly internationalist.

Through lack of internal restraints and the removal of all tariffs, an open national and international economy would be created. Markets would expand healthily, business enterprise —driven by the newly freed profit instinct of entrepreneurs— would flourish, and everyone would benefit. Eliminating privileges and aids for certain businessmen would have the double virtue of preventing exploitation and creating prosperity for all.

This economic theory was intimately linked to foreign policy. The elimination of tariffs and the presence of an international gold standard, Liberal-Democrats believed, would create an interdependent world of peace and order. Since no nation would have protected advantages and the market of each would be open to all, the several nations of the world would engage in the economic activities for which they were best suited. In light of their mutual advantages under this system, rivalries and hostilities would disappear. The whole world, not simply the nation, would benefit from the open—and therefore dynamic—economy.

Foreign policy, according to the Liberal-Democrats, should in every way encourage interdependence and equal status. Brotherhood was the proper principle for diplomacy, based not simply on respect for others and their rights, but on the message of love among all peoples. Minority groups should be given equal status within the nation—always with the exception of the Negro—and local self-government should be the basis of the Constitution. In the world, similarly, each nationality must be allowed self-government, and small nations must have equal rights and status with great ones. They regarded the world, as the nation itself, as a pluralistic community in which the principles of action were to be based on equal voice and rights for all, and a lack of privileges. Compassion, not arrogance, would be the rule in the nation's foreign policy. When great decisions were to be made, they should be made multilaterally—in Gladstone's term, by the Concert of Europe—not by one great nation acting imperiously in defense of its "interests."

The Liberal-Democrats would foster a sense of international community, so as to moderate and civilize the inherent passions of nationalism. Surrounding and controlling all international affairs should be the protection of international law and morality. By this means, Gladstone said, the particular interests of each would be fettered and bound up so that they followed the interests of the whole.

Within the nation itself, personal and civic rights and religious status would be completely separate. Every faith must be not indifferently but indeed positively tolerated, for each shared membership in universal Christendom—or was at any rate equally without the right to claim religious hegemony or the monopoly of truth. Similarly, social distinctions, between ranks and between ethnic groups, were to be wiped away. No group was to be privileged, and every man was to be given his chance for individual advancement in an open social and economic market place, limited only by the extent of his own capacities and the vigor of his own character.

Every means must be adopted for opening up to the common people the social and economic and political routes to self-respect. That a man was an Irishman or a German immigrant or a workingman or a Dissenter should be quite irrelevant to his chances in life. Each should be assessed only on the ground of his success in fulfilling the demands of sturdy individualism, asking and giving no favor. In the great decisions of state, moreover, the common people were a much sounder guide to action than the aristocracy, for the latter had been corrupted by power and wealth. Many of them, indeed, had insinuated themselves into the upper ranks by chicane, not by right. While the Republicans, as Tilden said, consisted of men who lived by their wits, the Democrats comprised those who worked in the open light of day, relying on their honest labor alone.

The crucial battleground in politics lay ultimately within each man's character. It is hardly a coincidence that in almost every case the Liberal-Democratic leaders discussed in this study were social moralists in search of an encompassing ethic that would make their countrymen unselfish and compassionate. For this reason the specific things they called for were largely negative in character. They may have condemned the moral activism of Tory-Republican supervision of the private lives of others, but they too preached a message of moral prohibitions remindful of the Decalogue. The important distinction was that the religious example they looked to was the Christ who angrily overturned the tables of the money-changers and condemned the wealthy and the proud. The sins that aroused them were social sins, not so much the sins of personal life. Even Mackenzie, a teetotaler, responded to the essential spirit of his party membership by retreating from his early prohibitionism as he entered middle age. Canadian Liberalism was far more Dissenting in character—and therefore more zealous in its personal moralism—than were its British and American counterparts, but this fact was reflected remarkably little in its policies.

In Canada as elsewhere in the Anglo-American community, Liberal-Democracy thought of itself as a movement struggling primarily with large social evils, embodied in the demands of self-seeking aristocracies, whether of business wealth, of landed power, or of vested religious privilege. The Liberal-Democratic goal was the creation of an unprivileged society that was incorrupt, open equally to all ethnic groups and creeds, including freethinking, devoted to an internationalist form of economics in which the government gave no favors, and moved by a vision, however inchoate and remote, of a pluralistic and equalitarian nation and world cleansed finally and completely of arrogance, exclusiveness, and the lust to dominate.

BIBLIOGRAPHY

For the reader's convenience, this selected bibliography is arranged in sections, rather than in a single alphabetical list. The field covered by this book is so wide that readers will doubtless have particular rather than general interests and will appreciate a compartmented listing.

THE ANGLO-AMERICAN CONNECTION

Allen, H. C.: *Conflict and Concord: The Anglo-American Relationship Since 1783*. New York, 1959.

Athearn, Robert G.: *Westward the Briton*. New York, 1954.

Berthoff, Rowland T.: *British Immigrants in Industrial America, 1790–1950*. Cambridge, Mass., 1953.

Brebner, John G.: *North Atlantic Triangle: The Interplay of Canada, the United States and Great Britain*. New Haven, Conn., 1945.

Bridenbaugh, Carl: *Mitre and Sceptre: Transatlantic Faiths, Ideas, Personalities, and Politics: 1689–1775*. New York, 1962.

Cowan, Helen I.: *British Emigration to British North America: The First Hundred Years*. Toronto, 1961.

Crook, David Paul: *American Democracy in English Politics 1815–1840*. Oxford, 1965.

Graham, Ian Charles Cargill: *Colonists from Scotland: Emigration to North America, 1707–1783*. Ithaca, N.Y., 1956.

Johnson, Stanley C.: *A History of Emigration from the United Kingdom of North America, 1763–1912*. New York, 1966.

Katz, Stanley Nider: *Newcastle's New York: Anglo-American Politics, 1732–1753*. Cambridge, Mass., 1968.

Kraus, Michael: *The Atlantic Civilization: Eighteenth-Century Origins*. Ithaca, N.Y., 1949.

Lillibridge, G. D.: *Beacon of Freedom: The Impact of American*

Democracy upon Great Britain, 1830–1870. Philadelphia, 1954.

Pelling, Henry: *America and the British Left: From Bright to Bevan.* New York, 1957.

Rapson, Richard L.: "The British Traveler in America, 1860–1935." Ph.D. dissertation, Columbia University, 1965; to be published by the University of Washington Press.

Russett, Bruce M.: *Community and Contention: Britain and America in the Twentieth Century.* Cambridge, Mass., 1963.

Thistlethwaite, Frank: *America and the Atlantic Community: Anglo-American Aspects, 1790–1850.* New York, 1951 and 1964.

Thomas, Brinley: *Migration and Economic Growth: A Study of Great Britain and the Atlantic Economy.* Cambridge, 1954.

Todd, Arthur Cecil: *The Cornish Miner in America.* Truro, Cornwall, and Glendale, Calif., 1967.

UNITED STATES, GENERAL

Beard, Charles A.: *The Rise of American Civilization.* New York, 1934.

Benson, Lee: *The Concept of Jacksonian Democracy: New York as a Test Case.* New York, 1964.

Buck, Paul H.: *The Road to Reunion, 1865–1900.* New York, 1959.

Carpenter, Jesse T.: *The South as a Conscious Minority, 1789–1861.* New York, 1930.

Christman, Henry: *Tin Horns and Calico: An Episode in the Emergence of American Democracy.* New York, 1961.

Craven, Avery O.: *The Growth of Southern Nationalism, 1848–1861.* New York, 1953.

Degler, Carl N.: "American Political Parties and the Rise of the City: An Interpretation." *Journal of American History,* LI (1964), 41–59.

Filler, Louis, ed.: *Democrats and Republicans: Ten Years of the Republic—From Harry Thurston Peck's Twenty Years of the Republic.* New York, 1964.

Fischer, David H.: *The Revolution of American Conservatism: The Federalist Party in the Era of Jacksonian Democracy.* New York, 1966.

Hammond, Bray: *Banks and Politics in America from the Revolution to the Civil War.* Princeton, N.J., 1957.

Hays, Samuel P.: *The Response to Industrialism: 1885–1914.* Chicago, 1957.

Hirsch, Mark D.: *William C. Whitney: Modern Warwick.* New York, 1948.

Hollingsworth, Rogers: *The Whirligig of Politics: The Democracy of Cleveland and Bryan.* Chicago and London, 1963.

Hoogenboom, Ari: *Outlawing the Spoils: A History of the Civil Service Reform Movement 1865–1883.* Urbana, Ill., 1961.

Jacobs, Wilbur R.: "Turner's Methodology: Multiple Working Hypotheses or Ruling Theory?" *The Journal of American History,* LIV (1968), 853–63.

———, ed.: *Frederick Jackson Turner's Legacy: Unpublished Writings in American History.* San Marino, Calif., 1965.

Kass, Alvin: *Politics in New York State, 1800–1830.* Syracuse, N.Y., 1965.

Keller, Morton: "Introduction" to E. L. Godkin, *Problems of Modern Democracy: Political and Economic Essays.* Cambridge, Mass., 1966.

Kelley, Robert: "Taming the Sacramento: Hamiltonianism in Action." *Pacific Historical Review,* XXXIV (1965), 21–49.

Marshall, Lynn L.: "The Strange Stillbirth of the Whig Party." *American Historical Review.* LXXII (1967), 445–68.

May, Ernest R.: *Imperial Democracy: The Emergence of America as a Great Power.* New York, 1961.

Miller, John C.: *Alexander Hamilton and the Growth of the New Nation.* New York, 1964.

———: *Origins of the American Revolution.* Boston, 1943.

———: *The Federalist Era, 1789–1801.* New York, 1960.

Nevins, Allan: *Ordeal of the Union.* 2 vols. New York, 1947.

Oberholzer, Ellis Paxson: *A History of the United States Since the Civil War.* New York, 1937.

Ogden, Rollo: "Edwin Lawrence Godkin," in Allen Johnson and Dumas Malone, eds., *Dictionary of American Biography,* Vol. VII. New York, 1931.

Rutman, Darrett B.: *The Old Dominion: Essays for Thomas Perkins Abernethy.* Charlottesville, Va., 1964.

Samuels, Ernest: *The Young Henry Adams.* Cambridge, Mass., 1948.

Schlesinger, Arthur M., Jr.: *The Age of Jackson.* Boston, 1945.

Sharkey, Robert: *Money, Class, and Party: An Economic Study of Civil War and Reconstruction.* Baltimore, Md., 1959.

Sievers, Harry J.: *Benjamin Harrison: Hoosier Warrior*. New York, 1960.
Taylor, George Rogers: *The Transportation Revolution: 1815–1860*. New York, 1951.
Tompkins, E. Berkeley: "Scylla and Charybdis: The Anti-Imperialist Dilemma in the Election of 1900." *Pacific Historical Review*. XXXVI (1967), 143–61.
Turner, Frederick Jackson: *The Significance of Sections in American History*. New York, 1932.
Unger, Irwin: *The Greenback Era: A Social and Political History of American Finance, 1865–1879*. Princeton, N.J., 1964.
Van Buren, Martin: *Inquiry into the Origin and Course of Political Parties in the United States*. New York, 1867.
———: "The Autobiography of Martin Van Buren," ed. John C. Fitzpatrick. *Annual Report of the American Historical Association for the Year 1918*. Washington, D.C., 1919.
Woodward, C. Vann: *Reunion and Reaction*. New York, 1956.

GREAT BRITAIN, GENERAL

Arnstein, Walter L.: *The Bradlaugh Case: A Study in Late Victorian Opinion and Politics*. Oxford, 1965.
Ausubel, Herman: *In Hard Times: Reformers Among the Late Victorians*. New York, 1960.
Bagehot, Walter: *Bagehot's Historical Essays*, ed. Norman St. John-Stevas. Garden City, N.Y., 1965.
Briggs, Asa: *The Making of Modern England, 1783–1867: The Age of Improvement*. New York, 1965.
Burn, W. L.: *The Age of Equipoise: A Study of the Mid-Victorian Generation*. New York, 1965.
Clark, G. Kitson: *The Making of Victorian England*. Cambridge, Mass., 1962.
Coupland, Reginald: *Welsh and Scottish Nationalism: A Study*. London, 1954.
Cowling, Maurice: *1867 Disraeli, Gladstone and Revolution: The Passing of the Second Reform Bill*. Cambridge, Eng., 1967.
Dicey, A. V.: *Law and Public Opinion in England During the Nineteenth Century*. London, 1914.
Gash, Norman: *Politics in the Age of Peel: A Study in the Techniques of Parliamentary Representation 1830–1850*. London, New York, and Toronto, 1953.

————: *Reaction and Reconstruction in English Politics, 1832–1852.* Oxford, 1965.

Glaser, J. F.: "English Nonconformity and the Decline of Liberalism." *American Historical Review,* LXIII (1958), 352–63.

Guttridge, G. H.: *The Early Career of Lord Rockingham, 1730–1765.* Berkeley and Los Angeles, 1952.

Halévy, Elie: *England in 1815.* New York, 1961.

————: *The Liberal Awakening, 1815–1830.* New York, 1961.

————: *The Triumph of Reform, 1830–1841.* New York, 1961.

————, with a supplementary section by R. B. McCallum: *Victorian Years, 1841–1895.* New York, 1961.

Himmelfarb, Gertrude: "The Politics of Democracy: The English Reform Act of 1867." *The Journal of British Studies,* VI (1966), 97–138.

James, Robert Rhodes: *Rosebery: A Biography of Archibald Philip, Fifth Earl of Rosebery.* New York, 1964.

Machin, G. I. T.: *The Catholic Question in English Politics, 1820 to 1830.* Oxford, 1964.

McCallum, R. B.: *The Liberal Party from Earl Grey to Asquith.* London, 1963.

————: "The Liberal Outlook," in Morris Ginsberg, ed., *Law and Opinion in England in the 20th Century.* Berkeley and Los Angeles, 1959.

McDowell, R. B.: *British Conservatism, 1832–1914.* London, 1959.

Morgan, Kenneth O.: *Wales in British Politics, 1868–1922.* Cardiff, 1963.

Read, Donald: *The English Provinces, c. 1760–1960: A Study in Influence.* New York, 1964.

Semmel, Bernard: *Imperialism and Social Reform, English Social-Imperial Thought 1895–1914.* Cambridge, Mass., 1960.

Southgate, Donald: *The Passing of the Whigs, 1832–1886.* London, 1962.

Vincent, John: *The Formation of the British Liberal Party.* New York, 1966.

Vincent, J. R.: *Pollbooks: How Victorians Voted.* Cambridge, Eng., 1967.

CANADA, GENERAL

Brebner, J. Bartlet: *Canada: A Modern History.* Ann Arbor, Mich., 1960.

Cartwright, Sir Richard: *Reminiscences*. Toronto, 1912.

Craig, Gerald M.: *Upper Canada: The Formative Years, 1784–1841*. Toronto, 1963.

Creighton, Donald: *John A. Macdonald: The Old Chieftain*. Boston, 1956.

———: *John A. Macdonald: The Young Politician*. Boston, 1953.

———: *The Road to Confederation: The Emergence of Canada, 1863–1867*. Boston, 1965.

Galbraith, John Kenneth: *The Scotch*. Boston, 1964.

Gates, Lillian F.: "*Mackenzie's Gazette*: An Aspect of W. L. Mackenzie's American Years." *Canadian Historical Review*, XLVI (1965), 323–45.

Lower, Arthur R. M.: *Canadians in the Making: A Social History of Canada*. Toronto, 1958.

MacLennan, Hugh: *Two Solitudes*. New York, 1945.

———: *The Precipice*. New York, 1948.

Morton, W. L.: *The Critical Years: The Union of British North America, 1857–73*. London and New York, 1964.

Ostry, Bernard: "Conservatives, Liberals, and Labour in the 1870's." *Canadian Historical Review*, XLI (1960), 87–100.

Skelton, O. D.: *Life and Letters of Sir Wilfrid Laurier*. Toronto, 1912.

Underhill, Frank H.: *In Search of Canadian Liberalism*. Toronto, 1960.

SCOTLAND

Dabney, William M.: "Letters from Norfolk: Scottish Merchants View the Revolutionary Crisis," in Darrett B. Rutman, ed., *The Old Dominion: Essays for Thomas Perkins Abernethy*. Charlottesville, Va., 1964.

Elliott, David C.: "The Liberal Party in Scotland from the Midlothian Election to the First World War." Ph.D. dissertation, Harvard University, 1950.

Finlay, Ian: *Scotland*. London, 1945.

Kellas, J. G.: "The Liberal Party in Scotland, 1885–1895." Ph.D. dissertation, University of London, 1961.

Lindsay, Maurice: *By Yon Bonnie Banks: A Gallimaufry*. London, 1961.

Notestein, Wallace: *The Scot in History: A Study of the Interplay of Character and History*. New Haven, Conn., 1947.

Pryde, George S.: *Scotland from 1603 to the Present Day.* Edinburgh, 1962.

SOCIAL HISTORY

Brown, Thomas N.: *Irish-American Nationalism, 1870–1890.* Philadelphia and New York, 1966.

Elkins, Stanley M.: *Slavery: A Problem in American Institutional and Intellectual Life.* New York, 1964.

Epstein, L. D.: "British Class Consciousness and the Labour Party." *The Journal of British Studies*, I (1962), 136–50.

Ernst, Robert: *Immigrant Life in New York City, 1825–1863.* Port Washington, N.Y., 1965.

Fox, Dixon Ryan: *Yankees and Yorkers.* New York and London, 1940.

Glazer, Nathan, and Daniel Patrick Moynihan: *Beyond the Melting Pot: The Negroes, Puerto Ricans, Jews, Italians, and Irish of New York City.* Cambridge, Mass., 1964.

Guttsman, W. L.: *The British Political Elite.* London, 1963.

Leyburn, James G.: *The Scotch-Irish: A Social History.* Chapel Hill, N.C., 1962.

Litwak, Leon. *North of Slavery: The Negro in the Free States.* Chicago, 1961.

Lofton, Williston H.: "Abolition and Labor." *Journal of Negro History*, XXXIII (1948), 249–83.

———: "Northern Labor and the Negro During the Civil War." *Journal of Negro History*, XXXIV (1949), 251–73.

Man, Albon P., Jr.: "Labor Competition and the New York Draft Riots of 1863." *Journal of Negro History*, XXXVI (1951), 375–405.

Mann, Arthur: *Yankee Reformers in the Urban Age: Social Reform in Boston, 1880–1900.* New York, 1966.

Rayback, Joseph G.: "The American Workingman and the Antislavery Crusade." *Journal of Economic History*, III (1943), 152–64.

Schofield, Robert E.: *The Lunar Society of Birmingham: A Social History of Provincial Science and Industry in Eighteenth-Century England.* Oxford, 1963.

Wolfinger, Raymond E.: "The Development and Persistence of Ethnic Voting." *American Political Science Review*, LIX (1965), 896–908.

INTELLECTUAL HISTORY

Alexander, Edward: *Matthew Arnold and John Stuart Mill.* New York and London, 1965.

Bailyn, Bernard: *The Ideological Origins of the American Revolution.* Cambridge, Mass., 1967.

Briggs, Asa: *Victorian People: A Reassessment of Persons and Themes, 1851–1867.* New York, 1963.

Bronowski, J., and Bruce Mazlish: *The Western Intellectual Tradition from Leonardo to Hegel.* New York, 1960.

Cash, W. J.: *The Mind of the South.* New York, 1941.

Colbourn, H. Trevor: *The Lamp of Experience: Whig History and the Intellectual Origins of the American Revolution.* Chapel Hill, N.C., 1965.

Curti, Merle: *The Growth of American Thought.* New York, Evanston, Ill., and London, 1964.

Fine, Sidney: *Laissez-Faire and the General-Welfare State: A Study of Conflict in American Thought, 1865–1901.* Ann Arbor, Mich., 1956.

Higham, John: *Strangers in the Land: Patterns of American Nativism, 1860–1925.* New York, 1963.

Hofstadter, Richard: *The Age of Reform, from Bryan to F.D.R.* New York, 1955.

——: *The American Political Tradition and the Men Who Made It.* New York, 1948.

——: *The Paranoid Style in American Politics.* New York, 1966.

Houghton, Walter E.: *The Victorian Frame of Mind, 1830–1870.* New Haven, Conn., 1957.

Meyers, Marvin: *The Jacksonian Persuasion: Politics and Belief.* New York, 1960.

Miller, Douglas T.: *Jacksonian Aristocracy: Class and Democracy in New York, 1830–1860.* New York, 1967.

Richter, Melvin: *The Politics of Conscience: T. H. Green and His Age.* Cambridge, Mass., 1964.

Schlesinger, Arthur M., Jr., and Morton White, eds.: *Paths of American Thought.* Boston, 1963.

Semmel, Bernard: *Imperialism and Social Reform: English Social-Imperial Thought 1895–1914.* Cambridge, Mass., 1960.

Stephen, Sir Leslie: *History of English Thought in the Eighteenth Century.* 2 vols. New York and Burlingame, Calif., 1962.

Thornton, A. P.: *The Habit of Authority: Paternalism in British History.* Toronto, 1964.

Van Deusen, Glyndon G.: "Some Aspects of Whig Thought and Theory in the Jacksonian Period." *American Historical Review,* LXIII (1958), 305–22.

Willey, Basil: *More Nineteenth Century Studies: A Group of Honest Doubters.* London, 1956.

RELIGIOUS HISTORY

Alexander, Archibald: *Thoughts of Religious Experience.* Philadelphia, 1844.

Briggs, Charles A.: *Whither? A Theological Question for the Times.* New York, 1889.

Brydon, George Maclaren: *Virginia's Mother Church: And the Political Conditions Under Which It Grew.* 2 vols. Philadelphia, 1948, 1952.

Burleigh, J. H. S.: *A Church History of Scotland.* Oxford, 1960.

Butler, Bishop Joseph: *The Analogy of Religion, Natural and Revealed, to the Constitution and Course of Nature.* London, 1736.

Cowherd, Raymond G.: *The Politics of English Dissent: The Religious Aspects of Liberal and Humanitarian Reform Movements from 1815–1848.* New York, 1956.

Cross, Arthur Lyon: *The Anglican Episcopate and the American Colonies.* New York, 1902.

Cross, Whitney R.: *The Burned-Over District: The Social and Intellectual History of Enthusiastic Religion in Western New York, 1800–1850.* Ithaca, N.Y., 1950, and New York, 1965.

Davis, Horton: *Worship and Theology in England: From Watts and Wesley to Maurice, 1690–1850.* 3 vols. Princeton, N.J., 1961.

Herklots, H. G. G.: *The Church of England and the American Episcopal Church, from the First Voyages of Discovery to the First Lambeth Conference.* London, 1966.

Hodge, Charles: *What Is Presbyterianism?* Philadelphia, 1855.

Humphrey, the Rev. H., ed.: *The New England Primer, Containing the Assembly's Catechism* . . . Worcester, Mass., ca. 1852.

Littell, Franklin Hamlin: *From State Church to Pluralism: A Protestant Interpretation of Religion in American History.* Garden City, N.Y., 1962.

Munz, Peter: *The Place of Hooker in the History of Thought.* London, 1952.

Rapson, Richard: "The Religious Feelings of the American People,

428   BIBLIOGRAPHY

1845–1935: A British View." *Church History*, XXXV (1966),
  3–19.
Smith, E. W.: *The Creed of Presbyterians*. Richmond, Va., 1901.
Smith, Timothy L.: *Revivalism and Social Reform: American
  Protestantism on the Eve of the Civil War*. New York, 1965.
Wilberforce, William: *A Practical View of the Prevailing Religious
  System of Professed Christians, in the Higher and Middle
  Classes in this Country, Contrasted with Real Christianity*.
  London, 1797.

BEHAVIORAL SCIENCES

Adorno, T. W., E. Frenkel-Brunswik, D. J. Levinson, and R. N.
  Sanford: *The Authoritarian Personality*. New York, 1950.
Alford, Robert T.: *Party and Society: The Anglo-American Democ-
  racies*. Chicago, 1963.
Allport, Gordon: *The Nature of Prejudice*. Garden City, N.Y., 1958.
———: *Pattern and Growth in Personality*. New York, 1961.
Berger, Peter: *Invitation to Sociology: A Humanistic Perspective*.
  Garden City, N.Y., 1963.
Erikson, Erik H.: *Childhood and Society*. New York, 1963.
———: *Young Man Luther: A Study in Psychoanalysis and His-
  tory*. New York, 1962.
Garraty, John A.: "The Interrelations of Psychology and Biog-
  raphy." *Psychological Bulletin*, LI (1954), 569–82.
Lasswell, Harold D., Daniel Lerner, and C. Easton Rothwell: *The
  Comparative Study of Elites*. Stanford, Calif., 1952.
Mannheim, Karl: *Ideology and Utopia*, tr. Louis Wirth and Ed-
  ward Shils. New York, 1936.
Merton, Robert K.: *Social Theory and Social Structure*. Glencoe,
  Ill., 1957.
Shibutani, Tomatsu: "Reference Groups and Social Control," in
  Arnold M. Rose, ed., *Human Behavior and Social Processes:
  An Interactionist Approach*. Boston, 1962.
———: *Society and Personality: An Interactionist Approach to
  Social Psychology*. Englewood Cliffs, N.J., 1961.

ADAM SMITH

Cropsey, Joseph: *Polity and Economy: An Interpretation of the
  Principles of Adam Smith*. The Hague, 1957.

Fay, C. R.: *Adam Smith and the Scotland of His Day.* Cambridge, Eng., 1956.

Ginzberg, Eli: *The House of Adam Smith.* New York, 1934.

Heilbroner, Robert L.: *The Worldly Philosophers: The Lives, Times and Ideas of the Great Economic Thinkers.* New York, 1961.

Letwin, William: *The Origins of Scientific Economics.* New York, 1965.

Schumpeter, Joseph A.: *A History of Economic Analysis.* New York, 1954.

Scott, W. R.: *Adam Smith as Student and Professor.* Glasgow, 1937.

Smith, Adam: *An Inquiry into the Nature and Causes of the Wealth of Nations,* ed. Edwin Cannan (Modern Library edn.). New York, 1937.

EDMUND BURKE

Barkan, Elliott Robert, ed.: *Edmund Burke on the American Revolution: Selected Speeches and Letters.* New York, 1966.

Bryant, Donald C.: "Edmund Burke: A Generation of Scholarship and Discovery." *The Journal of British Studies,* II (1962), 120–145.

Burke, Edmund: *Reflections on the Revolution in France,* ed. Thomas H. D. Mahoney. Indianapolis and New York, 1955.

Cone, Carl B.: *Burke and the Nature of Politics: The Age of the American Revolution.* Lexington, Ky., 1957.

Mahoney, Thomas H. D.: *Edmund Burke and Ireland.* Cambridge, Mass., 1960.

Morley, John: *Edmund Burke: A Historical Study.* London, 1866, New York, 1924.

Stanlis, Peter J.: *Edmund Burke and the Natural Law.* Ann Arbor, Mich., 1958.

———, ed.: *Edmund Burke: Selected Writings and Speeches.* Garden City, N.Y., 1963.

———, ed.: *The Relevance of Edmund Burke.* New York, 1964.

Sutherland, L. Stuart: "Edmund Burke and the First Rockingham Ministry." *English Historical Review,* XLVII (1932), 46–72.

THOMAS JEFFERSON

Chinard, Gilbert: *The Literary Bible of Thomas Jefferson: His Commonplace Book of Philosophers and Poets.* Baltimore and Paris, 1928.

Ford, Paul Leicester, ed.: *The Works of Thomas Jefferson.* New York and London, 1904.

Ganter, Herbert L.: "William Small, Jefferson's Beloved Teacher." *William and Mary Quarterly* (1947), pp. 505–11.

Jefferson, Thomas: *Notes on the State of Virginia.* New York, 1964.

Koch, Adrienne: *Jefferson and Madison: The Great Collaboration.* New York, 1953.

———: *The Philosophy of Thomas Jefferson.* Chicago, 1964.

Malone, Dumas: *Jefferson the Virginian.* Boston, 1948.

Peterson, Merrill D.: *The Jefferson Image in the American Mind.* New York, 1962.

Roche, O. I. A., ed.: *The Jefferson Bible, with Annotated Commentaries on Religion of Thomas Jefferson.* New York, 1964.

Schachner, Nathan: *Thomas Jefferson: A Biography.* 2 vols. New York, 1951.

WILLIAM GLADSTONE

Garratt, G. T.: *The Two Mr. Gladstones.* London, 1936.

Gladstone, William Ewart: *Address and Speeches Delivered at Manchester on the 23rd and 24th of April, 1862.* Pamphlet. London, 1862.

———: *Correspondence on Church and Religion of William Ewart Gladstone,* selected and arranged by D. C. Lathbury. 2 vols. London, 1910.

———: "Course of Commercial Policy at Home and Abroad." *Foreign and Colonial Quarterly Review* (1843). Reprinted London, 1919.

———: *Home Rule Manifesto: Address to the Electors of Midlothian, May 1, 1886.* Pamphlet. London, 1886.

———: *Midlothian Campaign: Political Speeches Delivered in November and December 1879 and March and April 1880.* Edinburgh, 1880.

———: *Speeches of the Right Hon. W. E. Gladstone, M.P., with a Sketch of His Life,* ed. Henry W. Lucy. London and New York, 1885.

———: *Speeches on Parliamentary Reform in 1866*. London, 1866.

———: *Speech of the Right Hon. W. E. Gladstone on the War and Negotiations, Commons, Aug. 3, 1855*. Pamphlet. London, 1855.

———: *Studies Subsidiary to the Works of Bishop Butler*. New York, 1896.

———: *Substance of a Speech on the Motion of Lord John Russell for a Committee of the Whole House, with a View to the Removal of the Remaining Jewish Disabilities, Commons, Dec. 16, 1847*. Pamphlet. London, 1848.

———: *Substance of the Speech of the Right Hon. W. E. Gladstone, the Affairs of Greece, and the Foreign Policy of the Administration. Commons, June 27, 1850*. Pamphlet. London, 1850.

———: *Gleanings of Past Years, 1843–78*. 7 vols. New York, 1878.

———: *The Home Rule Bill. Speech, Commons, February 13, 1893*. Pamphlet. London, 1893.

———: *Two Letters to the Earl of Aberdeen on the State Prosecutions of the Neapolitan Government*. Pamphlet. New York, 1851.

———: *War in China. Speech, Commons, Mar. 3, 1857*. Pamphlet. London, 1857.

Hammond, J. L. and M. R. D. Foot: *Gladstone and Liberalism*. London, 1952; 2d edn., New York, 1966.

Hammond, J. L. B.: *Gladstone and the Irish Nation*. London, 1938 and 1964.

Hirst, F. W.: *Gladstone as Financier and Economist*. London, 1931.

Kelley, Robert: "Midlothian: A Study in Politics and Ideas." *Victorian Studies*, IV (1960), 119–40.

Magnus, Philip M.: *Gladstone, a Biography*. New York, 1954.

Morley, John: *The Life of William Ewart Gladstone*. 3 vols. London, 1903.

Shannon, R. T.: *Gladstone and the Bulgarian Agitation 1876*. London, 1963.

SAMUEL TILDEN

Bigelow, John: *Life of Samuel J. Tilden*. 2 vols. New York, 1895.

———, ed.: *Letters and Literary Memorials of Samuel J. Tilden*. 2 vols. New York, 1908.

————, ed.: *The Writings and Speeches of Samuel J. Tilden.* 2 vols. New York, 1885.

Callow, Alexander B., Jr.: *The Tweed Ring.* New York, 1966.

Flick, Alexander C.: *Samuel J. Tilden.* New York, 1939.

George, Henry: *The Question before the People. What Is the Real Issue in the Presidential Campaign?* Pamphlet. San Francisco, 1876.

Hirsch, Mark D.: "Samuel J. Tilden: The Story of a Lost Opportunity." *American Historical Review,* LVI (1951), 788–802.

Society for the Diffusion of Political Knowledge. *Papers of the Society.*

GROVER CLEVELAND

Bergh, Albert Ellery, ed.: *Grover Cleveland: Addresses, State Papers and Letters.* New York, 1909.

Cleveland, Grover: *The Self-Made Man in American Life.* New York, 1897.

————: *Presidential Problems.* New York, 1904.

Merrill, Horace Samuel: *Bourbon Leader: Grover Cleveland and the Democratic Party.* Boston, 1957.

Nevins, Allan: *Grover Cleveland: A Study in Courage.* New York, 1932.

————: *Letters of Grover Cleveland, 1850–1908.* Boston, 1933.

Parker, George F., ed.: *The Writings and Speeches of Grover Cleveland.* New York, 1892.

Bradford, Gamaliel: "Grover Cleveland," *Atlantic,* CXXVI (1920), 650–70.

Gilder, Richard Watson: "Grover Cleveland: A Record of Friendship." *Century,* LXXVIII (1909), 483–501, 687–705, 846–60; LXXIX (1910), 24–31.

Schurz, Carl: "Grover Cleveland's Second Administration." *McClure's Magazine,* IX (1897), 633–44.

State of New York: *Public Papers of Grover Cleveland, Governor.* Albany, 1883.

————: *Public Papers of Grover Cleveland, Governor.* Albany, 1884.

White, William Allen: "Cleveland." *McClure's Magazine,* XVIII (1902), 322–30.

Wilson, Woodrow: "Mr. Cleveland as President." *Atlantic Monthly,* LXXIX (1897), 289–300.

GEORGE BROWN AND ALEXANDER MACKENZIE

Buckingham, William, and G. W. Ross: *The Hon. Alexander Mackenzie: His Life and Times*. Toronto, 1892.

Careless, J. M. S.: *Brown of the Globe*. 2 vols. Toronto, 1963.

Thomson, Dale C.: *Alexander Mackenzie: Clear Grit*. Toronto, 1960.

Mackenzie, Alexander: *Speeches of the Hon. Alexander Mackenzie During His Visit to Scotland with his Principal Speeches in Canada Since the Session of 1875*. Toronto, 1876.

————: *The Life and Speeches of Hon. George Brown*. Toronto, 1882.

————, *et al.: Reform Government in the Dominion: The Pic-Nic Speeches Delivered in the Province of Ontario During the Summer of 1877*. Toronto, 1878.

INDEX

Christianity (*cont.*)
  Bolingbroke and Jefferson on,
  113–121; Gladstone on, 177
church and state, 50–2, 309,
  365, 370, 372
Church of England, 165, 194,
  217, 404; in U.K., 22; in
  Ireland, 23; theology, 93; in
  colonies, 107–13; disestablishment of in Virginia, 115–16;
  and Church of Scotland, 152;
  discussed, 156; Evangelicalism in, 156–62; and Oxford,
  168; and Gladstone, 174–6; in
  Canada, 355, 371, 390
Church of Ireland, 212, 214–15
Church of Scotland, 151, 384,
  390; Disruption, 362–5
Church of Scotland Free, 364
churches: in U.S. politics, 48–
  53, 307–17; Church of Scotland split, 362–5; *see also*
  Christianity; Church of England; Dissenters; religion in
  politics; Roman Catholicism
civil liberties, 174–5
civil service, 211, 217, 277, 300,
  324, 346, 407, 411; purpose
  of, 17–18
Civil War, 130, 181, 205, 206,
  244, 271
Clear Grits, 369, 372, 379, 380
Clergy Reserves, 355, 371, 373,
  374, 390
Cleveland, Grover, xix, 41, 101,
  238, 278, 289, 291, 362, 379,
  385–6, 394 *n.*, 396, 404, 410;
  life and ideas, 293–350 *passim*
Cleveland, Richard Falley, 311
Cobbett, William, 13, 187, 248
Cobden, Richard, 191–2, 247,
  369, 389
coercion, 412; Burke on, 87;
  Gladstone on, 174, 214, 230,
  231
Coercion Acts, 228–9
Colbourne, H. Trevor, 121
Cole, G. D. H., 29
Coleridge, J. D., 145
collectivism, 294
colonies, feelings toward
  England, 103–4

Concert of Europe, 224, 416
Cone, Carl B., 83
Confederation movement, 315,
  380
Congregationalists, 51, 108, 219,
  250, 309, 311
Connecticut, 240
conservation, 346
Conservative Party (Canada),
  41, 357, 368–9, 371, 374, 378–
  9, 387, 354
Conservative Party (U.K.), 200,
  207, 231; and Burke, 80; and
  Scots, 151; Peel creates, 181;
  preference for authority, 185;
  split over repeal of Corn Laws,
  192–4, 196–7; *see also* Tories
conspiracy theories, 242, 253;
  Anglican Plot, 110; Tory Plot,
  110–11
Constitution, Jefferson on, 132
consumers, and currency, 193,
  289, 340–1; 405
Cornish miners, 39
Cornwall, 4–5
corporations: Adam Smith on,
  73; Gladstone on, 188; general
  incorporation law, 261–3;
  Cleveland on, 296–7, 326
corrupt practices acts, 277
corruption, 206, 256, 350, 366,
  370, 378–9, 383, 395–6; Jacksonian fears of, 12–13; Adam
  Smith on, 77; Burke and Rockingham Whigs on, 83–4;
  colonial fears of, 110–11;
  Jefferson on, 123; Democratic
  fears of, 242; general discussion of, 276–9; Cleveland era,
  294–5, 325, 330–2; Mackenzie
  on, 386–8, 397–9; issue
  summarized, 411
Cowling, Maurice, 207
Craig, Gerald M., 354
Cranmer, Archbishop Thomas,
  173
Crimean War, 200, 223
Cross, Whitney R., 308
currency, 257, 288–9, 340–1, 379,
  405; Jacksonians on, 13, 243;
  ideas on, 14; Jefferson on, 127–
  8; early controversies over,

A Note About the Author

ROBERT L. KELLEY was born in Santa Barbara, California, in 1925. He received his B.A. from the University of California at Santa Barbara and his M.A. and Ph.D. from Stanford University. Aside from five years as an Air Force officer he has been in the academic world all his life. Since 1955 he has taught at the University of California at Santa Barbara, where he is a professor of history and has developed the first undergraduate and graduate program in this country on Anglo-American intellectual history. He won the Harold J. Plous Memorial Award for teaching and research in 1962 and the Louis Knott Koontz Annual Award of the Pacific Coast branch of the American Historical Association for the best article to appear in the *Pacific Historical Review* in 1965.

Mr. Kelley is the author of *Gold Versus Grain* (1959) and co-author, with Leland D. Baldwin, of *The Stream of American History* (1965) and *Survey of American History* (1967). He is a contributor to *Victorian Studies, The Journal of British Studies, American Quarterly, The Historian,* and the *Encyclopædia Britannica,* for which he prepared the biographical article on Dwight D. Eisenhower. Mr. Kelley is married and lives in Santa Barbara with his wife and four children.

A Note on the Type

THE TEXT OF THIS BOOK was set in a typeface called Primer, designed by Rudolph Ruzicka for the Mergenthaler Linotype Company and first made available in 1949. Primer, a modified modern face based on Century broadface, has the virtue of great legibility and was designed especially for today's methods of composition and printing.

Primer is Ruzicka's third typeface. In 1940 he designed Fairfield, and in 1947 Fairfield Medium, both for the Mergenthaler Linotype Company.

Ruzicka was born in Bohemia in 1883 and came to the United States at the age of eleven. He attended public schools in Chicago and later the Chicago Art Institute. During his long career he has been a wood engraver, etcher, cartographer, and book designer. For many years he was associated with Daniel Berkeley Updike and produced the annual keepsakes for The Merrymount Press from 1911 until 1941.

Ruzicka has been honored by many distinguished organizations, and in 1936 he was awarded the gold medal of the American Institute of Graphic Arts. From his home in New Hampshire, Ruzicka continues to be active in the graphic arts.

Composed, printed, and bound by The Haddon Craftsmen, Inc., Scranton, Pennsylvania. Typography and binding design by Golda Fishbein.